Marine Pollution, Shipping Waste and International Law

Waste management poses increasing challenges to both the protection of the environment and to human health. To face these challenges, this book claims that environmental law needs to shift attention from media-specific pollution regimes to integrative life-cycle approaches of waste management, *i.e.*, from the prevention of waste generation to the actual handling of wastes. Furthermore, the cooperation of States and the establishment of coordinated activities are essential because States can no longer have separate standards for wastes posing transboundary risks and for 'purely domestic' wastes.

Drawing upon both International and EU law, the book provides a detailed analysis of the regimes set up to deal with the transboundary movement of wastes and ship-source pollution, so as to elucidate the obligations and legal principles governing such regimes. It concludes that treaty obligations concerning transboundary movements of wastes are inapplicable to ship wastes while on board ships and on land. However, despite the limitations of the transboundary movement of wastes regime, the principle of Environmentally Sound Management (ESM) embodied in this regime has gradually transformed into a legal principle. ESM works to address the legal gaps in the regulation of wastes, and consequently, it provides the desired coherence to the legal system since it acts as a bridge between several regulatory and sectoral levels. Furthermore, ESM offers a new light with which to understand and interpret existing obligations, and it provides a renewed impetus to regimes that directly and indirectly govern wastes. This impetus translates into greater coordination and the establishment of cross-sectional policies.

By offering alternative ways to solve problems linked to the management of ship wastes in the sea-land interface, this book will appeal to anyone with an interest in International Environmental Law.

Gabriela Argüello holds a doctoral degree in Maritime and Transport Law from the University of Gothenburg and a master's in Maritime Law from Lund University (Sweden). Her research interests relate to environmental global challenges in relation to the marine environment and the governance of the oceans. Currently, Gabriela is a Postdoctoral Research Fellow in Law with a focus on Large-Scale Collective Action at the Centre for Collective Action Research (CeCAR). Gabriela has published refereed articles in areas of waste management and ship recycling in international journals.

Routledge Research in International Environmental Law

The Precautionary Principle in Marine Environmental Law
With Special Reference to High Risk Vessels
Bénédicte Sage-Fuller

International Environmental Law and Distributive Justice
The Equitable Distribution of CDM Projects under the Kyoto Protocol
Tomilola Akanle Eni-Ibukun

Environmental Governance in Europe and Asia
A Comparative Study of Institutional and Legislative Frameworks
Jona Razzaque

Climate Change, Forests and REDD
Lessons for Institutional Design
Edited by Joyeeta Gupta, Nicolien van der Grijp and Onno Kuik

International Environmental Law and the Conservation of Coral Reefs
Edward J. Goodwin

International Environmental Law and the International Court of Justice
Aleksandra Cavoski

Enforcement of International Environmental Law
Challenges and Responses at the International Level
Martin Hedemann-Robinson

Marine Pollution, Shipping Waste and International Law
Gabriela Argüello

https://www.routledge.com/Routledge-Research-in-International-Environmental-Law/book-series/INTENVLAW

Marine Pollution, Shipping Waste and International Law

Gabriela Argüello

LONDON AND NEW YORK

First published 2020
by Routledge
2 Park Square, Milton Park, Abingdon, Oxon OX14 4RN

and by Routledge
605 Third Avenue, New York, NY 10017

Routledge is an imprint of the Taylor & Francis Group, an informa business

First issued in paperback 2021

© 2020 Gabriela Argüello

The right of Gabriela Argüello to be identified as author of this work has been asserted by her in accordance with sections 77 and 78 of the Copyright, Designs and Patents Act 1988.

All rights reserved. No part of this book may be reprinted or reproduced or utilised in any form or by any electronic, mechanical, or other means, now known or hereafter invented, including photocopying and recording, or in any information storage or retrieval system, without permission in writing from the publishers.

Trademark notice: Product or corporate names may be trademarks or registered trademarks, and are used only for identification and explanation without intent to infringe.

Publisher's Note
The publisher has gone to great lengths to ensure the quality of this reprint but points out that some imperfections in the original copies may be apparent.

British Library Cataloguing-in-Publication Data
A catalogue record for this book is available from the British Library

Library of Congress Cataloging-in-Publication Data
Names: Arguello Moncayo, Gabriela, 1983– author.
Title: Marine pollution, shipping waste and international law / Gabriela Arguello.
Description: Abingdon, Oxon; New York, NY: Routledge, 2020. | Series: Routledge research in international environmental law | Based on author's thesis (doctoral - Gèoteborgs universitet, 2017) issued under title: Environmentally sound management: its status and role in the sea-land interface regulation of wastes. | Includes bibliographical references.
Identifiers: LCCN 2019017105 (print) | LCCN 2019018282 (ebook) | ISBN 9780429059513 (ebk) | ISBN 9780367180980 (hbk)
Subjects: LCSH: Ships—Waste disposal—Law and legislation.
Classification: LCC K3592.5 (ebook) | LCC K3592.5 .A74 2020 (print) | DDC 344.04/6343—dc23
LC record available at https://lccn.loc.gov/2019017105

ISBN: 978-0-367-18098-0 (hbk)
ISBN: 978-1-03-224067-1 (pbk)
ISBN: 978-0-429-05951-3 (ebk)

DOI: 10.4324/9780429059513

Typeset in Galliard
by codeMantra

Contents

List of figures	viii
List of tables	ix
List of abbreviations	x

PART I
Preliminaries   1

1 Introduction   3
Background 3
The relevance of international law in the regulation of wastes 6
ESM and ship wastes 7
ESM and sustainable development 8
Theoretical framework 9

2 Environmentally sound management of wastes (ESM)   12
ESM: its roles 12
*Legal status of ESM: from policy objective and
    treaty obligation to customary law 16*
ESM as a customary law and treaty obligation 30
ESM as a normative legal framework 31
Concluding remarks 32
Sovereignty and ESM 33
*Concluding remarks: ESM and permanent sovereignty over
    natural resources 39*

3 Wastes   40
A reexamination of the legal concept of waste 40
Ship wastes 43
Wastes subject to transboundary movements of wastes 50

vi *Contents*

*Transboundary movements of wastes and ship wastes: an
analysis of Article 195 of the LOSC 62*
Concluding remarks 63

PART II
Regulation of transboundary movements of wastes and ship wastes

65

4 Transboundary movements of wastes

67

From transboundary pollution to pollution transfer 67
The Basel Convention 69
*The OECD legal framework of transboundary
movements of wastes 81*
EU law and shipments of wastes 98
Concluding remarks 100

5 Ship-source pollution

101

Marine pollution 101
An overview on ship-source marine pollution 103
MARPOL 110
EU and ship wastes 115
Concluding remarks 118

PART III
The ESM of wastes

119

6 The sea/land interface waste management dilemma

121

Genesis of the controversy at the international level 121
*Blending operations on board ships: the initial
controversy 125*
*The management of ship wastes on land: the current
controversy 127*
*The EU and the management of ship wastes in their
sea/land interface 143*

7 ESM and the transboundary movement of waste regime

146

The growing importance of ESM within the Basel regime 146
Legal nature of the ESM obligation 147
ESM: substantive content 148

Contents vii

ESM at the OECD level 157
ESM at the EU level 161
Concluding remarks 163

8 The ESM of ship wastes: the sea/land interface   164
The ESM of ship wastes at the international level 164
The ESM of ship wastes at the EU level 184
Forthcoming regulation on port reception facilities 208

PART IV
Conclusions   211

9 The management of ship wastes: the sea-land interface   213
Conflicts of law 213

10 International law and waste management   219
The integrative function of ESM: possibilities
and limitations 219

Appendix I: management of cargo residues
(MARPOL, Annex II) in the Baltic Sea area   223
Appendix II: survey results concerning the collection
of cargo residues (MARPOL, Annex II) in the
Baltic Sea area   225

References   231
Bibliography   237
Index   261

Figures

2.1	ESM core meaning	26
4.1	Basel Convention	81
4.2	Movement of wastes according to Regulation 1013/2006/EC	99
7.1	Environmentally sound management of wastes	150
8.1	Port's fee system	169
8.2	Port reception facilities: cost recovery systems for ship-generated wastes	203
a.1	Response rate (%). Ports that receive liquid bulk cargoes in the Baltic Sea area	225
a.2	Does the port authority have information regarding the volume (m^3) of cargo residues 'actually delivered'?	226
a.3	Fee system: MARPOL – Annex II residues	227
a.4	Notification procedure regarding MARPOL Annex II residues	227
a.5	Who handles the collection of MARPOL – Annex II residues?	228
a.6	Types of external waste management operators	229
a.7	Ownership and operation of port reception facilities	229
a.8	Port involvement concerning handling or management of MARPOL – Annex II residues	230

Tables

3.1	Ship wastes MARPOL	44
4.1	Waste categories OECD and Basel Convention	87
4.2	Control procedures OECD Council Decision C(2001)107/FINAL	90
8.1	Special Areas MARPOL	172

Abbreviations

APS	Amsterdam Port Services
AFS Convention	International Convention on the Control of Harmful Anti-Fouling Systems of Ships
BAT	Best available techniques
BEP	Best environmental practices
BWM Convention	International Convention for the Control and Management of Ships' Ballast Water and Sediments
CIEL	Center for International Environmental Law
CLC Conventions	1969 International Convention on Civil Liability for Oil Pollution Damage Protocol of 1992 to Amend the International Convention on Civil Liability for Oil Pollution Damage
COP to the Basel Convention	Conference of the Parties to the Basel Convention on the Control of Transboundary Movements of Hazardous Wastes and Their Disposal
EC	European Community
Court of Justice	Court of Justice of the European Union
EEZ	Exclusive Economic Zone
EMSA	European Maritime Safety Agency
ESM	Environmentally Sound Management
EU	European Union
Fund Conventions	1971 International Convention on the Establishment of an International Fund for Compensation for Oil Pollution Damage 1992 Protocol to Amend the 1971 International Convention on the Establishment of an International Fund for Compensation for Oil Pollution Damage

	Protocol of 2003 to the International Convention on the Establishment of an International Fund for Compensation for Oil Pollution Damage, 1992
GAIRS	Generally accepted international rules and standards
GESAMP	Joint Group of Experts on the Scientific Aspects of Marine Environmental Protection
Helsinki Convention	Convention for the Protection of the Marine Environment of the Baltic Sea Area, 1992
HELCOM	Baltic Marine Environment Protection Commission
ICJ	International Court of Justice
ILA	International Law Association
ILC	International Law Commission
ILO	International Labor Organization
IMDG	International Maritime Dangerous Goods Code
IMO	International Maritime Organization
ITLOS	International Tribunal for the Law of the Sea
London Convention	Convention on the Prevention of Marine Pollution by Dumping of Wastes and Other Matter, 1972 and its 1996 Protocol
LOSC	United Nations Convention on the Law of the Sea, 1982
MARPOL	International Convention for the Prevention of Pollution from Ships 1973 as Modified by its 1978 Protocol
MEAs	Multilateral Environmental Agreements
MEPC	Marine Environment Protection Committee
MSC	Maritime Safety Committee
NGO	Nongovernmental Organization
OBO carrier	Ore-Bulk-Oil carrier
OECD	Organisation for Economic Cooperation and Development
OEWG	Open-ended Working Group of the Basel Convention
OILPOL 54	International Convention for the Prevention of Pollution of the Sea by Oil, 1954
OPRC 90	International Convention on Oil Pollution Preparedness, Response and Co-operation, 1990
OSPAR Convention	Convention for the Protection of the Marine Environment of the North-East Atlantic

xii *Abbreviations*

Paris MoU	Paris Memorandum of Understanding on Port State Control
PIC	Prior Informed Consent
PCIJ	Permanent Court of International Justice
Rio Declaration	Rio Declaration on Environment and Development
SOLAS Convention	International Convention for the Safety of Life at Sea, 1974 as amended
SSN	SafeSeaNet
TEU	Treaty on European Union
TFEU	Treaty on the Functioning of the European Union
UN	United Nations
UNCED	United Nations Conference on Environment and Development held in 1992
UNCSD	United Nations Conference on Sustainable Development 2012
UNEP	United Nations Environment Programme
UNGA	United Nations General Assembly
UNSG	United Nations Secretary-General
UNTS	United Nations Treaty Series
WSSD	World Summit on Sustainable Development 2012

Part I
Preliminaries

1 Introduction

Background

Human activities are increasingly putting pressure on the functioning and resilience of the Earth system, i.e., the biophysical and chemical processes happening on land, in the oceans, and in the atmosphere.[1] To grasp the anthropogenic influences on this system, scientists have identified nine planetary boundaries including climate and land-system changes, and biogeochemical flows, among others.[2] Within such planetary boundaries, the most pressing challenge is that of devising "safe operating spaces for humanity".[3] One key feature in establishing these planetary boundaries is the safeguarding of the capacity of the environment to "absorb and dissipate human waste".[4] Indeed, waste management is fundamental to maintaining human activities within the planetary boundaries and preserving the environment's capacity to sustain life. For instance, waste management has implications for the preservation of biodiversity and the maintenance of ecosystem services, e.g., by avoiding the discharge of hazardous waste into the ocean or emissions into the atmosphere.[5]

While essential for ensuring the Earth's resilience, waste management remains one of the greatest challenges for not only our generation but future ones too. Waste generation is closely interrelated "to population and income growth".[6]

---

1 Johan Rockström et al., "Planetary Boundaries: Exploring the Safe Operating Space for Humanity," *Ecology and Society* 14, no. 2 (2009). *See also* Will Steffen et al., "Planetary Boundaries: Guiding Human Development on a Changing Planet," *Science* 347, no. 6223 (2015).

2 Ibid.

3 Rockström et al., "Planetary Boundaries: Exploring the Safe Operating Space for Humanity."

4 *See* Johan Rockström and Jeffrey D. Sachs, "Sustainable Development and Planetary Boundaries," *High Level Panel on the Post-2015 Development Agenda* (2013), 4.

5 Ibid.

6 United Nations Environment Programme (UNEP) and GRID-Arendal, "Towards a Green Economy: Pathways to Sustainable Development and Poverty Eradication," (2011), 299. *See also* that according to the OECD, "Generally, waste in high-income countries tends to contain more packing materials and manufactured products/materials, and less organic waste. Conversely organic waste can make up 50–80% of municipal waste in lower income countries" Organisation for Economic Co-Operation and Development (OECD), "Material Resources, Productivity and the Environment," *OECD Green Growth Studies* (Paris, 2015), 90.

4 Preliminaries

According to the OECD's estimates, "12 billion metric tons (Gt) of wastes including over 0.4 Gt of hazardous waste" are generated each year.[7] Therefore, as societies experience further economic development and industrialization, waste management poses both challenges for the protection of the environment and human health, and opportunities for expanding markets of recyclable materials and energy recovery.[8]

A life-cycle approach to waste management

Traditionally, waste management dealt with downstream disposal operations. A life-cycle approach, by contrast, offers a new perspective that involves every phase, i.e., from the prevention and reduction of waste generation to the actual handling of wastes. Waste handling includes the collection, transport, monitoring, and treatment of wastes including the aftercare of waste facilities.

From a legal perspective, the regulation of waste is intrinsically intertwined with policy issues. At both international and regional levels, a life-cycle approach is promoted as a fundamental part of the transition from a "linear economy," to a "circular"[9] or "green economy".[10] A circular economy aims to achieve sustainable development by uniting economic development and environmental protection.[11] Waste management is vital to such a transition. In a linear econ-

---

7 The quantities of generated wastes must be carefully considered, since the definition of waste varies between States and information regarding some waste streams is not always available. Organisation for Economic Co-Operation and Development (OECD), "Material Resources, Productivity and the Environment," 90. A detailed explanation of the trends of waste generation is found in "Resource Productivity in the G8 and the OECD," *A Report in the Framework of the Kobe 3R Action Plan* (2011), 15–16.

8 Organisation for Economic Co-Operation and Development (OECD), "Material Resources, Productivity and the Environment," 41, 93. Secretariat of the Basel Convention, Zoï Environment Network, and GRID-Arendal, "Vital Waste Graphics 3," (France, 2012), 12–13. Katharina Kummer, "Turning Wastes into Valuable Resources: Promoting Compliance with Obligations?," *Environmental Policy and Law* 41, nos. 4–5 (2011). United Nations Environment Programme (UNEP) and GRID-Arendal, "Towards a Green Economy: Pathways to Sustainable Development and Poverty Eradication," 298.

9 *Note* that circular economy has its origin in "economy and ecology." Alan Murray, Keith Skene, and Kathryn Haynes, "The Circular Economy: An Interdisciplinary Exploration of the Concept and Application in a Global Context," *Journal of Business Ethics* 140, no. 3 (2017): 369.

10 At the international level, the United Nations Environment Programme (UNEP) has been a primary actor in the transition toward a "green economy." United Nations Environment Programme (UNEP) and GRID-Arendal, "Towards a Green Economy: Pathways to Sustainable Development and Poverty Eradication," 295. At the EU level, *See* "Com(2015) 614 Final: Closing the Loop – An EU Action for the Circular Economy," (Brussels, 2015), 8. *See also* "Com(2017) 33 Final, on the Implementation of the Circular Economy Action Plan," in *Report from the Commission to the European Parliament, the Council, the European Economic and Social Committee and the Committee of the Regions* (26.01.2017). Organisation for Economic Co-Operation and Development (OECD), "Material Resources, Productivity and the Environment," 41.

11 Murray, Skene, and Haynes, "The Circular Economy: An Interdisciplinary Exploration of the Concept and Application in a Global Context," 369. *See also* Chris Backes, *Law for a Circular Economy* (The Hague: Eleven International Publishing, 2017), 13. "The circular economy refers

omy, production is dependent on the exploitation of natural resources. Production is then followed by consumption and finally by waste disposal.[12] In a circular or green economy, the efficient use of resources becomes paramount. Consequently, the preservation and protection of resources entail a reexamination of the role of wastes in the economy. Waste becomes another stage in the production process; those substances or materials reenter the production process by several means, including reuse, recycling, or recovery.[13] The efficient use of resources also involves the prevention of waste generation.

Legal challenges for waste regulation from a life-cycle approach

From a legal perspective, applying a life-cycle approach to waste management raises two main challenges. First, international law regulates wastes incidentally, i.e., within media-specific pollution regimes, e.g., sea, air, land-based pollution; or in relation to hazardous substances, e.g., regulation of persistent organic pollutants. In cases where wastes are directly regulated, this regulation is concerned with a particular activity, i.e., transboundary movements or dumping. The incidental regulation of wastes involves a risk of transfer of pollution from one environmental medium to another, resulting in fragmentation. Such fragmentation produces a lack of coordination between different regimes and the proliferation of conflicting and inconsistent legal obligations.

The second challenge is that waste management has been traditionally considered as a national affair except in cases dealing with pollution transfer and transboundary movements of wastes. Within this traditional legal perspective, States are virtually free to generate and to dispose of wastes as they see fit, so long as such wastes do not cause harm beyond their national jurisdiction.[14]

---

to an economic concept which is rooted in the principle of sustainable development and whose objective is to produce goods and services while limiting the consumption and waste of raw materials, water and energy sources." This is a citation of the French Ministry of Environment, Energy and the Sea found in Eléonore Maitre-Ekern, "The Choice of Regulatory Instruments for a Circular Economy," in *Environmental Law and Economics*, ed. Mathis Klaus and Bruce R. Huber (Switzerland: Springer 2017), 311.

12 Richard Hughes, "The EU Circular Economy Package – Life Cycle Thinking to Life Cycle Law?" (paper presented at the the 24th CIRP Conference on Life Cycle Engineering, 2017), 10–11.

13 *Note* that a "circular economy is one that is restorative and regenerative by design, and which aims to keep products, components and materials at their highest utility and value at all times, distinguishing between technical and biological cycles. Therefore, the circular economy concept aims at optimising the value of the resources used and to minimise the amount of resources used." Backes, *Law for a Circular Economy*, 13. *See also* Maitre-Ekern, "The Choice of Regulatory Instruments for a Circular Economy."

14 *See*, for example, Rosemary Rayfuse, "Principles of International Environmental Law Applicable to Waste Management," in *Waste Management and the Green Economy: Law and Policy*, ed. Katharina Kummer, Andreas R. Ziegler, and Jorun Baumgartner (Cheltenham: Edward Elgar Publishing, 2016).

6 Preliminaries

Considering the challenges described above, the main legal problem concerning waste is the absence of a regulatory system that would enable the management of waste from a life-cycle approach. Such regulatory system should provide the tools to coordinate between the existing legal regimes that incidentally regulate wastes.

The relevance of international law in the regulation of wastes

A life-cycle approach to waste management requires the cooperation of States and the establishment of coordinated activities. States can no longer have separate standards for wastes posing transboundary risks and for "purely domestic" wastes. This dichotomy defeats the policy objective to regulate wastes from a life-cycle approach.

The Basel Convention

The Basel Convention on the Control of Transboundary Movements of Hazardous Wastes and their Disposal[15] is the most comprehensive treaty dealing with wastes. For several years, some advanced the proposition that this treaty had the potential to become the basic framework for waste regulation from a life-cycle approach.[16] The underlying argument is that although the Basel Convention governs a particular stage of the wastes' cycle, i.e., transboundary movements of wastes and their subsequent treatment, this instrument also incorporates several principles that could apply to every category of waste, such as waste minimization or environmentally sound management (ESM).[17] Thus, treaties incidentally dealing with wastes or with particular hazardous substances, or with a certain stage of the waste life-cycle, should conform with the basic principles established under the Basel Convention.

This book argues, however, that this Convention failed to become an overarching regime for dealing with wastes for two main reasons. First, its restrictive approach concerning movements of wastes, i.e., transboundary movements are

---

15 Hereafter the Basel Convention.
16 "It is submitted that the Basel Convention, to date the most advanced attempt at comprehensive global regulation of this issue, has the potential to form the basis on which to build this regime. The other rules, which effectively address some aspects of the hazardous waste cycle, have a useful and important role in complementing and enhancing the Basel Convention." Katharina Kummer, *International Management of Hazardous Wastes: The Basel Convention and Related Legal Rules* (Oxford: Oxford University Press, 1995), 29. Secretariat of the Basel Convention, "The Application of the Basel Convention to Hazardous Wastes and Other Wastes Generated on Board Ships," (4 April 2011), 23. "Third Legal Analysis of the Application of the Basel Convention to Hazardous Wastes and Other Wastes Generated on Board Ships," (30 April 2012), 29.
17 "The Basel Convention is based on a life-cycle approach: it sets out obligations pertaining to the generation of wastes and to the management of wastes, including their transboundary movements." Juliette Kohler, "A Paradigm Shift under the Basel Convention on Hazardous Wastes," in *Waste Management and the Green Economy: Law and Policy*, ed. Katharina Kummer, Andreas R. Ziegler, and Jorun Baumgartner (Cheltenham: Edward Elgar Publishing, 2016), 80.

the exception, not the rule, and even when such movements are allowed, the control mechanisms are stringent. Second, recyclable or recoverable wastes are subject to the same strict control mechanisms as wastes subject to final disposal.

The rise of ESM

Despite the limitations of the Basel Convention, which prevent it from becoming an overarching regime to deal with wastes, this book argues that the ESM embodied in this treaty has gradually transformed into a legal principle. The repercussions of such a transformation are twofold. First, waste management can no longer be categorized as an exclusive national affair. The ESM of wastes requires the treatment of wastes from a life-cycle approach. Second, ESM is the fundamental framework for the regulation of wastes. This principle has allowed the establishment of cross-sectional policies among several regimes, for instance, interactions between transboundary movement of wastes and ship-source pollution regimes. This coordination plays a crucial part in addressing the fragmentation of waste regulation, as well as in establishing international agreed standards of waste management. Overall, ESM is facilitating the development of a comprehensive waste regime.

ESM and ship wastes

To address the challenges involved in the regulation of waste, this book is concerned with the management of wastes generated on board vessels while at sea and after they are discharged on land to port reception facilities. Ship wastes were chosen for three reasons.

First, these wastes are incidentally regulated within the regime of marine pollution. At the international level, ship wastes are governed by the International Convention for the Prevention of Pollution from Ships 1973 as Modified by its 1978 Protocol (hereafter MARPOL). The consequence has been the development of a preventive regime that strictly regulates harmful substances (including wastes) while at sea, restricting discharges in the marine environment. Focusing on the prevention of pollution in specific environmental media (e.g., the sea) leaves little room for a life-cycle waste approach in relation to the management of wastes once they are discharged on land. Consequently, there is a risk of transforming ship-source marine pollution into land-based pollution.

Second, the prevention of ship-source pollution is heavily reliant on the "provision of adequate port reception facilities" for the discharge of wastes that otherwise would end up in the sea. The Parties to this treaty, however, have been reluctant to develop the meaning and extent of the obligation related to the provision of port reception facilities[18] and the relationship between

---

18 *See* Ronald B. Mitchell, *Intentional Oil Pollution at Sea: Environmental Policy and Treaty Compliance* (Cambridge: MIT Press, 1994), Chapter 6. Alan Khee-Jin Tan, *Vessel-Source Marine Pollution: The Law and Politics of International Regulation* (Cambridge: Cambridge University Press, 2006), 251–81.

8 *Preliminaries*

these facilities and further downstream management operations. Such reluctance could be understood from the traditional legal approach toward domestic wastes, i.e., once wastes are discharged on land, States manage these wastes at their discretion.

Finally, ship wastes were chosen due to incidents related to the unsafe management of ship wastes on land. In light of these incidents, scholars, States, and international organizations responded by examining the possible application of the Basel Convention to ship wastes while at sea and after their discharge on land. However, this book argues that the appropriate instrument for this task is not the Basel Convention, but rather the ESM principle. The rise of the ESM of wastes has been a catalyst for addressing the management of ship wastes once they enter national boundaries. As analyzed in Chapter 8, ESM is instrumental in categorizing *adequate* port reception facilities as those allowing the treatment of wastes on land.

ESM and sustainable development

Sustainable development is an environmental policy which captures the need to balance environmental, social, and economic needs. To achieve such balance, the 2030 Agenda for Sustainable Development set several goals. Although nonbinding, the adoption of these goals is not devoid of legal significance. In this case, the UN General Assembly was a unique forum that brought together all members of the UN, who articulated the values shared by the international community toward sustainable development and the actions that States are either taking or should be taking to achieve certain objectives.[19] Waste management is fundamental in achieving several of these goals, including water management and the development of sustainable cities.[20] Particularly, ESM is strongly related to Goal 12 "sustainable consumption and production patterns" which includes the ESM of wastes throughout their life-cycle in several of its targets.[21] This goal promotes the ESM of wastes in general, i.e., including both wastes that remain within national boundaries, as well as those posing potential transboundary risks. Today, ESM is included in a range of soft and hard law instruments that demonstrate the evolution of waste management from a purely domestic affair to an international one.

---

19 The relevance of this particular UN General Assembly is discussed in Chapter 2 in relation to the formation of customary law.

20 *See* Goals 6 and 11. *United Nations General Assembly, "A/Res/70/1. Transforming Our World: The 2030 Agenda for Sustainable Development," in Seventieth Session. Agenda Items 15 and 16 (2015), 22.*

21 The targets include: "[b]y 2020, achieve the environmentally sound management of chemicals and all wastes throughout their life-cycle, in accordance with agreed international frameworks, and significantly reduce their release to air, water and soil in order to minimize their adverse impacts on human health and the environment ... By 2030, substantially reduce waste generation through prevention, reduction, recycling and reuse." Ibid.

Introduction 9

Theoretical framework

On environmental legal principles

In international environmental law, the word "principle" can have several meanings. First, it can refer to two sources of international law. One of these sources is customary law as defined in Article 38(1)(b) of the Statute of the International Court of Justice (ICJ). Usually, customary norms are referred to as principles, e.g., the no-harm principle. Another source of a rather limited scope of application can be seen in the "general principles of law recognized by civilized nations".[22] Traditionally, general principles of law have had a modest role in solving *non-liquet* situations, i.e., when there is no applicable law.[23] Apart from these sources, there are some normative statements that have developed from public policy[24] (e.g., sustainable development), which do not easily fit into the traditional classification of sources of law since their legal status is controversial. Despite their uncertain legal status, these principles display some legal effects, as explained below.

Principles comprise both binding customary law as well as normative statements.[25] A common characteristic of principles relates to their broad manner of formulation, which makes their applicability flexible. The legal effects of principles are varied, e.g., binding obligations, normative frameworks,[26] or policies that "reflect courses of action adopted to secure ... a state of affairs conceived to be desirable".[27] Principles, such as the ESM of wastes, serve as evaluative standards by which to assess and interpret other norms and provide a guide for regulatory development. According to Birnie et al., principles "set limits, or provide guidance, or determine how conflicts between other rules or principles will be resolved".[28] Finally, principles have a close connection to the coherence of environmental law. They are the connecting thread between rules that become a

---

22 *See* Article 38(1)(c) of the Statute of the International Court of Justice.

23 Malcolm Shaw, *International Law*, 8th edn (Cambridge: Cambridge University Press, 2017), 73.

24 Nicolas de Sadeleer, *Environmental Principles: From Political Slogans to Legal Rules* (Oxford: Oxford University Press, 2002), 38.

25 Eloise Scotford, *Environmental Principles and the Evolution of Environmental Law* (Oxford: Hart Publishing, 2017), Chapter 6. Alexander Kiss and Dinah Shelton, *Guide to International Environmental Law* (Leiden: Martinus Nijhoff Publishers, 2007), 89–90.

26 Dupuy characterizes certain principles such as sustainable development and the precautionary approach as part of a "normative matrix" that "due to their extreme generality and vagueness, such concepts, as well as when they evolve into law, always remain dependent upon complementary sources for the clarification of their veritable content ... [T]hey should be viewed in terms of their normative potential rather than from the formal perspective of their legal status." Pierre-Marie Dupuy, "Formation of Customary International Law and General Principles," in *The Oxford Handbook of International Environmental Law*, ed. Daniel Bodansky, Jutta Brunnée, and Ellen Hey (Oxford: Oxford University Press, 2008), 462.

27 Scotford, *Environmental Principles and the Evolution of Environmental Law*, 6.

28 Patricia Birnie, Alan Boyle, and Catherine Redgwell, *International Law and the Environment*, 3rd edn (Oxford: Oxford University Press, 2009), 28.

10 *Preliminaries*

system rather than a collection of norms.[29] Principles play an important role not only in understanding the content and interaction between specific international obligations, but also in shaping the identity of environmental law as a legal field.

On regime interaction

The author discusses the interaction between the regimes dealing with transboundary movements of wastes and ship-source pollution. The term "regime" is understood as a body of specialized norms, principles, and institutions that regulate a particular issue, e.g., law of the sea. However, specialization differs from debates surrounding the notion of "self-contained regimes." As explained by Nele Matz-Lück, self-contained regimes could imply the emergence of branches of law that "exist independently from other international law".[30] However, no regime exists in isolation. One may argue that no matter the level of specialization, regimes are subject to the same sources of law, law-making processes, and general rules including *lex specialis* or *lex posteriori*.[31] Additionally, the study of regime interaction demands a diversity of approaches including a historical account of these specialized fields to find common grounds of collaboration in the creation, development, and enforcement of international law. Institutional analysis regarding the role of international organizations in the development of synergies between legal regimes is also fundamental to explain the emergence of legal principles connecting legal regimes. This book offers an array of such approaches toward regime interaction.

First, a doctrinal study related to the interpretation of sources of law together with understanding the meaning of legal material in its historical, social, economic, and politic contexts is required. Engaging in such analysis serves a dual purpose. The first is to achieve coherence[32] between the regimes dealing with transboundary movements of wastes and ship-source pollution. As analyzed in

---

29 On the role of principles and its relationship with coherence, *See* Kaarlo Tuori, *Ratio and Voluntas: The Tension between Reason and Will in Law*, Applied Legal Philosophy (Farnham: Ashgate, 2011), 164–66. Ronald Dworkin, *Law's Empire* (Cambridge, MA: Harvard University Press, 1986), 263.

30 Nele Matz-Lück, "Norm Interpretation across International Regimes: Competences and Legitimacy," in *Regime Interaction in International Law: Facing Fragmentation*, ed. Margaret Young (Cambridge: Cambridge University Press, 2012), 206–7.

31 International Law Commission, "Conclusions of the Work of the Study Group on the Fragmentation of International Law: Difficulties Arising from the Diversification and Expansion of International Law, (Fifty-Third Session a/56/10)," *Yearbook of the International Law Commission*, Part 2 (2006): 5.

32 Coherence "aims at presenting the law as a network of principles, rules, meta-rules, and exceptions, at different levels of abstraction, connected by support relations. The argumentation used in order to achieve coherence involves not only description and logic but also evaluative (normative) steps." Peczenik, "A Theory of Legal Doctrine," *Ratio Juris* 14, no. 1 (2001):79. "Coherence refers to the emanation of rules from principles of general application." Jürgen Friedrich, *International Environmental "Soft Law": The Functions and Limits of Nonbinding Instruments in International Environmental Governance and Law* (Berlin: Springer 2013), 255.

Chapter 6, international organizations and States have discussed the management of ship wastes in the sea/land interface solely as a matter of conflicting and competing norms. Addressing such conflict seeks to provide legal certainty and predictability, which is vital for the actors who must implement, enforce, and comply with these regulations. The second purpose is to address the fragmented regulation on wastes, which is currently subject to sectoral pollution regimes. Moving toward an overarching regime of waste management is possible due to the emergence of ESM as an international legal principle.

Second, the possibilities and limits of cooperation between international organizations and treaty organs dealing with specialized legal regimes are also addressed. The management of ship wastes, e.g., has fostered cooperation between the Conference of the Parties to the Basel Convention and the International Maritime Organization while at the European Union (EU) level, renewed attention is being given to Directive No. 2000/59/EC on Port Reception Facilities for Ship-Generated Waste and Cargo Residues concerning its functional integration with wider EU waste legislation. To this end, the book highlights on empirical evidence and maps the difficulties encountered in tracing ship wastes after their discharge to port reception facilities. The work draws on the European Maritime Safety Agency findings regarding the delivery of ship-generated waste and cargo residues to port reception facilities in EU ports.[33] From this study, it became evident that particular obstacles with regard to traceability emerge in relation to residues from noxious liquid substances carried in bulk. The author then chose to study ports in the Baltic Sea since, as a semi-enclosed sea, the Baltic is more vulnerable to environmental pressures, including ship-source pollution. There are 61 ports in the Baltic that receive noxious liquid bulk cargoes. A closed questionnaire, included in Appendix I, was sent to all these ports. Questions related to: (a) volume (m^3) of cargo residues "actually delivered"; (b) waste notification system; (c) how wastes are managed, i.e., by the port, an individual terminal or an external operator; (d) current practices regarding how external operators are chosen; and (e) channels of communication between the port and the individual terminal or external operator. This study provides evidence of normative development across regimes, but also it exposes normative overlaps and duplication of activities among international organizations.

---

33 Ramboll, "Final Report: EMSA Study on the Delivery of Ship-Generated Waste and Cargo Residues to Port Reception Facilities in EU Ports," in *EMSA/OP/06/2011* (European Maritime Safety Agency (EMSA), August 2012).

2 Environmentally sound management of wastes (ESM)

ESM: its roles

Waste management from a national to an international affair

Waste management was traditionally seen as a domestic matter. The Stockholm Conference, 1972, did not specifically address wastes, but its Principle 6 called States to cease the discharge of hazardous substances beyond the capacities of the environment.[1] The broad notion of hazardous substances included wastes. However, the initial concern in relation to hazardous substances was to halt their release, whereas today international law is focused also on preventing and minimizing waste generation.[2] In 1976, the OECD's Council adopted Recommendation C(76)155 FINAL on a Comprehensive Waste Management Policy. It was the first instrument to acknowledge wastes as a matter of international concern, due to: (a) the increasing generation of hazardous wastes; (b) the economic and regulatory challenges related to the management of varied hazardous waste streams and constituents; and (c) the possible unintended transfer of pollution from one sector of the environment to another.[3] The protection of human beings and the environment would be later translated as the foundation of ESM.

The ESM of wastes emerged in the early 1980s at the OECD level during initial efforts to regulate transboundary movements of wastes. While at the international level, developing States supported a complete prohibition on transboundary movements of wastes, OECD Member States focused instead on ESM as a basic principle for the management of hazardous wastes *within domestic boundaries*

---

1 Principle 6 of the Stockholm Declaration "is founded on the assumption that the environment has the capacity, to some extent, to assimilate substances so to render them harmless." The assimilative capacity has been replaced by the precautionary principle" Aruna Venkat, *Environmental Law and Policy* (India: PHI Learning Private Limited, 2011), 199–200.

2 COP to the Basel Convention, "Cartagena Declaration on the Prevention, Minimization and Recovery of Hazardous Wastes and Other Wastes," in *Annex IV: Report of the Conference of the Parties to the Basel Convention on the Control of Transboundary Movements of Hazardous Wastes and their Disposal on its Tenth Meeting (UNEP/CHW.10/28)* (Colombia, 2011).

3 *See* the preamble of Organisation for Economic Co-Operation and Development (OECD), "C(76)155/Final Recommendation of the Council on a Comprehensive Waste Management Policy," (1976).

and for those subject to transboundary movements. During the early 1980s, ESM was devised as a leading argument to legitimize transboundary movements of wastes. In fact, the fifth preambular paragraph of the OECD Council Decision and Recommendation C(83)180(Final) on Transfrontier Movements of Wastes mentions that "efficient and environmentally sound management of hazardous waste may justify some transfrontier movements of such waste".[4]

The OECD Council Decision and Recommendation C(83)180(Final) declared as a general principle that States should manage wastes within their jurisdiction in "such a way as to protect man[5] and the environment." Independently of the place where wastes are disposed, ESM is concerned with the protection of human health and the environment from the deleterious effects of hazardous wastes. These two objectives have been incorporated into the definition of ESM in several instruments at both international and regional levels, including, for instance, the Basel Convention and the working definition of ESM at the OECD level. The OECD Decisions and Recommendations controlling transboundary movements of wastes consistently include ESM as an overarching principle for the management of hazardous wastes.[6]

In a parallel effort, at the international level, UNEP's Montevideo Programme for the Development and Periodic Review of Environmental Law[7] developed the Cairo Guidelines and Principles for the Environmentally Sound Management of Hazardous Wastes (Cairo Guidelines) that were adopted by the Governing Council of UNEP in 1987.[8] Their aim was to assist States in developing strategies for the ESM of hazardous wastes from generation to final disposal. The Cairo Guidelines were based on "common elements and principles derived from relevant existing bilateral, regional and global agreements and national regulations"[9] regarding waste management.

---

4 This same paragraph was reproduced verbatim in the conclusions and recommendations of the OECD Conference on International Cooperation Concerning Transfrontier Movements of Hazardous Wastes (Basel, Switzerland, 26–27 March 1985). The text of this Conference can be found as an Annex of the OECD Resolution C(85) 100. "C(85)100 Council Resolution on International Co-Operation Concerning Transfrontier Movements of Hazardous Wastes" (1985).
5 The wording "man" was replaced in later instruments by "human health."
6 Organisation for Economic Co-Operation and Development (OECD), "C(83)180(Final) Council Decision and Recommendation on Transfrontier Movements of Hazardous Wastes." "C(85)100 Council Resolution on International Co-Operation Concerning Transfrontier Movements of Hazardous Wastes." "C(86) 64 (Final) Council Decision – Recommendation on Exports of Hazardous Wastes from the OECD Area" (1986). "C(90)178/Final Council Decision-Recommendation on the Reduction of Transfrontier Movements of Wastes" (1991). "C(92)39/Final Council Decision Concerning the Control of Transfrontier Movements of Wastes Destined for Recovery Operations" (1992).
7 *See* Governing Council of UNEP, "Decision 10/21: Adoption of the Programme for the Development and Periodic Review of Environmental Law," (31 May 1982). Ad Hoc Meeting of Senior Government Officials Expert in Environmental Law, "Montevideo Programme for the Development and Periodic Review of Environmental Law," in *Ad Hoc Meeting of Senior Government Officials Expert in Environmental Law* (6 November 1981).
8 United Nations Environment Programme (UNEP), "Cairo Guidelines and Principles for the Environmentally Sound Management of Hazardous Wastes," in *UNEP/GC.14/17* (1987).
9 Ibid.

14 *Preliminaries*

The contribution of the Cairo Guidelines is threefold. First, this instrument set the foundations for the development of ESM as a principle regarding hazardous wastes within national jurisdiction, as well as for those subject to transboundary movements. Second, the Cairo Guidelines and the OECD Decisions and Recommendations on transfrontier movements of wastes were the precursors of the Basel Convention. At that point in time, the regulation on movements of wastes was a developing area of international law, solely governed by customary law principles of transboundary pollution. Third, the Cairo guidelines are included in the 13th preambular paragraph of the Basel Convention. This inclusion is relevant for the purposes of treaty interpretation. Therefore, it sheds light on the substantive content of ESM,[10] including, among others: (a) preventive measures regarding waste generation, (b) monitoring and control of waste handling, (c) development of best available techniques (BAT) and best environmental practices (BEP), and (d) technical and safety measures for the operation and aftercare of management facilities.

Another landmark soft law instrument regarding ESM is the Rio Declaration, 1992. In particular, Agenda 21 includes ESM in several areas, ranging from chemicals to hazardous wastes,[11] while endorsing other principles as well, e.g., the precautionary approach and the polluter pays principle.

Chapter 3 of the Johannesburg Plan of Implementation[12] focuses on changing "unsustainable patterns of consumption and production" and its paragraphs 22 and 23 are concerned with ESM wastes. As with Agenda 21, it favors a precautionary approach. The first priority is the minimization of the generation of wastes in both quantitative and qualitative terms. Waste that is nevertheless generated should be reused or recycled. Final disposal, e.g., landfill, should be the last resort when designing the ESM of waste systems. The cooperation and participation of all stakeholders involved in waste management is also encouraged.

"The Future We Want"[13] recognizes the importance of developing the ESM of wastes at all levels, i.e., wastes within national jurisdiction and those crossing national borders. Like its predecessors, "The Future We Want" stressed the need

---

10 Soft law instruments are "mechanisms for authoritative interpretation or amplification of the terms of a treaty ... Cairo Guidelines ... can be regarded as an amplification of the obligation of 'environmentally sound management' provided for in the Basel Convention." Alan Boyle, "Some Reflections on the Relationship of Treaties and Soft Law," *International and Comparative Law Quarterly* 48, no. 4 (1999): 905.

11 *See* Chapters 19 and 20 General Assembly – United Nations, "Agenda 21 – UN Doc. A/CONF.151/ 26," (1992).

12 The Johannesburg Declaration and Johannesburg Plan of Implementation were adopted at the United Nations World Summit of Sustainable Development held in 2002, also known as Rio+10. United Nations General Assembly, "Political Declaration and Plan of Implementation of the World Summit in Sustainable Development (a/CONF.199/20*)," in *Report of the World Summit on Sustainable Development* (South Africa, 2002).

13 The United Nations Conference on Sustainable Development held in 2012 at Rio, also known as Rio+20, concluded with the adoption of this document. United Nations – General Assembly, "The Future We Want (a/Res/66/288 Distr. General. Sixty-Sixth Session – Agenda Item 19)," (2012).

to: (a) manage chemicals and wastes "throughout their life-cycle", (b) enhance institutional coordination and cooperation, and (c) support the participation of public and other stakeholders involved in chemical and waste management.

The soft law frameworks and policy instruments analyzed in this section show that the main objective of ESM is without doubt the protection of the environment and human health from the deleterious effects of hazardous wastes. However, these instruments also stress that waste management should be conducted in an efficient manner. In addition, waste disposal operations, with or without the possibility of recovery, present an opportunity for income generation. Thus, the emerging international waste policy can be seen as an attempt to strike a balance between environmental protection and economic development where the rational use of resources is of paramount importance.

Currently, ESM is also included in numerous treaties that explicitly include the ESM of wastes as an obligation.[14] The inclusion of ESM as a treaty obligation has also triggered the adoption of further soft law instruments, for instance, through the Conference of the Parties (COP) of these treaties. A notable example is the COP to the Basel Convention, which since the late 1990s has focused its attention on developing standards that facilitate the understanding and implementation of ESM. The decisions, resolutions, and further recommendations adopted by these COPs represent a guidance framework for interpreting treaty obligations, since the Parties are directly involved in giving substantial content to the obligations embodied in a treaty. Therefore, they become particularly salient in the operation and evolution of these treaties.[15] Dupuy and Viñuales have referred to the instruments adopted by treaty organs and other intergovernmental bodies as *droit derive*, since they are "regulations adopted by a body that is empowered to do so by a treaty".[16] The importance of these instruments is their role in the development of international standards.

ESM: the connecting thread of waste regulation

Several treaties deal incidentally with wastes to attain other objectives in relation to the prevention of environmental pollution or the control of certain hazardous substances, including the control of discharges and emissions of persistent organic pollutants, the control of discharges of ship-source pollutants, and air pollutants. Others deal with waste in a fragmentary form, including the London Convention

---

14 The Basel Convention; Bamako Convention; Minamata Convention on Mercury; the Protocol on the Prevention of Pollution of the Mediterranean Sea by Transboundary Movements of Hazardous Wastes and their Disposal; Stockholm Convention on Persistent Organic Pollutants (POPs Convention). A recent example concerns the International Convention for the Control and Management of Ships' Ballast Water and Sediments. Article 14(1)(b) refers to the environmentally safe disposal of ballast water and sediments.

15 Jutta Brunnée, "Coping with Consent: Law-Making under Multilateral Environmental Agreements," *Leiden Journal of International Law* 15 (2002): 51.

16 Pierre-Marie Dupuy and Jorge Viñuales, *International Environmental Law* (Cambridge: Cambridge University Press, 2015), 36.

16 *Preliminaries*

on the Prevention of Marine Pollution by Dumping of Wastes and Other Matter, 1972, and its 1996 Protocol. Although the regulation of wastes has become a matter of international concern, its regulation is highly fragmented. Yet this piecemeal approach finds common ground under the ESM umbrella. ESM attempts to give voice to several waste policy instruments at international and regional levels, proclaiming a paradigm shift in relation to wastes, i.e., from nuisances to resources. In fact, ESM has helped to establish synergies between sectoral treaties dealing directly or incidentally with wastes, including the Basel Convention and MARPOL.

Legal status of ESM: from policy objective and treaty obligation to customary law

The examination of the ESM of wastes, like that of any other contemporary principle in international environmental law, involves a discussion of its legal status and an assessment of whether it has passed into the general corpus of international customary law or remains limited to specific treaty obligations. This section analyzes customary international law and the indeterminacy around its formation. As will be outlined, there is some evidence in respect of the existence of State practice and *opinio juris* in relation to ESM.

One feature of international law is its decentralized character. Unlike municipal systems, international law lacks a legislative body. This absence raises questions around the mechanisms and legitimacy[17] of law-making processes in the international arena. It has also attracted criticism with regard to the nature of international law[18] and the difficulties encountered in the systematic development of law. As the International Law Association (ILA) has noted, customary law is the result of an "informal process of rule-creation".[19] Legal scholars have scrutinized this formation process since medieval times, and the debate surrounding its constitutive elements is ongoing.[20] Custom is traditionally characterized as a

---

17 Patrick Kelly, "Customary International Law in Historical Context: The Exercise of Power without General Acceptance," in *Reexamining Customary International Law*, ed. D. Brian Lepard (Cambridge: Cambridge University Press, 2017). Martti Koskenniemi, *From Apology to Utopia: The Structure of International Legal Argument* (Cambridge: Cambridge University Press, 2006), Chapter 6.

18 *See* Jack L. Goldsmith and Eric A. Posner, *The Limits of International Law* (New York: Oxford University Press, 2005). Anna Södersten and Dennis Patterson, "The Nature of International Law," in *A Companion to European Union Law and International Law*, ed. Anna Södersten and Dennis Patterson (Chichester: Wiley Blackwell, 2016). Anthony D'Amato, "Is International Law Really 'Law'?," *Northwestern University Law Review* 79, nos. 5–6 (1984–85).

19 Committee on Formation of Customary (General) International Law, "Statement of Principles to the Formation of General Customary International Law," (International Law Association, 2000), 2.

20 For a historic account of the discussions surrounding the formation of customary law, *See* Emily Kadens and Ernest A. Young, "How Customary is Customary International Law?," *William & Mary Law Review* 54, no. 3 (2013). *See also* Anthea Elizabeth Roberts, "Traditional and Modern Approaches to Customary International Law: A Reconciliation," *The American Journal of International Law* 95 (2001).

Environmentally sound management of wastes 17

source of law only if it fulfills two conditions prescribed in the ICJ statute, i.e., custom has to be a "general practice," and it must be "accepted as law." In other words, customary international law has two constitutive parameters. The first is State practice, also known as the material element of custom, which ought to be general, widespread, and uniform. Second, international custom has a subjective parameter known as *opinio juris*. Overall, the concept of custom refers to States' behavior, which must be accompanied by the internal conviction that a law exists and that it demands a particular performance.

The ICJ, on several occasions, has argued that the formation of customary law requires both a general practice and *opinio juris*.[21] The ICJ, however, has neither offered guidance on the methodology for assessing such parameters, nor has it been entirely consistent with respect to the constitutive characteristics of State practice and *opinio juris*. In 2016, the International Law Commission (ILC) presented its draft conclusions regarding the "Identification of Customary International Law." This draft also emphasizes the two constitutive elements of customary law[22] and stresses that both elements are to be assessed individually. Though the contemporary conception of customary law links the material and subjective elements of this source of law, as explained below, there is no clear legal pattern, either in international case law or in legal scholarship, that would provide the defining parameters of State practice and *opinio juris*. For example, it is still subject to debate whether claims or statements constitute evidence of State practice or whether treaties, for instance, are valuable resources in the assessment of *opinio juris*. Despite the constant emphasis given to State practice and *opinio juris* as intrinsically interrelated parameters in the formation of customary law, traditionally, State practice has been the predominant factor in the assessment of customary law, while contemporary customary law seems to place more emphasis on *opinio juris*.[23]

State practice

General considerations

State practice refers to the conduct of States, although, in some circumstances, the practice of international organizations may be relevant in the formation of international custom. Currently, there are two points of controversy surrounding the material part of international customary law. The first relates to its meaning and

---

21 *See*, for example, *Jurisdictional Immunities of the State (Germany v. Italy: Greece Intervening)*, ICJ Reports 2012, p. 99, para 55 (3 February 2012). *Case Concerning Military and Paramilitary Activities in and against Nicaragua (Nicaragua v. United States of America)*, ICJ Reports 1986, p. 14 (27 June 1986), 207. *See also North Sea Continental Shelf Cases, ICJ Rep. 3, para 77 (1969). Questions Relating to the Obligation to Prosecute or Extradite (Belgium v. Senegal) (Judgment)*, ICJ Reports 2012, p. 422, para 99 (20 July 2012).

22 International Law Commission, "Identification of Customary International Law (a/Cn.4/L.872)," in *Text of the Draft Conclusions Provisionally Adopted by the Drafting Committee*, ed. United Nations General Assembly (2016), Draft Conclusion 2.

23 Roberts, "Traditional and Modern Approaches to Customary International Law: A Reconciliation."

18 *Preliminaries*

extent, i.e., whether something other than what States do or refrain from doing[24] could constitute State practice. Closely related to this matter is the identification of evidence and further records of State practice. The second controversial point refers to the constitutive characteristic of "State practice," i.e., being *general*.

Meaning and evidence of State practice

In relation to State practice, D'Amato, for instance, refers exclusively to "actions of States." According to the author, claims are not part of State practice. Claims "may *articulate* a legal norm, [but] cannot constitute the material component of custom ... [T]he claim has little value as a prediction of what the state will actually do".[25] In the *Lotus* case, the Permanent Court of International Justice (PCIJ) submitted that the assessment of customary law requires "acts of State accomplished in the domain of international relations".[26] It seems that this case associates State practice with particular State's actions rather than statements. Nonetheless, the PCIJ failed to clarify the meaning of these "acts." In the *Fisheries* case, Judge Read's dissenting opinion sustained that claims may be relevant in assessing State practice only if they are coupled with physical acts.[27] Following this line of argument, it is reasonable to doubt the existence of "customary law norms," including the no-harm rule, where there is evidence that a State's physical actions do not conform to such a norm.[28] In relation to wastes, many could question whether ESM has passed into the corpus of international customary law when many States still face severe challenges over waste management. However, as explained below, State practice is not confined to physical acts, but also includes claims, including, for instance, legislation. The problems related to State practice go beyond evidentiary records of physical and verbal acts. They also concern the difficulties of distinguishing between the emergence of customary law and the challenges faced by States in implementing it. This is particularly evident in fields such as environmental law where the no-harm rule, for example, could be subject to multiple policy details and require the institutional, technical, and economic capacities to prevent, monitor, and eventually sanction deviations from the norm.

---

24 On the difficulties of omissions as the material component of customary law, *See* Anthony D'Amato, *Concept of Custom in International Law* (Ithaca, NY: Cornell University Press, 1971), 61–63.

25 Ibid., 88.

26 *The Lotus (France/Turkey)*, PCIJ, Ser. A No. 10 (1927).

27 "Customary international law is the generalization of the practice of States. This cannot be established by citing cases where coastal States have made extensive claims, but have not maintained their claims by the actual assertion of sovereignty over trespassing foreign ships ..." *Fisheries Case (United Kingdom v. Norway) (Dissenting Opinion of Judge J.E. Read)*, ICJ Reports 1951, p. 116, para 191 (18 December 1951).

28 Bodansky, for instance, is skeptical of the existence of various customary international law rules, since the "physical acts" of the State do not conform to the alleged rules. Daniel Bodansky, "Customary (and Not So Customary) International Environmental Law," *Global Legal Studies Journal* 3 (1995): 110–11.

Environmentally sound management of wastes 19

Other scholars, such as Akehurst, include acts and claims as State practice. For example, claims can refer to diplomatic exchanges, records of States' statements in international conferences, as well as statements "made by States in the context of concrete disputes ... in the same way as assertions made ... *in abstracto*".[29] Akehurst's account of State practice as actions and claims is widely recognized today since both are expressions of the will of States.[30] The ILC states that both "physical and verbal acts" are forms of State practice.[31] Verbal acts have been defined as oral statements. Although some have suggested that not all kinds of State practice carry the same weight,[32] the ILC considers that there is no "predetermined hierarchy" among different forms of State practice. These forms of State practice could be included in national legislation and decisions, national opinions of legal advisors, diplomatic correspondence and acts, policy documentation, and press releases. More controversial is whether policy statements made in international organizations and the resolutions adopted under the auspices of these organizations reflect State practice. While the Third Restatement[33] and the ILA[34] consider that statements of States in international organizations and further resolutions do constitute State practice, for the ILC, the resolutions of international organizations and intergovernmental conferences cannot be considered per se State practice. Instead, it is the conduct connected to such resolutions that constitutes State practice.[35] The ILC also clarifies that these resolutions do not create customary law, but may be used as evidence "for the existence and content of the customary law rule".[36]

This chapter described the efforts of the OECD and the COP to the Basel Convention in promoting ESM as a pillar of the management of wastes. As a result of such efforts, ESM is currently not only a policy objective or a treaty obligation exclusively related to transboundary movements of wastes. In fact,

---

29 Michael Akehurst, "Custom as a Source of International Law," *British Yearbook of International Law* 47, no. 1 (1976): 5.

30 "There is no inherent reason why verbal acts should not count as practice, whilst physical acts ... should ... [B]oth forms of conduct are manifestations of State will. Committee on Formation of Customary (General) International Law, "Statement of Principles to the Formation of General Customary International Law," 14.

31 International Law Commission, "Identification of Customary International Law (a/Cn.4/ L.872)," Draft Conclusion 6 (1). *See also* "[i]naction may constitute state practice, as when a state acquiesces." *Restatement of the Law, Third, of Foreign Relations Law of the United States*, Vol. I. §§1 to 488, §102, p. 25.

32 Shaw, *International Law*, 62.

33 State practice includes "official statements of policy, whether they are unilateral or undertaken in cooperation with other states, for example in organizations such as the ... OECD." *Restatement of the Law, Third, of Foreign Relations Law of the United States*, Vol. I. §§1 to 488, §102, p. 25.

34 ILA mentions: "statements in international organizations and the resolutions these bodies adopt – all of which are frequently cited as examples of State practice." Committee on Formation of Customary (General) International Law, "Statement of Principles to the Formation of General Customary International Law," 14.

35 International Law Commission, "Identification of Customary International Law (a/Cn.4/L.872)," Draft Conclusion 6 (2).

36 Ibid., Draft Conclusion 12.

20 *Preliminaries*

several States have included the ESM of wastes as an obligation in national waste legislation; these include Chile, Mexico, India, South Africa, and Spain.[37] At the EU level, Article 13 of the Waste Framework Directive provides for a general obligation that requires States to take "measures to ensure that waste management is carried out without endangering human health, without harming the environment." This obligation corresponds almost verbatim to the definition of the ESM of wastes as defined by, for instance, the OECD and the Basel Convention. The incorporation of ESM in national legislation is not only included in framework or general waste legislation; it also forms part of a range of norms, e.g., legislation dealing with particular waste streams or particular constituents. For instance, India has incorporated the ESM of wastes as a general obligation to deal with e-waste;[38] Brazil has included ESM in legislation dealing with solid wastes.[39]

However, it is more difficult to assess the role of treaties that have included the ESM of wastes as an obligation and their contribution to the formation of customary international law. Article 38 of the Vienna Convention on the Law of Treaties establishes: "[n]othing in articles 34 to 37 precludes a rule set forth in a treaty from becoming binding upon a third State as a customary rule of international law, recognized as such." This article is revealing insofar as customary and treaty law are not unrelated sources. In fact, both may have several interactions, e.g., a treaty can codify preexisting customary law or a treaty obligation could be the basis for the formation of new customary law.[40]

Considering the possibility of the constitutive effect of treaty norms in the formation of customary law, at first glance one could assume that the introduction of the ESM of wastes in a wide variety of treaties provides solid evidence of a growing State practice in respect of waste management. However, a counter-argument immediately arises, i.e., the incorporation of a certain obligation in treaties reveals the lack of *opinio juris* in relation to a specific norm. In this case, States are applying the ESM of wastes in order to fulfill their treaty obligations, rather than to meet an obligation under customary law. Both the ICJ and ILC have recognized that treaties may play a role in developing customary international law,[41] but the ILC clarifies that an obligation "set forth in a number of treaties may, but does not necessarily, indicate that the treaty rule reflects a rule

---

37 A summary of national legislation regarding wastes can be found at www.basel.int/Countries/NationalLegislation/tabid/1420/Default.aspx, last accessed 9 March 2019.

38 *See* Article 3(o) of the "E-Waste Management Rules," (Gazette of India, Extraordinary Part-II, Section-3, Sub-Section (i), October, 2016). Available at: www.basel.int/Countries/National Legislation/tabid/1420/Default.aspx, last accessed 9 March 2019.

39 *See* Article 3(VIII) of the "Law No. 12.305 Establishing National Policy on Solid Wastes," (DOU 3/8/2010, August 2010). Available at: www.basel.int/Countries/NationalLegislation/tabid/1420/Default.aspx, last accessed 9 March 2019.

40 Robert Kolb, *The Law of Treaties: An Introduction* (Cheltenham: Edward Elgar Publishing, 2016), 261–62.

41 "multilateral conventions may have an important role to play in recording and defining rules deriving from custom, or indeed in developing them." *Case Concerning the Continental Shelf (Libyan Arab Jamahiriya v. Malta)*, ICJ Reports 1985, p. 13, para 27 (3 June 1985).

of customary international law".[42] Nonetheless, not only is there an increasing number of treaties including the ESM of wastes in a wide range of areas, e.g., transboundary movements of wastes, ship recycling, mercury wastes, but one can also note the adoption of national legislation that includes ESM. Such inclusion is meant to apply to wastes in general and not simply to those subject to transboundary movements of wastes, or those derived from breaking a ship, or those containing mercury. As such, there are some indications that the ESM of wastes is not limited to a particular treaty regime; instead, it has gained a foothold as an obligation that is relevant to deal with waste from a life-cycle perspective. Additionally, the recurring incorporation of ESM in treaties that directly or indirectly regulate waste indicates that ESM has a general character and is not exclusively bound to the regime of the *transboundary movement* of wastes.

A treaty rule could become customary law, according to the ICJ, if it has a "*norm-creating character*".[43] D'Amato follows this dictum very closely by arguing that only a "*generalizable rule*" has the potential to transform into international custom.[44] The norm in question should be able to bind all States in general. Such a requirement could be fulfilled by ESM, since the abstract formulation of the treaty norm as established in the Basel Convention, i.e., "taking all practicable steps to ensure that hazardous wastes or other wastes are managed in a manner which will protect human health and the environment against the adverse effects which may result from such wastes," has the potential to be applicable to any category of waste beyond the treaty itself.[45] The norm, however, must not be analyzed solely *in abstracto*; one must also take into account the whole treaty. The conditions of and exceptions to a treaty norm could potentially affect their transition into customary international law. This is certainly not the case for the ESM of wastes, since ESM must always be ultimately achieved. The notion that a treaty rule must have a "norm-creation character" has been criticized because every rule that achieves its status as customary law has an inherent norm-creating character.[46] Additionally, this "test" could add another layer of uncertainty to the formation of customary law.

"General" State practice

State practice needs to be *general* in order to be relevant in the formation of customary international law. For a practice to be general, two elements are required. First, State practice requires the participation of a substantial

---

42 Draft Conclusion 11, "Identification of Customary International Law (a/Cn.4/L.872)."

43 *North Sea Continental Shelf Cases*, 71.

44 D'Amato, *Concept of Custom in International Law*, 105.

45 Norm-creation rules are abstract in nature because they can regulate "an abstract number of situations, rather than directed towards a concrete one." Mark E. Villiger, *Customary International Law and Treaties* (Leiden: Martinus Nijhoff Publishers, 1985), 190.

46 Richard Reeve Baxter, *Treaties and Customs*, Vol. 129 (The Hague: The Hague Academy of International Law, 1970), 62.

22 Preliminaries

number of States that "are specially affected." Moreover, such practice must be uniform/consistent.

One element that has gradually become less relevant in the assessment of "generality" relates to the period of time in which State practice must be performed.[47] According to the ILC, as long as the practice is general, "no particular duration is required".[48] Some attribute the declining importance of "time" in the analysis of general State practice to faster interactions between States, mainly due to technological developments, and more frequent State interactions, e.g., diplomacy, or within international organizations.[49] Another possible explanation, however, is the declining importance of State practice in the doctrine related to the formation of customary international law. *Opinio juris*, from a contemporary perspective, is more relevant than State practice because a strong emphasis on *normative* and general statements could transform custom "in a progressive source of law that can respond to issues and moral challenges".[50] Ensuring the protection of "fundamental human values"[51] is the central tenet of modern custom. This shift will explain the quick or even "instant" development of customary law in fields such as space, humanitarian, and environmental law. Yet, many commentators warn about favoring *opinio juris* or normative statements[52] in the formation process of customary law. In the absence of any evidence of State practice, or in cases where State practice contradicts such "normative statements," the result is the adoption of "putative" customary law. Such customary law will then be nothing more than political slogans or ideals, which add nothing to the achievement of such "fundamental human values" since "putative" customary law lacks any substantial content and says nothing about future States' action or

---

47 International law has experienced the development of "instant customary law." *See* Diego Mejía-Lemos, "Some Considerations Regarding '"Instant" International Customary Law', Fifty Years Later," *Indian Journal of International Law* 55, no. 1 (2015). Michael Byers, *Custom, Power and the Power of Rules: International Relations and Customary International Law* (Cambridge: Cambridge University Press, 1999), 160–65. Bing Cheng, *Studies in International Space Law* (Oxford: Oxford University Press, 1997), Chapter 7, 147.

48 *See* Draft Conclusion 8(2), International Law Commission, "Identification of Customary International Law (a/Cn.4/L.872)."

49 "In former days, practice, repetition and *opinio juris sive necessitatis*, … might be combined together in a very long and slow process extending over centuries. In the contemporary age of highly developed techniques of communication and information, the formation of a custom through the medium of international organizations is greatly facilitated." *South West Africa Cases (Ethiopia v. South Africa; Liberia v. South Africa) (Dissenting Opinion of Judge Tanaka)*, ICJ Reports 1966, p. 6, para 289 (8 July 1966).

50 Roberts, "Traditional and Modern Approaches to Customary International Law: A Reconciliation," 758.

51 "most lawyers would make an important distinction between customary rules which, for example, lay down the extent of a State's maritime jurisdiction and 'elementary considerations of humanity'. While the former … have a … connection with what States have done or accepted, arguing the latter by reference to State practice would seem intuitively artificial or even repulsive." Koskenniemi, *From Apology to Utopia*, 401.

52 Fernando Tesón, "Fake Custom," in *Reexamining Customary International Law*, ed. D. Brian Lepard (Cambridge: Cambridge University Press, 2017), 109–10.

Environmentally sound management of wastes 23

any other legal development. Some have pointed out that recognizing customary law that has no parallel in State practice delegitimizes international law and can even be labelled as "normative chauvinism," since what is usually taken as constituting "fundamental human values" may actually represent Western values.[53]

The following passage from the *North Continental Shelf* cases summarizes the contemporary notion of "*general*" State practice, i.e., consistent, widespread, and representative:

> [a]lthough the passage of only a short period of time is not necessarily, or of itself, a bar to the formation of a new rule of customary international law ... an indispensable requirement would be that within the period in question, short though it might be, State practice, including that of States whose interests are specially affected, should have been both extensive and virtually uniform in the sense of the provision invoked ...[54]

The standard of "widespread practice" inevitably leaves room for interpretation and subjective assessment. In relation to the ESM of wastes, would the requirement of generality be satisfied if a *simple majority* of sovereign States were to adhere to ESM as an obligation in terms of the treatment of wastes? In other words, should one State equate to "one vote"? The answer should be in the negative, since the principle of sovereign equality of States seems to bar the notion that a majority legislates for the minority.

The most common argument when analyzing "widespread practice" is whether powerful States conform to the alleged "norm".[55] It could be said that on account of their political influence, powerful States may become "leaders" and their practice could impact the practice of other, less influential nations. In other words, acceptance of the "norm" by a greater number of States could be guaranteed when powerful States also conform to a specific practice. So, would it be enough to focus on the practice of a few "powerful" States so as to assess whether ESM has become a general practice? The answer here must also be in the negative because behind the arguments that correlate power with the

53 Bruno Simma and Philip Alston, "The Sources of Human Rights Law: Custom, Jus Cogens, and General Principles," *Australian Yearbook of International Law* 12 (1988–89): 94. Roberts, "Traditional and Modern Approaches to Customary International Law: A Reconciliation," 769.

54 *North Sea Continental Shelf Cases*, 74. *See also Maritime Delimitation and Territorial Questions between Qatar and Bahrain (Merits), ICJ reports 2001, p. 40 (16 March 2001). Delimitation of the Maritime Boundary in the Gulf of Maine Area, Judgment,* ICJ Reports 1984, p. 246, 111 (12 October 1984).

55 "Many customs owe their origin wholly to decisions or acts of great Powers which by their repetition or sequence, and above all by the idea of order that finally grows out of them." Charles De Visscher, *Theory and Reality in Public International Law* (Princeton, NJ: Princeton University Press, 1957), 150. "One can conclude by stating that for a custom to be accepted and recognized it must have the concurrence of the major powers in that particular field ... [t]his follows from the nature of the international system where all may participate, but the views of those with greater power carry greater weight." Shaw, *International Law*, 59. Karol Wolfke, *Custom in Present International Law* (Wroclaw: Zaklad Narodowy, 1964), 81–82.

24   *Preliminaries*

successful emergence of customary law lies a subtle denial of the sovereign equality of states. Additionally, "general State practice" is neither a quantitative test, e.g., simple majority rule, nor the practice of a few States disguised as the extensive practice of the international community. Judge Weeremantry's dissenting opinion in the advisory opinion concerning the *Legality of the Threat or Use of Nuclear Weapons* summarizes this position: "[f]rom the standpoint of the creation of international custom, the practice and policies of five States out of 185 seem to be an insufficient basis on which to assert the creation of custom, whatever be the global influence of those five".[56] The emphasis on the practice of powerful States in the formation of customary international law promotes the interests of a few and imposes those interests as law.

Establishing the "States that are specially affected" is another parameter that requires analysis. In relation to the ESM of wastes, it could be argued that every State is "specially affected," since the management of wastes has direct effects on human health and the environment independently of their political standing in the international arena. Others will again argue that, given their "global influence" and widespread involvement in varied activities at the international level, powerful States will generally satisfy this criterion. In the course of this research, the inquiry into evidence related to State practice and the ESM of wastes, e.g., national legislation, has not been confined to "powerful" States. However, the task is a daunting one. The ILC stipulates a high standard by which to assess State practice, i.e., "[a]ccount is to be taken of *all available practice of a particular State*, which is to be assessed as a whole" (emphasis added). The difficulties surrounding the analysis of all available practice of over 190 States have prompted strong criticisms of the "material element" of custom, since the identification of customary law remains limited to the practice of certain States. In some circumstances, customary law has been assessed solely in the light of decisions of tribunals and teachings,[57] despite the fact that the ILC characterizes the latter as subsidiary means for the determination of customary law.[58] Thus, in the absence of a person embodying the capacities of Dworkin's Judge Hercules, judges, practitioners, and scholars are faced with fragments of State practice.[59]

---

56 *Legality of the Threat or Use of Nuclear Weapons, Advisory Opinion (Dissenting Opinion of Judge Weeramantry)*, ICJ Reports 1996, p. 226, para 311.

57 "The Tribunal further agrees ... that in principle the content of a rule of customary international law ... can best be determined on the basis of evidence of actual State practice establishing custom that also shows that the States have accepted such practice as law (*opinio juris*). However, the Tribunal notes that neither Party has produced such evidence in this arbitration. In the circumstances, the Tribunal must rely on other, indirect evidence in order to ascertain the content of the customary international law minimum standard of treatment; the Tribunal cannot simply declare *non liquet*. Such indirect evidence includes, in the Tribunal's view, decisions taken by other NAFTA tribunals ... as well as relevant legal scholarship." *Windstream Energy LLC v. Government of Canada, Award*, PCA – Case No. 2013-22, para 351 (27 September 2016).

58 *See* Draft Conclusions 13 and 14, International Law Commission, "Identification of Customary International Law (a/Cn.4/L.872)."

59 This is the case even when quantitative research methods are used to collect and analyze State practice. Worster provides an overview of the challenges and opportunities involved in sampling

Environmentally sound management of wastes 25

A final remark on general State practice concerns its consistency. The ICJ has stressed the importance of evaluating whether the material element of customary law is "virtually uniform".[60] The ILA emphasizes that consistency must be internal and collective.[61] Internal consistency means a regular behavior of a particular State, while collective consistency means a regular behavior among the States engaged in a certain practice.[62] Overall, as stated in the *Asylum* case, if practice among States reflects "so much uncertainty and contradiction, so much fluctuation and discrepancy ... it is not possible to discern in all this any constant and uniform usage".[63] To establish, for instance, whether States exhibit a consistent practice in relation to the ESM of wastes, it is crucial to determine whether there are comparable circumstances that allow one to find some evidence of behavior regularities. ESM is defined in very wide terms. While the ESM of wastes has been consistently included in Resolutions of the UN General Assembly, one could argue that the definition of ESM is so broad in its scope as to allow States to enjoy a significant degree of latitude of discretion in deciding the parameters of the ESM of wastes. This could include a varied set of policies. Consequently, it would not be possible to ascertain either the "core meaning" of ESM or "comparable situations." However, this is not the case. The OECD and the COP to the Basel Convention, e.g., have endeavored to develop a framework for the *common understanding* of the ESM of wastes in general.[64] Although the status of these resolutions as an expression of State practice remains controversial, these documents are still relevant in identifying the content and substantive elements of ESM. The "core meaning" of ESM relates to the life-cycle approach to wastes. The following graphic summarizes such an approach (Figure 2.1):

State practice and the subsequent analysis of sufficient evidence. William Thomas Worster, "The Inductive and Deductive Methods in Customary International Law Analysis: Traditional and Modern Approaches," *Georgetown Journal of International Law* 45 (2014): 496–501. William Thomas Worster, "The Transformation of Quantity into Quality: Critical Mass in the Formation of Customary International Law," *Boston University International Law Journal* 31 (2013): 77–78.

60 *Case Concerning Military and Paramilitary Activities in and against Nicaragua (Nicaragua v. United States of America)*, para 186. *Case Concerning Right of Passage over Indian Territory (Portugal v. India) (Merits)*, ICJ Reports, p. 6, para 40 (12 April 1960).

61 Committee on Formation of Customary (General) International Law, "Statement of Principles to the Formation of General Customary International Law," 21.

62 Ibid.

63 *Colombian-Peruvian Asylum Case (Judgment)*, ICJ Reports, 1950, p. 266, para 277 (20 November 1950).

64 Organisation for Economic Co-Operation and Development (OECD), "Guidance Manual on Environmentally Sound Management of Waste." United Nations Environment Programme (UNEP), "UNEP/CHW.11/3/Add.1/REV.1. Framework for the Environmentally Sound Management of Hazardous Wastes and Other Wastes," *Conference of the Parties to the Basel Convention on the Control of Transboundary Movements of Hazardous Wastes and their Disposal. Eleventh Meeting* (Geneva, 2013).

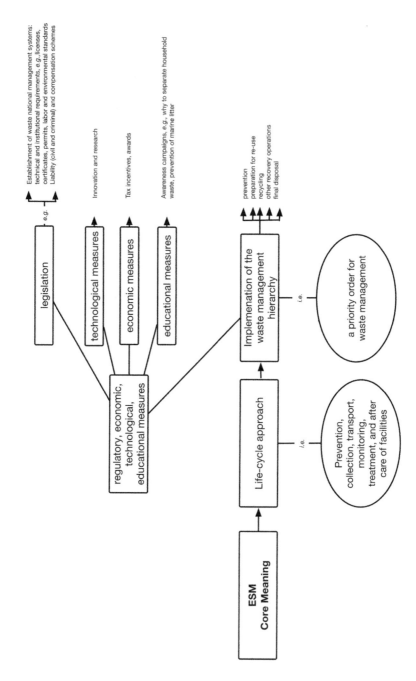

Figure 2.1 ESM core meaning.

The international efforts to develop the substantive elements of the ESM of wastes constitute a blueprint for the "core meaning" of this principle that enables a comparison of State practice among the members of the international community.

Opinio juris

Besides State practice, the formation of customary law requires *opinio juris*, also known as the subjective element of international custom. *Opinio juris* is a theoretical device for distinguishing between practice that can give rise to legal obligations and practice displayed for comity or diplomacy, for instance. *Opinio juris* can be understood in a twofold manner.

First, voluntarists explain that *opinio juris* is an objective manifestation of States' consent and will, rather than a subjective process of "inner reasoning".[65] The voluntarist approach has been criticized because it equates customary law with tacit treaty law and carries misconceptions regarding the role of consent in the international legal order.[66]

Second, *opinio juris* is an internal conviction, or a *belief* that a certain practice must be conducted because it is required by law. This has been the position of the ICJ in several cases.[67] However, the assessment of beliefs is a difficult task that raises questions as to the identification of the authorities or officials that are capable of articulating such belief on behalf of the State. So, according to the ILA, those who read *opinio juris* in terms of a subjective belief are preoccupied not with uncovering the inner motives of a State, but rather with what a State "*says* it believes, or what can reasonably be implied from its conduct".[68]

Treating *opinio juris* as an internal belief, however, poses serious difficulties in the formation of new customary law, especially when such State practice contradicts previous customary law. In the *Case Concerning Military and Paramilitary Activities in and against Nicaragua*, the ICJ stated:

---

65 Cheng, *Studies in International Space Law*, 137. Maurice Mendelson, "The Subjective Element in Customary International Law," *British Yearbook of International Law* 66, no. 1 (1996): 184–94.

66 Voluntarists made assumptions regarding "the role of consent in the international legal system *as a whole*. It is commonly said that international law is based on the consent of sovereign States; *ergo* customary law, which is part of that *corpus*, must equally depend on consent. ... At the most general, systemic level, it is certainly true that, if States chose to dispense with international law as a whole, and to operate on anarchic principles ... they could do so. But given that States have in fact consented to the existence of a system of international law as a whole, and continue to do so, it does not necessarily follow that the creation and binding force of each individual rule in the system is dependent on the consent of each and every subject" Mendelson, "The Subjective Element in Customary International Law," 189–90.

67 *North Sea Continental Shelf Cases*, para 77. *Territorial and Maritime Dispute (Nicaragua v. Colombia)* Judgment ICJ Reports 2012, p. 624, para 207 (19 November 2012). *The Lotus (France/Turkey)*, 28.

68 Committee on the Formation of Customary (General) International Law, "Statement of Principles to the Formation of General Customary International Law," 33.

28 *Preliminaries*

the Court deems it sufficient that the conduct of States should, in general, be consistent with such rules, and that instances of State conduct inconsistent with a given rule should generally have been treated as breaches of that rule, not as indications of the recognition of a new rule. If a State acts in a way prima facie incompatible with a recognized rule, but defends its conduct by appealing to exceptions or justifications contained within the rule itself, then whether or not the State's conduct is in fact justifiable on that basis, the significance of that attitude is to confirm rather than to weaken the rule.[69]

The previously cited case establishes a general rule regarding State practice that contradicts an established customary law. Inconsistencies must be treated as breaches. However, the ICJ does not deny the possibility that a certain contradictory State practice could be the starting point of a new customary law rule. Therefore, as Shaw explains:

> [b]ehaviour contrary to a custom contains within itself the seeds of a new rule and if it is endorsed by other nations, the previous law will disappear and be replaced, or alternatively there could be a period of time during which the two customs co-exist until one of them is generally accepted.[70]

The formation of new customary law evinces that *opinio juris is essentially a process.* It develops as States conform to a certain practice. For this reason, Shaw accurately defines *opinio juris* as a belief that a certain behavior "is law or is becoming law".[71] Other scholars closely follow this understanding too, including Lepard who conceptualizes this subjective element as a "requirement that states generally believe that is desirable now or in the near future to have an authoritative legal principle or rule prescribing, permitting, or prohibiting certain state practice".[72]

Currently, the ILC has defined *opinio juris* as a "sense of legal right or obligation".[73] This sense of legality could certainly include a current belief that the practice is law or that is becoming law. The inclusion of the terms "becoming

---

69 *Case Concerning Military and Paramilitary Activities in and against Nicaragua (Nicaragua v. United States of America)*, para 186.

70 Shaw, *International Law*, 68.

71 Ibid., 64. *See also* Byers, *Custom, Power and the Power of Rules: International Relations and Customary International Law*, 151. *Opinio juris* "may be, not a belief that the practice is already legally binding, but a claim that it *ought* to be legally binding. In other words, those who follow the practice, and treat it as a legal standard of behaviour, may be doing so with deliberate legislative intention." Raphael Walden, "Customary International Law: A Jurisprudential Analysis," *Israel Law Review* 13, no. 1 (1978): 97.

72 D. Brian Lepard, *Customary International Law: A New Theory with Practical Implications* (Cambridge: Cambridge University Press, 2010), 112.

73 Draft Conclusion 9, International Law Commission, "Identification of Customary International Law (a/Cn.4/L.872)."

Environmentally sound management of wastes 29

law" implies something more than a long-term aspiration. Since *opinio juris* is a process, its assessment, according to Lepard, includes a temporal dimension, i.e., "now or in the near future".[74]

The forms of evidence that the ILC identified in relation to *opinio juris* are:

> public statements made on behalf of States; official publications; government legal opinions; diplomatic correspondence; decisions of national courts; treaty provisions; and conduct in connection with resolutions adopted by an international organization or at an intergovernmental conference.[75]

An apparent problem with these forms of evidence is their close relationship with evidence of State practice.[76] It could be challenging to explicitly differentiate the grounds on which one of these evidentiary forms could be considered as evidence of State practice, or *opinio juris*, or both. In light of the practical difficulties of assessing *opinio juris*, it is no surprise that the ICJ and scholars alike are relying on resolutions adopted by international organizations, especially those of the UN General Assembly, to identify *opinio juris*.[77] Of course, not all resolutions have evidentiary value or even carry the same weight. The ILC's Second Report on Identification of Customary International Law explains that a State's attitude and consensus may be revealed "by voting ... on the resolution, by joining a consensus, or by statements made in connection with the resolution".[78]

Concerning the ESM of wastes, this chapter already discussed the relevance of the inclusion of this principle in several UN General Assembly resolutions dealing with sustainable development. The most recent of these resolutions is the 2030 Agenda for Sustainable Development. The 193 UN Member States unanimously adopted this resolution. In this case, the UN General Assembly provided a unique forum for achieving international consensus in relation to the most pressing challenges facing sustainable development. Although the UN General Assembly resolutions are not binding and cannot create customary law, they could, as previously explored, evince *opinio juris*. Some of the targets included in the Sustainable Development Goals are framed as general aspirations

---

74 Lepard, *Customary International Law: A New Theory with Practical Implications*, 113.

75 Draft Conclusion 10(2), International Law Commission, "Identification of Customary International Law (a/Cn.4/L.872)."

76 "In a sense, all that states can do or omit to do can be classified as 'state practice', because their behaviour is what they do (the 'objective element') and it is also our only guide as to what they want, or 'believe', to be the law." Jörg Kammerhofer, "Uncertainty in the Formal Sources of International Law: Customary International Law and Some of Its Problems," *EJIL* 15, no. 3 (2004).

77 "*opinio juris* may, though with all due caution, be deduced from, *inter alia*, the attitude of the Parties and the attitude of States towards certain General Assembly resolutions ... *Case Concerning Military and Paramilitary Activities in and against Nicaragua (Nicaragua v. United States of America)*, para 188. *See also Legality of the Threat or Use of Nuclear Weapons, ICJ Reports 226, para 29 (1996). para 70.*

78 International Law Commission, "Second Report on the Identification of Customary International Law (a/Cn.4/672*)," 65.

30 *Preliminaries*

of the international community, rather than any sort of articulation of legal obligations or rights. Others, instead, include a temporal dimension in order to achieve certain specific targets, e.g., the ESM of chemicals and wastes. For instance, Goal 12, "sustainable consumption and production patterns" that includes ESM as one of targets, aims, by 2020, to achieve the ESM of chemicals and wastes, and, by 2030, to "substantially reduce waste generation." The language used in the formulation of these targets is also revealing insofar as they are not phrased as a recommendation, aspiration, or encouragement. On the contrary, they are phrased as a prescription. The timeframe for achieving the ESM of chemicals and wastes could also be an indication of the development of *opinio juris* in accordance with Lepard's understanding that a belief is law "now or in the near future." This does not mean, however, that every target that includes a timeframe, or is phrased as prescribing a certain conduct, should immediately be taken as evidence of customary law. Following the established definition of customary law, State practice is also required. Overall, there is evidence of State practice and *opinio juris* in relation to the ESM of wastes.

ESM as a customary law and treaty obligation

The identification of ESM as customary law does not mean that the Basel Convention in general or the obligations related to ESM as established in such a treaty are customary law. Both remain distinct. This is the position expressed in the *Case Concerning Military and Paramilitary Activities in and against Nicaragua* where the ICJ explained:

> even if two norms belonging to two sources of international law appear identical in content, and even if the States in question are bound by these rules both on the level of treaty-law and on that of customary international law, these norms retain a separate existence. This is so from the standpoint of their applicability ... [r]ules which are identical in treaty law and in customary international law are also distinguishable by reference to the methods of interpretation and application.[79]

The *Case Concerning Military and Paramilitary Activities in and against Nicaragua* dealt with preexisting customary law incorporated in treaties. The codifying treaty does not "subsume" or "supervene" such customary law. In the case of ESM, the Basel Convention had a constitutive effect, since the incorporation of ESM as a treaty norm was the point of departure for the development of ESM as a customary law principle. However, the legal consequences are the same, i.e., the obligations established in the Basel Convention maintain their treaty law nature and co-exist with the emerging customary principle. In the *North Sea*

---

79 *Case Concerning Military and Paramilitary Activities in and against Nicaragua (Nicaragua v. United States of America)*, para 178.

Environmentally sound management of wastes 31

Continental Shelf Cases, the ICJ clarified that a treaty norm could have a "crystallizing" effect, i.e., being the final step in the formation of a customary law that was already developing. Nonetheless, it was emphatic in clarifying that the conventional rule as such is not applicable to a non-Party.[80]

ESM exists simultaneously as a treaty norm embodied in the Basel Convention and as customary law principle. Both overlap in their general conceptualization brought by the treaty, i.e., ESM is "taking all practicable steps to ensure that ... wastes are managed in a manner which will protect human health and the environment against the adverse effects which may result from such wastes".[81] A core meaning of this obligation relates to the life-cycle approach to waste. Such an approach means that waste management is guided by a priority order, i.e., prevention of waste generation, reuse, recycling, recovery, and disposal. The application of this priority order requires the adoption of legal, technological, economic, and educational measures. ESM is comprehensive, since it requires the participation of governments, waste operators, civil society organizations, and the population at large.

This core meaning of ESM is shared between the treaty norm and the customary law. However, the Basel Convention establishes ancillary obligations identifying the specific rights and obligations of Parties involved in the transboundary movement of wastes. Such obligations are unique to the regime governing transboundary movements of wastes.

ESM as a normative legal framework

Even if the legal status of the ESM of wastes could be subject to debate, this principle is not devoid of legal significance. International environmental law is driven by principles whose outward legal effects are varied. ESM is one example of a principle that provides a normative framework for both attaining legal coherence in the regulation of wastes and shaping further legal developments in this field.

ESM as a normative legal framework guides the actions of States and international organizations in relation to the regulation of wastes. For instance, ESM is what has prompted concerted efforts between the COP to the Basel Convention and the IMO, which try to shed light on the obligations concerning the management of ship wastes in the sea/land interface. This principle is the foundation for cooperation and synergies between different regimes, since it offers a renewed perspective on waste management from a life-cycle approach regardless of whether those wastes are managed domestically or elsewhere.

Following de Sadeleer's seminal work on environmental principles, it is important to distinguish between political and environmental law principles. While both provide "legislative and regulatory"[82] guidance, the former can be set

---

80 *North Sea Continental Shelf Cases*, para 69.
81 *See* Article 2(8) of the Basel Convention.
82 de Sadeleer, *Environmental Principles: From Political Slogans to Legal Rules*, 310.

32 *Preliminaries*

aside, while the latter have "autonomous normative value" and "autonomous applicability".[83] Autonomy implies that environmental principles produce legal effects. Two requirements are necessary to infer normative autonomy. First, a principle must be included in a binding legal text, and second, its formulation must be "sufficiently prescriptive".[84] ESM fulfills both requirements.

As to the first requirement, the inclusion of a principle in a treaty is a necessary step in the transformation from a policy goal or long-term aspiration into a normative legal framework. ESM has been included as a legal obligation in the operative sections[85] of several treaties (e.g., the Basel Convention,[86] and the Minamata Convention on Mercury).[87] The normative autonomy of ESM is also inferred from the range of treaties that have incorporated it. The origins of ESM are traced back to the regulation of transboundary movements of wastes. Today, ESM is included in conventions that directly or indirectly deal with wastes, e.g., ship recycling.[88] As to the second requirement, de Sadeleer explains that the prescriptive formulation of a principle must indicate its binding character.[89] As such, a case-by-case analysis is required. With regard to ESM, its inclusion in the Basel Convention shows, e.g., that the principle's degree of abstraction decreases as more content is added. Article 2(8) of the Basel Convention when defining ESM sets out the environmental goal, i.e., to protect human health and the environment against the adverse effects of hazardous wastes. Furthermore, the ESM principle is operationalized through more detailed rules that demonstrate its normative value, e.g., States shall ensure the availability of disposal facilities for ESM.[90]

Overall, the inclusion of ESM in the Basel Convention and its prescriptive character fostered its normative value as one of the main legal pillars of the regulation of transboundary movements of wastes. It was also the catalyst for the development of ESM as a normative framework for the regulation of wastes from a life-cycle approach.

Concluding remarks

The author argues that ESM is a principle that fosters cooperation between subjects of international law and prompts the development of further soft and hard law actions. Principles are fundamental in a field such as international

---

83 Ibid.

84 Ibid., 311 and 68.

85 "A distinction should be drawn between the principles found in the preambular sections of treaties and those elaborated in the operational parts. A principle can be normative only to the extent that it is affirmed by an operative provision of a convention." Ibid., 314.

86 *See* Article 2(8).

87 *See* Article 11(3)(a).

88 *See* Regulations 15(1) and 20 of the International Convention for the Safe and Environmentally Sound Recycling of Ships, Hong Kong.

89 de Sadeleer, *Environmental Principles: From Political Slogans to Legal Rules*, 314–15.

90 *See* Article 4(2)(b).

Environmentally sound management of wastes 33

environmental law, where cooperation and consensus are paramount. Additionally, environmental principles are usually presented as general and broad formulations. Such broad formulations make them flexible, so that they might be adapted to changing circumstances.

Although the ESM of wastes has an autonomous normative value, independent of its legal status, a discussion of international custom is not misplaced. The role of customary law is still relevant in two respects. First, customs (unlike treaties) could potentially bind all States, while treaties are only binding on States that express their consent to becoming Parties to a particular instrument, as established in the *North Sea Continental Shelf* cases, for example.[91] Thus, in the absence of treaty law, customary law and general principles of law may be the only sources available to highlight a legal problem. Second, in third party dispute resolutions, the question of whether a certain principle fulfills the criteria of customary law is fundamental, since courts are bound to enforce *legal* rights and obligations.[92]

Sovereignty and ESM

ESM challenges the traditional perspective on waste management, i.e., States are "free" to generate wastes and dispose of them as they see fit so long as the generating States comply with their duty to prevent transboundary harm. The study of ESM and "domestic" environments has implications for the concept of sovereignty. Despite being a topic of some controversy, sovereignty remains central to public international law. Contemporarily, this concept is discussed in relation to statehood[93] and is closely associated with territory.[94] Rather than an

---

91 *North Sea Continental Shelf Cases.* On the role of consent in international law in general and in treaties in particular, *See* Louis Henkin, *International Law: Politics and Values.* Vol. 18, Developments in International Law (Leiden: Martinus Nijhoff Publishers, 1995), 27–29. Anthony Aust, *Modern Treaty Law and Practice*, 3rd edn (Cambridge: Cambridge University Press, 2013), 87, Chapter 7.

92 *Note* that the ICJ has denied any law-making capacity. *Legality of the Threat or Use of Nuclear Weapons*, 237, para 18. The ICJ has also expressed that "as a court of law, cannot render judgment *sub specie legis ferendae*, or anticipate the law before the legislator has laid it down" *Fisheries Jurisdiction Case (Federal Republic of Germany v. Iceland) (Merits)*, ICJ Reports 1974, p. 175, para 45 (25 July 1974). On law-making and judicial decision-making, *See* Carlo Focarelli, *International Law as a Social Construct: The Struggle for Global Justice* (Oxford: Oxford University Press, 2012), 317–19.

93 "In brief, 'sovereignty' is shorthand for legal personality of a certain kind, that of statehood; 'jurisdiction' refers to particular aspects of the substance, especially rights (or claims), liberties, and powers." James Crawford, *Brownlie's Principles of Public International Law*, 8th edn (Oxford: Oxford University Press, 2012), 204.

94 "sovereignty itself, with its retinue of legal rights and duties, is founded upon the fact of territory." Shaw, *International Law*, 361. *See also* James Crawford, *The Creation of States in International Law*, 2nd edn (Oxford: Oxford University Press, 2006), 32. Malcolm Shaw, "The International Court of Justice and the Law of Territory," in *The Development of International Law by the International Court of Justice*, ed. Christian Tams and James Sloan (Oxford: Oxford University Press, 2013).

34 *Preliminaries*

unlimited and unquestionable power of States,[95] sovereignty comprises the most comprehensive set of rights and obligations attributed to a State *in accordance with international law* as stated by the International Court of Justice (ICJ) in the advisory opinion concerning the *Reparation for injuries suffered in the service of the United Nations.*[96]

Relative nature of "purely domestic affairs"

Traditionally, sovereignty has been described as autonomy, independence, and freedom of States to regulate and control "purely domestic affairs." According to Henkin, independence implies the recognition of States as "separate entities" both "physically and politically".[97] Nonetheless, being independent does not prevent States from agreeing on binding obligations, nor does independence protect States from external scrutiny when such obligations are not complied with. Independence is closely related to the customary principle of nonintervention, defined by the ICJ in the *Case Concerning Military and Paramilitary Activities in and against Nicaragua* as:

> A prohibited intervention must accordingly be one bearing on matters in which each State is permitted, by the principle of State sovereignty, to decide freely. One of these is the choice of a political, economic, social and cultural system, and the formulation of foreign policy.[98]

The notion of independence may lead to the conclusion that there is a sharp distinction between national and international law.[99] Nowadays, however, many areas traditionally considered within the sphere of national affairs, e.g., waste

---

95 "sovereignty degenerated into a principle postulating the total independence and freedom from higher binding norms ... it slowly grew into a territorial principle." Franz Xaver Perrez, *Cooperative Sovereignty: From Independence to Interdependece in the Structure of International Environmental Law* (The Hague: Kluwer Law International, 2000), 40. Louis Henkin, "That 'S' Word: Sovereignty, and Globalization, and Human Rights, Et Cetera," *Fordham Law Review* 68, no. 1 (1999): 2.

96 *Advisory Opinion Reparation for Injuries Suffered in the Service of the United Nations*, ICJ Rep 174, ICGJ 232 180 (11 April 1949).

97 Henkin, *International Law: Politics and Values*, 18, 10.

98 *Case Concerning Military and Paramilitary Activities in and against Nicaragua (Nicaragua v. United States of America)*, para 205.

99 While explaining the origin of internal sovereignty, Lessafer explains: "[i]nternal sovereignty goes hand in hand with an abstract or depersonalised notion of the state. All this is a precondition to the dualism between the international and internal legal orders that became central to the modern law of nations." Randall Lesaffer, "Peace Treaties from Lodi to Westphalia," in *Peace Treaties and International Law in European History: From the Late Middle Ages to World War One*, ed. Randall Lesaffer (Cambridge: Cambridge University Press, 2004), 14. *See also*, Philip Allot, "The Emerging Universal Legal System," in *New Perspectives on the Divide between National and International Law*, ed. Janne Nijman and André Nollkaemper (Oxford: Oxford University Press, 2007), 79.

Environmentally sound management of wastes 35

management, conservation of biodiversity, ship recycling, are increasingly subject to international law. The increasing expansion of international law in relation to both fields (e.g., economy, environment, human rights) and actors (e.g., international organizations, civil society, proliferation of international courts) evinces interdependence and a shift away from a legal system exclusively concerned with co-existence. The growing interdependence[100] among the subjects of international law influences the understanding of sovereignty, shifting it from independence and autonomy toward "authority and responsibility to participate and cooperate in the global community".[101] This is the concept of sovereignty supported in this book. Furthermore, the emergence of the ESM of waste as a principle should not be considered as a limitation on or interference in territorial sovereignty, but rather as an example of the growing interdependence of States to deal with challenges that cannot be addressed individually but instead require concerted efforts.

Sovereignty and the environment

ESM embraces a life-cycle approach to wastes. Such an approach includes the minimization of waste generation, which has an impact on resource conservation and exploitation. So, ESM could be construed as a limitation on States' sovereignty over their natural resources.

Permanent sovereignty over natural resources: an overview

Initially, newly independent States formulated the principle related to "permanent sovereignty over natural resources" so as to safeguard their economic independence from colonial powers,[102] and ultimately to consolidate their right of self-determination.[103] After the adoption of United Nations General Assembly

---

100 Franz Xaver Perrez, "Efficiency of Cooperation: A Functional Analysis of Sovereignty," *Arizona Journal of International and Comparative Law* 15, no. 2 (1998): 578.

101 Perrez, *Cooperative Sovereignty: From Independence to Interdependece in the Structure of International Environmental Law*, 332.

102 *See* Nico Schrijver, "Fifty Years Permanent Sovereignty over Natural Resources: The 1962 UN Declaration as the Opinio Iuris Communis," in *Permanent Sovereignty over Natural Resources*, ed. Marc Bungenberg and Stephan Hobe (Switzerland: Springer, 2015). Stephan Hobe, "Evolution of the Principle on Permanent Sovereignty over Natural Resources," in *Permanent Sovereignty over Natural Resources*, ed. Marc Bungenberg and Stephan Hobe (Switzerland: Springer, 2015). Virginie Barral, "National Sovereignty over Natural Resources: Environmental Challenges and Sustainable Development," in *Research Handbook on International Law and Natural Resources*, ed. Elisa Morgera and Kati Kulovesi (Cheltenham: Edward Elgar Publishing, 2016). Nico Schrijver, *Sovereignty over Natural Resources: Balancing Rights and Duties* (Cambridge: Cambridge University Press, 1997), Chapters 2 and 3.

103 "The right of peoples and nations to permanent sovereignty over natural resources must be exercised in the interest of their national development and the well-being of the people concerned." "United Nations General Assembly: Resolution on Permanent Sovereignty over Natural Resources a/Res/1803/Xvii," in *Seventeeth Session* (1962). *See also*, Catherine Redgwell,

36 Preliminaries

(UNGA) Resolution 1803 (XVII) on Permanent Sovereignty over Natural Resources in 1962, this principle transformed into customary law. The ICJ, for instance, recognized this status in the *Democratic Republic of the Congo v. Uganda* case.[104] During the decades following the adoption of Resolution 1803 (XVII), the protection and preservation of the environment became a leading concern within the international community as evinced, for instance, by the adoption of the Stockholm Declaration by the United Nations Conference on the Human Environment, 1972. This Conference led to the establishment of United Nations Environment Programme (UNEP) in the same year[105] and laid the foundations for the development of contemporary environmental law[106] where cooperation is a fundamental duty in order to achieve environmental protection. Principle 21 of the Stockholm Declaration indicates:

> States have, in accordance with the Charter of the United Nations and the principles of international law, the sovereign right to exploit their own resources *pursuant to their own environmental policies, and the responsibility to ensure that activities within their jurisdiction or control do not cause damage to the environment of other States or of areas beyond the limits of national jurisdiction.* (emphasis added)

A key contribution of the Conference was to situate "permanent sovereignty over natural resources" in an environmental perspective.[107] This principle was no longer conceived in terms of absolute independence or as a means to devise clear-cut divisions between domestic, international, or shared environments,

---

"Sustainable Development of National Energy Resources: What Has International Law Got to Do with It?," *AFE Babalola University: The Journal of Sustainable Development Law and Policy* 8, no. 1 (2017): 381–82.

104 *Armed Activities on the Territory of the Congo (Democratic Republic of the Congo v. Uganda)*, ICJ Reports, p. 168, para 244 (2005).

105 UNEP was established in 1972. *See* United Nations General Assembly, "Institutional and Financial Arrangements for International Environmental Cooperation (Resolution No. 2997 (XXVII) Twenty-Seventh Session, Agenda Item 47)," (15 December, 1972).

106 The term "contemporary environmental law" is used here to reveal the transition from resource management to the treatment of the environment in a holistic way, i.e., considering the different interrelationships and interdependence of ecosystems.

107 "In 1974, two years after the Stockholm Conference, the General Assembly adopted two further resolutions. The 'Declaration on the Establishment of a New International Economic Order' (NIEO) ... [t]he Charter of Economic Rights and Duties of States ... [b]y emphasizing the apparently untrammelled sovereignty of states over natural resources, these resolutions might be thought to imply that any restrictions would for the most part require agreement between the states concerned. In reality, however, these resolutions ... were primarily directed at asserting the right to nationalize or control foreign-owned resources and industries." Birnie, Boyle, and Redgwell, *International Law and the Environment*, 191. *See also* United Nations General Assembly, "Resolution 3201 (S-VI): Declaration on the Establishment of a New International Economic Order," in *Resolutions adopted on the Report of the Ad Hoc Committee of the Sixth Special Session* (1974). "A/Res/29/3281: Charter of Economic Rights and Duties of States," in *Resolutions adopted in the Twenty-Ninth Session – Agenda Item 48* (1974).

Environmentally sound management of wastes 37

but rather as the departure point for assessing rights and obligations concerning the environment. Thus, along with the sovereign right of exploitation of natural resources, correlated obligations were developed, including the no-harm rule, "diligence and due care, good-neighbourliness, and State responsibility with regard to extraterritorial damage".[108] The no-harm rule is discussed in more detail in Chapter 4. However, here it suffices to note that while managing their resources States must take measures to *prevent* harm[109] to the territory of other States and to *collaborate* in preserving the environment beyond national boundaries.

As Schrijver has pointed out, permanent sovereignty over natural resources was gradually "supplemented by concerns with respect to the conservation and rational use of natural resources".[110] This gradual evolution is illustrated in Principle 2 of the Rio Declaration on Environment and Development that qualifies the sovereign right of a State to exploit its own resources "according to their own environmental or development policies." Principle 2 bespeaks the notion of balance between economic growth and environmental protection within and outside national boundaries. The UNGA Resolution Transforming our World: The 2030 Agenda for Sustainable Development, adopted in 2015, reaffirms the right of States to "freely exercise, full permanent sovereignty over all ... natural resources".[111] The concept of sovereignty remains pertinent in analyzing not only the rights but also the obligations of States in respect of natural resources within and beyond national jurisdiction. Although States have comprehensive rights to manage resources in their territories, domestic environments have not been immune to international regulation since States have gradually agreed on obligations that limit this sovereignty, e.g., the Convention on Biological Diversity, 1992.

Sustainable development and the blurring boundaries of "domestic" environments

Sustainable development has also influenced the understanding of the principle concerning permanent sovereignty over natural resources. The World Commission on Environment and Development, in its report "Our Common Future" defined sustainability as the development that "meets the needs of

---

108 Schrijver, "Fifty Years Permanent Sovereignty over Natural Resources: The 1962 UN Declaration as the Opinio Iuris Communis," 19.

109 The no-harm rule "is directly related to sovereignty equality ... [t]he rule seeks to reconcile one State's sovereign right to use its territory and resources with another State's defensive invocation of the very same sovereignty-based right." Günther Handl, "Transboundary Impacts," in *The Oxford Handbook of International Environmental Law*, ed. Daniel Bodansky, Jutta Brunnée, and Ellen Hey (Oxford: Oxford University Press, 2007), 534.

110 Schrijver, "Fifty Years Permanent Sovereignty over Natural Resources: The 1962 UN Declaration as the Opinio Iuris Communis," 20.

111 United Nations General Assembly, "A/Res/70/1. Transforming Our World: The 2030 Agenda for Sustainable Development," para 18.

38 Preliminaries

the present without compromising the ability of future generations to meet their own needs".[112] At the heart of sustainable development lie integration and a balance between economy, society, and environment. The ICJ, in the *Gabčíkovo-Nagymaros Project* and the *Pulp Mill* cases, has referred to sustainable development as a "concept" that expresses the "need to reconcile economic development with protection of the environment".[113] Although the ICJ has not yet recognized it as a legal principle, in the Final Report on Sustainable Development, the International Law Commission (ILC) emphasized that:

> sustainable use of natural resources is increasingly a rule of general customary international law notwithstanding the geographical location and/or legal status of the natural resource involved. This is also demonstrated by the evolution of the principle of sovereignty over natural resources from a merely rights-based into a duties as well as rights-based principle.[114]

In a separate opinion of the *Gabčíkovo-Nagymaros Project*, Judge Weeremantry regretted that the ICJ considered sustainable development as a concept instead of a "principle with normative value".[115] Likewise, in the *Iron Rhine ("Ijzeren Rijn") Railway* arbitration, the Tribunal analyzed both the design and the implementation of economic activities and highlighted the influence of the Stockholm Conference, 1972, and principle 4 of the Rio Declaration on Environment and Development, 1992, concerning the protection of the environment. In particular, the Tribunal considered that economic development activities and environment are interrelated and cannot be considered in isolation. Then, the Tribunal noted:

> [e]nvironmental law and the law on development stand not as alternatives but as mutually reinforcing, integral concepts, which require that where

---

112 United Nations General Assembly, "Brundtland Report of the World Commission on Environment and Development (Distr. General a/42/427)," (1987), para 27. For an overview of sustainable development, *See* Daniel Magraw and Lisa D. Hawke, "Sustainable Development," in *The Oxford Handbook of International Environmental Law*, ed. Daniel Bodansky, Jutta Brunnée, and Ellen Hey (Oxford: Oxford University Press, 2007).

113 *Gabčíkovo Nagymaros Dam (Hungary/Slovakia)*, ICJ Rep, p. 7, para 140 (1997). *Pulp Mills on the River Uruguay (Argentina v. Uruguay)*, General List No. 135, ICJ 2010, p. 14, paras 76 and 177 (Judgment of 20 April 2010).

114 International Law Association (ILA), "International Law on Sustainable Development: Final Report. Sofia Conference 2012," in *75 Int'lL. Ass'n Rep. CONF. 821, 879 (2012)* (United Kingdom, 2012), 837–38. *See also* the "duty of States to ensure sustainable use of natural resources" in "New Delhi Declaration of Principles of International Law Relating to Sustainable Development," in *70th Conference of the International Law Association (ILA)* (India: International Environmental Agreements: Politics, Law and Economics 2. Kluwer Academic Publishers, 2002).

115 *Gabčíkovo Nagymaros Dam (Hungary/Slovakia) (Separate Opinion of Vice-President Weeramantry)*, ICJ Rep, p. 7, para 85 (1997).

Environmentally sound management of wastes 39

development may cause significant harm to the environment there is a duty to prevent, or at least mitigate, such harm ... [s]uch duty in the opinion of the Tribunal, has now become a principle of general international law.[116]

Notwithstanding the controversies surrounding the legal status of sustainable development, it has increasingly pervaded "domestic" environments in relation to, e.g., waste management, biodiversity conservation, and climate change. Concerning permanent sovereignty over natural resources, sustainable development evokes the need to strike a *balance* between the right of States to exploit their resources and their obligations toward the environment.

Concluding remarks: ESM and permanent sovereignty over natural resources

The development of the ESM is an example of the agreed limits to the exercise of States' permanent sovereignty over natural resources. Such sovereignty is not an absolute *laissez-faire* scheme, but rather a set of rights and obligations of States in respect of natural resources within and beyond national jurisdiction. In exercising such rights, due consideration must be given to economic, social, and environmental matters. The ESM of wastes calls for the minimization of waste generation, and therefore to an efficient use of natural resources. As further discussed in this book, from an international law perspective, States enjoy significant discretion about what measures to take in response to waste minimization, e.g., regulation about product standards or binding targets of waste minimization. At a regional level, the EU has enacted several pieces of legislation concerning products, e.g., on packaging, and electronic equipment. Regarding ship wastes, minimization practices on board vessels and incentives to promote such minimization are still under development. Overall, waste minimization remains one of the biggest challenges in the area of waste management, since increased waste generation is closely correlated with economic development.

---

116 *Award in the Arbitration Regarding the Iron Rhine ("Ijzeren Rijn") Railway between the Kingdom of Belgium and the Kingdom of the Netherlands*, RIAA XXVII, pp. 35–125, para 59 (24 May 2005).

3 Wastes

A reexamination of the legal concept of waste

The use of "waste" as a legal category and its influence in regulation

Some initial guidance in understanding the everyday uses of the word "waste" can be gleaned from dictionaries. For instance, the Merriam-Webster dictionary defines waste as "defective, superfluous material ... an unwanted by-product of a manufacturing process, chemical laboratory, or nuclear reactor ... refuse from places of human or animal habitation, as garbage, rubbish ... sewage".[1] This definition shows that a common feature related to waste is its negative content, i.e., something useless and undesirable, having no value at all. Another common feature is the perception of waste as toxic, hazardous, or polluting. The definition illustrates a broad range of what is usually considered as waste. On the one hand, sewage or garbage can fall into the category of municipal waste, by-products of chemical laboratories are hazardous wastes, and by-products of nuclear reactors are ultra-hazardous wastes. Thus, wastes are polluting or contaminating substances or materials that may have deleterious effects on human health and the environment. Of course, when talking about the environment, deleterious effects of wastes can cause environmental degradation of land, watercourses, sea, and air, within or beyond national boundaries.

This negative conception of waste transcends the everyday usage of the word and has a direct impact on waste policy issues.[2] For instance, disposal activities may encounter strong public objections that can be better described as "not in

---

1 Frederick C. Mish, ed. *Merriam-Webster's Collegiate Dictionary* (Springfield, MA: Merriam-Webster's Collegiate, 2011), 1412.

2 "[t]he process of obtaining the consents ... required to permit the yard's waste management activities, is not purely one of demonstrating the necessary technical capacity. It also has a political component, especially where the grant of such consents is open to public scrutiny." Colin De La Rue and Charles B. Anderson, *Shipping and the Environment: Law and Practice*, 2nd (London: Informa Law, 2009), 1042.

Wastes 41

my backyard syndrome".[3] The so-called "ghost ships" offer a prime example of this metaphor. The ghost ships were decommissioned naval ships from the United States of America that were sent to the United Kingdom for dismantling. Despite the disposal yard's technical capacity to break them, the ships were not dismantled in the United Kingdom due to[4] civil society pressures, i.e., Friends of the Earth and the Basel Action Network, which successfully associated these ships with toxic waste.[5] While these ships were precleaned and had no toxic cargo, their structures were found to contain asbestos. Indeed, the categorization of a substance or material as "waste" is significant, since such categorization is usually translated into stringent controls and stronger public reactions in relation to its management. Thus, "waste" becomes a powerful tool with which to raise public concerns, encourage political debate, and promote the adoption of stringent regulation.

The Janus-like nature of wastes

The definition of waste reveals it as something useless and without value. But to whom is this "waste" nonvaluable? Considering wastes as worthless per se is inaccurate. It is submitted that no substance or material has intrinsic features that can be objectively identified as waste. Even sewage and organic waste (compost) are further used to produce energy, i.e., electricity or heat.[6] In sociological terms, waste has been conceived as a "production resource and a consumption good: a bipolar object [and] wasting ... as a regulated exchange of value between objects".[7] A ship owner disposing a vessel may consider it a waste because the vessel requires high maintenance; it has reached the end of its operative life, or a regulation has imposed higher construction and safety standards that such

---

3 *Note* that "[t]he holders of the waste in the state of generation are faced with an increasing scarcity of disposal facilities, growing public opposition to the establishment and operation of such facilities as a result of what has been termed NIMBY (Not In My Back Yard) syndrome." Kummer, *International Management of Hazardous Wastes: The Basel Convention and Related Legal Rules*, 6. *Note* also that in relation to landfills in Western countries, "[p]ublic opposition to waste management facilities, in view of the increasing awareness, has equally intensified." Cyril Uchenna Gwam, "*Travaux Preparatoires* of the Basel Convention on the Control of Transboundary Movements of Hazardous Wastes and their Disposal," *Journal of Natural Resources and Environmental Law* 18 (2003): 6.

4 *See* the case *R. (on the Application of Friends of the Earth) v. Environment Agency*, Env. L.R. 31 (2003). Tony Puthucherril, *From Ship Breaking to Sustainable Ship Recycling: Evolution of a Legal Regime*, ed. David Freestone, Vol. 5, Legal Aspects of Sustainable Development (Leiden: Martinus Nijhoff Publishers, 2010), 46–51.

5 Basel Action Network (BAN), "Needless Risk: The Bush Administration's Scheme to Export Toxic Waste Ships to Europe," (20 October 2003). Friends of the Earth, "Ghost Fleet Ships, Toxicity and PCBs," (December 2003).

6 Secretariat of the Basel Convention, Zoï Environment Network, and GRID-Arendal, "Vital Waste Graphics 3," 20.

7 Martin O'Brien, "Rubbish Values: Reflections on the Political Economy of Waste," *Science as Culture* 8, no. 3 (1999): 271.

42 *Preliminaries*

a vessel can no longer satisfy. On the other hand, a ship-scrapping yard in Alang, India, considers this vessel as a valuable good from which raw materials, e.g., steel, can be recovered.[8] Similar considerations may apply to the transboundary movement of wastes in general, where there are emerging markets not only for recycling wastes, but also for waste disposal as an economic activity.[9] Thus, subjective understandings of waste have influenced the development of waste-value concepts or utilitarian perspectives, which imply that materials or substances that can be recycled, reused, and recovered should not fall into the category of waste.[10] Indeed, a trend has emerged that seeks to move away from waste categorizations by considering these substances or materials as just another stage of the economic system. At the same time, concerns have been raised regarding treating wastes differently if they are destined for final disposal or recycling. This is because differentiation in wastes could encourage façade-recycling operations and divergences among states over what recovery or recycling operations entail.[11]

Another alternative approach when addressing wastes is to dismiss the use of this word altogether, since the driving force behind the regulation of wastes is the risk that these substances or materials pose. This is the position of Wilkinson, who suggests turning to the "ideas of environmental hazard and risk".[12] In other words, wastes should not be treated any differently from any other good or product with hazardous characteristics.[13] Despite the merits of this argument,

---

8 *Note* that around "80–90 percent of a ship [as a percentage of the empty vessel's weight] represents a valuable source of scrap steel for construction, for example." Secretariat of the Basel Convention, Zoï Environment Network, and GRID-Arendal, "Vital Waste Graphics 3," 18.

9 *Note* that the value of wastes is not given exclusively when those substances and materials can be recycled or re-used; they are also valuable for businesses engaged in final disposal operations. O'Brien, "Rubbish Values: Reflections on the Political Economy of Waste," 287. *Note* also that wastes are valued for "disposal industries. Specialized waste plants generally require costly and continuous maintenance ... it is not surprising that waste disposal facilities may start to import foreign wastes" as is the case in Germany. Mirina Grosz, *Sustainable Waste Trade under WTO Law: Chances and Risks of the Legal Framework's Regulation of Transboundary Movement of Wastes*, ed. Mads Andenas, Vol. 4, Nijhoff International Trade Law Series (Leiden: Martinus Nijhoff Publishers, 2011), 17.

10 For an account of value concepts of wastes, *See* David Wilkinson, "Time to Discard the Concept of Waste," *Environmental Law Review* 1 (1999): 191–94. Grosz, *Sustainable Waste Trade under WTO Law*, 4, 11–18.

11 J. Wylie Donald, "The Bamako Convention as a Solution to the Problem of Hazardous Waste Exports to Less Developed Countries," *Columbia Journal of Environmental Law* 17 (1992): 449. *See also* the opinion of Greenpeace regarding the Ban Amendment: "waste traders will no longer be able to justify hazardous waste exports by sending them to sham or dirty recycling operations." Jim Puckett and Cathy Fogel, "A Victory for Environment and Justice: The Basel Ban and How It Happened," in *Greenpeace International* (Washington, 1994), 1.

12 Wilkinson, "Time to Discard the Concept of Waste," 195.

13 It is noteworthy that certain regulatory bodies make a distinction between hazard and risk. *See,* e.g., The Presidential/Congressional Commission on Risk Assessment and Risk Management, "Framework for Environmental-Health Risk Management," (United States of America, 1997), 1. On the other hand, for instance, the ILC defines risk in terms of probability of harm: "Risk ...

Wastes 43

it underestimates the extent to which materials, products, objects, or substances at some point in a production process, or in a household, become unwanted, unhygienic, and useless. Consequently, the category of waste arises even if someone else sees this waste as valuable or as constituting raw material. This duality of waste/product can be summarized as follows: waste is "a resource and not a resource, a potential value and a potential nonvalue simultaneously ... the 'final' residue is never reached for there is never a *final residue of value*".[14] Additionally, if wastes are treated like any other hazardous material or substance, e.g., oil, the primary responsibility for their management rests on the importing States, while in transboundary movements of wastes, exporting States remain responsible for managing those wastes.[15]

When addressing waste in its legal context, its definition is no less problematic. Whether a substance or material is considered waste varies according to a specific regulatory scheme and at different regulatory levels, i.e., international, regional, and national. One should bear in mind that wastes can be generated on land or at sea, within or outside national boundaries, and this generation or disposal may only affect a particular State or it may provoke transboundary pollution. Furthermore, many regimes do not use the word "waste," or they use it only incidentally as is the case with MARPOL.

Ship wastes

International law

It is important to note that several treaties regulate wastes arising from shipping activities, e.g., the International Convention on the Control of Harmful Anti-Fouling Systems of Ships (AFS Convention), and the International Convention for the Control and Management of Ships' Ballast Water and Sediments (BWM Convention). Ships at the end of their operative life could be classified as wastes, but their regulation is transitioning from the realm of transboundary movements of wastes to a specialized regime, i.e., the Hong Kong International Convention for the Safe and Environmentally Sound Recycling of Ships (Hong Kong Convention). This section examines which substances fall into the category of ship wastes.

---

includes risks taking the form of a high probability of causing significant transboundary harm and a low probability of causing disastrous transboundary harm." International Law Commission (Fifty-Third Session A/56/10), "Draft Articles on Prevention of Transboundary Harm from Hazardous Activities, with Commentaries," (2001), Article 2.

14 O'Brien, "Rubbish Values: Reflections on the Political Economy of Waste," 291.

15 Handl and Lutz discuss the trade of hazardous materials and incidentally make comparisons with waste trade. Günter Handl and Robert Lutz, "An International Policy Perspective on the Trade of Hazardous Materials and Technologies," *Harvard International Law Journal* 30 (1989).

MARPOL

MARPOL regulates, among other things, operational residues generated in: (a) machinery spaces, (b) cargo spaces, and (c) living spaces of a ship. MARPOL is the most comprehensive regime dealing with ship-source pollution, both operational and accidental. This instrument relates to the prevention of "pollution of the marine environment by the discharge of harmful substances or effluents containing such substances".[16] Harmful substances under MARPOL are polluting materials of any kind, i.e., liquid, gas, or solid, whose introduction into the environment is detrimental to both human health and the environment. Nonetheless, the *harmful substances* regulated by MARPOL comprise a wider category than waste, since the concept of "harmful substances" includes, for instance, bunkers and hazardous cargoes, such as oil or chemicals, as well as the residues of such cargo. Article 1(1) of MARPOL defines harmful substances as "any substance … liable to create hazards to human health, to harm living resources and marine life, to damage amenities or to interfere with other legitimate uses of the sea".[17] This Convention has six annexes, which deal with oil; noxious substances carried in bulk, i.e., chemicals; harmful substances carried in packaged form; sewage; garbage; and air pollution. The day-to-day operations of ships will generate ship wastes in relation to each of MARPOL's annexes. Those wastes are summarized in Table 3.1:

Table 3.1 Ship wastes MARPOL

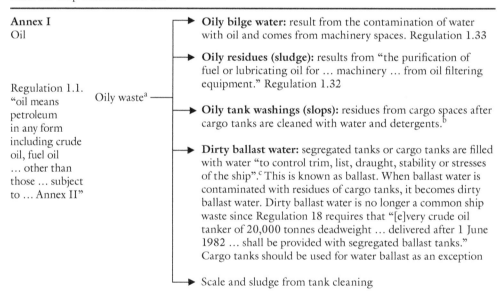

---

16 *See* Article 1(1) of MARPOL.
17 Ibid., Article 2(2).

Annex II
Noxious substances carried in bulk

Regulation 1(10) Substances falling into the category X, Y, or Z of the (IBC Code)[d]

Residues from cargo Regulation 1(10)

→ **Residues from Category X:** Substances falling into category X present "major hazard to either to marine resources or human health." Regulation 6(1)

→ **Residues from Category Y:** Substances falling into category Y present "hazard to either marine resources or human health or cause harm to amenities or other legitimate uses of the sea." Regulation 6(2)

→ **Residues from Category Z:** Substances falling into category Z present "a minor hazard either to marine resources or human health." Regulation 6(3)

Residues that are mixed with water Regulation 1(11)

→ Tank washing

→ Dirty ballast water

→ Bilge slops

Annex IV
Sewage
Regulation 1(3)

- Drainage and other wastes from any form of toilets and urinal
- Drainage from medical premises
- Drainage from spaces containing living animals
- Mixtures of the above drainages
- Grey water, i.e., residues from bathing, laundry, or dishwashing, is not covered by this Annex

Annex V[c]
Garbage

Regulation 1(1)

- Animal carcasses, i.e., animals carried as cargo that died during the voyage
- Cargo residues that are not covered by other Annexes
- Cooking oil
- Domestic wastes are residues from living spaces of the ship
- Fishing gear
- Food wastes means any spoiled or unspoiled food substances and includes fruits
- Incinerator ashes
- Operational wastes are residues that are not covered by other Annexes
- Plastics

Annex VI
Air pollution

- Ozone depleting substances (Regulation 12) from refrigeration, air conditioning, and fire extinguishing equipment
- Exhaust gas cleaning residues arising from scrubbers. (Regulations 4 and 17.2) Exhaust gas cleaning systems are also known as scrubbers and are used to reduce the amount of sulfur oxide (SO_X) in fuels[f]

---

a Marine Environment Protection Committee (MEPC), "Revised Guidelines for Systems for Handling Oily Wastes in Machinery Spaces of Ships Incorporating Guidance Notes for an Integrated Bilge Water Treatment System (IBTS), as Amended," (MEPC.1/Circ.642, 12 November 2008).

b MARPOL does not define slops, but numeral 16 of Regulation 1 of Annex I of MARPOL defines slop tank as a "tank specifically designated for the collection of tank drainings, tank washings and other oily mixtures."

c Article 1(2) of the International Convention for the Control and Management of Ships' Ballast Water and Sediments. CE Delft and CHEW, "The Management of Ship-Generated Waste On-Board Ships. EMSA/Op/02/2016," (European Maritime Safety Agency (EMSA), 2017), 58.

d "International Code for the Construction and Equipment of Ships Carrying Dangerous Chemicals in Bulk. (IBC Code)," International Maritime Organization (IMO).

e Marine Environment Protection Committee (MEPC), "Resolution MEPC.201(62) Revised MARPOL Annex V."

f Marine Environment Protection Committee (MEPC), "Resolution MEPC.184(59): 2009 Guidelines for Exhaust Gas Cleaning Systems," (MEPC 59/24/Add.1, 17 July 2009).

46 *Preliminaries*

Based on several discharge criteria, some residues can, under limited circumstances, be disposed of at sea, after being subject to other waste treatment operations, including oil-water separation in the case of bilge water,[18] and the disinfection and comminution of sewage.[19] The vast majority of ship wastes, however, remain on board vessels. These residues are constantly generated due to ships operations, and they can only be kept on board for a limited time before its discharge becomes a necessity. The provision of adequate port reception facilities becomes essential within the waste management process of ship wastes. As further analyzed in Chapter 8, the compliance with ESM includes the integration of wastes into national waste plans.

International convention on the control of harmful anti-fouling systems of ships

The AFS Convention is also relevant in the regulation of ship wastes. Since marine organisms become attached to ships, their hulls are often given surface treatments or coatings of paint designed to prevent any organisms from attaching. These organisms could reduce a ship's speed and increase fuel consumption.[20] The treatments are known as anti-fouling systems and may contain harmful substances, e.g., tributyltin (TBT, persistent organotin compound). The introduction of TBT into the marine environment causes severe damage to marine life and can also enter the food chain.[21] The AFS Convention restricts and prohibits the use of certain anti-fouling systems. Article 5 of the Convention prescribes that a State Party must:

> take appropriate measures in its territory to require that wastes from the application or removal of an anti-fouling system controlled in Annex 1 are collected, handled, treated and disposed of in a *safe and environmentally sound manner* to protect human health and the environment. (emphasis added)

The application and removal of anti-fouling systems occur at specific periods during the operative life of a vessel, i.e., "maintenance, repairs or conversion

---

18 *See* MARPOL, Annex I – Oil, Regulation 30(4) related to pumping, piping, and discharge arrangement. *See also* Regulation 32 "oil/water interface detector."

19 *See* MARPOL, Annex IV – Sewage, Regulation 9(2) "sewage systems"; Regulation 11(1.1) "Discharge of Sewage."

20 Rue and Anderson, *Shipping and the Environment: Law and Practice*, 847–50.

21 "TBT is further found to bioaccumulate in fish, dolphins, seals, whales, and other sea mammals, and it negatively affects a range of invertebrates, causing sterility in them and sometimes, even death … [w]ashing, scraping, and repainting of boat hulls may also cause harmful health effects on shipyard workers." Lena Gipperth, "The Legal Design of the International and European Union Ban on Tributyltin Antifouling Paint: Direct and Indirect Effects," *Journal of Environmental Management*, 90 (2009): 87.

operation".[22] This will also take place during the process of tearing down a vessel at the end of its operative life, i.e., recycling. IMO's manual on port reception facilities includes recommendations with regard to the handling, storage, and treatment of wastes resulting from the application or removal of anti-fouling systems on land. The manual focuses on the capabilities of ship repair/conversion yards and/or ship recycling yards,[23] and not on the provision of port reception facilities, because the application and removal of anti-fouling systems is not a regular activity in respect of day-to-day ship operations.

International convention for the control and management of ships' ballast water and sediments

The BWM Convention deals with the management of ballast water[24] in order to eliminate the transfer of harmful aquatic organisms and pathogens. In tanks designated to carry ballast water, sediments accumulate that contain organisms that may have harmful effects on the environment and human health. These sediments are ship-generated wastes, and every port and terminal *where ballast tanks are cleaned and repaired* must provide adequate port reception facilities for the reception of such sediments according to Article 5 of the Convention. This provision does not include the obligation to provide port reception facilities to receive ballast water. In addition, ports that do not engage in cleaning and repairing ballast tanks are not required to provide a reception facility of sediments either. The IMO, however, has developed guidelines for the provision of water ballast reception facilities,[25] and the manual on Port Reception Facilities provides recommendations for the collection, storage, and treatment of both ballast water and sediments.

EU law

Unlike MARPOL, which refers, in general terms, to harmful substances, Directive 2000/59/EC on Port Reception Facilities explicitly employs the terminology of "ship-generated waste" in reference to residues regulated under

---

22 International Maritime Organization (IMO), "Port Reception Facilities – How to Do It," in *Inadequacy of Reception Facilities, Updated Version of the Draft Manual on Port Reception Facilities* (London: MEPC 69/11, 2016), 11.

23 This does not entail that these yards will be always responsible for the treatment of the wastes. Specialized companies could be in charge of disposal or recovery operations. *See* Chapter 8.6.3. Ibid.

24 According to Article 1(3) of the BWM Convention, "ballast water management means mechanical, physical, chemical, and biological processes, either singularly or in combination, to remove, render harmless, or avoid the uptake or discharge of Harmful Aquatic Organisms and Pathogens within Ballast Water and Sediments."

25 Marine Environment Protection Committee (MEPC), "Resolution MEPC.153(55) Guidelines for Ballast Water Reception Facilities (G5)," (MEPC\55\23. Fifty-Fifth Session – Agenda Item 23, 13 October 2006).

48 *Preliminaries*

MARPOL's Annexes I, IV, and V,[26] i.e., oil, sewage, and garbage. Other wastes regulated by the Directive include "cargo residues" defined as "remnants of any cargo material on board in cargo holds or tanks which remain after unloading procedures and cleaning operations are completed and shall include loading/unloading excesses and spillage".[27] These wastes include substances regulated under MARPOL's Annexes I and II. There is an important caveat in relation to MARPOL Annex V, i.e., garbage. This Annex was comprehensively revised in 2011[28] when new categories of garbage were developed, including "cargo residues." Regulation 1(2) of said Annex defines cargo residues as:

> any remnants of any cargo which are not covered by other Annexes to the present Convention and which remain on the deck or in holds following loading or unloading, including loading and unloading excess or spillage, whether in wet or dry condition or entrained in wash water but does not include cargo dust remaining on the deck after sweeping or dust on the external surfaces of the ship.

According to Article 7(1) of Directive 2000/59/EC, mandatory discharge standards are only applicable to ship-generated wastes, but not to cargo residues. The category of "cargo residues" under MARPOL, Annex V, could potentially create difficulties for port users calling at an EU port, since it is not entirely clear whether those wastes are subject to mandatory discharge criteria. However, all residues under MARPOL, Annex V, must be considered ship-generated wastes for the purposes of Directive 2000/59/EC.[29] In relation to the Baltic Sea area, Regulation 6 of Annex IV of the Helsinki Convention also distinguishes between ship-generated wastes and cargo residues.

Practical reasons triggered the distinction between ship-generated wastes and cargo residues. Cargo residues come from a vast variety of cargoes, e.g., hazardous chemicals. Some residues remain property of the cargo owner. Others require specialized facilities for collection, storage, and treatment.[30] As such, it is

---

26 *See* Article 2(c) of Directive 2000/59/ on Port Reception Facilities for Ship-Generated Waste and Cargo Residues.

27 Ibid., Article 2(d).

28 (MEPC), "Resolution MEPC.201(62) Revised MARPOL Annex V." The revised Annex entered into force on 1 January 2013. Before the amendment, garbage was defined as "all kind of victual, domestic, and operational waste excluding fresh fish and parts thereof, generated during the normal operation of the ship and liable to be disposed continuously or periodically except those substances which are defined or listed in other Annexes of the Convention."

29 Article 2(c) of Directive 2000/59/ provides: "'ship-generated waste' shall mean all waste, including sewage, and residues other than cargo residues, which are generated during the service of a ship and fall under the scope of Annexes I, IV and V to MARPOL 73/78 and cargo-associated waste as defined in the Guidelines for the implementation of Annex V to MARPOL 73/7." *See also* "C/2016/1759 Commission Notice – Guidelines for the Interpretation of Directive 2000/59/ on Port Reception Facilities for Ship-Generated Waste and Cargo Residues," (OJ C 115, p. 5.16, 2016), 9–10.

30 European Maritime Safety Agency (EMSA), "Horizontal Assessment Report – Port Reception Facilities (Directive 2000/59/EC)," (December 2010), 42.

common practice for ship operators to contact private waste management operators with little or no involvement of the port authorities. In fact, port authorities in Europe generally consider that cargo residues are somehow outside the scope of their responsibilities, placing accountability on the ship operator and the "individual terminal".[31]

Article 6 of Directive 2000/59/EC obliges shipmasters to notify in advance the amount of ship-generated wastes *and cargo residues* to be delivered at port reception facilities or that are kept on board before entering an EU port. Such information must be available to the relevant authorities. Despite this obligation, the communication between the port authorities and the individual terminals regarding cargo residues is limited.[32] In the Baltic Sea area, e.g., many ports do not have information concerning the collection, transportation, and subsequent management of cargo residues because such activities are handled between the ship and the terminal or waste operators.[33] Consequently, information about the collection of cargo residues is scarce. This has a negative impact on the implementation and enforcement of Directive 2000/59/EC. If the relevant authorities have little or no knowledge of cargo residues, it is not possible for them to assess whether ships are complying with their discharge obligations as provided in Articles 10 and 11 of Directive 2000/59/EC. Moreover, the lack of information also hinders the compliance of obligations set out in the Waste Framework Directive, including the obligation to ensure the traceability of hazardous wastes.[34] Overall, the control and monitoring of the reception and further management of cargo residues on land are weak.

The distinction between ship-generated waste and cargo residues has generated complications for port users. Shipmasters find difficulties in assessing the different categories of wastes according to MARPOL and Directive 2000/59/EC. In fact, shipmasters are subject to different notification forms depending on

---

31 Horizontal Assessment Report – Port Reception Facilities (Directive 2000/59/EC), 42. *See also:* "[p]orts using private operators often have an informal waste notification system in place where direct contact is established between the agent and the operators, and thus without any direct involvement from the ports ... Although waste handling is outsourced to the terminals it is still the overall responsibility of the Port Authority to ensure compliance with Directive 2000/59/EC." Ramboll, "Final Report: EMSA Study on the Delivery of Ship-Generated Waste and Cargo Residues to Port Reception Facilities in EU Ports," 32.

32 Panteia and PWC, "Ex-Post Evaluation of Directive 2000/59/EC on Port Reception Facilities for Ship-Generated Waste and Cargo Residues (Final Report)," (European Commission, 2015), 66.

33 *See Infra,* Appendix II. Even in cases where port authorities have access to this information, it is rarely subject to any kind of analysis or assessment. In relation to the survey conducted for this book, the ports of Copenhagen and Malmö indicated that: "We are notified via the Swedish Maritime Administration standard template for waste notification. We require this 24 hours in advance. In this template, they state if they will discharge cargo residues, *but we do not take any action*" (emphasis added).

34 *See* Article 17 of Directive 2008/98/EC.

50 *Preliminaries*

whether they call at an EU port or a port located elsewhere.[35] For this reason, in 2015, the notification form set forth in Directive 2000/59/EC was amended.[36] The amended form follows closely the IMO Advanced Notification Form for Waste Delivery to Port Reception Facilities.[37] This amendment aims to avoid administrative burdens for port users as well as reflect the amendments of MARPOL, Annex V. It is expected that ships notify the quantities of wastes "actually delivered at port." The information could potentially be used to develop waste management plans.

Wastes subject to transboundary movements of wastes

Basel Convention

Legal definitions of waste will vary according to the legal instrument. For instance, these definitions can be guided by: (a) the identification of certain constituents that could have harmful effects on human health and/or the environment; (b) the description of the activities that a substance or object will be subject to, i.e., recycling, reuse, reclamation, or disposal; and (c) the distinction between wastes and nonwastes subject to certain criteria of value. The Basel Convention adopts two of the three approaches described above. Under this regime, whether or not a substance or material is deemed valuable does not affect the classification of waste.

Waste is defined in Article 2(1) of the Basel Convention as: "substances or objects which are disposed of or are intended to be disposed of or are required to be disposed of by the provisions of national law." From this definition, it is possible to conclude that waste can be any kind of gas, liquid, or solid material, but there is an important qualification here, namely that the classification of substances or objects as wastes is determined by their disposal or what Grosz describes as the operational approach.[38] Disposal under the Basel Convention not only encompasses the actual process of disposal or compulsory disposal under national legislation, but also incorporates a subjective element by including the intention of disposal. Nonetheless, the Convention is silent with regard to whose intention is relevant when categorizing a substance or object as waste, and in respect of how one can determine the content of an intention, as well as the moment when such an intention to dispose arises. It is unclear whether the "relevant"

---

35 European Commission, "Com(2016) 168 Final REFIT Evaluation of Directive 2000/59/EC on Port Reception Facilities for Ship-Generated Waste and Cargo Residues," in *Report from the Commission to the European Parliament and the Council* (2016), 12.

36 "Commission Directive (EU) 2015/2087 Amending Annex II to Directive 2000/59/EC on Port Reception Facilities for Ship-Generated Waste and Cargo Residues," (OJ L 302, pp. 99–102, 19.11.2015).

37 "Consolidated Guidance for Port Reception Facility Providers and Users," (MEPC.1/Circ.834, 15 April 2014).

38 Grosz, *Sustainable Waste Trade under WTO Law*, 4, 19.

Wastes 51

intention is to be found in the generator, exporter, importer, or carrier, or whether all such intentions are relevant.[39]

Disposal, according to Article 2(4) of the Basel Convention, covers "any operation specified in Annex IV." This annex includes a wide range of operations that fall into two categories. The first, Section A, refers to operations with no possibility of resource recovery, recycling, reclamation, direct reuse, or alternative uses, e.g., deposit in landfills, release into the ocean, biological treatments, deep injection, physical chemical treatment, permanent storage, and incineration.[40] The second category, Section B, refers to operations that may lead to resource recovery, recycling, reclamation, direct reuse, or alternative uses, such as reclamation of metals, solvents, or fuel, regeneration of acids, recovery of components from catalysts, or land treatment resulting in benefits to agriculture or ecological improvement. Sections A and B of Annex IV exemplify the operations to which wastes could be subject, but the lists are not exhaustive. According to Grosz, an open list is beneficial for keeping up "with potential technological and scientific developments",[41] but it also weakens the concept of wastes that is heavily reliant on the idea and content of disposal operations. Achieving a harmonized legal concept of wastes seems unlikely, since both disposal operations and hazardous wastes could also be established under national legislation.[42]

It is noteworthy that under the Basel Convention, disposal operations include activities such as reuse, recycling, recovery, reclamation, and alternative uses, yet none of these terms is defined under the Convention. Some guidance about reuse can be found in a footnote in Annex IX, which addresses reuse as "repair, refurbishment or upgrading, but not major reassembly." Additional assistance regarding the content of these operations can be found in the technical guidelines developed by the Open-ended Working Group and adopted by the COP to the Basel Convention.

The definition of wastes is far from clear. First, it could be argued that all substances or objects that are subject to disposal operations and that fall under the classification of hazardous or other wastes are immediately governed by the Basel Convention, except those wastes that are excluded from its scope, i.e., wastes derived from the normal operation of ships and radioactive wastes. However, "[a]n additional requirement for any waste to fall under the Convention's definition of wastes is that it is subject to transboundary movement".[43] If no transboundary movement occurs, the application of the entire Convention is not triggered.

---

39 Ibid., 74. Grosz mentions that, as with other international regimes, "their primary subjects are states. States are presumably not in a position to form their own volition or to assess whether certain materials constitute waste and are suitable for disposal or recovery operations."

40 *See* Annex IV of the Basel Convention.

41 Grosz, *Sustainable Waste Trade under WTO Law*, 4, 21.

42 *See* Articles 2(1) and 2(4) of the Basel Convention.

43 David Langlet, *Prior Informed Consent and Hazardous Trade: Regulating Trade in Hazardous Goods at the Intersection of Sovereignty, Free Trade, and Environmental Protection* (Austin, TX: Wolters Kluwer Law & Business, 2009), 78.

52 *Preliminaries*

Hazardous wastes and other wastes

Article 1 of the Basel Convention confines its scope of application *to hazardous and other* wastes subject to transboundary movements. Both waste streams and waste constituents are criteria used to identify whether a waste falls under the category of hazardous wastes according to Annex I. This annex establishes several waste streams, including clinical waste, industrial waste, hydrocarbon waste, and those substances containing hazardous constituents, e.g., cadmium, selenium, arsenic, mercury, lead thallium, inorganic cyanides, and asbestos. The Basel Convention governs all wastes established in Annex I unless they do not possess the hazardous characteristics established in Annex III, e.g., flammability, explosiveness, corrosiveness, toxicity, and infectiousness. The list of hazardous characteristics of Annex III is the result of the categories developed by the United Nations Recommendations on the Transport of Dangerous Goods.[44]

The classification of hazardous wastes, as adopted in the Basel Convention, was heavily criticized because the range of substances included in Annex I was too extensive and no consideration was given to wastes containing minor quantities of hazardous constituents.[45] Additionally, some of the hazardous characteristics listed in Annex III were vague and hard to define.[46] For these reasons, in its Fourth Meeting, held in 1998, the COP to the Basel Convention proposed an amendment of the Treaty. As a result, Annexes VIII and IX were adopted to facilitate the Convention's practical application.[47] Annex VIII establishes a more detailed waste list that falls within the category of hazardous wastes according to Article 1, paragraph 1 (a) of the Basel Convention. Wastes subject to this annex are classified into: (a) metal and metal-bearing wastes; (b) wastes containing principally inorganic constituents, which may contain metals and organic materials;

---

44 *See* the revised edition of these recommendations, available at: <www.unece.org/trans/danger/publi/unrec/rev17/17files_e.html>, last accessed 9 March 2019. United Nations, "UN Recommendations on the Transport of Dangerous Goods – Model Regulations," (2011). *Note* also that Tolba explains that in the process of negotiation of the Basel Convention, there was no accepted and global definition of hazardous wastes. Mostafa K. Tolba and Iwona Rummel-Bulska, *Global Environmental Diplomacy: Negotiating Environmental Agreements for the World, 1973–1992*, ed. Nazli Choucri, Global Environmental Accords (Cambridge: The MIT Press, 2008), 98.

45 Kummer, *International Management of Hazardous Wastes: The Basel Convention and Related Legal Rules*, 50–51.

46 Ibid.

47 Secretariat of the Basel Convention, "Amendment and Adoption of Annexes to the Convention (Decision IV/9)," in *Conference of the Parties to the Basel Convention on the Control of Transboundary Movements of Hazardous Wastes and their Disposal: Fourth Meeting (UNEP/CHW.4/35)* (Kuching, 23–27 February 1998), para 53. The amendment entered into force on 6 November 1998. Annex VIII has been amended twice by the Sixth and Seventh Meetings of the Conference of the Parties, "Review or Adjustment of the Lists of Wastes Contained in Annexes VIII and IX to the Basel Convention," in *Conference of the Parties to the Basel Convention on the Control of Transboundary Movements of Hazardous Wastes and Their Disposal: Seventh Meeting, Item 6 of the Provisional Agenda (UNEP/CHW.7/15)* (Geneva, 2004). Those amendments entered into force on 20 November 2003 and 8 October 2005, respectively.

Wastes   53

(c) wastes containing principally organic constituents, which may contain metals and inorganic materials; and (d) wastes that may contain either inorganic or organic constituents. It is notable that while the wastes listed in Annex VIII are *prima facie* considered hazardous, wastes that do not possess the hazardous characteristics contained in Annex III could still be classified as nonhazardous.

Annex IX includes metal and metal-bearing wastes containing, e.g., copper, nickel, and iron. These wastes are *prima facie* not considered hazardous except when they contain the constituents of Annex I in "an extent causing them to exhibit an Annex III characteristic." Finally, according to Article 1(1) (b) of the Basel Convention, transit, exporting, and importing states can characterize wastes as hazardous under their national legislation. "Other wastes" are divided into two categories listed in Annex II, i.e., household waste and residues from the incineration of household waste.

The distinction between hazardous and other wastes has no real significance because both categories are subject to the same strict control mechanisms. Indeed, the "other wastes" category was included in the Fifth Negotiation Session of the Basel Convention so as to remove uncertainties regarding the possibility of classifying municipal waste as hazardous and to fulfill the requirements of certain negotiating states to incorporate household waste and the residues of its incineration in the scope of the Convention.[48]

OECD level

The scope of OECD Council Decision C(2001)107/FINAL is the regulation of transboundary movements of hazardous wastes *destined for recovery* among OECD states. The OECD Council Decision mirrors the Basel Convention by adopting an operational approach to the definition of wastes.

Wastes

Chapter A.3 of the Council Decision establishes that wastes are:

> substances or objects, other than radioactive materials covered by other international agreements, which: i) are disposed of or are being recovered; or ii) are intended to be disposed of or recovered; or iii) are required, by the provisions of national law, to be disposed of or recovered.

As soon as a substance or object is subject to a disposal or recovery operation, it will become waste. Disposal and recovery operations established in

---

48 Kummer, *International Management of Hazardous Wastes: The Basel Convention and Related Legal Rules*, 50. *Note* also that the United States was concerned with the possible classification of municipal waste as hazardous and the subsequent conflicts with national laws. Gwam, "*Travaux Preparatoires* of the Basel Convention on the Control of Transboundary Movements of Hazardous Wastes and their Disposal," 42–43.

54 *Preliminaries*

Appendices 5.A and 5.B, respectively, are identical to Annexes IV.A and IV.B of the Basel Convention. The main difference is that under the Basel Convention disposal encompasses what the OECD regime defines as recovery operations. Since the recycling potential and further economic use of wastes do not have any significance in relation to the control procedures established in the Basel Convention, it was deemed unnecessary to distinguish between disposal with or without the possibility of recovery. This recycling dilemma was addressed in the OECD Council Decision by introducing a distinct regulatory framework for wastes subject to recovery operations.

Wastes under national legislation, however, can be defined and classified differently from those wastes subject to transboundary movements of wastes for several reasons. This could be the result of: (a) inadequate coordination between agencies dealing with wastes; (b) dispersed legislation on the matter; or (c) lack of resources to identify and classify substances or objects as wastes. Additionally, States could maintain distinct definitions of wastes under national legislation if the characterization of wastes for transboundary movements is considered restrictive or overinclusive. So, a substance or object may be considered a raw material or by-product when managed or traded within the boundaries of a certain jurisdiction, and that same object or substance could be classified as hazardous waste if subject to exportation. One should keep in mind that waste regulation is certainly more stringent than the regulation of other materials classified as products or goods, even hazardous ones. This speaks to the inherently negative connotations of the word "waste," in common parlance, and that is carried over to public policy and law. In fact, classifying a substance or material as something else could be a mechanism through which to unburden or promote, for instance, recycling industries or circular economies.[49] In the Communication Com(2015) 614 final, the European Commission stressed the need to strengthen the market for "secondary raw materials." The emphasis on materials instead of waste goes beyond mere terminology; it is the first step toward revising existing legislation "to determine when a secondary raw material should no longer be legally considered as 'waste', by clarifying existing rules on 'end-of-waste'".[50] Excluding certain objects or substances from the categorization of waste due to their potential reuse or economic value constitutes a utilitarian approach toward the definition of waste.

As with the Basel Convention, the OECD Council Decision C(2001)107/FINAL includes an operational approach in its definition of wastes, i.e., substances or objects that *are* disposed/recovered or *are required* to be disposed/recovered,

---

49 At the EU level, circular economies have been understood as "materials that can be recycled are injected back into the economy as new raw materials thus increasing the security of supply." "Com(2015) 614 Final: Closing the Loop – An EU Action for the Circular Economy." *See also*, Commission of the European Communities, "Communication from the Commission Com(2003) 301 Final," in *Towards a Thematic Strategy on the Prevention and Recycling of Waste* (Brussels, 2003).

50 "Com(2015) 614 Final: Closing the Loop – An EU Action for the Circular Economy," 11.

but it also includes a subjective criterion when referring to substances or objects *"intended"* to be disposed/recovered. This intention is certainly subjective and can be concealed. At the EU level, where a very similar definition has been adopted, this matter has been addressed through an objective test, which aims to "infer" the intention from the actions of the holder,[51] and it does not preclude further "economic re-use by others".[52]

Although the OECD Council Decision C(2001)107/FINAL defines wastes as those substances subject to disposal operations, these are actually excluded from its scope of application.[53] In the disposal operations of hazardous wastes, the applicable regime will become the Basel Convention. On the other hand, from the wording of the OECD Council Decision C(2001)107/FINAL, it becomes apparent that it applies both to hazardous and nonhazardous wastes if they are subject to recovery operations. Since the OECD Council Decision develops a framework that encourages the trade of recyclable wastes, it is reasonable to suggest that the decision has a general application without excluding wastes due to their characteristics and composition.

Hazardous wastes

A listing approach determines whether or not a waste is hazardous. Chapter A.2 defines hazardous wastes as those listed in Appendix 1 "unless they do not possess any of the characteristics contained in Appendix 2." The definition closely follows the wording of the Basel Convention, and Appendix 1 is identical to Annex I of the Convention. It corresponds to the control of both waste streams (Y1–Y18) and waste constituents (Y19–Y45). Appendix II, on the other hand, is identical to Annex III of the Basel Convention dealing with the hazardous characteristics of wastes. The list of hazardous wastes is not an exhaustive one, since Member States, through national legislation, can characterize more wastes as "hazardous." The introduction of the definition of hazardous wastes in the OECD Council Decision is somewhat confusing, since the control procedures are not established in relation to the stated definition, but instead refer to "green- and amber-listed wastes." Those lists do not make any direct reference either to hazardous wastes as defined in the Decision, or to Appendix 1 or 2. Nonetheless, it is important to consider that Annexes I and III of the Basel Convention, which are identical to Appendices 1 and 2 of the OECD Council Decision, were modified by the introduction of Annexes VIII and IX of the Basel Convention. As explained below, Annexes VIII and IX of the Basel Convention are taken into account in order to establish both green and amber lists of wastes under the OECD Council Decision C(2001)107/FINAL in an effort to make it congruent with the Basel Convention.

---

51 European Commission, "Guidance on the Interpretation of Key Provisions of Directive 2008/98/EC on Waste," ed. Directorate-General Environment (2012), 10.
52 Jürgen Fluck, "The Term 'Waste' in EU Law," *European Environmental Law Review* (1994).
53 *See* Chapter B.1 of OECD Council Decision C(2001)107/FINAL.

56 Preliminaries

Wastes subject to the green control procedure are *prima facie* considered nonhazardous, since they do not "exhibit hazardous characteristics and are deemed to pose negligible risks for human health and the environment".[54] These wastes are listed in Appendix 3 of the OECD Council Decision, which is divided into two parts. Part I one refers to Annex IX of the Basel Convention (B list), i.e., metal and metal-bearing wastes, and wastes containing principally inorganic constituents, which may contain metals and organic materials. Appendix 3 slightly modifies some of the entries established in Annex IX of the Basel Convention. Part II, on the other hand, includes wastes previously listed as green wastes in the OECD Council Decision C(92)39/FINAL,[55] and these entries have no parallel in the Basel Convention. While wastes under Annex IX of the Basel Convention are considered nonhazardous if they do not exhibit the hazardous characteristics of Annex III, the OECD Council Decision has changed the chapeau of Appendix 3 with the following wording:

> [r]egardless of whether or not wastes are included on this list, they may not be subject to the Green control procedure if they are contaminated by other materials to an extent which (a) increases the risks associated with the wastes sufficiently to render them appropriate for submission to the Amber control procedure, when taking into account the criteria in Appendix 6, or (b) prevents the recovery of the wastes in an environmentally sound manner.

This is a significant departure from the Basel Convention, since the chapeau of Appendix 3 implies that a substance exhibiting hazardous characteristics could still follow the green control procedure.[56] In fact, Appendix 3 has broadened the criteria to assess the risk associated with wastes by referring both to Appendix 6 and to the capacity to recover such wastes in an environmentally sound manner. Appendix 6 presents a set of questions that include not only the hazardous characteristics of the wastes, but also the economic value of the waste, the frequency of transboundary movements to which such waste is subject, as well as management implications. Grosz raises some concerns regarding the criteria established in Appendix 6, since the criteria do not "only address questions on materials' hazardousness" and risks toward human health and the environment, but

---

54 Organisation for Economic Co-Operation and Development (OECD), "Guidance Manual for the Control of Transboundary Movements of Recoverable Wastes," (2009) 12.

55 Ibid.

56 The OECD Guidance Manual confirms this interpretation: "the chapeau attached to Annex IX of the Basel Convention is not applicable to Appendix 3 within the OECD Decision. Consequently, under the OECD Decision, it is possible, though highly unlikely, that a waste listed in Appendix 3 exhibits a hazardous characteristic but still benefits from the Green control procedure." Organisation for Economic Co-Operation and Development (OECD), "Guidance Manual for the Control of Transboundary Movements of Recoverable Wastes," 12.

include economic implications as well.[57] In other words, "hazardous wastes," as defined in the Basel Convention, could be subject to transboundary movements in contravention of the control procedure established in the Convention. If this is the case, the OECD Council Decision cannot take precedence over the Basel regime, since, as Kummer notes, "[t]he regulation of the management of wastes figuring on the green list, to the extent that they are not hazardous in terms of the Basel Convention, is exempt from its requirements".[58]

One should remember that nonhazardous wastes do not fall within the scope of the Basel Convention, meaning that the OECD Council could tailor a regime that would be fit for trading recoverable nonhazardous wastes among their Member States. This has been done through the establishment of green-listed wastes (Appendix 3), whose transboundary movements are, to a great extent, free and do not follow the principles of the Basel Convention, e.g., PIC procedure, self-sufficiency, proximity, among others. But as soon as those wastes are categorized as hazardous according to the Basel Convention, State Parties have two alternatives: (a) comply with the regulatory control established in this instrument; or (b) conclude an arrangement under Article 11 of the Basel Convention. The OECD Council, through the adoption of the amber control procedure, has opted for the latter choice.

Appendix 4 contains the lists of wastes subject to the amber control procedure and it is divided into two parts. Part I includes wastes listed in Annexes II and VIII of the Basel Convention, but some waste entries are modified. According to the Basel Convention, if wastes included in Annex VIII do not exhibit the hazardous characteristics of Annex III, they will be regarded as nonhazardous wastes, and therefore will not fall within the scope of application of the Convention. This chapeau is not included in the OECD Council Decision, so the amber control, which to some extent is compatible with the Basel Convention, could be applicable to nonhazardous wastes. In this particular case, there is no space for conflict between the two regimes since the Basel Convention seeks to ensure the strict control of transboundary movements of hazardous and other wastes, while the regulation on nonhazardous wastes is left entirely to State Parties.

Part II of Appendix 4 of the OECD Council Decision includes wastes previously categorized as amber- or red-listed wastes as defined in Decision C(92)39/FINAL, and these have no parallel in the Basel Convention. These wastes have been included after Member States have assessed the risks according to the set of questions established in Appendix 6. Such assessments are based on trade, the management implications of wastes, and their hazardous characteristics.

---

57 According to this author, while these criteria "may provide for valuable information regarding the market's efficiency, they do not necessarily inform about the risk in question." Grosz, *Sustainable Waste Trade under WTO Law*, 4, 31.

58 This is a comment made in relation to the OECD Council Decision C(92)39/FINAL, but it is still applicable to the current Council Decision. Kummer, *International Management of Hazardous Wastes: The Basel Convention and Related Legal Rules*, 166.

58 *Preliminaries*

EU law

Wastes

Regulation 1013/2006/EC on Shipments of Wastes must be read alongside the Waste Framework Directive[59] that defines "waste" in its Article 3(1) as: "any substance or object which the holder discards or intends or is required to discard".[60] This definition of waste was first introduced in Directive 75/442/EEC as amended by Directive 91/156/EEC. Before the 1991 amendment, the Directive referred to the term "dispose of" in line with the definition of wastes provided in the Basel Convention. However, it was uncertain whether substances or objects with further economic value, e.g., reuse or recycling, would fall within the definition of wastes. In the *Vessoso and Zanetti* case,[61] the Court of Justice determined that the Directive did not "intend to exclude all economic reutilization" of the wastes. Thus, the subjective criterion of value offers no ground to distinguish between waste and nonwaste. In the case *C-422/92*, the Court of Justice rejected the submission of the German Government that tried to exclude subjects and objects that are "capable of remaining within the economic circuit" from the concept of waste.[62]

At present, EU law focuses on the notion of discarding. The concept of discarding has evolved through case law. The Advocate General in the *Euro Tombesi* case[63] did not define the word "discarding" but instead only referred to operations involved in discarding, i.e., disposal and recovery. Article 3(15) of the Waste Framework Directive defines recovery as operations that mainly result in "serving a useful purpose" by employing them in an economic activity instead of other materials. On the other hand, Article 3(19) defines disposal as "any operation which is not recovery." As with the Basel Convention, a substance or

---

59 This Directive repealed Directive 2006/12/EC on waste (which repealed Directive 75/442/EEC as amended), hazardous waste Directive 91/689/EEC, and Waste Oils Directive 75/439/EEC.

60 *Note* that Article 2 of Regulation 1013/2006/EC mentions that waste is defined in Article 1(1) (a) of Directive 2006/12/EC and hazardous wastes is defined in Article 1(4) of the Council Directive 91/689/EEC on hazardous wastes. However, both pieces of regulation were repealed from 12 December 2010. *See* Article 41 of the "Directive 2008/98/EC on Waste and Repealing Certain Directives."

61 *See* para 11. *Joined Cases C-206/88 and C-207/88*, ECR (I-01461) (1990).

62 *See* paras 21 and 22. *C-422/92 Commision of the European Communities v. Germany*, ECR I-01097 (1995).

63 *Euro Tombesi* ECR I-03561 (1997). *See also* "discard means something more than getting rid of something worthless. AG Jacobs ... put forward that is not worth trying to interpret the term 'discard' according to its normal meaning. Instead, he suggested that the term 'waste' and the disposal and recovery operations listed in Annex II should be read together, and the term discard should therefore be accorded a special meaning defined by reference to those and analogous operations." Ilona Cheyne, "The Definition of Waste in EC Law," *Journal of Environmental Law* 14, no. 1 (2002): 66. In relation to the circularity of the argument see Satnam Choongh and Martha Grekos, "Finding a Workable Definition of Waste: Is It a Waste of Time?," *Journal of Planning & Environmental Law* (2006): 463–79.

material will be categorized as waste depending upon the operations to which such material or substance is subject, i.e., discarding. According to the *Euro Tombesi* case, whether a substance or material has any value or is capable of being recycled or reused is immaterial in the definition of wastes under EU law. Van Calster summarizes this position as follows:

> [u]sing the term "to discard" was aimed at ensuring that there would be no doubt as to the implication into the definition of waste which has an economic value. The critical aspect of the concept of discarding is not the fact that the holder intends to exclude any possibility of recovery.[64]

In the *Inter-environment Wallonie* case, the Court of Justice was asked whether a substance is excluded from its categorization of waste "if it directly or indirectly forms an integral part of an industrial production process".[65] The Court of Justice followed the opinion of Advocate General in the *Euro Tombesi* case and focused on disposal and recovery operations instead of the meaning of "discard." Then, it determined that disposal and recovery do not exclude operations included in an industrial production process.[66]

In the *ARCO Chemie-Nederland Ltd. and Epon* case, the Court of Justice focused on the meaning of "discard" and was not prepared to define wastes on the basis that a substance or object is subject to disposal and recovery operations.[67] The Court of Justice determined that several of the disposal and recovery operations described in the Annexes of the Directive do not refer explicitly to wastes, e.g., the use of certain substances as fuel to generate electricity, and that substances other than wastes can be subject to these operations.[68]

Discard is the decisive criterion that determines if a substance or object is waste, and it does not exclusively refer to disposal and recycling operations as stated in the opinion of Advocate General in the *Euro Tombesi* case. According to the Court of Justice, discard can be inferred from the following elements: (a) the substance is "commonly regarded as waste"[69]; (b) the substance

---

64 Geert Van Calster, "The EC Definition of Waste: The Euro Tombesi Bypass and the Basel Relief Routes," *European Business Law Review*, 8, nos. 5/6 (1997): 138.

65 Para 25. *C-129/96 Inter-Environnement Wallonie ASBL v. Région Wallonne*, ECR I-07411 (1997). However, as Van Calster explains, this case "did not undermine the distinction which must be drawn between waste recovery and 'normal' industry treatment of products which are not wastes." Geert van Calster, *EU Waste Law*, 2nd edn (Oxford: Oxford University Press, 2015), 14.

66 Paras 26–30. *C-129/96 Inter-Environnement Wallonie ASBL v. Région Wallonne.*

67 The case concerned the export of 15,000,000 kg of "LUWA-bottoms" that were ARCO's by-product and used as fuel in the cement industry. In relation to Epon, the court discussed wood chips used as fuel to generate electricity. *Joined Cases C-418/97 and C-419/97 Arco Chemie Nederland Ltd. v. Minister van Volkshuisvesting, Ruimtelijke Ordening en Milieubeheer and Directeur van de dienst Milieu en Water van de Provincie Gelderland*, ECR I-04475 (2000).

68 Paras 49 and 50. Ibid.

69 Para 71. Ibid.

60 Preliminaries

is subject to an operation that is commonly used for recovery or disposal of wastes[70]; (c) the substance or object is a production residue[71]; (d) the "substance is a residue for which no use other than disposal can be envisaged"[72]; (e) due to the composition of the substance, it cannot be used as originally intended; and (f) due to its hazardous characteristics, special precautions must be taken.[73]

The *ARCO Chemie-Nederland Ltd. and Epon* case also clarified that recovering substances in an "environmentally responsible manner" is not relevant in the definition of wastes,[74] but it is fundamental in relation to waste management. In the *Thames Water* case, the *Van de Walle* case, and the *Commune de Mesquer v. Total* case, the Court of Justice determined that accidental spillages of hazardous substances may be regarded as discarding.[75] Overall, the Court of Justice provided guidance to infer "discarding" according to the specific circumstances of the case. Thus, the factors discussed in these cases are not conclusive.

The determination of whether a substance or object is in fact waste must be determined "in the light of all the circumstances".[76] This case-by-case approach has been reiterated in several cases, e.g., the *Thames Water* case,[77] the *Van de Walle* case,[78] and *Palin Granit Oy* case.[79] EU law presents a flexible approach in relation to the definition of wastes. In assessing the particular circumstances of the case, the aim of the Waste Framework Directive, i.e., the protection of human health and the environment,[80] is paramount in

---

70 Para 73. Ibid.

71 Para 84. Ibid.

72 Para 86. Ibid.

73 Para 87. Ibid.

74 Paras 65 and 66. Ibid.

75 Para 28 of the *Thames Water* case indicates: "The escape of waste water from a sewerage network constitutes an event by which the sewerage undertaker, the holder of that waste water, 'discards' it. The fact that the waste waters spilled accidentally does not alter the outcome ... The Court also held that Directive 75/442 would be made redundant in part if hydrocarbons which cause contamination were not considered waste on the sole ground that they were spilled by accident." *Case C-252/05 Thames Water Utilities Ltd. v. South East London Division, Bromley Magistrates' Court*, ECR I-03883 (2007). *See also* paras 48 and 49, *Case C-1/03 Criminal Proceedings v. Paul Van De Walle, Daniel Laurent, Thierry Mersch, and Texaco Belgium SA*, ECR I-07613 (2004).

76 Para 88. *Joined Cases C-418/97 and C-419/97 Arco Chemie Nederland Ltd. v. Minister van Volkshuisvesting, Ruimtelijke Ordening en Milieubeheer and Directeur van de dienst Milieu en Water van de Provincie Gelderland.*

77 Para 27. *Case C-252/05 Thames Water Utilities Ltd. v. South East London Division, Bromley Magistrates' Court.*

78 Para 45. *Case C-1/03 Criminal Proceedings v. Paul Van De Walle, Daniel Laurent, Thierry Mersch, and Texaco Belgium SA.*

79 Paras 24 and 25. *Case C-9/00 Palin Granit Oy v. Vehmassalon Kansanterveystyön Kuntayhtymän Hallitus*, ECR I-3548 (2002).

80 *See* sixth paragraph of the recital of the Waste Framework Directive 2008/98/EC. In addition, the legal basis of this Directive is Article 192(1) of the Treaty on the Functioning of the European Union (TFEU).

Wastes 61

determining if a substance is categorized as waste. Having recourse to Article 191(2) of the Treaty on the Functioning of the European Union (TFEU), the Court of Justice has systematically rejected a restricted interpretation of waste, since the "European Union policy on the environment is to aim at a high level of protection and is to be based, in particular, on the precautionary principle and the principle that preventive action".[81] In conclusion, while the EU favors an open-textured definition of wastes, at the international level, the COP of the Parties to the Basel Convention adopted the Strategic framework for the implementation of the Basel Convention for 2012–2021, which includes, as one of its objectives, the harmonization and common understanding of wastes and nonwastes.[82]

Hazardous wastes

The Waste Framework Directive also defines hazardous wastes. Wastes are categorized as hazardous when they exhibit one or several of the properties established in Annex III of the Directive, e.g., toxic, flammable, irritant, and carcinogenic.[83] In contrast to the Basel Convention, this directive does not mention waste streams as a device through which to identify hazardous wastes. It is important to keep in mind these terminological differences, since, according to the Basel Convention, disposal includes operations with and without the possibility of recovery, and the chosen disposal operation has no impact on the control over transboundary movements of wastes. On the other hand, at the EU level, disposal or recovery has an impact on the level of control to which transboundary movements of wastes are subject.

According to Regulation 1013/2006/EC on Shipments of Wastes, in the case of wastes destined for recovery, both the identity of the importer and the classification of green-listed and amber-listed wastes become relevant. This classification corresponds to the degree of hazard to human health and the environment. Green-listed wastes will generally not exhibit properties that are harmful to the environment or human health. According to Annex I, part I of Regulation 1013/2006/EC on Shipments of Wastes, green-listed wastes include those established in Annex IX of the Basel Convention. These wastes are *prima facie* not considered as hazardous except when they contain the constituents of Annex I in "an extent causing them to exhibit an Annex III characteristic." On the other hand, amber-listed waste covers, e.g., wastes categorized as hazardous under the

---

81 Para 38. *Joined Cases C-241/12 and C-242/12. Shell Nederland Verkoopmaatschappij BV and Belgian Shell NV*, ECLI:EU:C:2013:821 (2013). Paras 38 and 39, *Case C-188/07. Commune de Mesquer v. Total France SA and Total International Ltd.*

82 *See* objective 1.1. COP to the Basel Convention, "Decision BC-10/2: New Strategic Framework for the Implementation of the Basel Convention for 2012–2021 (UNEP/CHW.10/3)," in *Conference of the Parties to the Basel Convention on the Control of Transboundary Movements of Hazardous Wastes and Their Disposal. Tenth Meeting* (Cartagena, October 2011)."

83 *See* Article 3(2) of the Waste Framework Directive 2008/98/EC.

62 *Preliminaries*

Basel Convention. The scope of Regulation 1013/2006/EC on Shipments of Wastes is confined to "shipments of wastes" between member and third States. The control procedures applied to different categories of wastes are further examined in Chapter 4.

Transboundary movements of wastes and ship wastes: an analysis of Article 195 of the LOSC

Article 195 of the United Nations Convention on the Law of the Sea, 1982 (LOSC) is relevant to transboundary movements of wastes carried by sea. This article prescribes that: "in taking measures to prevent, reduce and control pollution of the marine environment, states shall act so as not to *transfer, directly or indirectly, damage or hazards from one area to another or transform one type of pollution into another.*" No guidance is found in the records of the negotiations of the Convention in relation to the meaning and extent of the terms "transfer" or "transform".[84]

The interpretation of this provision is not entirely clear, but following the objective approach of treaty interpretation, "transfer" means "[t]o convey or take from one place, person, etc. to another; to transmit, transport; to give or hand over from one to another".[85] This article acknowledges that polluting agents, e.g., wastes, may not stay at their place of generation, and their transference within and beyond national boundaries implies a potential risk of pollution to the marine environment. Some authors use the words "transfer" and "transform" without distinction and argue that Article 195 of the LOSC is relevant not only in relation to waste trade, but also regarding transfer of a pollutant "from one medium to another",[86] e.g., incineration of waste generated on land that causes air pollution. However, transform means "to change the form of ... into another shape or form ... to change in character or condition; to alter in function or nature, to undergo a change of form or nature".[87] Transform refers to "the quality or nature of the pollution".[88] In this regard, one may consider that to transform is: (a) *to change the source of pollution*, for instance, from land-based pollution to marine pollution, by disposing land pollutants into the sea; or (b) *to alter the composition of the pollutant*, e.g., by incinerating industrial waste, which generates by-products or other types of

---

84 Myron H. Nordquist et al., eds., *United Nations Convention on the Law of the Sea 1982: A Commentary*, V vols., Vol. IV (Leiden: Martinus Nijhoff Publishers, 1991), 72.

85 Fiona McPherson and Richard Holden, eds., *Oxford English Dictionary Online* (Oxford: Oxford University Press, 2013).

86 Ludwik A. Teclaff and Eileen Teclaff, "Transfers of Pollution and the Marine Environment Conventions," *Natural Resources Journal* 31 (1991): 190–92.

87 McPherson and Holden, *Oxford English Dictionary Online*.

88 Nordquist et al., *United Nations Convention on the Law of the Sea 1982: A Commentary*, 72.

pollutants.[89] Article 195 of the LOSC has a direct impact on the regulation of transboundary movements of wastes. The Basel Convention gives substantive content to this obligation.

Concluding remarks

This chapter has highlighted the Janus-like nature of wastes, i.e., their simultaneous status as resource and nonresource. As a legal category, waste is dynamic, since its conceptualization at the international, regional, and national levels will vary according to subjective and objective criteria, as set out in this chapter. In relation to ship wastes, for instance, wastes are not specifically regulated; instead, they are subsumed under the category of "harmful substances."

---

89 *See* that "matter is indestructible, it does not go anywhere. Modern pollution laws that fragment the environment into air, land, and water have created a legacy of transformations and transfers. Discharge limitations in one medium, such as air, often do little more than shift the pollution from air to land." Lakshman Guruswamy, "The Promise of the United Nations Convention on the Law of the Sea (UNCLOS): Justice in Trade and Environment Disputes," *Ecology Law Quarterly* 25 (1998–99): 217–18.

Part II
Regulation of transboundary movements of wastes and ship wastes

4   Transboundary movements
of wastes

From transboundary pollution to pollution transfer

Before the advent of the Basel Convention, customary law offered little guidance beyond traditional principles of transboundary pollution to deal with the waste trade phenomenon. Considering that wastes pose pollution risks, their transboundary movement could be identified as a form of transboundary pollution, but as will become clear in this section, movements of wastes cannot be subsumed under this notion.

To discuss transboundary pollution, one might imagine by-products of industrialization, including fumes or chemicals that are introduced, e.g., into the air or watercourses. These by-products are not restricted by national boundaries and are able to travel across jurisdictions, e.g., through the air or sea. Transboundary pollution illustrates that States are "not self-contained units, but contingent on actions taken by others"[1] and, as such, absolute notions of territorial integrity and sovereignty come under pressure.

Transboundary effects triggered the development of good neighborship law and enshrined the principle of States' "sovereign right to exploit their own resources ... and the responsibility to ensure that activities within their jurisdiction or control do not cause damage to the environment of other states or areas beyond the limits of national jurisdiction".[2] The no-harm rule is the foundation for promoting the prevention and regulation of activities carried out within jurisdictional boundaries that pose a significant threat of causing deleterious transboundary impacts on the environment of other States, common areas, or shared resources. Although transboundary pollution generally presupposes the use of a State territory,[3] the no-harm rule also extends to activities *under the control* of States. The significance and extent of the word "control" is not without

---

1 Wolfgang Sachs, "Environment," in *The Development Dictionary: A Guide to Knowledge as Power*, ed. Wolfgang Sachs (London: Zed Books Ltd., 1992), 27.
2 *See* principle 2 of the Rio Declaration 1992. *See also* principle 21 of the Stockholm Declaration, and paragraph 8 of the Johannesburg Declaration.
3 *See* Articles 1 and 2 of the ILC's draft articles on the prevention of transboundary harm. International Law Commission (Fifty-Third session A/56/10), "Draft Articles on Prevention of Transboundary Harm from Hazardous Activities, with Commentaries."

68 *Transboundary movements of wastes*

controversy, but some useful guidance can be found in the commentaries on the ILC's draft articles on the prevention of transboundary harm. Control involves activities carried out in areas where a State does not enjoy territorial jurisdiction (e.g., EEZ, high seas).[4]

The no-harm rule can be traced back to the *Trail Smelter Arbitration* where the Tribunal affirmed that States do not have an absolute freedom to pollute. It is worth noting that in the *Trail Smelter*, pollution was not rendered illegitimate or unlawful as long as polluting activities were carried out within territorial boundaries and did not cause *serious* injury to other States.[5] In other words, the right to pollute was endorsed, but was also restricted in relation to the rights of other States. However, the *Trail Smelter* has nothing to say on pollution abatement within national boundaries because environmental and health issues were not central in this case.

The main duty in terms of transboundary pollution is not the compensation of harm, but rather its prevention. Harm has usually been identified with "physical consequences" to property, resources, and persons of the State likely to be affected. This restrictive vision of harm has been qualified in the *Trail Smelter* as one posing a "serious consequence," and in the *Lac Lanoux* as "seriously to injure a neighboring state".[6] Article 1 of the ILC's draft articles on transboundary harm uses the term "significant."

The duty to prevent transboundary harm is one of due diligence, i.e., "adoption and enforcement of measures that a State can reasonably be expected to adopt" and, in the words of the ILC, what is expected of a "good government".[7] In relation to the prevention of environmental harm, the standards of due diligence remain ambiguous. Guidance in assessing compliance can be found in multilateral treaties endorsing "accepted or recognized international standards." For instance, Article 8 of the Basel Convention incorporates by reference, among others, the International Maritime Dangerous Goods (IMDG) Code in relation to packing, labeling, and transportation of wastes.

Customary law of transboundary pollution has come a long way since its inception in the *Trail Smelter*. The no-harm rule has evolved to include the prevention of environmental harm. However, traditional principles of transboundary pollution say little about the specific rights and obligations of States involved in transboundary movements of wastes. The Basel Convention has not only given content to specific rights and obligations, but also gone beyond the procedural counterpart of customary law of transboundary pollution, especially with the adoption of the PIC procedure which is unusual in international law. In the *Lac Lanoux* arbitration, the Tribunal explained the following:

---

4 Ibid.

5 *Trail Smelter (Canada v. United States)*, 3 RIAA 716 (1938 and 1941).

6 *Lac Lanoux Arbitration (France v. Spain)*, 24 ILR 101 (1957).

7 *See* the comments to Article 3 of the ILC's draft articles on the prevention of transboundary harm.

Transboundary movements of wastes 69

[t]o admit that jurisdiction in a certain field can no longer be exercised except on the condition of ... an agreement between two states, is to place an essential restriction on the sovereignty of a state ... This amounts to admitting a "right of assent", a "right of veto", which at the discretion of one state paralyses the exercise of the territorial jurisdiction of another.

The *Lac Lanoux* arbitration rejects a prior informed consent duty because, traditionally, the law of transboundary pollution deals with the control of activities within a territory that *incidentally* cause damage to other States, especially neighboring states. Consequently, third States have no right to approve or disapprove of activities carried out in neighboring States. The no-harm rule is operationalized through cooperation. According to Parrish, "the good neighborliness principle is derived directly from the permanent sovereignty concept because it requires that a state consider the interests, and respect the rights, of other states".[8]

On the other hand, the PIC procedure is the cornerstone of the transboundary movements of wastes regime. The PIC procedure within the Basel Convention is not an expression of predominance of environmental considerations regarding activities involving a risk of pollution; rather, it endorses the sovereignty and territorial integrity of the State likely to be affected. Unlike traditional transboundary pollution, *States likely to be affected by a transboundary movement of wastes are not incidentally affected by an activity carried out within the territorial boundaries of other States.* Indeed, transboundary movements of wastes presuppose the deliberate *transfer* of pollutants from one place to another. In this case, pollution substances travel across national boundaries not through a natural medium, such as air or watercourses, but rather through human intervention. Thus, wastes subject to a transboundary movement could be disposed far away from their source of generation, and States in which wastes are intended to be managed have the right to decide how their territories and resources are used.

The Basel Convention

The Basel Convention is a regulatory instrument designed to strictly control and eventually minimize transboundary movements of hazardous and other wastes. It also deals with the ESM of wastes subject to transboundary movements. One of the main objectives of the Convention is the protection of human health and the environment from the risks associated with the generation, unsafe transport, and inadequate management of wastes. Despite the almost worldwide

---

8 Austen L. Parrish, "Sovereignty's Continuing Importance: Traces of *Trail Smelter* in the International Law Governing Hazardous Waste Transport," in *Transboundary Harm in International Law: Lessons from the Trail Smelter Arbitration*, ed. Rebecca M. Bratspies and Russell A. Miller (Cambridge: Cambridge University Press, 2006), 185.

70 *Transboundary movements of wastes*

ratification[9] of this instrument, its success remains modest, since the obligations imposed by the Convention are in many cases "modified" by the adoption of a multitude of regional agreements that regulate transboundary movements of hazardous wastes.[10] Suffice it to say that the Basel Convention has become an umbrella instrument against which the validity of subsequent rules is judged. What is particularly revealing from these regional agreements is the latent conflict between two opposing views that were not satisfactorily addressed by the Basel Convention. On the one hand, developing States argued for a complete ban on transboundary movements of wastes.[11] On the other hand, developed States argued for a regulatory system that would allow the trading of wastes, especially when those wastes have a potential value or could be reused through recycling or recovery.

The following subsections scrutinize the "compromise approach" reached in the Basel Convention. This approach resulted in the strict control of transboundary movements of wastes based on a predominant conception of waste, i.e., an undesirable side effect of industrialization that is illegitimately transferred to developing countries. Currently, transfers of wastes from developed to developing States (at least of those reported)[12] are not prevalent; however, international outcry over the unsafe disposal of wastes in developing countries has not subsided. For instance, the management of specific waste categories (e.g., ship wastes, ships at the end of their operative life, and obsolete electronic devices) has reopened the debate over the legitimacy of transboundary movements of wastes.

Regulatory tensions within the Basel Convention

Since the late 1960s and early 1970s, the increased awareness of the threats that hazardous wastes pose prompted the enactment of stringent environmental legislation in relation to waste disposal in industrialized countries

---

9 As of March 2019, there are 187 parties to this instrument. For the status of the Convention, *See* <https://treaties.un.org/pages/ViewDetails.aspx?src=TREATY&mtdsg_no=XXVII-3& chapter=27&lang=en>, last accessed 12 March 2019.

10 For instance, the Bamako Convention on the Ban of Import into Africa and the Control of Transboundary Movement and Management of Hazardous Waste Within Africa, the Waigani Convention, the Protocol on the Prevention of Pollution of the Mediterranean Sea by Transboundary Movements of Hazardous Wastes and their Disposal (Izmir Protocol), the OECD Council Decision C(2001)107/FINAL Concerning the Control of Transboundary Movements of Wastes Destined for Recovery Operations and Regulation (EC) No 1013/2006 on Shipments of Wastes.

11 *See* Rozelia Park, "An Examination of International Environmental Racism through the Lens of Transboundary Movement of Hazardous Wastes," *Global Legal Studies Journal* 5 (1997–98). *See also* Nisha Thakker, "India's Toxic Landfills: A Dumping Ground for the World's Electronic Waste," *Sustainable Development Law & Policy* 58 (2006).

12 "Unlike 20 years ago, wastes are no longer shipped only from North to South. There has been a significant increase in South-North and South-South shipments." Secretariat of the Basel Convention, Zoï Environment Network, and GRID-Arendal, "Vital Waste Graphics 3."

Transboundary movements of wastes 71

such as Japan, the United Kingdom, and the United States.[13] The dichotomy between States with strict environmental standards and those with weak regulation, enforcement, and lower waste disposal costs promoted movements of wastes beyond national frontiers from industrialized countries to developing countries, for instance, to Africa, Eastern Europe, and Latin America.[14] Concerns among the international community regarding transboundary movements of wastes increased as a result of some well-known incidents of unsafe disposal of hazardous wastes, such as the *Khian Sea*, which in 1986 left the United States with "15,000 tons of incinerator ash".[15] The ash was partially discharged in Haiti as fertilizer, and in 1988 the rest of the cargo was dumped illegally in the Atlantic and Indian Oceans after the vessel tried to discharge it in different ports in Africa, Asia, and Europe.[16] The legacy of these scandals was the idea that waste trade is inherently harmful, discriminatory, and unwanted. Indeed, in 1988 the Organization of African Unity declared: "dumping of ... industrial wastes in Africa is a crime against Africa and the African people".[17] In the same year, approximately 2.5 million metric tons of hazardous waste was subject to transboundary movements from Europe and between 200,000 and 300,000 million tons were destined for Eastern Europe.[18] These figures serve only as an estimation, because the characterization of "waste" plus its adjective "hazardous" varies significantly not only on account of the definition of waste given by national legislation, but also because the categorization of waste as "hazardous" is based on wastes' streams, components or constituents, harmful characteristics, or management requirements. In 2006, according to the Secretariat of the Basel Convention, approximately 10 million tons of hazardous and other wastes were subject to transboundary movement.[19]

The strong discourse of transboundary movements of wastes as inherently illegitimate, coupled with the stigmatizing nature of the concept of "waste," overshadowed other legitimate reasons for encouraging transboundary

13 Roger Batstone, James E. Smith, and David Wilson, eds., *The Safe Disposal of Hazardous Wastes: The Special Needs and Problems of Developing Countries*, Vol. 1, World Bank Technical Paper No. 93 (Washington: The World Bank, WTO, and UNEP, 1989), 1.

14 "According to a study carried out in the late 1980s, the average disposal costs for one ton of hazardous waste in Africa was between US$ 2.50 and US$ 50 ... in industrialized nations ranging from US$ 100 to US$ 2,000." Kummer, *International Management of Hazardous Wastes: The Basel Convention and Related Legal Rules*, 6–7."

15 Rue and Anderson, *Shipping and the Environment: Law and Practice*, 1016.

16 Ibid., 1017.

17 Council of Ministers of the Organization of African Unity, "Dumping of Nuclear Wastes in Africa Cm/Res.1153 (XlVIII)," (Ethiopia, 1988). *Note* that the Organization of African Unity has been replaced by the organization called African Union.

18 Tolba and Rummel-Bulska, *Global Environmental Diplomacy: Negotiating Environmental Agreements for the World, 1973–1992*, 99.

19 Kees Wielenga, "Waste without Frontiers: Global Trends in Generation and Transboundary Movements of Hazardous Wastes and Other Wastes," ed. Secretariat of the Basel Convention (Geneva, 2010), 12.

72 Transboundary movements of wastes

movements of wastes between industrialized countries. As Kummer has argued, although "the vast majority of waste transport took place between industrialized nations [this fact] was widely ignored".[20] Waste trade continues to occur among OECD countries for two reasons: (a) some countries have developed technologies that allow for wastes to managed in an environmentally sound manner; and (b) wastes are not simply nuisances, but also potentially valuable resources.

The struggles between these two positions paved the way for the adoption of the Basel Convention. Within this scenario, wastes became a priority for the UNEP since their inclusion in the Montevideo Programme for the Development and Periodic Review of Environmental Law in 1981.[21] In this document, the UNEP was urged to adopt guidelines or agreements regarding the "transport, handling and disposal of toxic and dangerous wastes".[22] In 1987, the Governing Council of the UNEP adopted the Cairo Guidelines and Principles for the Environmentally Sound Management of Hazardous Wastes.[23] The Cairo Guidelines are a soft law instrument that served as the basis for the development of the Basel Convention. These guidelines recommended the disposal of wastes as close as possible to their generation source and the application of the prior informed consent procedure. The regulatory efforts of the OECD Council through both Decisions and Recommendations also played a fundamental role in shaping the Basel Convention. The Basel Convention was adopted in 1989 and entered into force in 1992.[24]

Principles governing transboundary movements of wastes

Principles regarding the transboundary movements of wastes are concerned with the minimization of waste generation, the minimization of transboundary movements, the management of wastes as close as possible to their generation source, prior informed consent, and the ESM of wastes.

---

20 Katharina Kummer, "The Basel Convention on the Control of Transboundary Movements of Hazardous Wastes and their Disposal," (United Nations Audiovisual Library of International Law, 2011), 2.

21 Ad Hoc Meeting of Senior Government Officials Expert in Environmental Law, "Montevideo Programme for the Development and Periodic Review of Environmental Law," 1–5.

22 Ibid., 1.

23 United Nations Environment Programme (UNEP), "Compilation of Environmentally Sound Management Criteria and Core Performance Elements under the Work of the Basel Convention and Other Relevant Organizations UNEP/CHW/Cli_Teg.1/INF/4," in *Technical Expert Group to Develop a Framework for the Environmentally Sound Management of Wastes: Item 3 of the Provisional Agenda* (Tokyo, 12 April 2012).

24 For a detailed explanation of the negotiations of the Basel Convention, *See* Tolba and Rummel-Bulska, *Global Environmental Diplomacy: Negotiating Environmental Agreements for the World, 1973–1992*; Barbara Kwiatkowska and Alfred Soons, eds., *Transboundary Movements and Disposal of Hazardous Wastes in International Law: Basic Documents*, International Environmental Law and Policy Series (Leiden: Martinus Nijhoff Publishers, 1993).

Minimization of waste generation

Article 4(2)(a) of the Basel Convention requires states to take "appropriate measures" to reduce the generation of hazardous and other wastes. By introducing the phrase "appropriate measures," Parties have been given significant latitude of discretion in carrying out such a duty. This obligation seems to encompass the reduction not only in the quantity of hazardous wastes, but also in their hazardous characteristics. Waste minimization can be achieved by: (a) cleaner production processes, including manufacturing products by minimizing the use of hazardous substance like asbestos or mercury; and (b) changing consumption patterns, although this approach is certainly more challenging. Through Decision BC-10/02, the COP to the Basel Convention, in its Tenth Meeting, adopted a new Strategic Plan for the period 2012–2021.[25] This strategic plan gives substantial content to the obligation established in Article 10(2)(c) of the Basel Convention that requires State Parties to cooperate in the development and implementation of both new and existent technologies in order to reduce the generation of hazardous and other wastes.

Despite these efforts, the Secretariat of the Basel Convention reported that between 2004 and 2006 the generation of hazardous waste increased by 12 percent.[26] Moreover, in 2009, the value of the waste industry worldwide was said to be approximately US$3 billion.[27] Overall, waste minimization continues to be a challenge due to the growth of the waste industry, as well as the "catch-up" industrialization of developing countries that brings with it increasing levels of waste generation.[28]

The obligation to minimize the generation of waste is not an absolute one, since State Parties shall "take into account social, technological and economic aspects".[29] The introduction of this qualification basically creates a different standard between developing and developed States on the basis of their capabilities. In other words, the Convention allows a more lenient commitment for developing States regarding waste minimization that has no parallel in any other obligation prescribed in the Basel Convention. According to Matsui, "this

---

25 Conference of the Parties to the Basel Convention, "Report of the Conference of the Parties to the Basel Convention on the Control of Transboundary Movements of Hazardous Wastes and their Disposal on Its Tenth Meeting," in *Tenth Meeting (UNEP/CHW.10/28)* (Cartagena, 2011).

26 This figure says little about worldwide trends in the generation of hazardous wastes because the percentage presented here corresponds to data provided by 43 parties to the Basel Convention that provided information between 2004 and 2006. It is relevant to note that 37 of the above-mentioned parties are classed as high and upper middle income. Wielenga, "Waste without Frontiers: Global Trends in Generation and Transboundary Movements of Hazardous Wastes and Other Wastes," 10.

27 Basel Secretariat (UNEP), Zoï Environment Network, and GRID-Arendal, "Vital Waste Graphics 3," 16.

28 Wielenga, "Waste without Frontiers: Global Trends in Generation and Transboundary Movements of Hazardous Wastes and Other Wastes," 16.

29 *See* Article 4(2)(a) of the Basel Convention.

74 Transboundary movements of wastes

provision may be regarded as a reflection of the principle of common but differentiated responsibilities"[30] as reflected in Principle 7 of Agenda 21.

Common but differentiated responsibility is a guiding principle with which to negotiate international treaties or to interpret the obligations of treaty law *where contextual differences have been acknowledged*. When negotiating international obligations, this principle has two manifestations: (a) imposing different standards for developing states, and (b) conditioning the compliance "on the provision of solidarity assistance by developed states".[31] The former manifestation of Principle 7 is endorsed in Article 4(2)(a) of the Basel Convention.

Minimization of transboundary movements of wastes

According to Article 4(2)(d) of the Basel Convention, State Parties must reduce transboundary movements of wastes. *Thus, transboundary movements of wastes are the exception*. This is a marked difference from the OECD regime that seeks to promote movements of wastes for recovery. The different approaches found in the Basel Convention and in the OECD Council Decision C(2001)107/FINAL have been "brought together" in Regulation 1013/2006/EC on Shipments of Wastes.

As a general rule, no exportation or importation is allowed to or from a non-Party to the Basel Convention unless State Parties enter into transboundary movement of wastes agreements with non-Parties, and provided that such agreements are in conformity with the environmentally sound management requirements of the Basel Convention.[32] This "limited ban," as Kummer has described it, implies that States entering into multilateral, regional, or bilateral agreements must take into consideration the basic principles of the Basel Convention, such as ESM, proximity, and self-sufficiency.[33] Imposing a general prohibition on trade with non-Parties has a dual objective. First, it is an incentive for non-Parties to ratify or accede to the Convention,[34] but it is not an effective one since State Parties can still enter into agreements with non-Parties if the conditions established in Article 11 are met.[35] Second, this prohibition is a mechanism to avoid State Parties bypassing their obligations by trading with non-Parties. Instead, in order to avoid the application of the Basel Convention, a substance or material can be classified as something other than waste.

---

30 Yoshiro Matsui, "Some Aspects of the Principle of 'Common but Differentiated Responsibilities'," *International Environmental Agreements: Politics, Law and Economics* 2 (2002): 165.

31 Ibid., 133.

32 Articles 4(5) and 11 of the Basel Convention.

33 Kummer, *International Management of Hazardous Wastes: The Basel Convention and Related Legal Rules*, 61–62, 88–99.

34 Jonathan Krueger, *International Trade and the Basel Convention* (London: Earthscan Publications Ltd., 1999), 45.

35 David Abrams, "Regulating the International Hazardous Waste Trade: A Proposed Global Solution," *Columbia Journal of Transnational Law* 28, no. 3 (1990): 822.

Another restriction established in Article 4(6) of the Convention is the absolute prohibition on the exporting of wastes to the Antarctica. Transboundary movements of wastes between Parties are also allowed under restricted circumstances. Since the Basel Convention strengthens the principle of territorial sovereignty, States may, under national legislation, prohibit all importation of hazardous and other wastes.

Proximity principle

Wastes have to be managed close to their generation source. This is known as the "proximity principle," which should eventually lead to the "self-sufficiency" of States to manage wastes generated within their jurisdictions. To this end, Article 4(2)(b) of the Basel Convention requires State Parties to take appropriate measures to ensure the availability of suitable disposal facilities to manage wastes in an environmentally sound manner. Disposal facilities are those performing all waste management operations including recovery.

Proximity and self-sufficiency have been criticized on environmental and financial grounds. These principles do not guarantee per se that wastes will be managed in an environmentally sound manner. If States lack the adequate facilities, a transboundary movement is justified even when considerable distance is involved. Furthermore, in cases where certain wastes are generated in low quantities or if their management cost is restrictive, State Parties could encounter difficulties in ensuring the availability of adequate disposal facilities. In this scenario, the establishment of regional disposal facilities is a viable alternative. Under EU law, the application of the proximity principle is not absolute since Member States are not obliged to manage all the generated waste within their own jurisdictions. In fact, the proximity and self-sufficiency principles have been conceived on a regional basis.

Prior informed consent (PIC) procedure

During the negotiations of the Convention, it became apparent that the regulation of transboundary movements of wastes should enable States of import to assess whether or not to accept wastes in their jurisdictions. Two alternatives were discussed by the Ad Hoc Working Group of Legal and Technical Experts with a Mandate to Prepare a Global Convention on the Control of Transboundary Movements of Hazardous Wastes (Working Group).[36]

---

36 During the negotiation of the Basel Convention, the Ad Hoc Working Group held an organization meeting and another five sessions between February 1988 and March 1989. Ad Hoc Working Group of Legal and Technical Experts with a Mandate to Prepare a Global Convention on the Control of Transboundary Movements of Hazardous Wastes, "Organizational Meeting – UNEP/Wg.180/3," (Budapest: UNEP, 1987). Ad Hoc Working Group of Legal and Technical Experts with a Mandate to Prepare a Global Convention on the Control of Transboundary Movements of Hazardous Wastes, "Report of the Working Group: First Session – UNEP/

76 *Transboundary movements of wastes*

The first position was to introduce the PIC procedure, which had been previously incorporated in section 26 of the Cairo Guidelines. Other experts held that the PIC procedure "could be relaxed to tacit consent, which could be covered under bilateral agreement rather than in an international convention".[37] At the second session of the Working Group, the Executive Director of the UNEP brought to the attention of the Working Group several options to protect developing States, including: (a) the right of States of import to receive information and (b) making sure States of import have the capacity to assess the received information.[38]

The suggestion made by the Executive Director of the UNEP was relevant because the right to receive information is meaningless if States of import lack the technical and institutional capacity needed to evaluate the information. In fact, such evaluation and further consent could be subject to many considerations, including those of economic welfare, the environment, or health. However, the sole application of the PIC procedure is not evidence of the application of certain environmental or health standards.[39] For this reason, the PIC procedure alone *is a formal requirement* that is lacking in substance without the incorporation of substantial obligations, such as ESM. By the third session of the Working Group, Article 6 of the revised draft Convention established the right of States of import not only to receive information, but also to give consent to the movement.[40]

Before a transboundary movement of wastes takes place, the Parties and States involved in the movement shall apply the PIC procedure to hazardous and other wastes, whether they are intended to be recycled, reused, recovered, or subject to final disposal operations, such as landfill or incineration.[41] It also applies to every movement of wastes irrespective of the identity of the State of import, i.e., developing or developed State. In other words, the same strict regulatory procedure applies regardless of the disposal operation to which wastes will be subject and regardless of the State in which the disposal will occur.

Wg.182/L.1," (UNEP, 1988). Ad Hoc Working Group of Legal and Technical Experts with a Mandate to Prepare a Global Convention on the Control of Transboundary Movements of Hazardous Wastes, "Second Session: Note from the Executive Director. UNEP/Wg.186/2," (Caracas: UNEP, 1988). "Third Session: Fourth Revised Draft Convention on the Control of Transboundary Movements of Wastes. UNEP/Wg.189/L.2/REV.1," (Geneva: UNEP, 1988). "Fourth Session. Explanatory Notes with Recommendations for Amending Annexes I–IV of the Fifth Revised Draft Convention. UNEP/Wg.190/3/Add.1," (Luxembourg: UNEP, 1988). "Fifth Session – Item 4 of the Provisional Agenda. Draft Convention on the Control of Transboundary Movements of Wastes. UNEP/Wg.191/4," (Basel: UNEP, 1989).

37 "Organizational Meeting – UNEP/Wg.180/3," 8.

38 "Second Session: Note from the Executive Director. UNEP/Wg.186/2," 2.

39 Langlet, *Prior Informed Consent and Hazardous Trade*, 296.

40 Wastes, "Third Session: Fourth Revised Draft Convention on the Control of Transboundary Movements of Wastes. UNEP/Wg.189/L.2/REV.1."

41 *See* Article 6 of the Basel Convention.

The application of the same regulatory system to every waste falling within the scope of the Basel Convention proved to be unsatisfactory for some Parties, many of whom circumvented the strict regime established in the Convention by entering into agreements and arrangements as established in Article 11 of the Basel Convention. The development of these regional agreements exemplifies the opposite views regarding the application of a single control system, including the PIC procedure. For developed States, control systems should take into account the waste's level of hazard, the disposal operation, and the identity of the importing State. For developing countries, the PIC procedure was perceived as a weak regulatory approach.

LEGAL NATURE OF THE PIC PROCEDURE: COMMENTS REGARDING
ITS RELATIONSHIP WITH PRIOR INFORMED CONSULTATION

Some of the literature addressing the PIC procedure describes it as an "intensification of the principle of prior notice and consultation",[42] but prior consultation and prior informed consent are different. While prior informed consultation is a procedure through which the concerns of States affected by transboundary pollution are taken into account by the State engaged in a harmful activity, the PIC procedure is a concrete expression of sovereignty, since a State has the right to decide what impacts and hazardous substances will be accepted on its territory.[43]

In international law, prior informed consultation is a procedural obligation following from transboundary impacts as established in Principle 19 of the Rio Declaration. The application of this obligation has found strong support in several cases, including: *Lac Lanoux Arbitration, Nuclear Tests Cases, Pulp Mills,* and *Mox Plant Cases.* Consultation is conducted in cases related to: (a) the preservation, exploitation, utilization, and management of shared resources and (b) potentially harmful activities, carried out within the jurisdiction or control of a State, that pose a substantial risk of transboundary pollution.[44] States conducting potentially harmful activities are not required to carry out PIC procedures under customary law as expressed in the *Lac Lanoux* case.

As already discussed in this chapter, transboundary movements of wastes supposes the *deliberate transfer* of hazardous substances. The PIC procedure has been incorporated in MEAs dealing with these deliberate transfers, e.g., Basel Convention, and the Rotterdam Convention on the Prior Informed Consent Procedure for Certain Hazardous Chemicals and Pesticides in International Trade. Functioning and enforcement mechanisms of the PIC procedure are dependent on the MEA incorporating the procedure.

---

42 Grosz, *Sustainable Waste Trade under WTO Law,* 4, 135.
43 Birnie, Boyle, and Redgwell, *International Law and the Environment,* 473. *Note also* that "[i]t cannot be assumed that waste disposal in other states is permissible unless shown to be harmful."
44 Philippe Sands et al., *Principles of International Environmental Law,* 3rd edn (Cambridge: Cambridge University Press, 2012), 637–38.

78   Transboundary movements of wastes

What prior informed consultation and prior informed consent have in common is their procedural nature. When these obligations are coupled with other substantive obligations relating to the environment, they become "instrumental, in so far as they are designed to ensure that the substantive decisions reached take into account anticipated environmental harm".[45]

CRITICISMS OF THE PIC PROCEDURE

Several grounded criticisms have been made of the PIC procedure, particularly in respect of: (a) the relativeness of the "consent" given by developing countries when these States lack the adequate capacity and infrastructure to evaluate the information given about intended transboundary movements; (b) the weak role of the Secretariat of the Basel Convention in monitoring the PIC procedure since the notifications are not sent to the Secretariat unless a Party requests it according to Article 13(4) of the Basel Convention; and (c) recurrent practices used to avoid the PIC procedure.[46]

Conditions for transboundary movements of wastes and control procedure

Transboundary movements of wastes between State Parties are allowed under restricted circumstances. This trade restrictive approach draws on the aspiration of developing States that argued for the establishment of a self-sufficiency principle within the Basel Convention. Developing States intended that all negative externalities of wastes be internalized by the waste generator. First, pursuant to Article 4(9)(a) and (b) of the Basel Convention, movements of wastes can take place if the State of export does not have the technological capacities and facilities to dispose of the wastes in an environmentally sound and efficient manner. Second, if wastes are required as raw material for recycling or recovery operations in importing States, then transboundary movements may take place. Finally, according to Article 4(9)(c), transboundary movements of wastes could be allowed according to criteria established by the Parties involved in a transboundary movement considering that such criteria fulfill the objectives of the Basel regime, e.g., principle of proximity or the ESM of wastes. Louka criticizes Article 4(9)(c) because the reference "to the convention's goals is circular and does not provide any further clarification" as to the conditions for allowing a transboundary movement of wastes.[47] Overall, transboundary movements will only be allowed between State Parties if the transfer represents the best available

---

45 Phoebe N. Okowa, "Procedural Obligations in International Environmental Agreements," *British Yearbook of International Law* 67, no. 1 (1997): 275.

46 Jonathan Krueger, "Prior Informed Consent and the Basel Convention: The Hazards of What Isn't Known," *The Journal of Environment & Development* 7, no. 2 (1998): 122.

47 Elli Louka, *International Environmental Law: Fairness, Effectiveness, and World Order* (Cambridge: Cambridge University Press, 2006), 429.

solution for disposing of the wastes. The "best available solution" should not be understood in strictly economic terms, because disposal of wastes includes their ESM, i.e., treatment of wastes, the protection of human health and the environment.

Transboundary movements of wastes occur in four stages: notification; consent; transboundary movement; and confirmation of disposal.[48] The Basel Convention has chosen the PIC procedure as its cornerstone regulatory mechanism because it operationalizes the sovereign right of States to accept or deny the entrance of hazardous substances into their jurisdictions. Thus, the application of the PIC procedure begins with a single or general notification.

The State of export, the generator, or the exporter must notify to States of transit and import every proposed transboundary movement.[49] The notification includes the information required in Annex V(A) of the Basel Convention, e.g., reasons for exportation, identification of the exporter, disposer, carrier, itinerary, competent authorities, means of transport, and methods of disposal. A general notification for multiple transboundary movements is also possible if the following conditions are met. First, the proposed movements involve wastes with the same physical and chemical characteristics. Second, the wastes must be sent to the same disposer. Lastly, wastes must follow the same trading route and involve the same customs offices in the State of export, import, and transit. The general notification covers several transboundary movements of wastes during a period of twelve months.[50]

The second stage in the control of transboundary movements is obtaining consent from the State of import and transit. These States have the prerogative to request further information, deny or allow a movement subject to conditions.[51] Pursuant to Article 6(3)(b) of the Basel Convention, the State of import must also "confirm the existence of a contract between the exporter and the disposer specifying environmentally sound management of the wastes in question." This provision imposes a rather weak obligation, since the Convention is silent on the substantive content of the contract and focuses only on its formal existence. It is noteworthy that importing States have no time limit within which to answer requests for transboundary movements, and no tacit consent can be implied. However, if transit States do not respond to a request within sixty (60) days, the consent is inferred and the transboundary movement can proceed.[52] In the case of multiple transboundary movements of wastes covered by a general notification, the consent of the State of import and export could be subject to the supply of specific information, including "exact quantities or periodical lists

---

48 *See* Secretariat of the Basel Convention, "Controlling Transboundary Movements of Hazardous Wastes," (Switzerland: United Nations, 2011).

49 *See* Article 6(1) of the Basel Convention.

50 *See* Articles 6(6) and 6(8) of the Basel Convention.

51 *See* Articles 6(2) and 6(4) of the Basel Convention.

52 *See* Article 6(4) of the Basel Convention.

80 *Transboundary movements of wastes*

of ... wastes to be shipped".[53] This general notification simplifies to some extent the control procedure established under the Basel Convention.

In relation to the PIC procedure, the position of States of transit is certainly weaker than the position of States of import. While the consent given by the State of import must always be explicit, the consent of the State of transit may be tacit. Additionally, only the State of transit may waive the requirement of prior written consent "either generally or under specific conditions" pursuant to Article 6(4) of the Convention. During the negotiation of the Basel Convention, developing States argued that States of import and transit should have the same rights in relation to the PIC procedure. Nonetheless, developed States like Japan, the United States, and several European countries did not support the application of the PIC procedure to States of transit. In particular, developed States wanted to avoid the imposition of more bureaucratic burdens on the State of export, and to prevent possible conflicts over navigational rights.[54]

Once the consent of the State of export and import has been received, the third stage is the initiation of the transboundary movement of wastes. Wastes are monitored during their carriage from the moment they leave the generator until their reception by the disposer. For this purpose, wastes must be accompanied by a "movement document," signed by every person in charge of the wastes.[55] During the carriage, safety issues concerning loading, labeling, packaging, and intermediate storage of wastes must be supervised. Keeping records of the person in charge of wastes during their carriage is also relevant so as to establish potential liabilities for damages caused in transit. The COP to the Basel Convention, at its Eighth Meeting, adopted a revised version of the "forms for the notification and movement documents" together with a set of instructions for their use.[56] These revised forms include the requirements of not only the Basel Convention, but also the OECD Council Decision C(2001)107/FINAL and Regulation 1013/2006/EC on Shipments of Wastes.[57] When the disposal of wastes is carried out according to the information provided in the notification and the contract, the disposer must inform the State of export about it. Finally, the following graphic summarizes the most notable features of the control procedure established in the Basel Convention (Figure 4.1).

---

53 *See* Article 6(7) of the Basel Convention.

54 Gwam, "*Travaux Preparatoires* of the Basel Convention on the Control of Transboundary Movements of Hazardous Wastes and Their Disposal," 60–61.

55 *See* Article 4 (2)(7)(c) and Article 6 (9) of the Basel Convention.

56 COP to the Basel Convention, "Decision VIII/18: Harmonization of Forms for Notification and Movement Documents and Related Instructions. UNEP/CHW.8/16*," in *Eighth Meeting – Agenda Item 12* (Nairobi, 2006), 48–49.

57 Secretariat of the Basel Convention, "Revised Notification and Movement Documents for the Control of Transboundary Movement of Hazardous Wastes and Instructions for Completing These Documents," (2006).

Transboundary movements of wastes 81

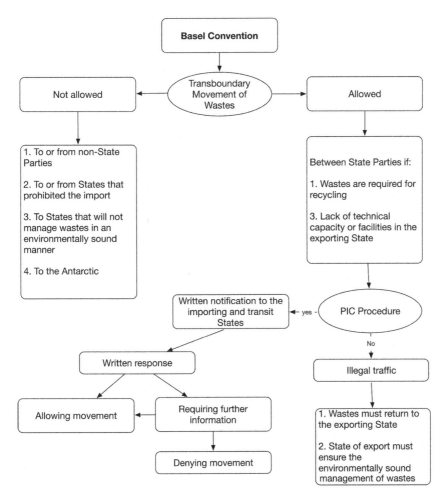

Figure 4.1 Basel Convention.

The OECD legal framework of transboundary movements of wastes

The understanding of the development of Regulation 1013/2006/EC on Shipments of Wastes would not be complete without an overview of the OECD Council Decision C(2001)107/Final, which together with the Basel Convention are the foundations of EU legislation on transboundary movements of wastes. The OECD Council Decision is the result of the revision of the OECD Council Decision C(92)39/FINAL, which follows the principles established under the Basel Convention, but with some fundamental differences, as will be explored in what follows.

82 *Transboundary movements of wastes*

The OECD Decision limits its application to wastes including hazardous wastes destined for recovery operations. As with the Basel Convention, the categorization of waste is determined by the operation to which a substance or object is subject. However, the OECD Decision drew upon the premise that transboundary movements of wastes, between Member States, that could be reused, recycled, or recovered should not be subject to the same stringent regulations as wastes that are subject to disposal operations. The rationale behind enabling transboundary movements instead of restricting them is twofold. First, there are States with the technological capabilities and willingness to manage wastes in an environmentally sound manner. Second, the transboundary movement of wastes is, indeed, a lucrative, efficient, and environmentally sound business within many industrialized States, e.g., OECD Member States.

In the wake of the international outcry in response to the unsafe management of hazardous wastes in developing countries, it was overlooked that most hazardous wastes were exported from OECD States to other OECD States and mostly on a regional basis.[58] This trend seems to have continued, and waste markets are certainly booming. For instance, in the European Union, exports of wastes, including hazardous wastes, increased from 3.99 million tons in 2001 to 6 million tons in 2015. Furthermore, hazardous wastes exports take place primarily between States of the European Union.[59] The consolidation of much needed international waste markets coupled with the increasing generation of wastes on a global scale puts pressure on some of the Basel Convention objectives, such as the self-sufficiency principle, the proximity principle, and the minimization of the generation of hazardous wastes. It also reveals that under certain circumstances it is neither possible nor desirable to prevent transboundary movements of wastes, since these movements could be the best way to manage wastes.

Origins of the OECD regulation on transboundary movements of wastes

OECD States paid close attention to transboundary movements of wastes, especially those movements from developed to developing States since the 1980s. That decade saw the exposure of the dangers of unsafe disposal of hazardous wastes in developing countries. However, industrialized States did not avoid the deleterious consequences of unreported movements of wastes either. The Seveso (1976) accident involved the release of hazardous chemicals from a plant located in the North of Milan.[60] The cleaning operations required the management of hazardous waste. Chemicals were stored in 41 drums that were illegally deposited in France, instead of being disposed of at a waste management facility as arranged

---

58 Kummer, *International Management of Hazardous Wastes: The Basel Convention and Related Legal Rules*, 8.

59 Eurostat: Statistics Explained, "Waste Shipment Statistics," <https://ec.europa.eu/eurostat/statistics-explained/index.php/Waste_shipment_statistics>. Last accessed 14 March 2019.

60 A detailed account of the incident can be found in Henrik Harjula, "Hazardous Waste," *Annals of the New York Academy of Sciences* 1076 (2006).

by the Italian Government.[61] Even more worrisome was the proliferation of pollution havens in developing States where spurious waste markets were flourishing, such as Guinea-Bissau, Congo, Equatorial Guinea, Gabon, Benin, and Nigeria.[62]

In the late 1980s and early 1990s, the OECD noted that transboundary movements of wastes were taking place among OECD States "because there is no local disposal capacity for these wastes or because legal disposal in a foreign country may be more environmentally sound".[63] Today, these reasons constitute some of the legal exceptions under the Basel Convention that allow a transboundary movement of wastes between State Parties.[64] The OECD also recognized that exports of wastes from OECD States to developing States were mostly "highly hazardous wastes",[65] and that those movements did not just save costs, but were very profitable in the "short run".[66] Due to well-founded concerns over spurious movements of hazardous wastes from developed to developing States, the OECD decided to develop guidelines to regulate such shipments between OECD States and third States. There were multiple reasons for undertaking such an endeavor. First, it was an immediate response to ease the growing outrage of developing States and civil society organizations, which declared such movements criminal and required an immediate and complete international ban on transboundary movements of wastes. Second, it was an attempt to establish guiding principles regarding the responsibilities of States involved in a transboundary movement of wastes. Third, there was a concern to prevent illegitimate movements of wastes without compromising well-established waste markets among developed States. Finally, upon the forthcoming international regulation on transboundary movements of wastes, the OECD was a forum in which industrialized States could adopt a shared position on the matter and influence international negotiations.

OECD Council Decision/Recommendation C(83)180(Final)

Before the Basel Convention entered into force in 1992, the OECD adopted four Council Decisions/Recommendations[67] and three Resolutions[68] for the

---

61 Ibid.
62 Lillian Pinzon, "Criminalization of the Transboundary Movement of Hazardous Waste and the Effect on Corporations," *DePaul Business Law Journal 7* (1994–95): 177.
63 Organisation for Economic Co-Operation and Development (OECD), "Monitoring and Control of Transfrontier Movements of Hazardous Wastes," in *Environment Monographs N.34* (1993), 11.
64 *See* Article 9(a) of the Basel Convention
65 Organisation for Economic Co-Operation and Development (OECD), "Monitoring and Control of Transfrontier Movements of Hazardous Wastes," 12.
66 Ibid., 11–12.
67 Organisation for Economic Co-Operation and Development (OECD), "C(83)180(Final) Council Decision and Recommendation on Transfrontier Movements of Hazardous Wastes." "C(86)64(Final) Council Decision – Recommendation on Exports of Hazardous Wastes from the OECD Area." "C(88)90(Final) Council Decision on Transfrontier Movements of Hazardous Waste" (1988); "C(90)178/Final Council Decision-Recommendation on the Reduction of Transfrontier Movements of Wastes."
68 Organisation for Economic Co-Operation and Development (OECD), "C(85)100: Resolution on the International Co-Operation Concerning Transfrontier Movements of Hazardous Wastes" (1985). "C(89)112(Final) Council Resolution on the Control of Transfrontier Movements of

84 Transboundary movements of wastes

regulation of transfrontier[69] movements of wastes. The OECD Council Decision and Recommendation C(83)180(Final) did not make any distinction between transboundary movements to OECD or non-OECD States. Nonetheless, the inception of major principles governing shipments of wastes and their further management can be found in this instrument. For instance, self-sufficiency regarding waste management is still one of the major methods through which to control and potentially reduce transboundary movements of wastes. For this reason, States were required to promote the installation of "appropriate disposal installations."

At the same time, the preamble of the OECD Council Decision C(83)180(Final) recognized that "efficient and environmentally sound management of hazardous waste may justify some transfrontier movements of such waste to make use of appropriate disposal facilities in other countries." In addition, principle 5 of Council Decision/Recommendation C(83)180(Final) suggested the implementation of an international "pre-notification system" to give accurate and useful information to importing States. The latter, on the other hand, could deny such importation. This notification system marks the beginnings of the PIC procedure. The Council Decision/Recommendation did not expressly require a movement of wastes to begin after obtaining the consent of the importing State. This express consent was, however, implied in the prerogative of States to refuse the importation.

Another interesting feature of Council Decision/Recommendation C(83) 180(Final) was its requirement for exporting States to accept reimportation of wastes. This requirement hints toward identifying who remains responsible for the wastes, even when a transboundary movement has begun. The notion of reimportation or return of wastes also involves the ultimate responsibility to manage wastes in an environmentally sound manner. Today, such responsibility rests on exporting States and cannot be transferred to any other State.

OECD Council Decision/Recommendation C(86)64(Final)

As a result of the OECD Conference on International Co-Operation Concerning Transfrontier Movements of Hazardous Wastes held in Basel in 1985, the Member States reaffirmed their commitment to regulate transfrontier movements of wastes including those to or from non-OECD States.[70] This implied that controls should be implemented under the principle of nondiscrimination. In other words, the OECD States "will not apply any less strict controls on transfrontier movements of hazardous wastes involving non-Member countries".[71]

Hazardous Wastes," (1989). Organisation for Economic Co-Operation and Development (OECD), "C(89)1(Final) Council Resolution on the Control of Transfrontier Movements of Hazardous Wastes," (1989).

69 This term was replaced with "transboundary" after the adoption of the Council Decision C(2001)107/FINAL to conform to the terminology employed in the Basel Convention.

70 The proceedings can be found as an Annex of the OECD Resolution C(85)100.

71 Ibid., Recommendation V.

The principle of nondiscrimination was implemented in the OECD Council Decision/Recommendation C(86)64(Final). According to this instrument, a movement could not be allowed without the consent of the importing State, and movements were prohibited in cases where non-Member States lacked adequate disposal facilities.

OECD Council Decision C(88)90(Final)

The OECD undertook the titanic task of defining hazardous wastes. Previous OECD acts relied on national legislation to identify which substances, objects, or gases were wastes and hazardous wastes. However, definitions of wastes could vary greatly between exporting, transit, and importing States. For this reason, transfrontier movements of wastes were defined as "any shipment of waste from one country to another, where the waste is considered as being hazardous waste in at least one of the countries concerned".[72] Relying on the identification of hazardous wastes in the legislation of at least one of the States concerned, i.e., exporting, transit, and importing States, rather than demanding exporting States to comply exclusively with the legislation of importing States was a positive mechanism by which to control the movement of wastes to non-OECD States. One should bear in mind that during the years preceding the conclusion of the Basel Convention, several developing countries had incipient or no legislation regarding hazardous waste management, while others had turned a blind eye and avoided strict regulations.[73]

The inconsistency surrounding the definition of waste and hazardous waste in different jurisdictions was problematic, to say the least. The OECD made a cross-reference of the legislation of several Member States alongside international agreements dealing with the transport of dangerous goods and the management of harmful substances.[74] The work concluded with the adoption of the OECD Council Decision C(88)90(Final). It was the first time that the operational approach was used to define wastes as any material other than radioactive material subject to disposal operations. The meaning of "hazardous" and disposal operations followed a listing approach. The OECD Council Decision C(88)90(Final) adopted a core list of wastes to be controlled on the basis of the International

---

72 Concerned countries should be understood as exporting, importing, and transit States. The definition of "concerned countries" is expressly included in the OECD Council Decision/Recommendation C(83)180(Final), but not in the OECD Council/Decision C(86)64(Final). Nonetheless, from the text of both Acts it is clear that before allowing a transfrontier movement of wastes to take place, the exporter should take into consideration if the intended shipment is considered hazardous wastes "in a country where it is situated or through or to which it is conveyed."

73 Information regarding importing States and companies involved in transboundary shipments is found in Jang B. Singh and V. Chris Lakhan, "Business Ethics and the International Trade in Hazardous Wastes," *Journal of Business Ethics* 8 (1989).

74 *See* Organisation for Economic Co-Operation and Development (OECD), "Monitoring and Control of Transfrontier Movements of Hazardous Wastes," 17.

86 Transboundary movements of wastes

Waste Identification Code (IWIC). Additionally, Member States had the prerogative to define hazardous wastes within their national legislation. The IWIC system has six codes from which the core list of wastes was developed. The core list comprises 17 waste types (Y1–Y17) and 27 waste constituents (Y18–Y44).[75] This international classification system is relevant since it was later taken over by the Basel Convention.

In the light of the adoption of the Basel Convention under the auspices of the UNEP, the OECD decided to support such a global initiative and ceased its work on concluding an international agreement.[76] However, *from the OECD Decision/Recommendation C(90)178/FINAL onwards, the OECD considered it appropriate to monitor rather than minimize the transboundary movement of wastes destined for recovery operations among Member States.* This is certainly a departure from the Basel Convention. Since all OECD members are Parties to the Basel Convention, with the exception of the United States, the relationship between the OECD Council Decision C(2001)107/FINAL must be scrutinized in light of Article 11 of the Basel Convention. Suffice it to mention here that Parties to the Basel Convention are allowed to conclude agreements and "arrangements" in relation to transboundary movements of hazardous wastes only if such instruments do not derogate from the environmentally sound management of wastes obligation.

Initial efforts to harmonize OECD regulations on shipments of wastes and the Basel Convention

The OECD Council Decision C(92)39/FINAL was concluded as an arrangement under Article 11 of the Basel Convention. Consequently, this regime delimited its scope of application to wastes destined to recovery operations taking place to and from Member States. The Council Decision marked an attempt by industrialized States to counteract the strict regulatory system imposed by the Basel Convention to hazardous and other wastes destined for recovery operations, while trying, at the same time, to align with the principles and obligations established in the Basel Convention.[77] The Council Decision preserved the definition of: (a) wastes; (b) recovery operations; and (c) the International Waste Identification Code (IWIC) classification system as established in the OECD Council Decision C(88)90(Final). The OECD system of waste classification was compatible with the Basel Convention as summarized as follows (Table 4.1).

---

75 The entire list and IWIC codes can be found as an Annex of the OECD Council Decision C(88)90(Final).

76 *See* OECD Resolutions C(89)1(Final) and C(89)112(Final).

77 Organisation for Economic Co-Operation and Development (OECD), "Trade Measures in the Basel Convention on the Control of Transboundary Movements of Hazardous Wastes and their Disposal," in COM/ENV/TD(97)41/FINAL, ed. Joint Session of Trade and Environment Experts (1998), 4 and 30.

Table 4.1 Waste categories OECD and Basel Convention

OECD Council Decision C(92)39/FINAL	*Basel Convention*[a]
Y List Core list	**Annex I** Categories of wastes to be controlled. Based on the Y List **Annex II** Categories of wastes requiring special consideration. Based on the Y List. Includes household wastes and residues generated due to incineration of household wastes
List 1 (Q code) Reasons why materials are intended for disposal	
List 2 (D and R codes) Disposal operations. D code corresponds to operations without the possibility of recovery and R code correspond to operations with the possibility of recovery	**Annex IV** (D and R codes) Disposal operations
List 3 (L – liquid; S – solid; G – gaseous codes) Generic types of potentially hazardous wastes (extracted from the Y List)	
List 4 Constituents of potentially hazardous wastes (extracted from the Y List)	
List 5 (H code) List of hazardous characteristics	**Annex III** (H code) List of hazardous characteristics
List 6 Activities which may generate potentially hazardous wastes	

a   This table does not include Annexes VIII and IX of the Basel Convention, which were adopted at the Fourth Meeting by the Conference of the Parties to the Basel Convention (Decision IV/9). (A thorough explanation relating to the identification of hazardous wastes and equivalences in different regimes can be found in Noel Duffy et al., "Procedure for the Identification of the Hazardous Components of Waste" (Cork: Clean Technology Centre, Cork Institute of Technology, 2001): 3–10. Introducing this table is intended to provide the reader with an overview of the equivalence between the definition of wastes in the Basel Convention and in the OECD regime.)

In terms of the definition of wastes, there was no room for any conflict between the OECD Council Decision C(92)39/FINAL and the Basel Convention, since the latter instrument took over the OECD work on classification of "hazardous wastes." Nonetheless, some codes, e.g., Q code, were not included in the Basel Convention, while other codes, such as L, S, or G, are subsumed under the Y List. What proved problematic was presenting "waste lists" in different ways and under different headings. These dissimilarities hinder both monitoring and reporting activities in relation to transboundary movements of wastes at both regional and international levels, since data sets can vary according to the classification system employed. Since the adoption of the OECD Council Decision C(2001)107/FINAL, further harmonization with the Basel Convention has been undertaken. However, there remain potential problems with "listing wastes" according to different classification systems. For instance, "the OECD list has 150 codes; the detailed Basel list has 120 and the aggregated Basel list has 47 Y codes".[78] Further

78 Grosz, *Sustainable Waste Trade under WTO Law*, 4, 93.

88 *Transboundary movements of wastes*

complications may be encountered when wastes under national law are classified differently from wastes subject to transboundary movements.[79] Overall, assessing the current state of hazardous waste generation and its transboundary movement is hampered by the asymmetry of available data.

The OECD Council Decision C(92)39/FINAL established three lists of wastes with three corresponding control procedures, i.e., green, amber, and red. These lists provide a gradual classification of wastes depending on the risks they pose to human health and to the environment.

Green list wastes are materials that do not exhibit the hazardous characteristics (H code) of the OECD Council Decision C(88)90(Final). In other words, these materials are *prima facie*[80] nonhazardous wastes. Apart from complying with controls "normally applied in commercial transactions," movements of "green list waste" were not subject to any specific principle related to transboundary movements. It is noteworthy that nonhazardous wastes fall outside the scope of the Basel Convention, and international law does not impose any obligation or restriction in respect of nonhazardous waste trade. Nonetheless, during the years when the OECD Council Decision C(92)39/FINAL was in force, Greenpeace claimed that several materials classified as green list waste were actually hazardous under the Basel Convention.[81] In this instance, the Basel Convention should take precedence over the OECD regime. Claims concerning potential conflicts between regional agreements and arrangements dealing with transboundary movements of waste and the Basel Convention reveal a persistent problem with listing and classifying wastes according to different specifications and codes.

Amber and red lists included hazardous wastes, but the latter list was subject to more stringent controls not only due to the hazardous constituents exhibited by these wastes but also because of the risks they pose to the environment and human health while being transported and managed. In short, both amber and red control procedures included compliance with the PIC procedure as established in the OECD Council Decision C(92)39/FINAL,[82] and required a valid contract with the facility in charge of managing the wastes.[83] While transboundary movements of amber list wastes could proceed with "tacit" acceptance, movements of red list

---

79 An exhaustive compilation of the meaning of hazardous wastes at international, OECD, and EU level and selected jurisdictions can be found in Duffy et al., "Procedure for the Identification of the Hazardous Components of Waste," 43.

80 According to Annex I (II) 2.a of OECD Council Decision C(92)39/FINAL, if green list wastes are contaminated by other materials to an extent that renders them hazardous, those should be included in the amber or red lists.

81 Kummer, *International Management of Hazardous Wastes: The Basel Convention and Related Legal Rules*, 166.

82 Annex I (IV) 2 of OECD Council Decision C(92)39/FINAL established two options to obtain previous consent before starting any movement of amber-listed waste. The first case is: "Provisions concerning transactions requiring specific consent," and the second case is: "Provisions relating to pre-consent by competent authorities for shipments to specific recovery."

83 Ibid., Annex I (IV) 1.

could only commence after having received written consent.[84] Green, amber, and red lists were periodically revised in light of the criteria established in Annex II regarding wastes' hazardous characteristics and management implications. The current OECD Council Decision C(2001)107/FINAL continues with this listing approach, but it has only two lists with two corresponding controls procedures.

At the time of the adoption of the Basel Convention, the definition of "hazardous wastes" came under attack for being over-inclusive and difficult to implement, especially for States without the technology to test whether or not certain waste exhibits the hazardous characteristics established in the Convention. This perceived flaw was addressed with the adoption of Annexes VIII and IX, and it was the catalyst to revise OECD Council Decision C(92)39/FINAL and to further advance the harmonization of the OECD regime with the Basel Convention.[85]

Control procedures: general considerations

The control procedures established in the OECD Council Decision C(2001)107/FINAL, i.e., green and amber, seek to ensure not only the ESM of wastes, but also their management in an economically efficient manner.[86] This approach is reasonable considering that the OECD Council Decision is predominantly concerned with enabling trade of recyclable wastes among OECD States. In general, green and amber procedures are gradual mechanisms through which to monitor transboundary movements of recoverable wastes depending on their potential risks to the environment, human health, previous trade patterns, and management implications. Thus, nonhazardous wastes will usually be subject to the green control procedure which does not impose any substantial restrictions on the movement of wastes,[87] while hazardous wastes will typically be subject to the amber control procedure,[88] which is more stringent.

Before discussing the main features of the green and amber control procedures in greater depth, it is worth mentioning that Member States have the right, under their national legislation, to classify as hazardous wastes other than those defined in the OECD Council Decision C(2001)107/FINAL.[89] The same right is preserved under Articles 1 and 3 of the Basel Convention. Additionally, according to Chapter II, Sections B.3. and B.4. of the OECD Council Decision, a State can choose, under certain circumstances, a different level of control.

The reasons why such differences may arise are manifold. First, in an effort to protect human health and the environment, States may define a certain substance or object as hazardous waste and thereby require it to be subject to the

---

84 Ibid., Annex I (V) 2.
85 Organisation for Economic Co-Operation and Development (OECD), "Guidance Manual for the Control of Transboundary Movements of Recoverable Wastes," 6.
86 There are no references to economic efficiency in the management of wastes in the Basel Convention.
87 *See* section C of OECD Council Decision C(2001)107/FINAL.
88 Ibid., Section D.
89 Ibid., Chapter II, Section A.2.

90 *Transboundary movements of wastes*

amber control procedure as a way of effectively controlling the substances that will eventually enter their jurisdiction. Second, certain wastes may be included in green or amber lists after the risks they pose in accordance with Appendix 6 have been assessed. But the assessment could differ from one State to the next, due to, for instance, the available testing technologies and overall scientific knowledge. Finally, some States may have classified certain objects or substances as green or amber-listed wastes, while others could consider that those substances or objects are not wastes, and therefore outside the scope of the OECD Council Decision. One should remember that Appendix 4, Part II includes wastes' entries, which have no parallel in the Basel Convention. All in all, this translates into a classical conflict of laws whereby competing national legislations are potentially applicable to the same situation. Questions that arise in this scenario are usually related to the mechanisms available to choose between the *lex fori* or *lex causae*.

The OECD Council Decision C(2001)107/FINAL, while recognizing that Member States may define, under national legislation, hazardous wastes, also dictates that States "shall not be required to enforce laws other than their own".[90] A similar criterion is introduced in relation to the regulation of non-listed wastes.[91] Additionally, this OECD Council Decision dictates the level of control that is applicable and indicates the Parties responsible for complying with obligations of transboundary movements of wastes when wastes are subject to amber control only in the State of import. From the text of the OECD Council Decision, one can summarize how to deal with conflicting control procedures established under national legislation as follows (Table 4.2):

Table 4.2 Control procedures OECD Council Decision C(2001)107/FINAL

Control procedure established under national law of a certain waste	*Which level of control is applicable?*	*Which Party must comply with the obligations of the OECD Council Decision C(2001)107/ FINAL?*
Exporting State or exporting and transit States: amber control procedure	Amber control procedure	All the obligations shall be assumed by the exporting State including those assigned to the importing State
Importing State or importing and transit States: green control procedure		
Exporting State or exporting and transit States: green control procedure	Amber control procedure	All the obligations shall be assumed by the importing State, the importer, and the recovery facility, including those assigned to the exporting State

90 Ibid., Chapter II, Section A.2.ii.
91 Ibid., Chapter II, Section B.6.b.

Control procedure established under national law of a certain waste	Which level of control is applicable?	Which Party must comply with the obligations of the OECD Council Decision C(2001)107/ FINAL?
Importing State or importing and transit States: amber control procedure		
Exporting and Importing State: green control procedure	No guideline provided	No guideline provided
Transit State: amber control procedure		

The OECD Council Decision C(2001)107/FINAL is silent on the applicable level of control when only the State of transit considers certain waste subject to the amber control procedure. The OECD Guidance Manual for the Control of Transboundary Movements of Recoverable Wastes recommends that the State of export should arrange the compliance with the notification procedure in accordance with the OECD Council Decision.[92] If exporting States are unable to ensure the application of the notification procedure to transit States, a modification to the route should be considered so as to avoid potential conflicts. It is worth mentioning that Member States should know the different applicable levels of controls chosen under national legislation by other Member States because the relevant information is sent to the OECD Secretariat.[93] Of course, differences in classification systems and levels of specification could hinder the task of determining whether a specific waste is subject to a different level of control in other Member States.

Green control procedure

The green control procedure applies to wastes listed in Appendix 3, which includes wastes considered *prima facie* nonhazardous wastes under the Basel Convention in addition to other waste entries introduced after assessing them according to the risk criteria established in Appendix 6. Section C dictates that green-listed wastes shall "be subject to all existing controls normally applied in commercial transactions." There is no guidance regarding the meaning and extent of such control. In reality, Section C neither controls nor establishes any supervising mechanism regarding the transboundary movements of green-listed wastes, which can be traded freely. In other words, the OECD Council Decision C(2001)107/FINAL does not regulate transboundary movements of green-listed wastes. However, the inclusion of green-listed wastes is not inconsequential because according to Chapter II.B of the OECD Council Decision,

92 Organisation for Economic Co-Operation and Development (OECD), "Guidance Manual for the Control of Transboundary Movements of Recoverable Wastes," 29.
93 *See* Chapter II, Section B.5. of OECD Council Decision C(2001)107/FINAL.

92 Transboundary movements of wastes

all transboundary movements of wastes destined for recovery shall be recovered in an environmentally sound manner at recovery facilities having appropriate legal status. The standards to follow are those of the jurisdiction where the facility is located. Additionally, an international transport agreement (by any means of transport) shall be in place. Thus, the ultimate responsibility for the environmentally management of wastes rests on importing States.

Bearing in mind that the OECD Council Decision C(2001)107/FINAL is an arrangement concluded according to Article 11 of the Basel Convention, this latter instrument prevails in cases of conflict.[94] It is unlikely that potential conflicts between the OECD Council Decision and the Basel Convention will actually increase the probabilities of unsafe waste recovery, since trade of recoverable wastes follows well-established waste markets among OECD States.

Amber control procedure

The amber control procedure applies to wastes considered *prima facie* hazardous under the Basel Convention and to other wastes included as amber-listed after having been assessed for their characteristics, trade patterns, and management implications according to Appendix 6.[95] This control procedure attempts to conform to the principles of the Basel Convention, but it is adjusted to accommodate waste trade patterns taking place among OECD States. Chapter II, Section D of OECD Council Decision C(2001)107/FINAL establishes a system that includes notifying planned movements to transit and importing States, obtaining previous consent when required, and tracking the waste movements until the recovery has been completed. To avoid excessive burdens on the movement of wastes destined for recovery, the amber control procedure contemplates two different scenarios that Member States could encounter when planning a movement. The first is "individual transboundary movements or multiple shipments to a recovery facility and the second is transboundary movements to pre-consented recovery facilities." Both cases share common features in respect of contract requirements, financial guarantees, and certifications needed from the moment the transboundary movement starts until the recovery is performed. The differences between these two cases mainly pertain to the PIC procedure.

No transboundary movements of amber-listed wastes can commence without a valid contract between the exporter and the importer. If the importer and the recovery facility are not the same natural person or legal entity, then a valid contract is also required between the exporter and the facility.[96] The contract

---

94 Kummer explains that the "Basel Convention has the potential to serve as an umbrella for the waste management systems of … the OECD." Kummer, *International Management of Hazardous Wastes: The Basel Convention and Related Legal Rules*, 166, 168–69.

95 *See* Chapter II, Section B.2.b. of OECD Council Decision C(2001)107/FINAL.

96 "[n]ormally the importer would be the same as the recovery facility, but in some cases the importer can also be another person, for example a recognized trader." Organisation for Economic Co-Operation and Development (OECD), "Guidance Manual for the Control of Transboundary Movements of Recoverable Wastes," 21.

Transboundary movements of wastes 93

is a relevant tool to monitor transboundary movements of wastes since it shall identify the waste generator, the person having the legal control over the wastes, and the recovery facility. Both the Basel Convention and the OECD Council Decision C(2001)107/FINAL stipulate the duty to reexport wastes when, for example., the movement cannot be completed according to the terms of the contract.[97] These contractual clauses would enable the compliance with the duty to reexport wastes, but there are some instances related to illegal transboundary movements of wastes where compliance is much more complicated, especially when Parties involved in the movement try to conceal the shipment of wastes as something else, e.g., second-hand goods.

In both cases covered by the amber control procedure, after importing and/or transit States receive a notification of a planned transboundary movement, those States can request to review existing contracts.[98] This means that a valid contract should be in place even before the concerned States allow the transboundary movement. So, "the contract may need to include a caveat stating that its enforcement is subject to the consent given by the competent authorities".[99]

In cases where an alternative management of wastes needs to be arranged, and in accordance with international or national legislation, the exporter or the importer shall provide financial guarantees, such as insurance.[100] As far as international law is concerned, Article 6(11) of the Basel Convention requires that compulsory insurance or another financial guarantee covers every transboundary movement of wastes *as required by importing or transit States.* Consequently, both the Basel Convention and the OECD Council Decision C(2001)107/FINAL have left it to national law to determine the conditions of such bond. Needless to say, different jurisdictions could have diverse standards of liability, i.e., strict or subjective; they could stipulate (or not) mechanisms to channel liability; and the meaning and extent of compensable damage could also vary. The international *lege lata* regarding liability and compensation of damage resulting from transboundary movements of wastes is far from satisfactory. The Basel Protocol on Civil Liability, adopted in 1999, is not in force yet. Without an international regime on civil liability for damage caused by transboundary movements of wastes, the pollution pays principle could be circumvented, while the possibility of obtaining compensation relies on traditional principles of State responsibility and, if appropriate, other civil liability regimes, whether international or regional.[101]

---

97 The duty to return or re-export wastes is exclusive to amber-listed wastes. Chapter I, Section D.3 of OECD Council Decision C(2001)107/FINAL.

98 Ibid., Chapter II, Section D.2.2.

99 Organisation for Economic Co-Operation and Development (OECD), "Guidance Manual for the Control of Transboundary Movements of Recoverable Wastes," 22.

100 *See* Chapter II, Section D.2.1.b. of OECD Council Decision C(2001)107/FINAL.

101 Albers examines the potential application of several civil liability regimes when transboundary movements of wastes are carried by sea. Jan Albers, *Responsibility and Liability in the Context of Transboundary Movements of Hazardous Wastes by Sea: Existing Rules and the 1999*

94 *Transboundary movements of wastes*

Summing up, a financial guarantee intends to ensure that economic resources are promptly available to mitigate and compensate damage caused by a movement of wastes, e.g., personal injury, property damage, environmental damage, environmental reinstatement, among other things. In cases where no bond or insurance is available, pollution victims may not have the chance to institute legal proceedings in national or foreign courts. And even if they do, such cases are both time-consuming and costly, with further potential complications arising if the liability standard is a subjective one because the proof of *mens rea* or fault is quite problematic in cases involving environmental damage.

After the PIC procedure is complied with, another common feature of the amber control procedure is the tracking of a transboundary movement of waste through the "movement document".[102] According to Appendix 8.A. and B. of OECD Council Decision C(2001)107/FINAL, this document shall include the contact details of the exporter, importer, recycling facility, carriers, and authorities of all States involved in the movement. Also, it shall mention the means of transport, waste description, and identification of the intended recovery operation. The exporter must certify that the movement document is "complete and correct to the best of his knowledge." It is uncertain whether using the phrase "to the best of his knowledge" comprises something more or different from a due diligence obligation. The representative of the waste management facility should certify receipt of wastes, and after the recovery of wastes is completed, the facility issues a certificate of recovery that must be sent to the exporter and to the relevant authorities of the exporting and transit States. If the movement or recovery of wastes cannot be completed according to the contract and in compliance with the OECD Council Decision, the movement document identifies the holder of waste at any given time, e.g., exporter, carrier(s), waste management facility, which could be useful in determining further liabilities of the persons involved in the movement.

While similar, the PIC procedure under the Basel Convention is more rigorous and its application is the same for all transboundary movement of hazardous and other wastes. On the other hand, the OECD Council Decision distinguishes between two cases.

The first one is concerned with individual transboundary movements of wastes or multiple shipments to a recovery facility, which the OECD has labeled as the "standard case".[103] Before a single transboundary movement of wastes can take place, the exporter must send a "single notification" document to *all countries concerned*, i.e., *exporting, importing, and transit States*, with the information required in Appendix 8.A. In accordance with the Basel Convention, the

---

Liability Protocol to the Basel Convention, Vol. 29, Hamburg Studies on Maritime Affairs (Berlin: Springer, 2015): Chapter 3.

102 *See* Chapter II, Section D.2.1. Case 1: Individual transboundary movements of wastes or multiple shipments to a recovery facility, numerals (j), (k), and (l), and Section D.2.1. Case 2: Transboundary movements of wastes to pre-consented recovery facilities numeral f) of OECD Council Decision C(2001)107/FINAL.

103 Organisation for Economic Co-Operation and Development (OECD), "Guidance Manual for the Control of Transboundary Movements of Recoverable Wastes," 21.

exporter is not allowed to send the notification. The notification of an intended transboundary movement of wastes must be done by the exporting State, "or shall require the generator or exporter to notify, in writing, through the channel of the competent authority of the state of export".[104] In other words, the State of export, before making such notification, shall verify that the planned movement complies with the relevant international and national legislation. According to the OECD Council Decision C(2001)107/FINAL, the exporter is obliged to send the notification, and as such, not only can the importing and transit States object to such movement, but so too can the State of export. National legislation can require that "competent authorities of the country of export, instead of the exporter, may themselves transmit this notification".[105]

The difference between the information included in the single notification and in the movement document is that the latter specifies details of the transport itself, such as the date of the shipment, contact information of the carrier, and packaging requirements. The importing State, and, if appropriate, the exporting State, shall send an acknowledgment of the single notification document within three working days of receipt of the information to the exporter. Afterwards, the concerned States have 30 days to either accept the movement or to object to it in writing. If no objection is received within that period, the transboundary movement is considered tacitly accepted. The PIC procedure for single transboundary movements of wastes is most similar to the one established under the Basel Convention, but it is considerably less stringent. For instance, according to Article 6(2) of the Basel Convention, the importing State has no timeframe in which to respond in writing as to whether the movement is accepted, denied, or if more information is required. Accordingly, no tacit consent is applicable in this regime. Under certain circumstances established in Article 6(4) of the Basel Convention, tacit acceptance of the transit State(s) is presumed.

Amber control procedure, Case 1, also takes into consideration multiple transboundary movements of wastes sharing similar physical and chemical characteristics that are regularly sent to the same recovery facility. Since these wastes have already well-established trade routes, and the waste management facility frequently recovers a particular type of wastes, the OECD Council Decision C(2001)107/FINAL presumes that States involved in these movements have already assessed the risks associated with these types of wastes and their subsequent management. For this reason, the PIC procedure is simplified. If accepted by the concerned States, the exporter sends a "general notification" document specifying the number of transboundary movements of wastes to the intended recovery facility for the period of one year. However, concerned States can revoke this general acceptance at any time. The quantities of shipped wastes during this period of time is immaterial; what is relevant to determine whether certain waste types could benefit from the simplified PIC procedure is the physical and chemical characteristics of the wastes and the identity of the recovery facility.

---

104 *See* Article 6(1) of the Basel Convention.
105 *See* Chapter II, Section D.2.1. Case 1.a. of OECD Council Decision C(2001)107/FINAL.

96 Transboundary movements of wastes

Amber control procedure, Case 2, deals with transboundary movements of wastes to pre-consented recovery facilities. States where recovery facilities are located can designate (and revoke at any time) certain waste management facilities as "pre-consented" to enable the application of a simplified and faster PIC procedure. This pre-consent also applies to specific waste types and the technologies used to recover such wastes. The PIC procedure closely follows Case 1, with the following differences. In cases of single transboundary movement of wastes, each planned movement shall be notified with a "single notification" document and later acknowledged as provided in Case 1. However, exporting and transit States only have seven working days to object to the movement, or else it is considered tacitly accepted. This period can be extended to 30 days if the exporting State requires further information from the exporter. It is worth mentioning that importing States are only required to acknowledge receipt, but not to reply to the exporter notification, since it is presumed that the State of import has already given its consent by approving certain recovery facilities. Case 2 also covers multiple transboundary movements of wastes sharing similar physical and chemical characteristics that are regularly sent to the same recovery facility. The application of the PIC procedure is very similar to Case 1, but the "general notification" can cover multiple shipments for a period of up to three years. The general acceptance can be revoked at any time by any of the States concerned.

The PIC procedure established in the OECD Council Decision C(2001)107/FINAL is weak, since it resembles a notice system,[106] and the "tacit consent" is not equivalent to the requirements of the Basel Convention. By establishing a simplified PIC procedure, the OECD assured that the Basel Convention receives the necessary support for industrialized countries, which remain to this day the major exporters of wastes. It was also a mechanism to safeguard the waste industry among developed States, since during the negotiations of the Basel Convention, several industrial sectors qualified the PIC procedure as "inherently impractical, burdensome, and bureaucratic."[107]

Only transboundary movements of wastes subject to the amber control procedure shall be returned or reexported, if the movement or management is not carried out according to the terms of the contract,[108] e.g., an accident while in transit, *a force majeure* event has destroyed the recovery facility, and when the movement is illegal. The OECD Council Decision C(2001)107/FINAL does not define the circumstances under which a movement is deemed illegal. It is uncertain whether the breach of any obligation stipulated under this regime will render the movement illegal, or which of the persons and/or States involved in the movement are liable in that event. The obscurity surrounding this provision is not a coincidence, since

---

106 Notice systems "undermine the ability of importing states to know a product's potential risks." Cyrus Mehry, "Prior Informed Consent: An Emerging Compromise for Hazardous Export," *Cornell International Law Journal* 21 (1988): 383–84.

107 Ibid., 366.

108 *See* Chapter II, Section D.2.3. of OECD Council Decision C(2001)107/FINAL.

the definition of illegal movements and allocation of responsibility were highly controversial issues at the time when the Basel Convention was adopted.[109]

According to Chapter II, Section D.2.3. of the OECD Council Decision C(2001)107/FINAL, if wastes shall be returned, the competent authorities of the importing or transit States shall inform all other concerned countries. The State of export cannot refuse the return of the wastes when no alternative arrangements can be made in order to recover the wastes in an environmentally sound manner. The OECD Council Decision C(2001)107/FINAL is silent with regard to the person or competent authority in charge of arranging such alternative recovery management. If there is a contract covering the movement, it shall dictate the party responsible for making such arrangements, and, if necessary, for returning the wastes. If there is no contract, or it does not contain a clause regarding alternative arrangements, or if the responsible party under the contract cannot fulfill its obligations, the OECD Guidance Manual suggests that cooperation between States is necessary.[110] This is a coherent suggestion, since contemporary international environmental law recognizes the duty of States to cooperate in order to prevent, mitigate, and compensate for environmental damage.

Although the OECD Guidance Manual upholds the view that a generator of wastes is to be held responsible for the wastes, until their environmentally sound management is completed, one should ask whether or not the exporting State has any obligation for the management of wastes. A definitive answer cannot be found in the text of the OECD Council Decision; nevertheless, it seems that the exporting State is indeed responsible for the ESM of wastes. Such a conclusion can be inferred from Chapter II, Section D.2.3., which establishes that the exporting State cannot deny the return of the movement. Such obligation subsists irrespective of why the movement could not be completed. So, the exporting State cannot claim to have exercised its due diligence obligations to avoid the return of the wastes to its jurisdiction and ensure the ESM of such wastes. This interpretation is consistent with Article 4(10) of the Basel Convention, which assigns the exporting State as the main Party responsible for the ESM of wastes, and such an obligation cannot be transferred to other States.

Further attempts at harmonization with the Basel Convention

One of the goals of the OECD Council Decision C(2001)107/FINAL is to harmonize the procedures and requirements of this instrument with those of the Basel Convention,[111] especially in relation to waste lists. For this reason, the OECD Council Decision is periodically revised to incorporate the amendments adopted by the Conference of the Parties to the Basel Convention in relation to wastes listed in

---

109 Kummer, *International Management of Hazardous Wastes: The Basel Convention and Related Legal Rules*, 70–71.

110 Organisation for Economic Co-Operation and Development (OECD), "Guidance Manual for the Control of Transboundary Movements of Recoverable Wastes," 33.

111 *See* the preamble of OECD Council Decision C(2001)107/FINAL.

98 Transboundary movements of wastes

Annexes II, VIII, and IX. Amendments made to Annex II of the Basel Convention are incorporated in Part I of Appendix 3 of the OECD Council Decision, i.e., green-listed wastes. Amendments made to Annexes VIII and IX are incorporated in Part I of Appendix 4 of the OECD Council Decision, i.e., amber-listed wastes.[112]

The wastes lists established in the OECD Council Decision C(2001)107/ FINAL are not exclusively based on the Basel Convention because some waste entries could be amended or incorporated according to Appendix 6. The criteria listed in this Appendix take into consideration the characteristics of the wastes, the trade patterns, and management options. Based on these criteria, some Member States could oppose to the amendment proposed by the COP to the Basel Convention. In this case, the objecting State(s) shall also suggest to the OECD Secretariat an alternative proposal regarding the appropriate level of control of the waste in question. If Member States reach an agreement, the OECD Council Decision is amended accordingly, but if no consensus is reached, then the amendment made to the Basel Convention is not incorporated into the OECD Council Decision. In the latter scenario, the Member States have the prerogative to control such waste according to national or international law.[113] This amendment mechanism leaves room for potential conflicts between the OECD Council Decision and the Basel Convention, especially if hazardous wastes under the latter instrument are subject to the green control procedure.

EU law and shipments of wastes

Regulation 1013/2006/EC on Shipments of Wastes implements the Basel Convention, the OECD Council Decision C(2001)107/FINAL, and the Lomé Convention IV.[114] Following the OECD approach, waste trade is not always considered an undesirable activity under EU law. In fact, under certain circumstances it is deemed the best alternative to achieve the ESM of wastes in accordance with the Waste Framework Directive 2008/98/EC, i.e., the protection of human health and the environment from the negative effects of waste management. Taking this rationale into account, Regulation 1013/2006/EC on Shipments of Wastes establishes different control mechanisms. As a general rule, export of wastes for disposal outside the EU is prohibited, and within the EU it is subject to the PIC procedure.[115]

In cases of wastes destined for recovery, both the identity of the importer and the classification of green-listed and amber-listed wastes are relevant. This classification corresponds to the degree of hazard to human health and the

112 Ibid., Chapter II.B.3.
113 Ibid.
114 The Lomé Convention IV is no longer in force. It was concluded for a period of ten years since March 1990 according to its Article 366. In 2000, the Lomé Convention IV was replaced by the Cotonou Agreement. However, the Lomé Convention remains relevant because, due to this instrument, the EU restricted the export of hazardous and nuclear wastes to ACP States, i.e., African, Caribbean and the Pacific Group of States.
115 The prohibition of exports of wastes destined for disposal is the result of the implementation of the Ban Amendment into EU law. *See* Articles 31 and 34 of Regulation 1013/2006/EC.

environment. Green-listed wastes will generally not exhibit properties that are harmful to the environment or human health. According to Annex I, part I of Regulation 1013/2006/EC on Shipments of Wastes, green-listed wastes include those established in Annex IX of the Basel Convention, e.g., copper, nickel, iron, or steel scrap. On the other hand, amber-listed waste covers wastes categorized as hazardous under the Basel Convention. Transboundary movements of green-listed wastes to States that have adopted the OECD Decision C(2001)107/Final are subject to general information requirements according to Article 18 of Regulation 1013/2006/EC on Shipments of Wastes. Therefore, trade of these wastes is not strictly restricted or cumbersome. In the case of non-OECD States, the importing State can choose to: (a) prohibit the movement; (b) allow the movement after the PIC procedure is complied with; or (c) allow the movement subject to general information requirements. Finally, Article 3(1)(b) of Regulation 1013/2006/EC on Shipments of Wastes prescribes that amber-listed wastes can be exported to OECD Decision States after complying with the PIC procedure,[116] and, as a general rule, export to non-OECD Decision States is prohibited. This overview of the control procedure can be summarized as follows (Figure 4.2):

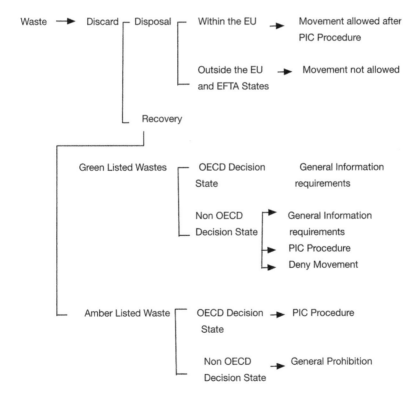

Figure 4.2 Movement of wastes according to Regulation 1013/2006/EC.

116 Ibid., Article 3(1)(b).

Concluding remarks

It is undeniable that the work undertaken by the OECD for the regulation of transboundary movements of wastes has influenced the development of the Basel Convention. However, this latter instrument was unable to strike a balance between the claims of developing States to ban transboundary movements of wastes and the desire of industrialized States to continue trading wastes, particularly among themselves.

Two mechanisms helped the Basel Convention receive almost worldwide support, ultimately becoming a landmark treaty in relation to the transboundary movements of wastes. First, the availability of Article 11 allowing State Parties to enter into agreements or arrangements dealing with transboundary movements of hazardous wastes, providing that certain conditions set out in the article are met. In this context, the OECD and ultimately the EU addressed the following: (a) the perceived rigidity of the Basel Convention in relation to recyclable or recoverable hazardous wastes; and (b) the rationale behind transboundary movements of wastes occurring between developed States. Second, the COP to the Basel Convention has given special attention to one of the pillars of the Convention, i.e., the ESM of wastes. This principle has provided a normative framework that fosters the development of both soft law and hard law standards regarding the management of wastes irrespective of their generation source. The ESM of wastes has become a coordinating principle from which to develop an international legal framework between different regimes.

5 Ship-source pollution

Marine pollution

Polluting substances may enter the oceans, from many sources, including land-based activities, dumping, operational or accidental discharges of harmful substances from ships, among others. Part XII of the LOSC is concerned with the protection and preservation of the marine environment. As Boyle explains, Part XII is a comprehensive and global "general framework ... that establishes ... responsibilities and powers of states in all matters of marine environmental protection".[1] Among its general obligations, Article 194 prescribes that States shall prevent, reduce, and control pollution of the marine environment. Pollution is a *human activity that has a detrimental impact.*

A specific definition of marine pollution was developed after realizing that the marine environment could not be considered as an everlasting receptacle of pollutants. In this sense, the Joint Group of Experts on the Scientific Aspects of Marine Environmental Protection (GESAMP) and UNESCO's Intergovernmental Oceanographic Commission (IOC) defined marine pollution as:

> the introduction by man, directly or indirectly, of substances or energy into the marine environment, including estuaries, resulting in such deleterious effects as harm to living resources, hazards to human health, hindrance to marine activities, including fishing, impairment of quality for use of sea water and reduction of amenities.[2]

This definition is incorporated, almost verbatim, in Article 1(4) of the LOSC. The GESAMP definition is strongly anthropocentric since it refers to resources and activities that have an impact on human life. The LOSC, on the other hand, considers that *marine life* in general and not only "resources" fall under the scope of pollution. In fact, Article 194(5) includes the protection and preservation from

---

1 Alan Boyle, "Marine Pollution under the Law of the Sea Convention," *The American Journal of International Law* 79, no. 2 (1985): 350.
2 Joint Group of Experts on the Scientific Aspects of Marine Environmental Protection (GESAMP), "Report of the First Session (Gesamp I/11)," (1969), 5.

102 Transboundary movements of wastes

pollution of "rare or fragile ecosystems as well as the habitat of depleted, threatened or endangered species and other forms of marine life." Therefore, "marine environment," which is the object to be protected from pollution, should be understood as a whole, including "the surface of the sea, the water column, the subsoil, the seabed, the atmosphere above them and everything comprised in that space, both physical and chemical components".[3]

Pollution, as defined in the LOSC, is derived only from human activities and does not include damage arising from natural phenomena. The description of pollution as the introduction of substances (oil, chemicals), alien species or energy (electricity, noise, radiation) leaves aside environmental harm caused by overexploitation or climate change. In other words, this definition could be criticized "for not taking sufficient account of the need to prevent changes in the marine environment".[4] Thus, pollution is only one type of environment harm and should be replaced by more inclusive terms, such as degradation.[5] In *the South China Sea Arbitration* case, the Arbitral Tribunal noted that Article 194(5) "confirms that Part XII is not limited to measures aimed strictly at controlling marine pollution," which while "certainly an important aspect of environmental protection … is by no means the only one".[6]

The increasing concern over marine pollution during the 1960s and 1970s, especially after disasters like the *Torrey Canyon* in 1967 and the *Amoco Cadiz* in 1978, served as catalysts to legislate it in a comprehensive manner. The umbrella provisions prescribed in the LOSC have endorsed many international regimes, such as MARPOL.[7] Furthermore, the LOSC has also allowed developments in respect of the protection of the marine environment from pollution. The concept of pollution is far from being uniform, and as such, it should be carefully examined, since its content could change among international, regional or national law. One common trend, however, is the slow but steady disappearance of the

---

3 Veronica Frank, *The European Community and Marine Environmental Protection in the International Law of the Sea: Implementing Global Obligations at the Regional Level* (Leiden: Martinus Nijhoff Publishers, 2007), 12. According to Frank, "[t]here is no definition of 'marine environment' under LOSC or other international instrument." In fact, the same can be said about the environment in general. *See also* Birnie, Boyle, and Redgwell, *International Law and the Environment*, 4–6 and 188–89.

4 Robin Rolf Churchill and Alan Vaughan Lowe, *The Law of the Sea*, 3rd edn (Manchester: Manchester University Press, 1999), 339.

5 "[t]he definition of marine pollution … is frequently interpreted restrictively as dealing with the release of harmful substances. The term 'degradation' rather than 'pollution' is used increasingly, *inter alia*, to ensure comprehensiveness: it includes all deleterious effects resulting from anthropogenic modification of the physical, chemical or biological characteristics of the environment, as well as environmental impacts of technology." United Nations Secretary-General (UNSG), "Developments Relating to the United Nations Convention on the Law of the Sea," in *Report of the Secretary-General (A/49/631) Forty-Ninth Session – Agenda Item 35* (16 November 1994), paras 74–76.

6 *Case No. 2013-19 the South China Sea Arbitration (the Republic of Philippines v. The People's Republic of China)*, para 945 (Permanent Court of Arbitration (PCA) 2016).

7 *See* Article 211 of the LOSC.

Ship-source pollution 103

term "pollution" and the emergence of new and more inclusive legal categories, such as degradation, adverse effects, or impacts.

An overview on ship-source marine pollution

Although oil pollution from ships has attracted more public attention than any other pollutant, ship-source pollution is not confined to oil spills, nor is it the greatest source of marine pollution.[8] Shipping activities cause atmospheric and marine pollution, and the latter can be operational or accidental. Operational discharges are *necessary* and "incidental to ... regular and normal operations"[9] of ships. For instance, a ship during its voyage will generate sewage, garbage, and oily wastes from machinery spaces. These substances and their discharge into the sea and/or into reception facilities are strictly regulated under MARPOL Annexes I to VI, which pertain to, respectively: oil, noxious liquid substances carried in bulk, harmful substances carried at sea in packaged form, sewage, garbage, and air pollution. Finally, accidental ship-source pollution results, e.g., from a collision or stranding, whereby the spillage of cargo could have disastrous effects in the marine environment, its living resources, and human health. Nevertheless, there are regulations in place to prevent accidental ship-source pollution and to take prompt and immediate action to mitigate the effects of accidental pollution. Particularly, preventive measures are prescribed under MARPOL (Annexes I and II), and the International Convention on Oil Pollution Preparedness, Response and Co-operation, 1990 (OPRC 90) has both preventive and mitigation measures.[10] In relation to public regulatory law, MARPOL is the most comprehensive and successful regime in relation to the prevention of ship-source pollution.

Currently, ship-source pollution is strictly regulated. Indeed, there is a comprehensive obligation to protect and preserve the marine environment *without hampering legitimate uses of sea*, e.g., *navigation, because shipping activities are vital to seaborne trade*. Finding a balance between environmental protection and protection of other legitimate uses of the sea is not an easy task. Despite the regulatory scheme in place, the negative impacts of shipping activities in the marine environment are not likely to decrease due to the continuous growth of the merchant fleet, that "reached almost 1.4 billion deadweight tons [dwt] in January 2011, an increase of 120 million dwt over 2010".[11]

---

8 According to the 1990 GESAMP report, shipping activities constitute 12 percent of marine pollution, while land-based activities make up 44 percent of marine pollution. Joint Group of Experts on the Scientific Aspects of Marine Environmental Protection (GESAMP), "The State of the Marine Environment: Report and Studies No. 39," (1990), 88.

9 Proshanto Mukherjee, "The Penal Law of Ship-Source Marine Pollution: Selected Issues in Perspective," in *The Law of the Sea, Environmental Law and Settlement of Disputes: Liber Amicorum Judge Thomas A. Mensah*, ed. Tafsir Ndiaye and Rüdiger Wolfrum (Leiden: Martinus Nijhoff Publishers, 2007), 466.

10 Ibid., 468. International Convention on Oil Pollution Preparedness, Response and Co-Operation, London, 30 November 1990, 1891 UNTS 51; 30 ILM 733. In force 13 May 1995.

11 UNCTAD, "Review of Maritime Transport," XV.

104 *Transboundary movements of wastes*

Customary law before the LOSC

Before the advent of the LOSC, the law of the sea was mainly concerned with the regulation of the different legitimate uses of the sea and little progress was made in relation to marine pollution. Nevertheless, there are customary law rules that could be applied to the protection of the marine environment from pollution. First, in the *Trail Smelter* arbitration, the tribunal stated that "no state has the right to use or permit the use of its territory in such a manner to cause injury by fumes in or to the territory of another"[12] State. Similarly, in the *Corfu Channel* case, the Court indicated that it is "every state's obligation not to allow knowingly its territory to be used contrary to the rights of other states".[13]

Authors like Abecassis and Jarashow,[14] and Churchill and Lowe[15] argue that these cases formed the basis of a general duty to protect the marine environment. So, States must ensure that their nationals, ships, and floating devices do not, e.g., discharge substances into the sea, which could affect other States. However, this general duty does not offer any concrete obligation regarding ship pollution or liability standards. Furthermore, it is undeniable that both the *Corfu Channel* and the *Trail Smelter* are concerned *with the use of a State's territory*. In this case, one can argue, as depicted in *The Lotus*, that a ship on the high seas is an extension of the territory of the State whose flag the ship is entitled to fly. But this proposition seems now to be archaic and has been extensively rejected.[16] Particularly, ships on the high seas are not subject to the law of the flag State as an extension of the territory; rather, as Colombos explains, vessels are "property in place where no local jurisdiction exists".[17] Overall, even the customary law analyzed here fell short of regulating and preventing ship-source pollution.

The abovementioned cases can also been interpreted in light of the doctrine of the abuse of rights, good neighborliness, and the maxim of *sic utere tuo ut alienum non laedas,* i.e., use your own as not to injure another's property. The doctrine of abuse of rights is also found in Article 300 of the LOSC that prescribes:

> states Parties shall fulfill in good faith the obligations assumed under this Convention and shall exercise the rights, jurisdiction and freedoms recognized in this Convention in a manner, which would not constitute an abuse of right.

---

12 *Trail Smelter (Canada v. United States)*, 3 RIAA (1938 and 1941).
13 *Corfu Channel (United Kingdom v. Albania)*, 3 ICJ Rep (1949).
14 David W. Abecassis and Richard L. Jarashow, *Oil Pollution from Ships: International, United Kingdom and United States Law and Practice*, 2nd edn (London: Stevens & Sons Ltd., 1985), 14.
15 Churchill and Lowe, *The Law of the Sea*, 332.
16 C. John Colombos, *The International Law of the Sea*, 6th edn (London: Longmans, 1967), 286–88. "There are practical reasons for the rule of subjection of ships to the laws of their state and it is unnecessary to employ the fiction of territoriality ... Moreover, such a fiction, if pushed to its logical conclusion, would lead to strange results. It would exclude the exercise of jurisdiction by a littoral state in its territorial waters."
17 Ibid., 285.

In this context, abuse of rights excludes the exercise of rights in a malicious manner,[18] but once again this doctrine does not provide any further content of rights and obligations in respect of prevention of ship marine pollution. The limited assistance of customary law has triggered the development of comprehensive treaty law.

The Geneva Convention on the High Seas, 1958: a license to pollute the oceans

Before the adoption and entering into force of the LOSC, in 1958, four treaties governing the law of the sea were adopted: (a) The Geneva Convention on the Territorial Sea and Contiguous Zone; (b) The Geneva Convention on the High Seas; The Geneva Convention on the Continental Shelf; and the Geneva Convention on Fishing and Conservation on the Living Resources of the High Seas. All these Conventions are in force and are still relevant since not all States are Parties to the LOSC. Between State Parties to the LOSC, this Convention prevails over the Geneva Conventions of 1958 according to Article 311(1) of the LOSC.

The Geneva Convention on the High Seas, 1958, provides little guidance about the principles that govern ship-source pollution other than an initial concern about oil pollution. Ship-source oil pollution gained attention for pollution damage to "fisheries resources" and encumbrances in navigable waters.[19] Concerns also grew due to the advent of Very Large Crude Carriers (VLCCs)[20] transporting huge amounts of oil worldwide. These vessels represented ticking bombs threatening coastal States with further oil spills. For these reasons, it is not surprising that Article 24 of the Geneva Convention on the High Seas, 1958, is the only reference regarding ship-source oil pollution. In fact, this article prescribes that: "[e]very state shall draw up regulations to prevent pollution of the seas by the discharge of oil from ships ... taking account of existing treaty provisions on the subject." It is interesting to note that this provision refers to "existing treaty provisions on the subject," but does not mention that States' oil pollution standards *must or shall* conform to such treaty provisions. Therefore, States were not bound to follow international provisions. In this context, it is obvious that regulations among States could be dissimilar, resulting in extensive freedom to pollute the marine environment. In this regard, Boyle notes that "important flag states were not parties to these [treaties] and adopted their own national regulations of a rather lower standard".[21]

---

18 *See* Birnie et al. who argue that the doctrine of abuse of rights can be understood in two ways: (a) as a concept "that limits the exercise of a rights in bad faith"; or (b) as "a doctrine of reasonableness or a balancing of interests." Birnie, Boyle, and Redgwell, *International Law and the Environment*, 204.

19 For an overview of the initial attempts to prevent ship-source oil pollution in the twentieth century, *See* Colombos, *The International Law of the Sea*, 430–36.

20 Rue and Anderson, *Shipping and the Environment: Law and Practice*, 10. *Note* that "[t]he focus of attention has been largely on crude oil, which although not necessarily the most dangerous substance carried by sea, is the most significant in tonnage terms."

21 Boyle, "Marine Pollution under the Law of the Sea Convention," 351.

106 *Transboundary movements of wastes*

The predecessor of MARPOL was the International Convention for the Prevention of Pollution of the Sea by Oil, 1954 (OILPOL 54), which was exclusively concerned with ship-source oil pollution. This latter instrument allowed operational oil discharges beyond prohibited zones, i.e., "generally speaking, the area lying within fifty miles of the nearest coast"[22] and even discharges into the sea when States lack port reception facilities.[23] Oil discharge standards became applicable beyond prohibited zones due to an amendment to OILPOL adopted in 1969.[24]

To fully understand Article 24 of the Geneva Convention on the High Seas, 1958, several aspects must be taken into consideration. First, vast areas of the sea, beyond the territorial sea, were subject to the high seas regime. Second, Article 6 of the Convention confirms that flag States exercise exclusive jurisdiction over their vessels on the high seas. Third, although the Territorial and Contiguous Zone Convention of 1958 does not establish the breadth of the territorial sea, by that time, most States claimed the territorial sea's breadth up to three, four, and six nautical miles.[25] All these circumstances made coastal States particularly vulnerable to ship-source pollution and a growing dissatisfaction regarding the regime governing the prevention of marine pollution triggered the development of Part XII of the LOSC. Additionally, as analyzed below, several changes were brought by the LOSC. Among the most distinguished are: (a) the advent of the EEZ and the retreat of vast areas from the high seas regime; (b) a comprehensive regime to deal with marine pollution; and (c) conservation of the principle of jurisdiction of the flag State to regulate pollution from ships with a strengthening of coastal and port State jurisdiction.

The vague obligation to regulate ship-source oil pollution established in Article 24 of the High Seas Convention of 1958 has to be analyzed in the light of Article 2 of the Convention. This article prescribes that the freedoms of the high seas, e.g., navigation, must be exercised with reasonable regard to other States' interests. Nonetheless, the term "reasonable regard" is not entirely clear because it does not stipulate the rights and obligations of States, so "there should be a case by case weighing of the actual interests involved ... in order to determine which use is reasonable".[26] Thus, it seems that the reasonable use deals with the competition of lawful activities on the high seas, but says little about protection of the marine environment and prevention of ship-source pollution.

---

22 Jan Schneider, "Pollution from Vessels," in *The Environmental Law of the Sea*, ed. Douglas Johnson (Switzerland: International Union for Conservation of Nature and Natural Resources IUCN, 1981), 205.

23 Colombos, *The International Law of the Sea*, 434.

24 Schneider, "Pollution from Vessels," 205.

25 Churchill and Lowe, *The Law of the Sea*, 77–81. *Note* that "[w]hereas in 1960 the great majority of states claimed territorial seas less than twelve miles, by the closing stages of UNCLOS III the position was dramatically reversed, and the great majority of states claimed territorial seas of twelve miles or more."

26 Churchill and Lowe, *The Law of the Sea*, 206.

Ship-source pollution 107

The LOSC: the constitution of the oceans

The LOSC has been regarded as the constitution of the oceans.[27] This accurate description is supported by the wide acceptance of the Convention, which as of March 2019 has 168 Parties.[28] Part XII of this instrument reflects the transition from a "freedom" to pollute to a duty to prevent, mitigate, and remedy the damage caused by all sources of marine pollution. Additionally, several parts of this comprehensive framework are considered as customary law "by courts, international organizations, and non-parties".[29] This view is strengthened by the language used in Part XII of the Convention that addresses States as the whole international community and not only "state parties." Regarding ship-source pollution, the LOSC contains general and particular principles dealing with this matter.

Article 192 provides that States have a duty to protect and preserve the marine environment. The Arbitral Tribunal in the *South China Sea Arbitration* case declared:

> This "general obligation" extends both to "protection" of the marine environment from future damage and "preservation" in the sense of maintaining or improving its present condition. Article 192 thus entails the positive obligation to take active measures to protect and preserve the marine environment, and by logical implication, entails the negative obligation not to degrade the marine environment.[30]

This article is also significant because it refers to the marine environment as a whole, meaning that States must protect the oceans, including the high seas, marine life, rare ecosystems, among others. Furthermore, Article 194(1) recognizes that measures to prevent, reduce, and control marine pollution from any source have to be taken by States using "the best practicable means at their disposal and in accordance with their capabilities, and they shall endeavor to harmonize their policies." This provision concedes some degree of discretion to States when adopting the required measures, by taking into consideration a State's capabilities and availability of resources. According to Birnie et al., this provision was established mainly for developing countries, and it is criticized for being vague and an "unhelpful generality".[31] Despite the accuracy of this

---

27 Tommy Koh, "A Constitution for the Oceans," (1982). The document is available at: <www.un.org/Depts/los/convention_agreements/texts/koh_english.pdf>, last accessed 17 March 2019.

28 United Nations, *Status of UNCLOS*, <www.un.org/depts/los/reference_files/chronological_lists_of_ratifications.htm>, last accessed 17 March 2019.

29 *Note* that "[u]nlike the earlier Geneva Conventions of 1958, the 1982 Convention was intended to be, as far as possible, comprehensive in scope and universal in participation ... Not only does it enjoy very wide participation, but on many issues it has been considered as customary law." Birnie, Boyle, and Redgwell, *International Law and the Environment*, 382.

30 *Case No. 2013-19 the South China Sea Arbitration (the Republic of Philippines v. The People's Republic of China).*

31 Birnie, Boyle, and Redgwell, *International Law and the Environment*, 389.

108 *Transboundary movements of wastes*

criticism, Articles 202 and 203 of the LOSC impose an obligation upon States to promote and provide technical and scientific assistance to developing States with a view to allocating resources and enhancing the adoption and enforcement of measures to protect the marine environment. However, the flexibility given in Article 194(1) is absent in relation to ship-source pollution because measures to prevent, reduce, and control pollution from ships *must* at least conform to "generally accepted international rules and standards".[32]

The general obligations established in Part XII of the LOSC relate to: (a) notification about imminent or actual damage of pollution to other States likely to be affected; (b) promotion of scientific research and maintaining of contingency plans; and (c) monitoring and carrying out environmental impact assessments.[33] Furthermore, Article 197 prescribes that States must cooperate on a global or regional basis, directly or through competent international organizations, e.g., IMO, in order to develop rules and standards regarding the protection of the marine environment. The obligation to cooperate acknowledges that marine pollution is international in nature because pollutants cross boundaries and have deleterious effects in the marine environment as a unit.[34]

Pollution from ships involves several aspects as established in Article 194(3) (b) of the LOSC including: (a) design, construction, and ship manning; (b) reduction and control of operational discharges; (c) prevention and mitigation of accidental pollution; and (d) safety of operations at sea. Furthermore, regulation regarding ship-source pollution also deals with: (a) prescription and enforcement of pollution standards; (b) cooperation to deal with pollution incidents and emergencies at sea; and (c) liability. On the whole, when dealing with ship-source pollution at the international, regional, and national levels, the trilogy described by Mukherjee as the "continuum of prevention, mitigation, and remedy" has to be in place.[35]

Article 211 of the LOSC deals exclusively with ship-source pollution and its aims are twofold. First, it provides a jurisdictional framework that balances the interests of flag, coastal, and port States. Second, it requires States to act through a general diplomatic conference or the competent international organization, i.e., IMO, to establish rules and standards to "prevent, reduce, and control pollution of the marine environment from vessels".[36] In fact, according to Article 211(2), the regulations and laws prescribed by the flag States must "at least have the same effect as that of generally accepted international rules and standards

---

32 *See* Article 211(2) of the LOSC.

33 *See* Articles 198, 199, 200, 201, 202, 204 and 206 of the LOSC.

34 *Mox Plant Case (Provisional Measures)*, ITLOS No. 10 (2001).

35 Mukherjee, "The Penal Law of Ship-Source Marine Pollution: Selected Issues in Perspective," 468–71. "[p]reventive measures are put into place with the object of eliminating or reducing the chances of the pollution occurring ... By contrast remedial measures ... in relation to operational discharges, they are pursued routinely because of the cumulative effect of the pollution occurring over an infinite period. In cases of accidental spills, the measures are deployed expeditiously. Remedial measures are introduced when preventive measures fail to materialize."

36 *See* Article 211(1) of the LOSC.

Ship-source pollution 109

established through the competent international organization or general diplomatic conference."

It has been widely accepted that "the competent international organization" is a reference to IMO.[37] However, establishing what count as generally accepted rules and standards is not entirely straightforward. As of March 2019, Parties to MARPOL Annexes I to VI represented the following percentages of the world's merchant shipping tonnage: both Annexes I and II 99.15 percent, Annex III 98.57 percent, Annex IV 96.33 percent, Annex V 98.73 percent, and Annex VI 96.68 percent.[38] The wide acceptance of MARPOL reveals that their Annexes can be regarded as generally accepted rules and standards under Article 211(2) of the LOSC. The difference between rules and standards, if any, is far from settled. While rules could be interpreted as treaty-based norms, "standards" could be construed as including soft law instruments or as technical provisions. Whether to include soft law instruments as part of the generally accepted rules and standards is a controversial issue. Nonetheless, these guidelines are legally relevant in the implementation of highly technical treaty law, or they could "provide evidence of *opinion juris* for the possible emergence of a rule of customary international law".[39] Authors like Churchill and Lowe,[40] Birnie,[41] and Rothwell and Stephens[42] argue that Article 211(2) may force flag States to follow rules adopted under the auspices the IMO even though they are not Parties to a particular Convention because States "have indirectly consented to be bound to these instruments"[43] through the LOSC. Even if this argument is accepted, the criteria with which to ascertain whether an instrument, hard or soft, has become "generally accepted" remain uncertain. Furthermore, if treaty law has not been transformed into customary law, it is quite difficult to oblige a sovereign State to

37 *Note* that the International Law Association (ILA) mentions that the use of the expression "competent international organization" in the singular "is no coincidence, but rather indicates that one particular organization has to be understood by this expression, namely the International Maritime Organization." Erik Franckx, ed. *Vessel-Source Pollution and Coastal State Jurisdiction: The Work of the ILA Committee on Coastal State Jurisdiction Relating to Marine Pollution (1991–2001)* (The Hague: Kluwer Law International, 2001), 20. Donald Rothwell and Tim Stephens, *The International Law of the Sea* (Oxford: Hart Publishing Ltd., 2010), 343–44.

38 International Maritime Organization, *Summary of the Status of Convention*, <www.imo.org/en/About/Conventions/StatusOfConventions/Pages/Default.aspx>, last accessed 17 March 2019.

39 Boyle, "Some Reflections on the Relationship of Treaties and Soft Law," 906.

40 Churchill and Lowe, *The Law of the Sea*, 347.

41 Birnie, Boyle, and Redgwell, *International Law and the Environment*, 404.

42 Rothwell and Stephens, *The International Law of the Sea*, 344.

43 "Some treaties give binding force to soft-law instruments by incorporating them into the terms of a treaty by implied reference. The 1982 UN Convention on the Law of the Sea makes extensive use of this technique, impliedly incorporating recommendations and resolutions of IMO, as well as treaties such as the 1973 MARPOL Convention, under provisions variously requiring or permitting states to apply generally accepted rules and standards ... Thus although IMO has no power under its constitution to take formally binding decisions, UNCLOS may indirectly render some of these decisions obligatory." Boyle, "Some Reflections on the Relationship of Treaties and Soft Law," 906.

110 *Transboundary movements of wastes*

follow a Convention if said State has not expressly consented to be bound by it. It is also difficult to argue that State Parties to the LOSC are per se bound by instruments of a technical nature because their implementation requires economic resources and sophisticated technical and administrative capacity.

The umbrella standards provided in the LOSC are envisioned to promote "harmonization" and effective prevention, control, and remedy of marine pollution without discouraging legitimate uses of the sea, such as shipping. Despite the difficulties encountered in setting global standards, the LOSC is the "reference point for the validity of subsequent rules on oceans matters".[44]

MARPOL

Within the preventive spectrum of ship-source pollution, unquestionably MARPOL is the most comprehensive regime that governs ship-source pollution. MARPOL was adopted under the auspices of the IMO. The Convention was the result of the International Conference on Marine Pollution convened in 1973.[45] This instrument acknowledged the need to prevent marine pollution from a range of other *harmful substances* through five Annexes dealing with oil, noxious liquid substances carried in bulk, harmful substances in packaged form, sewage, and garbage, respectively. Although the ratification of Annexes III, IV, and V was optional, MARPOL 73 was not successful in entering into force because of difficulties that States faced in implementing the obligatory Annexes I and II.[46] The implementation of port reception facilities and technological demands were particularly challenging.

The constraints encountered to enable the ratification of MARPOL 73, coupled with pressures from the United States to individually legislate ship-source pollution, prompted the adoption of the 1978 Protocol to MARPOL through the International Conference on Tanker Safety and Pollution Prevention of 1978.[47] At the Conference, the implementation of Annex II was postponed after three years from the entry into force of the Protocol. MARPOL 73 as modified by its 78 Protocol entered into force on 2 October 1983, and since that time the Convention has been known as MARPOL 73/78. Finally, in 1997, a sixth Annex related to air pollution was adopted.

---

44 *See* Richard Barnes, David Freestone, and David M. Ong, "The Law of the Sea: Progress and Prospects," in *The Law of the Sea*, ed. Richard Barnes, David Freestone, and David M. Ong (Oxford: Oxford University Press, 2006), 465.

45 Rue and Anderson, *Shipping and the Environment: Law and Practice*, 823.

46 "the fact that Annexes I and II were 'coupled' together and made compulsory for state parties introduced huge challenges, particularly because the many types of chemicals falling under Annex II made it extremely difficult to implement." Tan, *Vessel-Source Marine Pollution: The Law and Politics of International Regulation*, 134.

47 Tan, *Vessel-Source Marine Pollution: The Law and Politics of International Regulation*, 135. *See also* Jeff B. Curtis, "Vessel-Source Oil Pollution and MARPOL 73/78: An International Success Story?," *Environmental Law* 15 (1984): 698–700.

Ship-source pollution 111

All Annexes of MARPOL have been successfully updated in line with technological developments through the tacit amendment procedure prescribed in Article 16(f)(iii) of the Convention.[48] This procedure is quicker than requiring formal acceptance and it has contributed greatly to the success of MARPOL and other IMO Conventions. MARPOL's chief purpose is to preserve the marine environment from the *discharge of harmful substances* that have a deleterious effect on human health or the marine environment (including amenities), or that hamper legitimate uses of the sea, e.g., navigation or fishing.[49] Additionally, the Convention deals with both operational and accidental pollution from ships.[50] Activities such as dumping, pollution caused by seabed exploration and exploitation, and pollution caused by "legitimate scientific research into pollution abatement"[51] fall outside the scope of the Convention. In view of MARPOL's objectives, terminology, and operation, it is necessary to distinguish it from the scope of the Basel Convention. For this reason, a brief outline of the Annexes of MARPOL is given below.

Standards for the prevention of ship-source pollution

Annex I of MARPOL deals with oil pollution,[52] from cargo and machinery spaces. According to Regulation 2.1, Annex I applies to all ships. Nonetheless, under some circumstances, exceptions are established in relation to the ship's gross tonnage,[53] built date, and type. Oil pollution management under this Annex relates to the following issues. First, according to Chapter 2 of this Annex, the Flag State Maritime Administration must conduct certain prescribed surveys and issue an International Oil Pollution Prevention Certificate.[54] Second, according to the type of ship and its gross tonnage, there are regulations dealing with the construction and equipment for cargo spaces of oil tankers, such as segregated ballast tanks or double hulls, and for machinery spaces for all ships, such as oil filtering equipment or sludge tanks.[55] Third, strict discharge criteria for cargo and machinery spaces are applied on the basis of various parameters: (a) type of ship (tanker or nontanker); (b) geographical location and distance from the nearest land; (c) prohibition of discharge within Special Areas;[56] (d) ship's

---

48 See Article 16(2) of MARPOL. An Amendment to an annex is considered accepted "unless ... an objection is communicated ... by not less than one third of the Parties or by the Parties the combined merchant fleets of which constitute not less than 50 per cent of the gross tonnage of the world's merchant fleet."

49 Ibid., Article 2(2).

50 *See supra* Chapter 3.

51 Ibid., Article 2(3).

52 *See* Annex I, Chapter 1, Regulation 1.1. of MARPOL.

53 Gross tonnage is a measure of the internal volume of spaces within a ship including cargo spaces.

54 *See* Annex I, Chapter 2, Regulations 6 to 10 of MARPOL.

55 Rue and Anderson, *Shipping and the Environment: Law and Practice*, 825–33.

56 "[s]pecial area means a sea area where for recognized technical reasons ... and to the particular character of its traffic the adoption of special mandatory methods for the prevention of sea

112 *Transboundary movements of wastes*

gross tonnage; (e) ship's equipment; (f) oil content in parts per million; and (g) continuous discharge in liters per nautical mile when the vessel is *en route*.[57] Additionally, an Oil Record Book must be carried on all ships.[58] Finally, within the MARPOL regime, it is of fundamental importance that States provide adequate reception facilities to receive oil residues.[59] Nonetheless, implementing these facilities remains a challenge,[60] and, where available, private operators may be restrained from using them due to their cost or adequacy.

Annex II deals with pollution by noxious liquid substances carried in bulk. Regulation 6 classifies these substances into four categories (X, Y, Z, and other substances) according to their hazard degree to human health and the marine environment. Substances in category X are the most hazardous, while "other substances" are deemed to present no harm to the environment. Furthermore, the regulation applies to all ships "certified to carry noxious liquid substances in bulk".[61] Pollution prevention within this Annex is based on a survey and certification system in charge of the flag State Maritime Administration.[62] In principle, the discharge of substances under categories X, Y, and Z is prohibited,[63] and thus, adequate port facilities are necessary to effectively implement Annex II. When allowed, the discharge criteria depend on the following parameters: (a) the geographical location of the ship from the nearest land and within Special Areas; (b) the categorization of the noxious liquid substance; (c) discharges must be made below the water line and the ship must proceed *en route*; (d) type of ship (self-propelled or not); and (e) the substance's concentration in the effluent.[64] Chapter 4 of this Annex prescribes that ships built after 1986 carrying noxious liquid substances must be constructed and equipped in accordance with the International Bulk Chemical Code. Finally, all operational and accidental discharges must be documented in the Cargo Record Book as established in Chapter 5, Regulation 15.

Annex III relates to harmful substances carried in packaged form as defined in the IMDG Code.[65] The standards to prevent pollution from these substances include adequate packaging, marking, labeling, stowage, and quantity

---

pollution by oil is required." Some of special areas under Annex I include, for instance: the Baltic Sea, Oman Sea, the Red Sea. MARPOL, Annex I, Chapter 1, Regulation 1.

57 Edgar Gold, *Gard Handbook on the Protection of the Marine Environment*, 3rd edn (Norway: Gard AS, 2006), 204–5.

58 The Oil Record Book is for both machinery spaces operations and cargo ballast operations. *See* Annex I, Chapters 3 and 4, Regulations 17 and 36 of MARPOL.

59 Ibid., Chapter 6.

60 *See Infra*, Chapter 8.

61 *See* Annex II, Chapter 1, Regulation 2 of MARPOL.

62 Ibid, Chapter 3.

63 Ibid, Annex II, Chapter 5, Regulation 13(1).

64 Ibid., Regulation 13. *See also* Gold, *Gard Handbook on the Protection of the Marine Environment*, 213–25.

65 *See* Annex III, Regulation 1 of MARPOL.

Ship-source pollution 113

limitation.[66] Annex III does not follow the patterns of Annexes I and II related to surveys, certifications, and implementation of port reception facilities because the risk of pollution does not arise from operational discharges, "tank cleaning, ballasting operations, or cargo residues".[67] So, regulations must ensure instead a proper handling of these substances to avoid accidental pollution.

Annex IV governs the prevention of pollution by sewage. Surveys, certifications, treatment and disinfection systems, and the implementation of reception facilities are required to prevent pollution from sewage.[68] The discharge criteria are based on: (a) the ship's gross tonnage; (b) the number of people certified to be carried on board; (c) distance from the nearest land, measured from the baseline; and (d) equipment available on board.[69]

While operating, ships produce garbage such as residues from food, glass, plastic, and dunnage that requires being disposed of. Annex V deals with the prevention of garbage. The standards to prevent pollution by garbage oblige State Parties to provide adequate reception facilities.[70] Indeed, these facilities are of fundamental importance due to the general prohibition on discharge of garbage into the sea, which is subject to some exceptions.[71] The disposal of certain types of garbage into the sea depends on several factors, including: (a) distance from the nearest land and (b) geographical location of the ship, i.e., Special Areas.[72] Finally, a Garbage Management Plan must be kept on board ships certified to carry 15 people or more and ships of 100 gross tonnage or above, while a Garbage Record Book must be kept on board ships certified to carry 15 people or more and ships of 400 gross tonnage or above.[73]

Article 212 of the LOSC addresses atmospheric source pollution of the marine environment. This pollution source is a complex issue to deal with, since exhaust emissions from ships do not enter directly into the sea. Particularly, Articles 212 and 222 of the LOSC prescribe that States must: (a) enact and enforce regulations to prevent, control, and reduce pollution *from or through* the atmosphere in relation to ships entitled to fly their flag and (b) endeavor to establish and implement global rules through the competent international organization or diplomatic conference. Particularly, a ship's exhaust emissions of nitrogen oxides (No_x) and sulfur oxides (So_x) go into the atmosphere causing acid rain, which enters the sea and causes marine pollution.[74] Other substances, including halons, deplete the

---

66 Ibid., Regulations 2, 3, 5, and 6.

67 Gold, *Gard Handbook on the Protection of the Marine Environment*, 227.

68 "Annex IV is developed on the premise that sewage reception facilities will be available in almost all ports. This is, of course, not the case at this stage." Ibid., 229–30.

69 *See* Annex IV, Regulations 2, 9, 10 and 12 of MARPOL.

70 Ibid., Regulation 8.

71 Ibid, Regulation 3(1).

72 Ibid, Regulations 3–7.

73 Ibid., Regulation 10.

74 Proshanto Mukherjee and Jingjing Xu, "The Legal Framework of Exhausts Emissions from Ships: A Selective Examination from a Law and Economics Perspective," in *Impacts of Climate Change on the Maritime Industry: The Proceedings of the Conference on Impacts of Climate Change on*

114 *Transboundary movements of wastes*

ozone layer, which is responsible for the regulation of sunlight and ultraviolet radiation entering the earth. Furthermore, substances known as greenhouse gases, e.g., carbon dioxide (CO_2), contribute to climate change.[75] Ozone layer depletion increases ultraviolet radiation and causes, *inter alia*, detrimental effects on fisheries, and climate change contributes to ocean levels rising.[76]

The controversy surrounding the appropriate forum for regulating these substances, which have not been traditionally seen as pollutants, has been discussed elsewhere.[77] Suffice it to say that the IMO has addressed not only exhaust emissions from ships containing No_x and So_x through Annex VI of MARPOL, but also the control of certain ozone depleting substances found on board vessels. Furthermore, in July 2011 an amendment to Annex VI was adopted. The new Chapter 4 "Regulations on Energy Efficiency for Ships," which entered into force in January 2013, is intended to reduce greenhouse gases from shipping. Mukherjee and Jingjing Xu justify the IMO's efforts in the control of CO_2 emissions from ships since Article 2(2) of the Kyoto Protocol to the United Nations Framework Convention on Climate Change, 1997,[78] states that Parties must reduce greenhouse gases by working, *inter alia*, with the IMO.[79] The contribution of the IMO in relation to exhaust emissions, ozone depleting substances, and greenhouse gases represents a step toward a comprehensive treatment of the marine environment and also erodes the traditional conception of pollution. As with other Annexes, the prevention of "air pollution" is based on surveys, certification, and installation of equipment for controlling emissions. The limits of these emissions depend on the substance. Prevention of accidental pollution under MARPOL consists of standards for "ship construction, and equipment, as well as for emergency plans".[80]

MARPOL's Achilles heel: heavy reliance on the adequacy of port reception facilities

The previous section outlined the obligations related to the prevention of ship-source pollution. From this outline, it becomes apparent that MARPOL impinges

---

    the Maritime Industry, 2–4 June 2008, ed. Neil Bellefontaine and Olof Lindén (Malmö: WMU Publications, 2009), 72.

75 Ibid.

76 Philippe Sands, *Principles of International Environmental Law*, 2nd edn (Cambridge: Cambridge University Press, 2003), 343 and 58.

77 For a discussion of the inclusion in Annex VI of substances not characterized as pollutants, *See* Mukherjee and Xu, "The Legal Framework of Exhausts Emissions from Ships: A Selective Examination from a Law and Economics Perspective"; Phillip Linné, "Ships, Air Pollution, and Climate Change: Some Reflections on Recent Legal Developments in the Marine Environment Protection Committee," *SIMPLY: Scandinavian Institute of Maritime Law Yearbook* (2011): 13–32.

78 Kyoto Protocol to the United Nations Framework Convention on Climate Change, 11, December 1997. UN Doc FCCC/CP/1997/7/Add.1, December 10, 1997; 37 ILM 22 (1998).

79 Mukherjee and Xu, "The Legal Framework of Exhausts Emissions from Ships: A Selective Examination from a Law and Economics Perspective," 78.

80 Louise Angélique de La Fayette, "The Sound Management of Wastes Generated at Sea: MARPOL, Not Basel," *Environmental Policy and Law* 39, nos. 4–5 (2009): 210.

directly on private operators who are responsible for managing harmful substances generated during ship operations and who must minimize the risk of accidental pollution. Given that discharges in the marine environment are restricted or prohibited, the success of MARPOL is also heavily dependent on the availability of adequate port reception facilities. However, as analyzed in Chapter 8 of this book, State Parties to MARPOL are keen to establish detailed obligations in relation to ships, but are reluctant to clarify their own obligations in relation to the provision of port reception facilities. The result is a lack of integration between the management of ship wastes at sea and its downstream management on land. If such port reception facilities are not adequate, the inevitable result is the transformation of one source of pollution into another.

The problem is further exacerbated by the lack of enforcement mechanisms against States failing to ensure suitable reception facilities because the IMO "as a consultative organization ... has never been allowed to exercise enforcement powers against its members".[81] The restricted faculties of the IMO as a supervisory body is reflected in States failing to report about port reception facilities as prescribed in Article 11(d) of MARPOL. Approximately 50 percent of State Parties "have never responded to IMO requests for information".[82]

EU and ship wastes

To achieve a normative compatibility between international law instruments and their EU counterparts, one should ask about the relationship between international treaties, which the EU is a Party to, and the relationships between EU law and international treaties, which EU members are Parties to, but not the EU. These questions warrant their own research agenda and it is beyond the scope of this book to give a thorough answer to them. However, suffice it to say that the EU is an international organization with international personality. It has the capacity to conclude international agreements with other subjects of international law. As a subject of international law, the EU is bound by it.[83]

Legal status of MARPOL in the EU

The EU is a Party to the LOSC.[84] In this regard, and according to Article 216 of the Treaty on the Functioning of the European Union (TFEU), international

---

81 Tan, *Vessel-Source Marine Pollution: The Law and Politics of International Regulation*, 267.
82 Ibid., 271.
83 *C-286/90, Poulsen*, European Court Reports I-6019 (1992).
84 "The EU declared as a condition to join the LOSC that maritime transport, safety of shipping and the prevention of marine pollution contained inter alia in LOSC Parts II, III, V, VII and XII are considered to be areas of shared competences, but also subject to continuous development." Liu Nengye and Frank Maes, "The European Union and the International Maritime Organization: EU's External Influence on the Prevention of Vessel Source Pollution," *Journal of Maritime Law & Commerce* 41, no. 4 (2010): 581–94.

116 *Transboundary movements of wastes*

treaties to which the EU is a Party "are binding upon the institutions of the Union and on its Member States." Furthermore, these treaties "prevail over secondary sources of EU law".[85]

Regarding MARPOL, one should ask, what is the legal relevance of this treaty for the EU? Although the EU is not a Party to MARPOL, one could argue that since the EU is a Party of the LOSC, whose Part XII, i.e., the Protection and Preservation of the Marine Environment, incorporates MARPOL by "rules of reference," this Convention is relevant in the operationalization of the LOSC. In relation to the prevention and control of ship-source pollution, Part XII imposes on its Parties the obligation to observe and implement "generally accepted international rules and standards established through the competent international organization".[86]

However, from an EU law perspective, the LOSC is a mixed agreement where both the EU and their Member States are Parties to the same instrument. Furthermore, the EU has some exclusive competences and some shared competences in relation to the law of the sea. When the EU acceded the LOSC, it declared the following regarding Part XII:

> [w]ith regard to the provisions on maritime transport, safety of shipping and the prevention of marine pollution ... the Community has exclusive competence only to the extent that such provisions of the Convention or legal instruments adopted in implementation thereof affect common rules established by the Community. When Community rules exist but are not affected, in particular in cases of Community provisions establishing only minimum standards, the Member States have competence.[87]

In the *Intertanko* case,[88] the Court of Justice of the European Union was requested to assess the validity of certain articles of Directive 2005/35/EC on Ship-source Pollution and on the Introduction of Penalties for Infringements in light of the provisions of the LOSC and MARPOL. Considering that the EU is a Party to the LOSC, the Court of Justice recognized that the validity of "secondary Community legislation may be affected by the fact that it is incompatible with such rules of international law".[89] However, according to the Court of Justice of the European Union, the LOSC is not "sufficiently precise"[90] to assess the validity of Directive 2005/35/EC. In relation to MARPOL, the Court of

---

85 Alina Kaczorowska, *European Union Law*, 3rd edn (London: Routledge Taylor & Francis Group, 2013), 121–22. The author also provides an explanation of the supremacy of EU Law in Chapter 8.

86 *See* Article 211(2) of the LOSC.

87 <treaties.un.org/Pages/ViewDetailsIII.aspx?src=TREATY&mtdsg_no=XXI-6&chapter= 21&Temp=mtdsg3&clang=_en>, last accessed 17 March 2019.

88 CJEU, Case C-308/06, *Intertanko and Others* [2008], ECR I-4057.

89 Ibid., para 43.

90 Ibid., para 45. On the status of international treaties in EU law, *See* David Langlet and Said Mahmoudi, *EU Environmental Law and Policy* (Oxford: Oxford University Press, 2016), 128–29.

Justice argued that it could not assess the validity of Directive 2005/35/EC in the light of this treaty because: (a) the EU is not a Party to MARPOL;[91] (b) the EU has not assumed "the powers previously exercised by the Member States in the field to which MARPOL 73/78 applies"[92]; and (c) MARPOL is not a codification of customary law.[93] According to the Court of Justice, the EU is not bound by MARPOL even though all Member States are Parties to this instrument.[94] However, MARPOL is not inconsequential within EU law since it is binding on all Member States. In the *Intertanko* case, the Court of Justice argued that MARPOL:

> have consequences for the interpretation of, first, UNCLOS and, second, the provisions of secondary law which fall within the field of application of MARPOL 73/78. In view of the customary principle of good faith, which forms part of general international law.[95]

The EU's role as port State

Article 211(2) of the LOSC prescribe that regulations concerning the prevention of ship-source pollution "shall at least have the same effect as that of generally accepted international rules and standards". From the text of this provision, States are in principle allowed to adopt stricter regulations and enforce them on ships flying their flags. However, regulations of a third State may be applicable to ships voluntarily entering a port of that third State. Ports are located in internal waters, and this maritime zone is closely assimilated to land territory.[96] This means that States exercise territorial sovereignty and, consequently, have full legislative and enforcement jurisdiction.

Considering the territorial nature of internal waters, under customary law prior to the LOSC, Port States could legislate ship-source pollution for foreign vessels. For this reason, Port States can demand the compliance of ship-source pollution legislation as a condition to allow ships entering into ports. In this sense, the LOSC does not modify the legislative jurisdiction of Port States.

---

91 CJEU, Case C-308/06, *Intertanko and Others* [2008], ECR I-4057, para 47.

92 Ibid., para 48.

93 Ibid., paras 49–51.

94 "In this respect, a line of argument has been presented according to which the fact that all member states (but not the EU) have acceded to an international agreement results in a limitation of EU competences on the field covered by the agreement. This reasoning is based on Article 351(1) TFEU, whose object and purpose it is to prevent EU law, in accordance with the maxim *pacta sunt servanda*, from undermining the rights and obligations of the member states established by international treaties." Alexander Proelss, "The European Court of Justice and Its Role in (Re-)Defining EU Member States' Jurisdiction over Ships," in *Jurisdiction over Ships: Post-UNCLOS Developments in the Law of the Sea*, ed. Henrik Ringbom, Publications on Ocean Development (Leiden: Brill Nijhoff, 2015), 431–32.

95 CJEU, Case C-308/06, *Intertanko and Others* [2008], ECR I-4057, para 52.

96 *See* Article 2(1) of the LOSC.

118 *Transboundary movements of wastes*

Indeed, Articles 25(2) and 211(3) confirm the right of Port States to prescribe conditions to access their ports and their offshore terminals. In case of ship-source pollution, such conditions must be communicated to the IMO and Port States shall give due publicity of such requirements.

Overall, in the absence of a customary law right of access to ports,[97] it is generally accepted that States can impose certain obligations on ships, e.g., the master, the ship operator, voluntarily entering their ports.[98] Controversies over port State jurisdiction pertain not to the existence of such ample jurisdictional powers, but rather to their limits according to public international law. The jurisdictional powers and limits of port State jurisdiction in general and the EU in particular have been discussed elsewhere.[99] Suffice it to note here that the EU is increasingly making use of their jurisdictional powers as Port States to impose obligations on ship operators. Such obligations not only complement international obligations, but also establish standards that compete with their international counterparts. Limits of Port States jurisdiction have been analyzed on a case by case basis and in the light of specific treaties and general principles of international law, including good faith, proportionality, reasonableness, and nondiscrimination.[100]

Concluding remarks

The increased interest in the regulation of ship-source pollution has gradually reduced the possibility of disposing of ship wastes in the marine environment. Such developments have a twofold consequence. First, States have increasingly agreed on strict standards related to the design, construction, and equipment of ships to manage harmful substances at sea. Additionally, operational discharges at sea are restricted and even prohibited in some cases. However, not every ship waste can be managed on board vessels, so such wastes must be discharged on land. In addition, the growth of the merchant fleet entails further challenges for the management of wastes on land. If the transformation of one source of pollution into another is to be avoided, there needs to be greater integration of the management of wastes at sea and on land.

---

97 Louise de La Fayette, "Access to Ports in International Law," *The International Journal of Marine and Coastal Law* 11, no. 1 (1996). Bevan Marten, *Port State Jurisdiction and the Regulation of International Merchant Shipping*, Hamburg Studies on Maritime Affairs (Switzerland: Springer, 2014), 31–35. Robin Churchill, "Coastal Waters," in *The IMLI Manual on International Maritime Law: Volume I: The Law of the Sea*, ed. David Attard, Malgosia Fitzmaurice, and Norman Martínez Gutiérrez (Oxford: Oxford University Press, 2014), 10–12.

98 *See*, for instance, Articles 25(2) and 211(3) of the LOSC.

99 Henrik Ringbom, *The EU Maritime Safety Policy and International Law* (Leiden: Martinus Nijhoff Publishers, 2008), Chapter 5. Frank, *The European Community and Marine Environmental Protection in the International Law of the Sea: Implementing Global Obligations at the Regional Level*, 201–5. Iliana Christodoulou-Varotsi, *Maritime Safety Law and Policies of the European Union and the United States of America: Antagonism or Synergy?* (Berlin: Springer, 2009), Part I.

100 Marten, *Port State Jurisdiction and the Regulation of International Merchant Shipping*.

Part III
The ESM of wastes

6 The sea/land interface waste management dilemma

Genesis of the controversy at the international level

In the aftermath of the *Probo Koala* and *Probo Emu* incidents, uncertainties arose regarding the nature of wastes generated as a result of blending activities on board vessels. This section provides an overview of these incidents. On the morning of 20 August 2006, foul-smelling fumes polluted the air of Abidjan in the Ivory Coast; and this odor proved fatal. In urban areas of Abidjan, highly toxic combinations of caustic soda and petrochemical residues were dumped.[1] As a result, 15 people died while thousands experienced respiratory and skin related diseases.[2] In relation to the environment, this mixture caused air, land, and water pollution. Due to the presence of organochlorines (i.e., an organic pollutant that accumulates in the food chain and contaminates drinking water), livestock, fish, and crops were destroyed,[3] affecting the livelihood of hundreds of people.

In the wake of this disaster it was crucial to trace the source of the residues. The initial investigation revealed that the residues came from the *Probo Koala*. The vessel was registered in Panama, operated by a Greek company, and chartered by Trafigura Beheer BV. The charterer has its headquarters in London. Trafigura is a branch of a multinational company legally based in the Netherlands. In the months preceding the unsafe disposal of wastes in Abidjan, the *Probo Koala* was located on the high seas near to Gibraltar.[4] On board the vessel, coker naphtha

---

1 United Nations General Assembly, "Report of the Special Rapporteur on the Adverse Effects of the Movement and Dumping of Toxic and Dangerous Products and Wastes on the Enjoyment of Human Rights, Okechukwu Ibeanu, A/Hrc/12/26/Add.2," in *Human Rights Council, Twelfth session – Agenda Item 3* (2009). A map showing the dumping sites is provided in Greenpeace and Amnesty International, "The Toxic Truth about a Company Called Trafigura, a Ship Called the Probo Koala and the Dumping of Toxic Waste in Côte D'ivoire," (2012). Stephan Berndsen, "Between Error and Evil: The Dynamics of Deadly Governmental Accidents" (Amsterdam: Vrije Universiteit Amsterdam, 2015).

2 Greenpeace and Amnesty International, "The Toxic Truth about a Company Called Trafigura, a Ship Called the Probo Koala and the Dumping of Toxic Waste in Côte D'ivoire," 2–3.

3 Ibid., 52.

4 Berndsen, "Between Error and Evil: The Dynamics of Deadly Governmental Accidents," 141. *Cf.* Trafigura has also presented a detailed account of the facts of this case <https://www.trafigura.com/resource-centre/probo-koala/>, last accessed 17 March 2019.

122   *The ESM of wastes*

(i.e., an unrefined gasoline product containing high levels of sulfur and nitrogen) was mixed with caustic soda to refine it. This process, in general, is known as blending and the particular refining procedure carried out on board the *Probo Koala* is known as caustic washing. As a result of this process, around 554 m^3 of wastes were generated.[5] The refined gasoline was not delivered in Abidjan; only the residues of the cargo were discharged in this port. How did these residues end up in a city located in Africa where the *Probo Koala* was not even trading? The *Probo Koala* arrived at the Ivory Coast after an excruciating voyage around several jurisdictions, including the Netherlands, Estonia, and Nigeria where the vessel unsuccessfully tried to deliver its cargo residues at port reception facilities.

On 2 July 2006, the vessel arrived in Amsterdam where the *Probo Koala* made arrangements with the waste disposal company Amsterdam Port Services (APS) to dispose of "slops," i.e., residues generated after washing the cargo holds of ships, including, for instance, a mixture of oil, water and sediments. However, the residues generated were not just those that arise from tank washings. Around 250 m^3 of slops[6] were discharged, but the foul-smelling fumes coming from the slops caused alarm around the port. Based on samples taken from the slops, APS requested Afvalstoffen Terminal Moerdijk (ATM), a chemical-waste disposal company, to treat the slops.[7] The disposal was possible but at a higher price per m^3 than originally offered.[8] Trafigura declined the new offer.[9] In the days that followed, discussions were had about the legal possibility of pumping back the slops. These discussions involved several public authorities, including: (a) the port State Control of the Inspection for Transport, Public Works and Water Management; (b) the Environmental and Construction Supervisory Agency; and (c) the Ministry of Housing, Spatial Planning and the Environment.[10] The port State Control analyzed this particular matter according to Annex I of MARPOL that deals with the prevention of oil pollution. Since operational discharges of oil or oil mixtures from the cargo area of tankers into the sea are allowed in restricted circumstances,[11] States have the obligation to provide adequate reception facilities to receive cargo residues.[12] However, MARPOL does not stipulate the specific location where the residues shall be discharged, e.g., the facility where

---

5 Berndsen, "Between Error and Evil: The Dynamics of Deadly Governmental Accidents," 141.

6 Ibid.

7 Ibid.

8 Ibid., APS offered to dispose of the slops for €20 per m^3 and the offer was later raised to €1,000 per m^3.

9 According to an official declaration by Trafigura, "APS revised its charges on 3rd July 2006. No credible explanation was ever given. APS's claim about the increased Chemical Oxygen Demand of the slops was irrelevant, and besides it was not substantiated by any test results and was therefore considered completely unreasonable," <https://www.trafigura.com/media/3954/trafigura-and-the-probo-koala.pdf>, last accessed 18 March 2019.

10 Berndsen, "Between Error and Evil: The Dynamics of Deadly Governmental Accidents," 141–43.

11 *See* Regulation 34 of Annex I of MARPOL.

12 Ibid., Regulation 38.

Sea/land interface waste management dilemma   123

the cargo is unloaded. Article 10 of Directive 2000/59/EC on Port Reception Facilities establishes that cargo residues be "delivered to a port reception facility in accordance with the provisions of MARPOL 73/78." It follows that as long as the vessel has enough holding capacity to retain the residues on board, the master is able to choose between different reception facilities.[13] Based on this line of thought, the Port Authority found no legal basis to deny pumping back the slops of the *Probo Koala*.

However, at that point in time, the presence of caustic soda was overlooked.[14] Caustic soda falls into Annex II of MARPOL. This Annex is concerned with the prevention of pollution by noxious liquid substances in bulk. There are several categories of residues arising from carrying noxious liquid in bulk, including cargo residues and residues arising from tank cleaning or ballasting.[15] Regulations 6 and 7 of MARPOL, Annex II, establish at which point the tanks should be washed. If washing is required, the residues must be discharged at the port reception facility where the unloading of the cargo took place. From the chronology of events leading to the discharge of residues in Abidjan, there was no unloading port of the cargo carried on board the *Probo Koala*. While blending operations were carried out on board the *Probo Koala*, there were several ship-to-ship cargo transfer operations taking place between April and June 2006.[16]

The Ministry of Housing, Spatial Planning and the Environment analyzed the case in light of the Dutch Environmental Management Act. According to this piece of legislation, only authorized persons can discard industrial wastes,[17] and APS did not have the required license. The Environmental and Construction Supervisory Agency focused on whether or not APS had "accepted" the residues or commenced their disposal. There was no evidence suggesting that APS accepted the slops. Finally, the public authorities gave permission to reload the residues into the *Probo Koala*. On 19 August 2006, the voyage of the *Probo Kola* was completed when it berthed in Abidjan. With the assistance of Trafigura's subsidiary and a shipping agent, arrangements were made with a local waste

---

13 If tankers are carrying substances, which through their physical properties inhibit effective product/water separation, and monitoring, including asphalt and high-density oils, the residues must be discharged at the unloading port. This is an exception established in Annex I of MARPOL regarding the freedom to choose among different port reception facilities. *See* Regulations 2.4, 38 of Annex I of MARPOL and numerals 7 and 62 of the Unified Interpretations of Annex I of MARPOL.

14 When public authorities in the Netherlands took the decision to pump back the slops, the results of the samples taken from the slops were not ready. Berndsen, "Between Error and Evil: The Dynamics of Deadly Governmental Accidents," 142.

15 *See* Regulations 1.12, 1.13, and 13 of Annex II of MARPOL.

16 Greenpeace and Amnesty International, "The Toxic Truth about a Company Called Trafigura, a Ship Called the Probo Koala and the Dumping of Toxic Waste in Côte D'ivoire," 30.

17 *See* Section 10.37 of the Environmental Management Act. An English translation can be found at:<http://www.asser.nl/upload/eel-webroot/www/documents/national/netherlands/EMA052004.pdf>, last accessed 18 March 2019.

124   *The ESM of wastes*

disposal company called "Tommy".[18] The company loaded the residues in trucks and later that night dumped the residues around the city.[19]

In the aftermath of the *Probo Koala* affair, the media fueled an international public outcry by categorizing the incident as an illegal transport of *wastes* from Europe to Africa.[20] The discussion was no longer focused on the legal nature of the activities carried on board the *Probo Koala* or on the obligation for States to provide adequate reception facilities to receive ship wastes. In the eyes of the media, the *Probo Koala* was an example of how Africa had been used, yet again, as a cheap option for industrialized countries to dispose of their unwanted hazardous wastes. Civil society organizations, including Greenpeace,[21] claimed that the *Probo Koala* affair should be analyzed in light of the Basel Convention and Regulation 1013/2006/EC on Shipments of Wastes.

The legacy of the *Probo Koala* was loss of life, personal injury, damage to property, environmental damage, and pure economic loss.[22] Court cases were instituted in the Ivory Coast, the United Kingdom and the Netherlands. In the Ivory Coast, the representative of the company Tommy and the shipping agent were criminally prosecuted and sentenced in 2008,[23] while civil and criminal cases

18 "The company had made an offer of \$30 per m³ for waste falling under the MARPOL Convention and \$35 per m³ for chemical slops" United Nations General Assembly, "Report of the Special Rapporteur on the Adverse Effects of the Movement and Dumping of Toxic and Dangerous Products and Wastes on the Enjoyment of Human Rights, Okechukwu Ibeanu, A/Hrc/12/26/Add.2," 8.

19 Ibid.

20 Media headlines at the time of the incident attracted international attention on the *Probo Koala* affair. *See,* for instance, "Ivory Coast 'Toxic Ship' Inquiry," *BBC News* (September 2006); Quist-Arcton Ofeibea, "Ivory Coast Tragedy Exposes Toxic Flow to Poor," *NPR.org* (October 2006). Helena Spongeberg, "EU Prepares Environmental Crime Law after Africa Tragedy," *EU-observer* (October 2006). The District Court of Amsterdam in the case LJN: BN2149, Rechtbank Amsterdam, 13/846003-06 (PROMIS) brought against Trafigura discussed the idea of "trial by media." Berndsen translated certain fragments of the judgment. *See* Berndsen, "Between Error and Evil: The Dynamics of Deadly Governmental Accidents," 156.

21 Greenpeace became an active participant in the *Probo Koala* affair soon after the unsafe disposal took place. One of the early "demands" of Greenpeace was to ensure "that the ship is held until a full criminal investigation is carried out and those responsible for the illegal waste export." Greenpeace, "Toxic Death Ship Blocked," *Greenpeace International* (2006).

22 In the case brought against Trafigura in Amsterdam, LJN: BN2149, Rechtbank Amsterdam, 13/846003-06 (PROMIS), the District Court of Amsterdam declared that due to the composition of the wastes they were indeed dangerous to life and health, but "[w]hether that risk also materialized is irrelevant." Berndsen, "Between Error and Evil: The Dynamics of Deadly Governmental Accidents," 155. Here are some expert reports of the nature of the wastes carried on board the Probo Koala. Treharne & Davies Ltd. Minton, "The Minton Report: Caustic Tank Washing, Abidjan, Ivory Coast," (2006). Based on preliminary data regarding the *Probo Koala,* Trafigura commissioned this report currently known as the Minton Report. The Minton report was initially leaked by the organization Wikileaks and was later made publicly available. *See also* Dutch Forensic Institute, "Expert Report: Odour Nuisance Incident APS Amsterdam," (Ministry of Justice, 2007).

23 Jonathan Verschuuren, "Overcoming the Limitations of Environmental Law in a Globalised World," in *Handbook of Globalisation and Environmental Policy: National Government Interventions in a Global Arena,* ed. Frank Wijen et al. (Cheltenham: Edward Elgar Publishing, 2010), 634–36.

Sea/land interface waste management dilemma 125

against Trafigura's subsidiary in Abidjan were settled. In the United Kingdom, 30,000 victims logged a class action that was settled in 2009. Criminal and tort proceedings were instituted in the Netherlands against Trafigura, APS, and the master of the *Probo Koala*. In 2011, the Court of Appeal upheld a guilty verdict against Trafigura for breaching the Waste Shipment Regulation and imposed a fine of €1,000,000. The Court of Appeal considered that the *Probo Koala* affair fell within the scope of the Basel Convention and the Waste Shipment Regulation because the wastes were discharged to port reception facilities and later pumped back on board.[24] This action essentially triggered a transboundary movement of wastes as defined in these instruments. Whether the *Probo Koala* affair falls within the scope of the Basel Convention and the Waste Shipment Regulation could also be analyzed from two other perspectives. First, the nature of coker naphtha and whether it can be categorized as a hazardous waste under the Basel Convention. Second, whether blending operations on board vessels are "abnormal" and excluded from MARPOL.

The second incident involved the OBO carrier *Probo Emu*. In this case, Trafigura also performed blending operations on board the vessel. The ship called at the port of Sløvåg on the west coast of Norway and declared the presence of slops on board that required to be discharged into reception facilities.[25] In May 2007, an explosion occurred causing the release of harmful substances and further property damage, personal injury, economic loss, and environmental damage.

These incidents ignited an ongoing legal conflict between two regimes, i.e., MARPOL on the one hand, and the Basel Convention on the other hand. The following sections set out the initial controversy regarding blending operations on board vessels and the current controversy regarding the management of ship wastes while on board and after the discharge to port reception facilities.

Blending operations on board ships: the initial controversy

Blending operations should be distinguished from industrial processes carried out on board vessels. The former consists of mixing two substances into one, while the latter involves deliberate chemical reactions to create a new product with different properties than those of the substances originally processed. Blending operations of fuel at sea became a common practice since the growth in demand for bio-fuel blends. There were several reasons for this increase in demand, which included meeting customers' needs regarding the characteristic of a product and the lowering of costs.[26] So, the initial discussion between

24 Berndsen, "Between Error and Evil: The Dynamics of Deadly Governmental Accidents," 158–59.
25 Trygve Skjold et al., "Accident Investigation Following the Vest Tank Explosion at Sløvåg: Revision 03 – English Version," (Bergen: CMR Gexcon, 2008).
26 International Maritime Organization (IMO), "Application of the Requirements for the Carriage of Bio-Fuels and Bio-Fuel Blends: Guidelines for Blending on Board Submitted by Intertanko (Blg 13/4/2)," in *Sub-Committee on Bulk Liquids and Gases: Thirteenth Session – Agenda Item 4* (9 January 2009).

126   *The ESM of wastes*

MARPOL and the Basel Convention centered on whether blending operations and the management of their residues fall within the exclusion contained in Article 1(4) of the Basel Convention.

Due to the *Probo Koala* affair, the Secretariat of the Basel Convention requested the IMO to identify and address possible gaps between MARPOL and the Basel Convention.[27] In this particular case, coker naphtha was blended with caustic soda on board the vessel, and the IMO informed the Secretariat of the Basel Convention that the cargo of gasoline falls under Annex I of MARPOL while the cargo of caustic soda falls under Annex II of this Convention.[28] Furthermore, when the *Probo Koala* and the *Probo Emu* incidents took place, blending operations on board vessels were neither regulated nor illegal.[29]

In this scenario, one could think that regulating blending operations on board vessels at sea and in ports would close the "gap" between MARPOL and the Basel Convention and avoid further conflicts between these regimes. The regulation of blending operations on board vessels was an IMO undertaking. In the thirteenth session of the Sub-Committee on Liquids and Gases, provisional guidelines were developed to ensure the safety of blending operations on board ships during the sea voyage.[30] In the eighty-ninth session of the Maritime Safety Committee held in May 2011, an amendment to the SOLAS Convention, Chapter VI: Carriage of Cargoes was proposed to prohibit blending operations on board ships during the sea voyage.[31] No proposal has been made in respect of blending operations on board vessels in port. Nonetheless, ports are situated in internal waters where the coastal State enjoys full territorial sovereignty and, thus, national legislation would apply in this respect.

Moreover, in the eighty-ninth session of the Maritime Safety Committee, a proposal to prohibit not only blending operations, but also "production processes on board ships that result in new products"[32] was required by the Netherlands. This proposal was considered in the sixteenth session of the Sub-Committee on Liquids and Gases, where "clarification with respect of Offshore Support

---

27 United Nations (UNEP), "Cooperation between the Basel Convention and the International Maritime Organization (UNEP/CHW.8/16*, Decision VIII/9)," in *Report of the Conference of the Parties to the Basel Convention on the Control of Transboundary Movements of Hazardous Wastes and their Disposal on Its Eighth Meeting – Agenda Item 12* (Nairobi, 5 January 2007), 35.

28 "Implementation of the Decision VIII/9 on Cooperation between the Basel Convention and the International Maritime Organization: Comments Received from the International Maritime Organization (UNEP/Sbc/Bureau/8/1/INF/1)."

29 Verschuuren and Kuchta, "Victims of Environmental Pollution in the Slipstream of Globalization," 157.

30 International Maritime Organization (IMO), "Report to the Maritime Safety Committee and the Marine Environment Protection Committee (Blg 13/18)," in *Sub-Committee on Bulk Liquids and Gases. Thirteenth Session – Agenda Item 18* (6 March 2009), 10–13.

31 "Prohibition of the Blending of Bulk Liquid Cargoes during the Sea Voyage (MSC 89/25)," in *Report of the Maritime Safety Committee on Its Eighty-Ninth Session – Agenda Item 25* (27 May 2011), 56.

32 International Maritime Organization (IMO), "Prohibition of the Blending of Bulk Liquid Cargoes during the Sea Voyage (MSC 89/25)."

Vessels" was also taken into account to draft the amendment.[33] Finally, the ninetieth session of the Maritime Safety Committee held in May 2012 adopted the SOLAS regulation VI/5.2 to prohibit blending operations of bulk liquid cargoes during the sea voyage and production processes on board ships.[34] In conclusion, blending operations and industrial processes became a loophole in relation to the management of harmful substances generated at sea in the face of a scandal.

The management of ship wastes on land: the current controversy

The *Probo Koala* and *Probo Emu* revealed a gap between the law of the sea and the law of the land concerning the management of ship wastes after they are discharged to port reception facilities. Currently, there is a problem of regarding both the integration of ship wastes into national waste management systems and the *traceability* of ship wastes on land, particularly in relation to residues subject to MARPOL, Annex II, noxious liquid bulk cargoes.

Doubts over the Basel Convention and MARPOL remain because of the potential application of the Basel Convention to ship wastes, especially after they are discharged in port reception facilities. The following subsections analyze the relation between these two regimes. Regarding the management of ship wastes while on board a vessel, the extent of the exclusion contained in Article 1(4) of the Basel Convention is analyzed. Concerning the interface between sea and land, the application of the ESM principle is also evaluated as an alternative to assess the obligations of States regarding the management of ship wastes on land.

The exclusion of ship wastes from the transboundary movements of wastes regime

In the midst of the controversy between the Basel Convention and MARPOL lies Article 1(4) of the Basel Convention, which excludes from its scope of application:

> [w]astes which derive from the normal operations of a ship, the discharge of which is covered by another international instrument, are excluded from the scope of this Convention.

---

33 "Report to the Maritime Safety Committee and the Marine Environment Protection Committee: Outcomes of MSC 89 and MEPC 62 (Blg 16/16)," in *Sub-Committee on Bulk Liquids and Gases. Sixteenth Session – Agenda Item 16* (20 February 2012), 9.

34 "Regulation 5.2 – Prohibition of Blending of Bulk Liquid Cargoes During the Sea Voyage (MSC 90/28)," in *Report of the Maritime Safety Committee on Its Ninetieth Session – Agenda Item 28* (31 May 2012), 11–12. *See also* "Prohibition of Production Processes during the Sea Voyage – Exemption for Offshore Service Activities: Submitted by Liberia, the United States, Vanuatu, IADC, IMCA and OCIMF (MSC 90/14/2)," in *Maritime Safety Committe Ninetieth Session – Agenda Item 14* (13 March 2012).

128 *The ESM of wastes*

Before the *Probo Koala* and *Probo Emu* incidents gained notoriety, this exclusion raised no serious doubts about its extent and meaning. It was generally understood that it meant MARPOL. Regarding the phrase "normal operations," it can be argued that the categorization of ships' operations as "normal" or "abnormal" does not have any real significance because its introduction was exclusively intended to identify MARPOL as the governing instrument with respect to operations that formed an integral part of a ship's functions. According to the *travaux préparatoires* of the Basel Convention, this exclusion was drafted to preserve the scope of MARPOL's application.[35] In fact, Article 1(4) of the Basel Convention was incorporated into the Convention by request of the IMO.[36] The text of the exclusion as proposed by the IMO explains the use of terminology that is extraneous to the Basel Convention. Particularly, the term *discharge* is of fundamental importance within MARPOL, but it is incidental and not defined under the Basel Convention. A similar exclusion is also found in Article 1(4)(2) of the London Dumping Convention 1972 as amended by its 1996 Protocol.

On the other hand, it can also be argued that operations of ships can in fact be categorized as "normal" or "abnormal" in relation to a particular ship type and its functions. In this regard, Mukherjee explains that:

> what may be a normal operation for a fishing vessel may not be a normal operation for a container ship. Besides, there is an established rule that an exclusion or exception clause in any legal instrument must be given a narrow and strict construction. In other words, if an operation was not considered to be "normal" in respect of a certain ship, the exclusion would not be available to that ship.[37]

In this book, the author considers that although the operations of ships could be categorized as "normal or abnormal" or even not covered by MARPOL, a closer examination of the obligations of the Basel Convention reveals that this regime is unsuitable to effectively deal with operations of ships in general. For instance, while the Basel Convention establishes that States shall take measures to reduce transboundary movements of wastes to a minimum, this obligation is not applicable to ships. In fact, vessels operate at sea and wastes are continuously

---

35 Conference of Plenipotentiaries on the Global Convention on the Control of Transboundary Movements of Wastes, "Final Report of the Ad Hoc Working Group of Legal and Technical Experts with a Mandate to Prepare a Global Convention on the Control of Transboundary Movements of Hazardous Wastes. UNEP/Ig.80/4," (Basel: UNEP, 1989), para 15.

36 "[t]he text of article 1, paragraph 4 was drafted by a representative of the IMO Secretariat and submitted at a late stage of the negotiations of the Basel Convention." Secretariat of the Basel Convention, "The Application of the Basel Convention to Hazardous Wastes and Other Wastes Generated on Board Ships," 20.

37 Personal interview with Professor Proshanto K. Mukherjee, visiting professor at Dalian Maritime University (China), Chung Ang University (Seoul, S. Korea) and National University of Juridical Sciences (Kolkata, India). (Gothenburg, Sweden, 12 February 2014).

generated on board ships while crossing through national boundaries. Thus, transboundary movements of wastes generated at sea is the rule, not the exception.[38] In this sense, MARPOL has been successful in providing a scheme to reduce and control operational and accidental discharges of "wastes" generated during ships' operations, but cannot demand the minimization of transboundary movements because it will hamper trading by sea.

Another obligation of the Basel Convention that is mutually exclusive in terms of MARPOL relates to the principle of proximity. According to the Basel Convention, wastes should be disposed as close as possible to the source of generation. Evidently, ships *constantly* generate wastes during their operation. Thus, it is not feasible to precisely determine their place of generation and in which jurisdiction those wastes should be disposed of. The scenario is further complicated if wastes are generated on the high seas. In this sense, MARPOL's success depends heavily on the State Parties' provision of adequate reception facilities to receive "wastes" from vessels calling at their ports.

Article 4(1) of the Basel Convention prescribes the right of States to prohibit the importation of hazardous wastes to be disposed of into their territories. This is the result of States' sovereignty regarding the use of their territory and the risks they are willing to assume. This sovereign right has been waived in relation to ship wastes because States have the obligation to prevent and control marine pollution. Therefore, in an exercise of sovereignty, States have agreed to receive into their jurisdictions ship wastes and consequently be responsible for their subsequent management. As further analyzed in Chapter 8, the obligation to provide port reception facilities also includes the obligation to manage wastes on land and to avoid the transformation of one source of pollution into another one.[39]

Finally, the categorization regarding "normal or abnormal" operations should not be significant because it could also disrupt the legal certainty regarding the regime applicable to ships, i.e., MARPOL, and the suitable forum to deal with ship-related matters, i.e., IMO. In the following subsections, the Secretariat of the Basel Convention's interpretations of the exclusion contained in Article 1(4) of the Basel regime are examined alongside the comments provided by State Parties and civil society organizations.

First legal analysis provided by the Secretariat of the Basel Convention (April 2011)

After the *Probo Koala* incident, the Open-ended Working Group (OEWG) of the Basel Convention, in its seventh session, required the Secretariat of the Basel Convention to provide a legal analysis regarding the application of the Basel Convention to wastes generated on board ships.[40] The Secretariat of the Basel Convention

---

38 de La Fayette, "The Sound Management of Wastes Generated at Sea: MARPOL, Not Basel," 212.

39 *See* Article 195 of the LOSC.

40 Secretariat of the Basel Convention, "Cooperation between the Basel Convention and the International Maritime Organization (OEWG-VII/13)," in *Report of the Open-ended Working Group*

130 *The ESM of wastes*

supported the view that the phrase "normal operations" refers exclusively to MARPOL being irrelevant to differentiate between "normal" or "abnormal" operations within or outside a ship.[41] So, the exclusion, according to this point of view, prevents the application of the Basel Convention to ship wastes as long as they are subject to MARPOL. Following this argument, it is natural to conclude that all wastes generated on board ships, which MARPOL does not cover, will be subject to the Basel Convention. However, the Secretariat of the Basel Convention has also recognized that the generation of wastes on board vessels is inherent to ships' operations and it is "an ongoing activity ... within and outside the national jurisdiction of states. The generation of such wastes ... is a transboundary process".[42] For this reason, it is not feasible to apply obligations such as the PIC procedure established in the Basel Convention to wastes generated on board ships.[43]

Furthermore, the Secretariat of the Basel Convention argues that the cycle of wastes as addressed in the Basel Convention has the following pillars: (a) the reduction of waste generation; (b) the minimization of transboundary movements; and (c) the ESM of such wastes. Thus, although the requirements for transboundary movements cannot be applied to wastes generated on board ships, the ESM[44] applies to wastes once they are discharged from the ship. The accuracy of this statement is examined below.

The opinions expressed by the Basel Secretariat are not legally binding on the Parties who may or may not accept this analysis. The European Union and its Member States[45] did not agree that the phrase "normal operations" lacks significance and found difficulties in understanding the Secretariat's suggestion regarding MARPOL as an instrument that has to support the Basel Convention. The latter opinion of the Secretariat of the Basel Convention seems to be based on the idea advanced by Kummer, who sees the Basel Convention as a global attempt to regulate waste cycles without focusing on a particular environment, i.e., air, sea or land.[46] So, other rules, including MARPOL, "have a useful and important role in complementing and enhancing the Basel Convention".[47] Nonetheless, this conclusion fails to acknowledge that the Basel Convention is mainly focused on transboundary movements of wastes.

---

of the Basel Convention on the Control of Transboundary Movements of Hazardous Wastes and their Disposal. Seventh Session. (UNEP/CHW/OEWG/7/21) (Geneva, 2010), 37.

41 Secretariat of the Basel Convention, "The Application of the Basel Convention to Hazardous Wastes and Other Wastes Generated on Board Ships," 18–21.

42 Ibid., 22.

43 Ibid., 24.

44 Ibid., 24–25.

45 European Union, "Submission of the EU and Its 27 Member States on the First Legal Analysis Regarding the Application of the Basel Convention to Hazardous Wastes and Other Wastes Generated on Board Ships," (2011). The document is available at: <http://archive.basel.int/legalmatters/coop-IMO/oewgVII13-comments/index.html>, last accessed 19 March 2019.

46 Kummer, *International Management of Hazardous Wastes: The Basel Convention and Related Legal Rules*, 28–29.

47 Ibid., 29.

Sea/land interface waste management dilemma 131

Second legal analysis provided by the Secretariat of the Basel Convention (October 2011)

A revised document that superseded[48] the legal analysis referred to above was prepared by the Secretariat of the Basel Convention. The revised document creates complex and confusing scenarios that reveal the difficulties in applying principles of the Basel regime that are extraneous to MARPOL. In particular, regarding the phrase "normal operations," it is explained that wastes generated due to industrial processes carried on board vessels are neither unavoidable nor inherent to a ship's operation. Consequently, those activities should be characterized as "abnormal operations" of ships.[49] In this sense, the phrase "normal operations" is significant and it is defined as:

> those operations that are in conformity with Chapter IX of the SOLAS Convention (Management of safe operation of ships) which mandates that ships shall comply with ... auditing and certification by the flag state of a ship and of its managing company.[50]

The SOLAS Convention governs the construction, equipment, and operation of vessels to ensure safety of life at sea. Although it is undeniable that the safe operation of ships minimizes the chances of accidents and therefore pollution occurring, the main concern of the SOLAS Convention is not the prevention of pollution from ships. Thus, the definition provided is inaccurate and it is difficult to envisage how an instrument that does not deal directly with transboundary movements of wastes or marine pollution can elucidate the conflict between MARPOL and the Basel Convention.

The Secretariat of the Basel Convention also suggests that ship operations that are not categorized as "normal" shall be subject to the Basel Convention. In this sense, the obligations related to transboundary movements will apply to wastes from abnormal operations of ships, but it is recognized that practical difficulties may prevent the application of such obligations, e.g., PIC procedure. It is notable that the Secretariat of the Basel Convention does not propose any solutions to overcome these "practical difficulties."

Some Parties have also submitted their comments regarding this document. Canada expressed its concerns relating to the categorization of normal and abnormal operations of ships and the difficulties in applying the PIC procedure established in the Basel Convention to wastes generated at sea. In this regard,

---

48 Secretariat of the Basel Convention, "Revised Legal Analysis on the Application of the Basel Convention to Hazardous Wastes and Other Wastes Generated on Board a Ship (UNEP/CHW.10/INF/16)," in *Conference of the Parties to the Basel Convention on the Control of Transboundary Movements of Hazardous Wastes and their Disposal. Tenth Meeting – Item 3 (c) (vi)* (Cartagena, 7 October 2011).

49 Ibid., 7. Nonetheless, not all industrial processes are abnormal because Floating Production and Storage and Offloading are authorized to carry industrial processes on board.

50 Ibid.

132 *The ESM of wastes*

Canada suggests that any gaps should be dealt with through MARPOL due to "its central role in regulating ships".[51] The European Union and its Member States also raised concerns because the analysis scrutinizes the application of the Basel Convention to wastes generated on board ships without specifically clarifying the meaning and extent of the exclusion of "normal operations" of ships from the scope of this instrument.[52]

Third legal analysis provided by the Secretariat of the Basel Convention (April 2012)

The revised legal analysis of October 2011 was put into consideration of the COP to the Basel Convention at its Tenth Meeting, which requested another analysis on the subject by Decision BC-10/16.[53] As a result of this decision, the Secretariat of the Basel Convention prepared a reviewed legal analysis in April 2012.

According to the Secretariat, while the Basel Convention defines wastes, it does not confine the application of the Convention to specific generation processes or by identifying waste generators.[54] For this reason, the Secretariat of the Basel Secretariat considers that it is immaterial to distinguish "from 'normal' or 'abnormal' operations, whether on board or off board of ships".[55] The exclusion from the scope of the Basel Convention of wastes derived from the normal operations of ships, whose discharge is covered by another instrument, seems to be concerned with identifying the regime dealing with waste generated on board vessels independently of extraneous characterizations of normality. Thus, this exclusion should be read as "MARPOL wastes".[56]

---

51 Waste Reduction and Management Division Environment Canada, "Comments to the Revised Legal Analysis on the Application of the Basel Convention to Hazardous Wastes and Other Wastes Generated on Board a Ship (K1A 0H3)," (2012). Available at: <archive.basel.int/legal matters/coop-IMO/cop10-comments/canada.pdf>, last accessed 19 March 2019.

52 European Union, "Submission of the EU and Its Member States on the Legal Analysis of the Application of the Basel Convention to Hazardous Wastes and Other Wastes Generated on Board Ships (Document UNEP/CHW.10/INF/16)."

53 United Nations (UNEP), "Report of the Conference of the Parties to the Basel Convention on the Control of Transboundary Movements of Hazardous Wastes and their Disposal on Its Tenth Meeting," in *Conference of the Parties to the Basel Convention on the Control of Transboundary Movements of Hazardous Wastes and their Disposal. Tenth Meeting (UNEP/CHW.10/28)* (Cartagena, 2011), 51–52.

54 Secretariat of the Basel Convention, "Third Legal Analysis of the Application of the Basel Convention to Hazardous Wastes and Other Wastes Generated on Board Ships," para 22.

55 Ibid.

56 *Note* that "[w]hereas a specific reference to MARPOL was not included in Article 1, paragraph 4 of the Basel Convention, resorting to the term 'normal' was a way to clarify that it is the wastes falling within the scope of MARPOL that were targeted by the exclusion provision," Ibid., paras 23 and 25, p. 15. *See also* that "[t]his exclusion, proposed by IMO, is understood to exclude wastes generated at sea because they are covered by MARPOL. That was the distinction, not any esoteric definition of 'normality', which must be interpreted in context." de La Fayette, "The Sound Management of Wastes Generated at Sea: MARPOL, Not Basel," 209.

Sea/land interface waste management dilemma 133

This third legal analysis and its predecessors have received much criticism. Regarding the meaning of wastes derived from normal operations, the Center for International Environmental Law (CIEL) agrees that the international agreement in question is MARPOL and its legal analysis revolves around the full applicability of the Basel Convention to non-MARPOL wastes. Additionally, CIEL considers that "the assertion in the *Revised Legal Analysis* that MARPOL does not distinguish between 'normal' and 'abnormal' wastes misses a key point of MARPOL's *travaux*, which show that its scope was intended to address, inter alia, the normal operations of a ship".[57] In respect of this statement, it is noteworthy that both the Basel Convention and MARPOL are concerned with certain wastes or harmful substances. The juridical treatment of these substances is not dependent on their process of generation that could be categorized as normal or abnormal.

Although the *travaux preparatoires* of MARPOL do not define normal operations, according to CIEL, during the negotiations of this instrument, certain substances, such as oil, sewage, garbage, and noxious substances carried in bulk and in packaged form, were addressed and thus they give an indication of what should be understood as the normal operations of ships.[58] However, during the negotiations, industrial processes carried on board were not considered. "In other words, 'normal operations of a ship' does not cover industrial processes onboard vessels".[59] The government of Colombia also argues that blending operations and industrial activities do not fall under the exclusion contemplated in Article 1(4) of the Basel Convention because "MARPOL never intended ... to include factory type waste generated on board the ship"[60]; thus, in this scenario, the Basel Convention applies in full. These conclusions appear inexact for the following reasons.

First, when an international instrument is negotiated, it is not possible to foresee all factual scenarios or relevant issues that should or will be covered in the future by a certain instrument. Likewise, even if some issues could be considered relevant, negotiations of international instruments are generally lengthy processes where several political, economic, social and environmental considerations play an important role when shaping an international regime. In this sense, many compromises are necessary in order to achieve consensus. Second, it takes several years for an international instrument to enter into force since its adoption and, within this period, many of the factual, social, economic, environmental, and political scenarios could change. Therefore, not all activities that were unforeseen during the negotiation of MARPOL can be considered *ipso facto* as

---

57 The Center for International Environmental Law (CIEL), "Comments on the Analysis of the Basel Convention's Secretariat Regarding Hazardous and Other Wastes Generated on Board Ships," (1 December 2012), 15.

58 The Center for International Environmental Law (CIEL), "CIEL Issue Brief: 'Normal Operations of a Ship' in MARPOL: A Review of MARPOL's *Travaux*," (26 June 2012).

59 Ibid., 2.

60 Ministerio de Relaciones Exteriores de la República de Colombia, "Colombian Submission on the Third Analysis of the Basel Convention's Secretariat Regarding Hazardous and Other Wastes Generated on Board Ships," 1. Available at: <www.basel.int/Implementation/LegalMatters/Ships/tabid/2405/Default.aspx>.

134   *The ESM of wastes*

abnormal operations of ships because no legal instrument could anticipate every possible situation in advance. Indeed, international instruments, such as the Basel Convention or MARPOL, are dynamic in nature and evolve, for instance, due to State practices, related agreements, soft law, technological and scientific developments, and, of course, amendments.

Concluding remarks

The exclusion from the scope of the Basel Convention of wastes generated from normal operations of ships, whose discharge is covered by another international instrument, must be understood as MARPOL. It is inconsequential to characterize operations on board ships as normal or abnormal for the following reasons. First, the introduction of the phrase "normal operations" was requested by the IMO to preserve the scope of application of MARPOL. Second, the scope of application of MARPOL is not restricted by any characterization of ships' operations as normal or abnormal. Third, even if some activities can be characterized as abnormal or if those activities are not covered by MARPOL, it is crucial to recognize that obligations regarding transboundary movements of wastes and prior informed consent cannot be applied to ships. The Secretariat of the Basel Convention has noted certain practical difficulties in this regard, but one should be aware that those practical deterrents are caused by the mutually exclusive obligations that govern ship-source pollution and transboundary movements of wastes. For instance, while the Basel Convention discourages transboundary movements of wastes, under MARPOL transboundary movements are the rule.

The author believes that the actual debate lies not in defining normal or abnormal operations of ships, but rather in the characterization of the Basel Convention as an overarching framework to deal with hazardous wastes from generation to disposal where other norms have to enhance its objectives. *The real dilemma is how to deal with the sea/land interface.*

Ship operations: its transboundary essence and the inapplicability of obligations related to transboundary movement of wastes

It is the very nature of shipping that precludes the applicability of the Basel Convention to ship wastes while onboard. This inapplicability appears irrespective of any characterization of "normality" or even when these wastes are not covered, for instance, by MARPOL. Particularly problematic is the identification of State of export and the application of the PIC procedure. To fully grasp the difficulties encountered, it is necessary to explore what constitutes a transboundary movement of waste. According to Article 2(3) of the Basel Convention, a transboundary movement of wastes is:

> any movement of hazardous wastes or other wastes from an area under the national jurisdiction of one state to or through an area under the national

Sea/land interface waste management dilemma   135

jurisdiction of another state or to or through an area not under the national jurisdiction of any state, provided at least two states are involved in the movement.

The interpretation of this definition faces two issues that stem from: (a) the determination of the moment when a transboundary movement of wastes is triggered according to the Basel Convention; and (b) the rights of the States involved in a transboundary movement. The rather ambiguous expression "area under national jurisdiction of a state" is a key element in identifying when a transboundary movement occurs. Article 2(9) of the Basel Convention describes an "area under national jurisdiction" as "any land, *marine area* ... within which a state exercises administrative and regulatory responsibility ... in regard to the protection of human health or the environment." The reference regarding marine areas does not entirely clarify which maritime zones are covered by this provision. The imprecise language used to define transboundary movements is the result of disagreements during the negotiation process over the inclusion of precise references, e.g., to the exclusive economic zone (EEZ).[61] There was also disagreement over how to balance States' rights to prevent pollution of maritime zones under their jurisdiction without conflicting with navigational freedoms.

The Basel Convention confines the definition of the transboundary movement of wastes to transfers that commence from, to or through *areas under national jurisdiction*. This is due to the pivotal role[62] of exporting States within the Basel Convention. Exporting States remain responsible for the ESM of wastes. Indeed, this obligation cannot be transferred to importing or transit States according to Article 4(10) of the Convention. Additionally, if transboundary movements, carried out in conformity with the Convention, cannot be completed, wastes must be reimported to the State of export according to Article 8 of the Convention. This obligation endorses the primary obligation of the exporting State regarding the ESM of wastes, notwithstanding the compliance of the controls and procedures under the Basel Convention.

Ships inherently operate at sea and it is extremely difficult to establish where a transboundary movement begins and which is the exporting State. Consider a vessel flying an Ecuadorian flag and operating in Africa that is engaged in blending operations. During ship operations, wastes from cargo and machinery spaces are constantly generated within several territorial seas and EEZs. Furthermore,

---

61 Iwona Rummel-Bulska, "The Basel Convention and the UN Convention on the Law of the Sea," in *Competing Norms in the Law of Marine Environmental Protection*, ed. Henrik Ringbom, International Environmental Law and Policy Series (The Hague: Kluwer Law International, 1997), 88.

62 During the second negotiation session of the Basel Convention (Caracas, June 1988), the Group of 77 emphasized that "[a]lthough the role of the exporter and the producer has to be taken into account, the transboundary movement of hazardous waste must engage the responsibility of the country of export." Tolba and Rummel-Bulska, *Global Environmental Diplomacy: Negotiating Environmental Agreements for the World, 1973–1992*, 102.

136 *The ESM of wastes*

blending operations are carried out in the high seas. In this scenario, it is not feasible to distinguish where the transboundary movement begins because wastes are *continuously* being generated. Additionally, the Basel Convention would not cover waste transfers from the high seas. If it is argued that wastes arising from abnormal operations of ships fall within the scope of the Basel Convention, the ship in the example must comply with the PIC procedure, or else the movement is illegal and the wastes have to be reimported to the exporting State, which is nonexistent. In this case, the ship operator has no option but to discharge wastes in the sea. This is contrary to the provisions established in MARPOL and the LOSC.

Transit States' rights versus innocent passage and freedom of navigation

Considering that a transboundary movement must commence within an "area under the national jurisdiction of a state," it can be argued, e.g., that movements that begin within the territorial sea and the EEZ are transboundary movements of wastes for the purposes of the Basel Convention. However, a potential conflict between navigational rights and the obligations established in the Basel Convention may occur. A legal transboundary movement requires the prior consent for such movement from importing and transit States alike.[63] On the other hand, Article 4(12) of the Basel Convention establishes that:

> [n]*othing in this Convention shall affect* ... the *exercise by ships* ... *of navigational rights and freedoms* as provided for in international law and as reflected in relevant international instruments (Emphasis added).

This article endorses the view that the regulatory system prescribed in the Basel Convention must be exercised taking into consideration the customary rights and relevant provisions established in the LOSC regarding the freedoms of navigation and innocent passage. Therefore, as Kummer explains, this provision "gives priority to these rights, i.e., navigational, over any rule of the Basel Convention".[64]

Not all Parties to the Basel Convention share this interpretation. For instance, several Latin American States, e.g., Colombia, Ecuador, Mexico, Uruguay, and Venezuela, declared that the Basel Convention safeguards their rights as coastal States and, therefore, actions can be taken against ships involved in transboundary movements of wastes in their territorial seas and

---

63 *See* Article 2(3) of the Basel Convention.
64 Kummer, *International Management of Hazardous Wastes: The Basel Convention and Related Legal Rules*, 53. *Note* that, according to Kummer, Article 4(12) of the Basel Convention seems to imply that "a transit state's rights may be exercised only to the extent that they are not in conflict with the international law of the sea." *See also*, Alan Boyle, "Further Development of the 1982 Convention on the Law of the Sea: Mechanisms for Change," in *The Law of the Sea: Progress and Prospects*, ed. David Freestone, Richard Barnes, and David Ong (Oxford: Oxford University Press, 2006), 56.

Sea/land interface waste management dilemma   137

EEZs.[65] Furthermore, China has enacted legislation to prohibit the transit of ships carrying wastes through its territorial sea and EEZ.[66] On the other hand, States like Germany and Japan do not accept that the principles and obligations prescribed in the Basel Convention may curtail the freedom of navigation and innocent passage of ships[67] by requiring, for instance, previous consent. Wastes generated and transferred from the high seas do not fall under the definition of transboundary movements of the Basel Convention and are not covered by this instrument. The specific rights and obligations of coastal States regarding the territorial sea and EEZ are analyzed in greater depth below in relation to the rights of transit States involved in a transboundary movement of wastes.

According to the PIC procedure established in Article 6 of the Basel Convention, not only importing States but also transit States must consent to a transboundary movement of wastes. If those transboundary movements are carried out by sea, ships may navigate or transit through territorial seas and EEZs of several States before arriving at importing States. Furthermore, under customary law and treaty law, ships enjoy the right of innocent passage in the territorial sea and freedom of navigation in the EEZ.[68] In this scenario, uncertainties emerge as to whether the PIC procedure is applicable to ships exercising their rights of navigation while engaged in transboundary movements of wastes.

Although Article 4(12) of the Basel Convention seems to guarantee the navigational freedoms of ships engaged in the transboundary movement of wastes while passing through the territorial sea or the EEZ, there are still disagreements relating to the rights enjoyed by transit States under the Basel Convention. However, even in the absence of Article 4(12), the PIC procedure is inapplicable to transit States in cases where ships are exercising, for instance, their freedom of navigation within the EEZ. This is because *the PIC procedure is a manifestation of States' sovereignty over their territory.* In relation to the EEZ, Birnie et al. summarize: "[w]here transit takes place through maritime areas, however, no such basis in territorial sovereignty exists".[69]

States enjoy full sovereignty over their internal waters. Thus, ships engaged in a transboundary movement of wastes can transit within internal waters if there is compliance with the PIC procedure established in the Basel Convention. In the territorial sea, even though States enjoy sovereignty, the customary right of innocent passage limits this sovereignty. On the one hand, "passage" refers to foreign ships crossing through a territorial sea in a "continuous and expeditious"[70]

---

65 Rummel-Bulska, "The Basel Convention and the UN Convention on the Law of the Sea," 88–89.

66 Nengye Liu and Frank Maes, "Prevention of Vessel-Source Marine Pollution: A Note on the Challenges and Prospects for Chinese Practice under International Law," *Ocean Development & International Law* 42, no. 4 (2011): 361–62.

67 Ibid.

68 *See* Article 17 *et seq.* and Article 58(1) of the LOSC. *See also* Article 14 of the Geneva Convention on the Territorial Sea.

69 Birnie and Boyle, *International Law and the Environment*, 432.

70 *See* Articles 18(1) and (2) of the LOSC.

138   The ESM of wastes

manner without entering or proceeding from internal waters; or proceeding to or from internal waters or a call at such roadstead or port facility.[71] On the other hand, the term "innocent" refers to the passage of ships that is not detrimental "to the peace, good order or security of the coastal state".[72]

Determining which activities are prejudicial to the coastal State is not an easy task. In this sense, Article 19(2) of the LOSC provides a nonexhaustive list of activities that could render the passage noninnocent. Whether vessels carrying harmful substances, including hazardous wastes, are intrinsically prejudicial to the peace, good order or security of coastal States is doubtful. Indeed, Article 23 of the LOSC recognizes explicitly that ships carrying substances that are intrinsically harmful can exercise the innocent passage right, but must "carry documents and observe special precautionary measures established for such ships by international agreements." Such precautionary measures serve to, e.g., confine ships' passage to sea lines as prescribed in Article 22 of the LOSC. However, this article cannot be construed to include the PIC procedure established in the Basel Convention since it will potentially curtail the right of innocent passage of ships.

In the EEZ, coastal States do not enjoy sovereignty and this maritime zone does not "have a residual territorial character".[73] The EEZ is a *sui generis* maritime zone where coastal States have certain "sovereign rights" and jurisdiction regarding the protection of the marine environment, exploration, and exploitation of natural resources.[74] All in all, the PIC procedure enshrines the sovereignty of States over the use of their territories and resources, and within the EEZ no such sovereignty exists. Therefore, freedom of navigation cannot be curtailed by requiring previous notification and consent when ships are carrying harmful substances, including wastes regulated under the Basel Convention. In this regard, the following declaration made by the United States in relation to the position of transit States under the Basel Convention seems accurate:

> a state is a transit state only if wastes are moved or planned to be moved through ... its inland waters ... it will formally object to the declaration of any state to require its prior permissions or authorization of the passage of a vessel transporting hazardous wastes while exercising ... its right of innocent passage or freedom of navigation.[75]

Notwithstanding the foregoing analysis, this issue remains controversial. Many States have enacted legislation that requires previous notification and consent when ships carrying hazardous wastes intend to pass through their territorial sea or EEZ.[76]

---

71 Ibid.
72 Ibid., Article 19. *See also* Article 14(4) of the Geneva Convention on the Territorial Sea.
73 Churchill and Lowe, *The Law of the Sea*, 165.
74 *See* Article 56 of the LOSC.
75 Rummel-Bulska, "The Basel Convention and the UN Convention on the Law of the Sea," 100–101.
76 Ibid., 99.

The potential applicability of ESM to ship wastes

Ships have a timeframe within which harmful substances can be kept on board before discharge. For this reason: "[s]hip operators have a right and an obligation to discharge certain wastes into port reception facilities, while Port States have an obligation to provide suitable facilities".[77] While at sea, MARPOL provides detailed standards for managing ship wastes, e.g., prevention of waste generation, equipment on board, and discharge criteria. However, the Convention does not provide substantive content concerning the obligation to provide "adequate" port reception facilities. The history of MARPOL shows that its Parties have been reluctant to establish binding standards to assess whether these facilities are adequate. Instead, they have relied on soft law instruments developed under the auspices of the IMO.

In 2016, the IMO revised the Manual on Port Reception Facilities. This Manual is of fundamental importance because it qualifies port reception facilities as "adequate" if they "allow for the ultimate disposal of ship-generated wastes and residues to take place in an environmentally sound manner".[78] Thus, the IMO has taken a bold yet cautious step toward an international policy regarding the management of ship wastes. The Manual includes several alternatives for the downstream management of ship wastes, while clarifying that specific treatment operations of ship wastes on land is beyond the scope of MARPOL.[79]

The connection between the adequacy of port reception facilities and waste management on land is based on both Article 195 of the LOSC, which prohibits the transfer of pollution hazards from one place to another and the transformation of pollution sources, and the ESM principle. This Manual, like any other soft law instrument, is not mandatory. However, it provides guidance to State Parties to MARPOL as to what ensures the provision of adequate port reception facilities including some recommendations for achieving the ESM of wastes on land. It also provides further evidence on the emergence of an international legal framework regarding the management of wastes based on the ESM principle.

The Manual on Port Reception Facilities recognizes ESM as a thread that draws together several international instruments,[80] including the Basel Convention, MARPOL, the AFS Convention, and the BWM Convention. As discussed in Chapter 2, ESM transitioned from a policy objective to a customary law principle that is concerned with the life-cycle approach to wastes, i.e., from generation to final disposal independently of the generation source. ESM has been

---

77 de La Fayette, "The Sound Management of Wastes Generated at Sea: MARPOL, Not Basel," 211.

78 International Maritime Organization (IMO), "Port Reception Facilities – How to Do It," 21–22. This requirement was also established in Marine Environment Protection Committee (MEPC), "Resolution MEPC.83(44): Guidelines for Ensuring the Adequacy of Port Waste Reception Facilties," (MEPC 44 (20), 13 March 2000).

79 International Maritime Organization (IMO), "Port Reception Facilities – How to Do It," 16, 27 and Chapters 8–10.

80 Ibid., 17–18.

140 *The ESM of wastes*

the basis for establishing cross-sectoral policies between several regimes and for developing a wide range of regulatory developments, in relation to both hard law and soft law. The level of generalization of ESM comes from its formulation as a general principle and, as such, the determination of further standards should be assessed in an individual context.

Undoubtedly, the most prominent international instrument dealing with wastes is the Basel Convention. During the first years after the entry into force of this instrument, the Parties' emphasis was to restrict transboundary movements of wastes. In the early 1990s,[81] however, the focus shifted from restriction to the attainment of the ESM. This shift was precipitated by the realization that waste trade was a growing phenomenon and that well-established waste markets had been consolidated. In fact, according to a study commissioned by the Secretariat to the Basel Convention, "between 1993 and 2001 the amount of waste crisscrossing the globe increased from 2 million tonnes to more than 8.5 million tonnes".[82] Furthermore, legal transboundary movements of hazardous wastes from developed to developing countries was no longer on the increase.[83] Finally, this shift resulted from differences between jurisdictions in the concept of wastes and the blurring boundaries between waste and resource.[84]

The Basel Convention has incorporated ESM as one of its fundamental pillars. ESM is defined in general terms as: "taking all practicable steps to ensure that hazardous wastes or other wastes are managed in a manner which will protect human health and the environment against the adverse effects which may result from such wastes".[85] This treaty imposes several obligations to ensure the ESM in cases where wastes are subject to a transboundary movement in accordance with the Convention. These obligations relate to the identification of the party responsible for the ESM of wastes, i.e., the exporting State and the duty to reimport wastes in cases where wastes cannot be treated in an environmentally sound manner.[86] *These obligations established in the Basel Convention to ensure an ESM of wastes specifically address wastes that are subject to transboundary movement and are not applicable to ship wastes* as explained below.

---

81 In the Fifth Meeting of the COP to the Basel Convention, the parties adopted the Basel Declaration on Environmentally Sound Management. From then on, emphasis has been given to the development of a common framework to manage wastes, wherever the place of disposal. COP to the Basel Convention, "Decision V/1: Basel Declaration on Environmentally Sound Management," in *Conference of the Parties to the Basel Convention on the Control of Transboundary Movements of Hazardous Wastes and their Disposal – Fifth Meeting. UNEP/CHW.5/29* (Basel, 1999).

82 GRID-Arendal et al., "Vital Waste Graphics," (2004), 30.

83 "Approximately 75 percent of the total volume of waste is traded between developed countries." Ibid., A caveat is that the volume of trade refers to legal movements. Illegal movements of wastes are shipped to developing countries and followed by their unsound management. Tackling illegal movements is still one of the major challenges for the ESM of wastes.

84 Tarcísio Hardman Reis, "Waste and International Law: Towards a Resource-Based Approach?," in *Waste Management and the Green Economy: Law and Policy*, ed. Katharina Kummer, Andreas R. Ziegler, and Jorun Baumgartner (Cheltenham: Edward Elgar Publishing, 2016).

85 *See* Article 2(8) of the Basel Convention.

86 *See* Ibid., Articles 4(10) and 8.

The development of ESM as a principle is vital in developing an international legal framework of wastes in general and in envisaging legal developments concerning the management of ship wastes on land. *This is different from suggesting that the Basel Convention, as such, and the obligations contained in this instrument apply to ship wastes.* The Secretariat of the Basel Convention has suggested that "once ship-generated wastes are unloaded from a ship ... the requirement that they be managed in an environmentally sound manner in accordance with the provisions of the Basel Convention is fully applicable".[87] The Secretariat argues that the obligations relating to the ESM of wastes remain applicable to wastes generated on board vessels for the following reasons. First, the Basel Convention deals with the waste cycle from generation to disposal, while MARPOL applies to ship wastes until they have been unloaded.[88] Second, the ESM of wastes is an independent obligation, which must be complied with, even if no transboundary movement takes place.[89]

Compliance with ESM obligations as established in the Basel Convention impinges directly on Parties involved in a transboundary movement. Consequently, it is not possible to make a distinction between transboundary movements and ESM because these obligations are intrinsically linked, since waste management "applies to exporting, transit, and importing states alike".[90] If no transboundary movement takes place, no provision of the Basel Convention remains applicable. The Secretariat of IMO follows a similar argument, i.e., the application of the Basel Convention to ship wastes discharged to port reception facilities depends on whether such wastes are subsequently subject to a transboundary movement of wastes.[91]

What should be acknowledged is the role of the COP to the Basel Convention in the development of a common understanding of ESM and its continuous effort to adopt technical guidelines for the ESM of various categories of wastes. These technical guidelines usually focus on: (a) certain types of wastes, e.g., electronic waste, pneumatic tyres, ships; (b) wastes with hazardous characteristics as established in Annex III of the Basel Convention, e.g., delayed toxicity; (c) wastes having certain constituents as established in Annex I of the Basel Convention, e.g., wastes containing or contaminated with mercury; and (d) wastes belonging to certain waste streams as established in Annex I of the Basel Convention, e.g., waste oils. These technical guidelines could certainly assist States in managing wastes in an environmentally sound manner whether

---

87 Secretariat of the Basel Convention, "Third Legal Analysis of the Application of the Basel Convention to Hazardous Wastes and Other Wastes Generated on Board Ships," para 45.
88 "The Application of the Basel Convention to Hazardous Wastes and Other Wastes Generated on Board Ships," 22. "all of MARPOL annexes contain provisions for the environmentally sound management of wastes generated on board ships only whilst at sea, but not on land, once the waste is offloaded."
89 Ibid., 24.
90 Birnie and Boyle, *International Law and the Environment*, 433.
91 Secretariat of IMO, "Answer to the Invitation to IMO to Comment on the Draft Assessment on How Far the Current Basel Convention Technical Guidelines Cover MARPOL Wastes," (2015).

142 *The ESM of wastes*

or not those wastes have been subject to a transboundary movement. They could be particularly relevant for States that have yet to develop national waste management plans, or those that struggle to integrate ship wastes into national waste management. The Manual on Port Reception Facilities developed under the auspices of IMO suggests that guidance regarding the management of ship wastes on land can be found in the technical guidelines adopted by the COP to the Basel Convention.[92] In order to assess to what extent these technical guidelines cover MARPOL wastes, the COP to the Basel Convention invited the Parties to undertake such an assessment in close cooperation with the IMO.[93] The Public Waste Agency of Flanders, on behalf of Belgium, undertook such an evaluation that shed light on how to utilize the technical guidelines adopted by the COP to the Basel Convention in relation to ship wastes.[94]

The COP to the Basel Convention in its Twelfth Meeting, held in May 2015, adopted the Decision BC-12/16 on the "Cooperation between the Basel Convention and the IMO." Pursuant to this decision, the Secretariat of the Basel Convention developed a draft "Guidance Manual on How to Improve the Sea-Land Interface to Ensure that Wastes Falling Within the Scope of MARPOL, once Offloaded From a Ship, are Managed in an Environmentally Sound Manner" taking into account the Manual on Port Reception Facilities developed under the auspices of the IMO.[95] This Guidance Manual follows the third legal analysis of the Secretariat of the Basel Convention on the application of the Basel Convention to hazardous and other wastes generated on board ships. Therefore, the Guidance Manual argues for the application of "certain obligations" established in the Basel Convention to abnormal ship wastes when they are offloaded. This soft law instrument, however, appears more nuanced than previous legal analysis undertaken by the Secretariat of the Basel Convention, since rather than focusing on how to specifically apply the obligations contained in the Basel

---

92 International Maritime Organization (IMO), "Port Reception Facilities – How to Do It," 21.

93 *See* COP to the Basel Convention, "Decision BC-10/16: Cooperation between the Basel Convention and the International Maritime Organization," in *Report of the Conference of the Parties to the Basel Convention on the Control of Transboundary Movements of Hazardous Wastes and their Disposal on Its Tenth Meeting (UNEP/CHW.10/28)* (2011). "Decision BC-11/17: Cooperation between the Basel Convention and the International Maritime Organization," in *Report of the Conference of the Parties to the Basel Convention on the Control of Transboundary Movements of Hazardous Wastes and their Disposal on the Work of Its Eleventh Meeting (UNEP/CHW.11/24)* (2013).

94 (OVAM) Public Waste Agency of Flanders, "Revised Assessment Prepared by the Public Waste Agency of Flanders, on Behalf of Belgium, on How Far the Current Basel Convention Technical Guidelines Cover Wastes Covered by the International Convention for the Prevention of Pollution from Ships (UNEP/CHW.12/INF/29/REV.1)," in *Conference of the Parties to the Basel Convention on the Control of Transboundary Movements of Hazardous Wastes and their Disposal. Twelfth Meeting – Agenda Item 4 (e) (iii)* (13 July 2015).

95 "Revised Draft Guidance Manual on How to Improve the Sea-Land Interface (UNEP/CHW.13/INF/37)," in *Conference of the Parties to the Basel Convention on the Control of the Transboundary Movements of Hazardous Wastes and their Disposal. Thirteenth Meeting. Item 4 (e) (ii) of the Provisional Agenda* (5 April 2017).

Sea/land interface waste management dilemma   143

Convention to ship wastes, it devotes its attention to the downstream management of ship wastes on land by considering the broader meaning of the ESM of wastes. In 2017, at the Thirteenth Meeting, the COP to the Basel Convention took note of the Guidance Manual and requested that the Secretariat continue its collaboration with the IMO.[96]

Overall, the Basel Convention was a response to incidents of unsafe waste management in developing countries. As a result of these incidents, the Convention embraced a strict approach so as to restrict waste trade. This approach has proven to hinder the Convention in its quest to become an overarching regime to deal with hazardous wastes from a life-cycle approach. Nonetheless, the increasing relevance given by the COP to the Basel Convention to the principle of ESM is part of the intricate thread that seeks to bring together and coordinate different regimes dealing with wastes and to raise questions about international obligations concerning waste management regardless of their source.

The EU and the management of ship wastes in their sea/land interface

Ship wastes are also excluded from the scope of application of Regulation 1013/2006/EC on Shipments of Wastes. The Regulation has a similar, but more detailed exclusion than that prescribed in the Basel Convention. Article 1(3) of Regulation 1013/2006/EC on Shipments of Wastes establishes:

> [t]he following shall be excluded from the scope of this Regulation:
>
> (a) the offloading to shore of waste, including waste water and residues, generated by the normal operation of ships and offshore platforms, provided that such waste is subject to the requirements of ... MARPOL 73/78, or other binding international instruments;
>
> (b) waste generated on board vehicles, trains, aeroplanes and ships, until such waste is offloaded in order to be recovered or disposed of;

Since Regulation 1013/2006/EC on Shipments of Wastes implements the Basel Convention, it is likely that this exclusion has been included to reflect the text of its international counterpart.[97] The provision exclusively refers to the "offloading

---

96 "OEWG-10/11: Cooperation between the Basel Convention and the International Maritime Organization (UNEP/CHW/OEWG.10/13)," in *Open-ended Working Group of the Basel Convention on the Control of Transboundary Movements of Hazardous Wastes and their Disposal. Tenth Meeting* (Nairobi, 24 June 2016).

97 "The preparatory works of Regulation 259/93 are unusually quiet on the reason for the exclusion of 'ship waste'. This is most probably explained by the fact that the provision simply implements the relevant provision of the Basel Convention, namely Article 1(4)" Van Calster, *EU Waste Law*, 102.

144   *The ESM of wastes*

to shore of waste" while remaining silent on wastes while on board vessels. This could be interpreted as an indication that the Regulation does not pretend to impose further obligations regarding ship wastes while on board vessels, since these substances are covered by MARPOL.

Article 1(3)(a) of Regulation 1013/2006/EC on Shipments of Wastes raises once again the question of the applicability of MARPOL to wastes discharged to port reception facilities, especially in relation to the meaning and extent of the obligation to provide "adequate port reception facilities." These facilities are adequate if they "allow for the ultimate disposal of ships' wastes to take place in an environmentally appropriate way".[98] Although not a Party to MARPOL, the EU has transposed the international obligation to ensure the provision of adequate port reception facilities into EU legislation. Directive 2000/59/EC not only implements this particular obligation established in MARPOL, but also complements its international counterpart by establishing a number of detailed obligations,[99] including, for instance, the requirement to develop waste reception and handling plans.[100] What is particularly relevant for the management of ship wastes on land is Article 2 of Directive 2000/59/EC. Its final paragraph includes ship wastes within the scope of the Waste Framework Directive 2008/98/EC which establishes general measures for the prevention, reduction, and management of wastes. So, the scrutiny of the exclusion prescribed in Article 1(3) of Regulation 1013/2006/EC on Shipments of Wastes inevitably requires not only the interpretation of MARPOL's obligation regarding port reception facilities, but also the scrutiny of its EU counterpart, i.e., Directive 2000/59/EC. This Directive integrates ship wastes into the EU waste management system. Therefore, ship wastes are excluded from the application of Regulation 1013/2006/EC on Shipments of Wastes since the obligation to provide adequate port reception facilities as prescribed in MARPOL has been given substantive content at the EU level.

Despite the inclusion of ship wastes within the scope of application of the Waste Framework Directive, it is uncertain how the obligations of this Directive are applicable to ship wastes in practice. As discussed in Chapter 8, ports face several difficulties in the integration of ship wastes in the context of wider EU waste legislation. Certain obligations of the Waste Framework Directive that could be relevant for ship wastes – such as duties related to waste oils, separate collection and recovery targets for paper, metal, plastic, and glass, as well as hazardous wastes – were not drafted with due consideration given to the peculiarities of the reception, transport, and treatment of ship wastes on land.

In addition, Article 1(3)(b) excludes wastes generated on board of all means of transportation. This exclusion refers to operational wastes. From the Regulation's

---

98 Marine Environment Protection Committee (MEPC), "Resolution MEPC.83(44): Guidelines for Ensuring the Adequacy of Port Waste Reception Facilties," 5. "Resolution MEPC.83(44): Guidelines for Ensuring the Adequacy of Port Waste Reception Facilties."

99 These obligations have not raised doubts over the compatibility with MARPOL since, although tailored to meet the needs of the EU, they follow soft law instruments adopted under the auspices of the IMO.

100 *See* Article 5 of Directive 2000/59/EC.

travaux préparatoires, the introduction of this provision was justified because the requirements of the regulation would be "disproportionate with regard to waste generated on board vehicles, trains, ships, and aeroplanes".[101] This article provides evidence that the Regulation was not intended to regulate wastes derived from the daily operations of ships or any other means of transportation. It is concerned with regulating waste trade.

Article 1(3)(b) of Regulation 1013/2006/EC on Shipments of Wastes raises doubts over the applicability of the Regulation to ship wastes after they are discharged to port reception facilities. According to this article, ship wastes are excluded until they are "offloaded in order to be recovered or disposed of." The Regulation contains general obligations for ensuring the ESM of wastes.[102] Such obligations are impinged directly on the Parties involved in a shipment of wastes. As previously analyzed in relation to the Basel Convention, what is relevant is the applicability of the ESM as a principle rather than the application of specific obligations established in the Basel Convention or in Regulation 1013/2006/EC on Shipments of Wastes. To a certain extent, this seems to be the position of the European Commission. In the guidelines to interpret Directive 2000/59/EC on Port Reception Facilities, the Commission expressed the following:

> [p]rinciples of environmentally sound management of waste are also provided in the ... Basel Convention, that the Parties to that Convention must apply ... [t]he Commission considers that ... once the waste is delivered to a port reception facility, the Convention becomes applicable, and the facility must be managed in a way that upholds the principles enshrined in that Convention and in EU waste legislation.[103]

While the European Commission suggests that the Basel Convention is indeed applicable to wastes delivered to a port reception facility, the Commission immediately qualifies this assertion by requiring the facilities to be managed in accordance with the principles enshrined in the Basel Convention and further EU waste law. The following chapters analyze the content of ESM at both international and EU levels regarding wastes in general and ship wastes in particular.

---

101 "Com(2005) 641 Final: Opinion of the Commission Regarding the Proposal for a Regulation of the European Parliament and of the Council on Shipments of Waste," (Brussels: 2003/0139 (COD), 01.12.2005), 3.

102 *See* Article 49 of the Regulation on Shipment of Wastes 1013/2006/EC.

103 "C/2016/1759 Commission Notice – Guidelines for the Interpretation of Directive 2000/59/EC on Port Reception Facilities for Ship-Generated Waste and Cargo Residues," 7.

7 ESM and the transboundary movement of waste regime

The growing importance of ESM within the Basel regime

With transboundary movements on the rise, especially that of recyclable wastes,[1] the COP to the Basel Convention has increasingly focused on ESM.[2] The Parties recognized the need to support States, especially developing ones, in the implementation of national wastes management systems with the following hierarchical priority: prevention, minimization, recycling, recovery and disposal of waste.[3] This was also a response to a long-standing criticism of the Basel Convention, which imposes the same strict controls on hazardous and other wastes without taking into account whether those wastes can be recycled or recovered. Since ESM is a fundamental precondition for allowing a transboundary movement of wastes, the potential of wastes to be recycled becomes a criterion with which to assess a proposed movement.

In 2011, the COP to the Basel Convention, at its Tenth Meeting, adopted the Cartagena Declaration on the Prevention, Minimization and Recovery of Hazardous Wastes and Other Wastes. This instrument portrays ESM as an opportunity to balance the protection of the environment with economic development. The Parties acknowledged that the ESM of wastes is crucial to preserving resources, reducing pollution, and protecting human health, as well as being "an opportunity for the generation of employment, economic growth and the reduction of poverty".[4] Nonetheless, promoting the recovery of wastes as a

---

1 "Transboundary movements are increasing, but the vast majority of hazardous and other wastes is still treated within the country of origin and if waste is exported it stays, in most cases, within the same geographical region." Wielenga, "Waste without Frontiers: Global Trends in Generation and Transboundary Movements of Hazardous Wastes and Other Wastes," 4.

2 Pierre Portas, "The Basel Convention – A Promising Future," in *Chemicals, Environment, Health: A Global Management Perspective*, ed. Philip Wexler et al. (Boca Raton, FL: CRC Press, 2012).

3 COP to the Basel Convention, "Cartagena Declaration on the Prevention, Minimization and Recovery of Hazardous Wastes and Other Wastes."

4 *See* numeral 2 of: COP to the Basel Convention, "Cartagena Declaration on the Prevention, Minimization and Recovery of Hazardous Wastes and Other Wastes."

lucrative economic alternative undermines efforts directed toward preventing and minimizing waste. The New Strategic Framework for the Implementation of the Basel Convention for 2012–2021 was also adopted at the Tenth Meeting of the COP. This instrument endorses the life-cycle approach toward the ESM of waste and recognizes several principles that should guide the development of waste management systems, including: "sustainable use of resources; polluter-pays principle; extended producer responsibility; precautionary principle; proximity principle; cooperation and synergies; and sustainable consumption and production".[5] The strengthening of ESM continues to be a leading goal within the Strategic Framework.[6]

Legal nature of the ESM obligation

ESM is an obligation of conduct rather than one of result, and the relevant standard of liability is one of due diligence. According to Article 2(8) of the Basel Convention, ESM is defined as *"taking all practical steps* to ensure that hazardous wastes or other wastes are managed in a manner which will protect human health and the environment" (emphasis added). To this end, States *must perform certain activities of control and regulation* in order to fulfill their obligations under the Basel Convention. For instance: States will reimport wastes in cases where their disposal in an environmentally sound manner cannot be arranged.[7]

---

5 *See* Annex to Decision BC-10/2, Guiding Principles in "Decision BC-10/2: New Strategic Framework for the Implementation of the Basel Convention for 2012–2021 (UNEP/CHW.10/3)."

6 *See* Ibid., goals 2 and 3 A mid-term evaluation of the Strategic Framework took place at the Thirteenth Meeting of the COP to the Basel Convention, held in May 2017. However, the results are not conclusive since only 36 Parties to the Basel Convention submitted the required information. "Strategic Framework: Note by the Secretariat (UNEP/CHW.13/3)," in *Conference of the Parties to the Basel Convention on the Control of Transboundary Movements of Hazardous Wastes and their Disposal. Thirteenth Meeting* (Geneva, May 2017). The vast majority of the parties answering the questionnaire confirmed the implementation of ESM. Nonetheless, "the Framework indicators and the questionnaire did not permit any more detailed evaluation of which ESM guidelines", "Updated Report on the Creation of a Baseline for the Mid-Term and Final Evaluations of the Strategic Framework (UNEP/CHW.12/INF/5)," in *Conference of the Parties to the Basel Convention on the Control of Transboundary Movements of Hazardous Wastes and their Disposal. Twelfth Meeting* (May 2015).

7 *Note* also that due diligence is not a synonym for obligation of conduct: "[t]he determination of the applicable level of care is not to be confused with the question of whether the primary obligation is one of conduct or result. It rather concerns the question of whether the state is either absolutely responsible for the particular conduct or for the achievement of the particular result, or whether it is responsible for this outcome only within the realms of a certain degree of diligence taking account of the individual circumstances of the case", Albers, *Responsibility and Liability in the Context of Transboundary Movements of Hazardous Wastes by Sea*, 29, 88 and 98. René Lefeber, *Transboundary Environmental Interference and the Origin of State Liability* (The Hague: Kluwer Law International, 1996), 61–80.

148 *The ESM of wastes*

The soft law framework relating to ESM is also a guidance with which to assess whether States are complying with their due diligence obligation in relation to hazardous wastes. This soft law corpus gives substantive and procedural content to an obligation that is formulated in general terms. However, since ESM standards are developed exclusively through soft law, their implementation is still subject to States' discretion.

ESM: substantive content

The COP to the Basel Convention adopted two major "framework documents"[8] giving State Parties guidelines to establish, implement, and monitor waste management operations in their jurisdictions. Besides providing a common understanding of what ESM encompasses, the COP to the Basel Convention has adopted a significant number of technical guidelines for the ESM of wastes. The technical guidelines also focus on waste management alternatives, e.g., specially engineered landfill, incineration on land, physicochemical treatment.[9] The guidelines give a description of the waste, its environmental hazards, suitable management operations and technologies, and aftercare.

In 2013, the COP to the Basel Convention at its Eleventh Meeting adopted the Framework for the Environmentally Sound Management of Hazardous Wastes and Other Wastes (Framework Document). According to the chapeau of Chapter V.A. of the Framework Document, ESM includes "the entire waste management hierarchy." No reference can be found in the Basel Convention in respect of waste hierarchy, but this concept has been implemented in several jurisdictions and on a regional basis, including within the EU. At the EU level, the Waste Framework Directive introduces the waste hierarchy. The first aim of the waste hierarchy is to reduce[10] the generation of wastes, while the second aim is that when managing wastes, reuse, recycling, and recovery should be favored over final disposal.

Taking into account the "waste hierarchy," State Parties should have in place a regulatory framework coupled with financial and nonfinancial incentives to deal

---

8 These framework documents are: Secretariat of the Basel Convention, "Guidance Document on the Preparation of Technical Guidelines for the Environmentally Sound Management of Wastes Subject to the Basel Convention," (1994). United Nations Environment Programme (UNEP), "UNEP/CHW.11/3/Add.1/REV.1. Framework for the Environmentally Sound Management of Hazardous Wastes and Other Wastes."

9 The technical guidelines can be found at: <www.basel.int/TheConvention/Publications/TechnicalGuidelines/tabid/2362/Default.aspx>, last accessed 21 March 2019.

10 There have been discussions regarding two positions, one aiming to reduce the generation of waste, and the other aiming to eliminate the generation of wastes altogether. Alexander Gillespie, *Waste Policy: International Regulation, Comparative and Contextual Perspectives*, ed. Kurt Deketelaere and Zen Makuch, New Horizons in Environmental and Energy Law (Cheltenham: Edward Elgar Publishing, 2015), 74.

with the whole spectrum of waste including its prevention, collection, transport, and disposal or recovery. It should also include monitoring mechanisms and appropriate civil and criminal liability schemes. Regarding the functioning of waste management facilities, standards should be in place in terms of infrastructure, licensing schemes, occupational safety and environmental standards. Additionally, innovation and research should be promoted[11] in order: (a) to develop state of the art technology and processes with a view to managing wastes efficiently and boosting cleaner production initiatives; (b) to change consumption patterns; (c) to reduce the volume of consumption; and (d) to reduce waste generation at source.[12]

The implementation of the Framework Document can be achieved through legislation, certification schemes, codes of conduct, international cooperation, and educational and communicational programs, among other mechanisms.[13] Of particular note within this Framework Document is its commitment to several principles of the Rio Declaration, such as the polluter pays principle, and the precautionary approach.[14] At the same time, it recognizes the role that different stakeholders play in the pursuance of managing wastes in an environmental sound manner. Consequently, the engagement of public authorities, nongovernmental organizations, and public or private entities dealing with waste is pivotal in ensuring the ESM of wastes.[15]

According to the Framework for the Environmentally Sound Management of Hazardous Wastes and Other Wastes, several elements contribute to a common understanding of ESM. These include: (a) infrastructure; (b) development and implementation of the best available techniques and best environmental practices; (c) legal regulations ranging from licensing to the establishment of sanctions and liability schemes; (d) financial and nonfinancial incentives; (e) involvement of stakeholders; and (f) research and innovation. The following graph summarizes the elements of ESM (Figure 7.1):

11 United Nations Environment Programme (UNEP), "UNEP/CHW.11/3/Add.1/REV.1. Framework for the Environmentally Sound Management of Hazardous Wastes and Other Wastes." *See* numeral V.A. of the framework document.

12 Regarding changing consumer patterns, Gillespie notes that efforts have been directed towards transforming the consumer into a "green consumer" where "citizens can influence environmental policy by their individual purchasing power." However, according to the author "green consumerism was never really intended for people to consume less, but rather, to consume differently." Gillespie, *Waste Policy: International Regulation, Comparative and Contextual Perspectives*, 76–77.

13 Chapter V.B. United Nations Environment Programme (UNEP), "UNEP/CHW.11/3/Add.1/ REV.1. Framework for the Environmentally Sound Management of Hazardous Wastes and Other Wastes."

14 Ibid., 22. Annex I.

15 Ibid., 13–18.

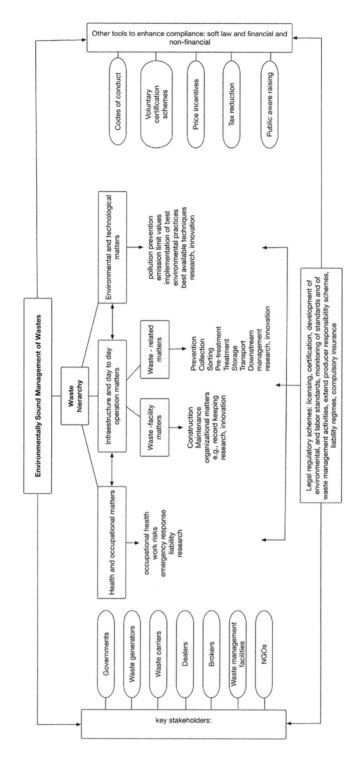

Figure 7.1 Environmentally sound management of wastes.

ESM and transboundary movement 151

The Framework Document proposes a common understanding of ESM. However, such understanding must not be construed as requiring States to have identical waste management systems, since "the capabilities and challenges faced by least developed countries, developing countries and countries with economies in transition"[16] are different, and the establishment of waste management systems will depend on several factors, including: (a) institutional and technical capabilities; (b) availability of economic resources; and (c) types and quantities of waste.

Compliance of ESM: the impact of the principle of nondiscrimination

There is a question that follows on from the discussion of the central role of ESM: How must State Parties to the Basel Convention discharge their ESM obligations if waste management standards are different in the State of export and the State of import? The determination of whether wastes will be managed in an environmentally sound manner could depend on not only the management standards applicable at the State of import, but also those applicable at the State of export.[17] As explained below, all the States involved in waste trade must be responsible for discharging the ESM obligations *without discrimination and in accordance with their obligations under international law.* In relation to transboundary movements of wastes, the principle of nondiscrimination implies that the State of import must be able to apply the similar or higher waste management standards than those applied in the State of export.[18] As explained in this section, the principle is particularly relevant when the exporting State has higher waste management standards than the State of import. However, when both jurisdictions have weak waste management standards, the nondiscrimination principle, per se, offers no guarantee in relation to the level of environmental or health protection.

The principle of nondiscrimination originated at the OECD level in relation to transboundary pollution.[19] It entails applying equivalent standards in relation

16 United Nations Environment Programme (UNEP), "UNEP/CHW.11/3/Add.1/REV.1. Framework for the Environmentally Sound Management of Hazardous Wastes and Other Wastes," 12.

17 "[w]hat is environmentally sound in the country of import may also depend on the level of technology and pollution control available in the exporting country: the implication is that it is unlikely to be environmentally sound to import wastes from states with higher standards of waste disposal." Birnie, Boyle, and Redgwell, *International Law and the Environment*, 480.

18 The principle of non-discrimination entails that "states should not substantially differentiate between their own environment and those of other states as regards the elaboration and application of laws and regulations in the areas of prevention, reparation and repression of pollution." Dupuy, "Soft Law and the International Law of the Environment," 426.

19 Organisation for Economic Co-Operation and Development (OECD), "C(74)224 Recommendation of the Council on Principles Concerning Transfrontier Pollution," (14 November 1974). "C (77) 28/Final Recommendation of the Council for the Implementation of a Regime of Equal Right of Access and Non-Discrimination in Relation to Transfrontier Pollution," (1977). Organisation for Economic Co-Operation and Development (OECD), "C(78)77/Final Recommendation of the Council for Strengthening International Co-Operation on Environmental Protection in Frontier Regions," (21 September 1978); Organisation for Economic Co-Operation

152   *The ESM of wastes*

to pollution regardless of whether it has domestic and/or transboundary effects. The OECD Council Recommendation C(74)224 described the following elements of the nondiscrimination principle:

- Transfrontier pollution cannot exceed the limits considered tolerable in relation to pollution levels within national jurisdiction, without prejudice of the application of international law standards.
- Polluters causing transboundary pollution should be subject to no less strict administrative, civil, or criminal procedures as those responsible for causing pollution in their own jurisdiction. By the same token, victims and persons likely to suffer damage due to transboundary pollution should be granted an equivalent treatment to those likely to suffer damage of pollution in their own jurisdiction.
- The polluter pays principle, if applicable within a jurisdiction, should be also applied in cases involving transboundary pollution.

This principle was operationalized through the development of standards for "equal right of access in relation to transboundary pollution" that includes, among other things: access to information; consultation; and access to justice.[20] Article 15 of the ILC Draft Articles on the Prevention of Transboundary Harm from Hazardous Activities describes the principle of nondiscrimination in a limited fashion; i.e., granting access to "persons ... who may be or are exposed to the risk of significant transboundary harm ... to judicial or other procedures to seek protection or other appropriate redress".[21] The principle has been applied in relation to transboundary pollution and transboundary movements of wastes.[22]

Whether the principle of nondiscrimination is fully applicable to the Parties to the Basel Convention is controversial. During the negotiations of this Convention, in respect of the ESM standards of waste management, there was no support for stipulating that standards in the State of import should be at least as

---

and Development (OECD), "C(79)116 Recommendation of the Council on the Assessment of Projects with Significant Impact on the Environment," (8 May 1979).

20 *See* Organisation for Economic Co-Operation and Development (OECD), "C (76) 55/Final Recommendation of the Council on Equal Right of Access in Relation to Transfrontier Pollution," (1976). "C (77) 28/Final Recommendation of the Council for the Implementation of a Regime of Equal Right of Access and Non-Discrimination in Relation to Transfrontier Pollution." OECD Secretariat, "Equal Right of Access in Matters of Transfrontier Pollution in OECD Member Countries," in *Legal Aspects of Transfrontier Pollution*, ed. OECD (Paris: OECD, 1977). Jean-Marc Bischoff, "The Territorial Limits of Public Law and their Implications in Regard to the Principles of Non-Discrimination and Equal Right of Access as Recognized in Connection with Transfrontier Pollution," in *Legal Aspects of Transfrontier Pollution*, ed. OECD (Paris: OECD, 1977).

21 International Law Commission (Fifty-Third Session A/56/10), "Draft Articles on Prevention of Transboundary Harm from Hazardous Activities, with Commentaries."

22 The non-discrimination principle "could have implications for such problems as trade in alien or endangered species, export of genetically modified organisms, or sustainable use of natural resources." Birnie, Boyle, and Redgwell, *International Law and the Environment*, 152.

ESM and transboundary movement 153

strict as those applicable in the State of export.[23] The negotiations culminated in the adoption of the rather ambiguous definition of ESM established in Article 2(8) of the Basel Convention, i.e., the management of wastes "in a manner which will protect human health and the environment against the adverse effects which may result from such wastes." The definition gives little guidance as to how to assess compliance with this obligation.

The nondiscrimination principle is arguably relevant in assessing whether the exporting State is complying with its ESM obligations under the Basel Convention, especially in relation to transboundary movements of wastes occurring between developed States and developing States with weak waste management standards. According to Article 4(10) of the Basel Convention, the State of export retains the responsibility for ensuring the management of wastes in an environmentally sound manner. This obligation cannot be transferred to States of import or transit. Additionally, according to Article 4(2)(e) the State of export has the obligation to prohibit a movement if it has reason to believe that the wastes will not be managed in an environmentally sound manner. ESM is "a precondition for legal transboundary movements of hazardous and other wastes".[24] The State of export must determine the suitable methods to dispose of the wastes and decide whether or not the proposed disposal activity complies with the ESM obligation under the Basel Convention. The assessment of whether the management of wastes is environmentally sound inevitably requires a case-by-case analysis taking into account the standards applicable in the State of export and those applicable in the State of import. Thus, having the authorization of the State of import to proceed with the movement is not enough and will not exempt the State of export from the obligation toward the ESM of wastes.

At the OECD level, the principle of nondiscrimination was included in the OECD Recommendations C(77)28 and C(83)100. It has also been included at the EU level, in Regulation 1013/2006/EC on Shipments of Wastes.[25] The principle of nondiscrimination, while relevant, is limited insofar as it does not provide any substantive standard regarding the level of protection. If transboundary movements of wastes occur between States without the capacities to manage wastes, the nondiscrimination principle does not provide any basis to avoid unsound waste management practices.

Ex ante *control of transboundary movements of wastes*

Although the State of export retains the responsibility for the ESM of wastes, the *ex ante* and *ex post facto* control of the management of wastes are quite limited. Article 4(2)(e) of the Basel Convention reduces the obligation of the State

---

23 Several delegations from Africa urged for the incorporation of the "no less strict" standard. "The 'no less strict' standard would have sharply curtailed the hazardous waste trade, but it was too far-reaching to be acceptable to leading waste exporting countries." Abrams, "Regulating the International Hazardous Waste Trade: A Proposed Global Solution," 828.
24 Grosz, *Sustainable Waste Trade under WTO Law*, 4, 143.
25 *See* Articles 11(1)(b), 12(1)(b) and (c) of Regulation 1013/2006/EC on Shipment of Wastes.

154 *The ESM of wastes*

of export to prohibit a transboundary movement of wastes, if it *has reason to believe* that wastes will not be managed in an environmentally sound manner. This "reason" is based exclusively on the information available of the proposed transboundary movement. Available information should be understood in general terms, including but not limited to the documentation provided by the exporter or generator in the notification document.

Article 4(2)(e) could be extensively criticized for its lack of guidance regarding the circumstances upon which a State of export must prohibit a movement and how it is going to exercise this "veto".[26] However, the State of export does not have the obligation to monitor, supervise, and control the management of wastes on account of the sovereignty and territorial integrity of States of import. Beyond national jurisdiction, States of export have no legal authority. Suggesting that the State of export could exercise an extra-territorial jurisdiction finds no support in the text of the Basel Convention, or in subsequent practice of State Parties. Additionally, other *ex ante* verification mechanisms, e.g., inspection of disposal sites, not only encounter difficulties in the exercise of extra-territorial competences, but these mechanisms can also be construed as a paternalistic interference.[27] During the negotiation of the Basel Convention, the Organization of African Unity (OAU) proposed the introduction of stringent verification processes, including the inspection of disposal sites.[28] However, the proposal found no support. Developed States, for instance, voiced their fear of environmental paternalism, but they also recognized that the ultimate responsibility for the management of wastes should not be placed exclusively on the State of import.

The Basel Convention allocates *ex ante* and *ex post facto* responsibilities for the ESM of wastes in all the States involved in a transboundary movement. Thus, States of import are also obliged to comply with ESM. The State of import does not have an absolute right to receive wastes since its acceptance is conditioned by the ESM of such wastes. However, as with the State of export, the *ex ante* obligation of the State of import is very weak. Article 4(2)(g) of the Basel Convention prescribes that States of import shall "[p]revent the import of hazardous wastes and other wastes if it has reason to believe that the wastes in question will not be managed in an environmentally sound manner." Thus, the importing State has considerable latitude in choosing how to implement and enforce its obligations ranging from formal verification of documentation to the active inspection of disposal sites (e.g., licensing of waste management facilities).

---

26 Abrams, "Regulating the International Hazardous Waste Trade: A Proposed Global Solution," 829.

27 For an ethical analysis and criticism of the paternalistic argument, *See* Frank B. Cross and Brenda J. Winslett, "'Export Death': Ethical Issues and the International Trade in Hazardous Products," *American Business Law Journal* 25, no. 3 (1987): 512–14. *See also* Abrams, "Regulating the International Hazardous Waste Trade: A Proposed Global Solution," 829. Handl and Lutz, "An International Policy Perspective on the Trade of Hazardous Materials and Technologies," 363.

28 Christoph Hilz and Mark Radka, "Environmental Negotiation and Policy: The Basel Convention on Transboundary Movement of Hazardous Wastes and their Disposal," *International Journal of Environment and Pollution* 1, nos. 1/2 (1991): 68.

If a State of import cannot ensure the environmentally sound management of wastes, it can seek international assistance according to Article 10 of the Basel Convention. In general, international assistance duties included in multilateral environmental agreements (MEAs) pursue: (a) the enhancement of institutional capabilities; (b) establishment of best practice; (c) transference of technology and know-how in the recipient State. One disadvantage of the cooperation duties to improve the ESM of wastes is that funding mechanisms are not compulsory, but voluntary.[29] The COP to the Basel Convention in its Fifth Meeting decided to enlarge the scope of the Technical Cooperation Trust Fund to assist developing States "in developing their capacity-building and transfer of technology and in putting in place measures to prevent accidents".[30] In 2002, at the Sixth Meeting, the COP to the Basel Convention established the "Interim Guidelines for the implementation of Decision V/32".[31] This documents specifies that resources to enhance capacity building will be destined to prevent accidents and damage to the environment, specifically: (a) safety, risk reduction, and accident prevention; and (b) emergency response and contingency planning. UNEP launched a consultative process for financing options for the safe and environmentally sound management of chemicals and wastes, including public-private partnerships, and the creation of a trust fund akin to the Multilateral Fund for the Implementation of the Montreal Protocol.[32] Finally, the Strategic Framework for the Implementation of the Basel Convention for 2012–2021 identified several funding mechanisms, e.g., domestic and external resources, regional cooperation, and the private sector.[33]

According to Article 14 of the Basel Convention, regional or sub-regional centers for training and technology transfers should be established. Currently there are 14 centers. The centers are located in Argentina, China, Egypt, El Salvador, Indonesia,

---

29 *See* Article 14 of the Basel Convention.

30 COP to the Basel Convention, "Decision V/32: Enlargement of the Scope of the Technical Cooperation Trust Fund," in *Conference of the Parties to the Basel Convention on the Control of Transboundary Movements of Hazardous Wastes and their Disposal. Fifth Meeting. UNEP/CHW.5/29* (Basel, 1999).

31 "Decision VI/14: Interim Guidelines for the Implementation of Decision V/32 on Enlargement of the Scope of the Trust Fund to Assist Developing and Other Countries in Need of Technical Assistance in the Implementation of the Basel Convention," in *Conference of the Parties to the Basel Convention on the Control of Transboundary Movements of Hazardous Wastes and their Disposal. Sixth Meeting. UNEP/CHW.6/40* (Geneva, 2002). The guidelines were amended at the Twelfth Meeting through Decision BC-12/11. "Decision BC-12/11: Implementation of Decision V/32 on the Enlargement of the Scope of the Trust Fund to Assist Developing and Other Countries in Need of Technical Assistance in the Implementation of the Basel Convention," in *Conference of the Parties to the Basel Convention on the Control of Transboundary Movements of Hazardous Wastes and their Disposal. Twelfth Meeting. UNEP/CHW.12/27* (Geneva, 2015).

32 "Outcome Document of the Consultative Process on Financing Options for Chemicals and Wastes (UNEP/CHW.10/INF/54)," in *Conference of the Parties to the Basel Convention on the Control of Transboundary Movements of Hazardous Wastes and their Disposal. Tenth Meeting* (Cartagena, October 2011).

33 *See* numeral IV. Means of Implementation of the Strategic Framework. "Decision BC-10/2: New Strategic Framework for the Implementation of the Basel Convention for 2012–2021 (UNEP/CHW.10/3)."

156 *The ESM of wastes*

Islamic Republic of Iran, Nigeria, Russian Federation, Senegal, Slovak Republic, South Pacific Regional Environment Program (Samoa), South Africa, Trinidad and Tobago, and Uruguay.[34] Although the Convention is global in nature, the needs of African countries, for instance, may differ from those of European States. Regional centers tend to foster further regional cooperation and attract funding.[35] Thus, having regional centers is important in addressing particular challenges that a region may be facing with regard to the implementation of the Basel Convention. Currently, the regional centers established under the Basel Convention deal with "three broad areas: raising awareness, strengthening administrative ability, and diffusing scientific and technical assistance and information".[36]

Best available techniques and best environmental practices

The Basel Convention makes no reference BAT and BEP. However, Article 10 calls upon State Parties to cooperate in the "development and implementation of new environmentally sound low-waste technologies" to ensure both the minimization and ESM of wastes. Although BAT and BEP are not explicitly mentioned in the Basel Convention, they have become an integral part of ESM. The Framework for the Environmentally Sound Management of Hazardous Wastes and Other Wastes calls for the application of BAT and BEP throughout the waste cycle. At the OECD level, Recommendation C(2004)100 on the Environmentally Sound Management of Wastes encourages States to use BAT. At the EU level, Article 16 of the Waste Framework Directive requires management facilities to "*take into account*" BAT.

BAT and BEP were coined to promote the prevention of environmental damage at source, rather than focusing on coping with the deleterious effects of human activities on the environment.[37] From binding and nonbinding instruments including BAT and BEP, some common features emerge to understand their meaning and content. BAT basically refers to the latest state of development of technology and methods of operation, which are most effective in achieving certain environmental goals. To determine BAT, scientific, economic, and social factors may be taken into consideration. BEP is commonly defined as the "most appropriate combination of environmental control measures and strategies." In addition, both BAT and BEP are dynamic in nature since they evolve according to scientific knowledge, as well as economic and social aspects. The substantive content of BAT and BEP will not be identical across developed and developing countries, they are generated and implemented in specific socio-economic environments.

---

34 General information regarding the activities of the centers can be found at: <www.basel.int/Partners/RegionalCentres/Overview/tabid/2334/Default.aspx>, last accessed 22 March 2019.

35 "Parties have set up regional centers in response to three partially overlapping sets of developing and industrialized country interests with respect to improving multilevel governance: expanding regional cooperation … attracting more resources for treaty implementation … and supporting implementation projects across smaller groups of countries." Henrik Selin, "Global Environmental Governance and Regional Centers," *Global Environmental Politics* 12, no. 3 (2012): 19.

36 Ibid., 28.

37 Tuomas Kuokkanen, *International Law and the Environment: Variations on a Theme*, Vol. 4 (The Hague: Kluwer Law International, 2002), 255.

ESM and transboundary movement 157

The legal nature of BAT and BEP varies according to the instrument into which they have been incorporated, ranging from policy guidance criteria to binding obligations, to being implemented and enforced by different States to varying degrees. In relation to transboundary movement of wastes at both international and OECD levels, BAT and BEP have been developed through soft law instruments. At the EU level, Regulation 1013/2006/EC on Shipments of Wastes requires waste facilities to apply BAT. If the facility does not apply BAT, the State of import can raise an objection to the movement.[38]

As previously discussed, ESM is an obligation of conduct subject to the standard of due diligence. In international environmental law, due diligence has been construed as entailing both BAT and BEP. Therefore, the application of BAT and BEP must be taken into account to determine whether or not a State Party to the Basel Convention has exercised due diligence in relation to the management of wastes in an environmentally sound manner. The ITLOS Seabed Dispute Chamber in its advisory opinion concerning the *Responsibilities and Obligations of States Sponsoring Persons and Entities with Respect to Activities in the Area* discussed the nature of due diligence. The Seabed Dispute Chamber explained that due diligence is a variable concept that evolves in light of "new scientific or technological knowledge".[39] In the *Pulp Mills* case, the International Court of Justice (ICJ) stated that the exercise of due diligence entails "careful consideration of the technology to be used".[40]

It appears that exercising due diligence is linked with the adoption of environmental control measures and the development of technology. Birnie et al. explain that:

> due diligence entails an evolving standard of technology and regulation, this is commonly expressed by reference to the use of best available techniques, best practices. Comparisons with standards followed by other states will often be a good guide in this context.[41]

Since transboundary movements of wastes involve several jurisdictions, i.e., State of export, State of import, and State of transit, the determination of BAT and BEP requires a comparative assessment. This is consistent with the principle of nondiscrimination. Finally, BAT and BEP are also intertwined with the precautionary approach.[42]

ESM at the OECD level

The OECD has chosen a soft law approach to give substance to this fundamental obligation that otherwise would have been left entirely to the discretion

---

38 *See* Articles 11(1)(h) and 12(1)(i) of Regulation 1013/2006/EC.
39 *Responsibilities and Obligations of States with Respect to Activities in the Area, Advisory Opinion,* 17 ITLOS Reports 10, para 117 (1 February 2011).
40 *Pulp Mills on the River Uruguay (Argentina v. Uruguay), Judgment of 20 April 2010,* General List No. 135, para 223 (2010).
41 Birnie, Boyle, and Redgwell, *International Law and the Environment,* 148.
42 *See* Owen McIntyre and Thomas Mosedale, "The Precautionary Principle as a Norm of Customary International Law," *Journal of Environmental Law* 9 (1997): 221

158   *The ESM of wastes*

of State Parties. Despite the fact that guidelines, recommendations, and codes of conduct are *prima facie* nonmandatory, one should not underestimate their effectiveness. Indeed, soft law instruments have become widely employed in environmental law to assist States in complying with and implementing their treaty obligations. Soft law may range from general aspirational declarations to specific and detailed technical guidelines that "can be measured and allow for monitoring of compliance",[43] for instance, through reporting or technical assistance.[44] Additionally, these instruments have proven to be particularly relevant in concretizing substantive obligations contained in treaty law, and thanks to their perceived flexibility they can be easily modified to keep up to date with technological or scientific developments if required. Flexibility of soft law instruments flows from their *prima facie* nonbinding nature. Grosz believes that the OECD Recommendation C(2004)100 on the Environmentally Sound Management of Wastes was chosen "in view of the different situations prevailing in different countries and facilities in the OECD Region".[45] Nonetheless, flexibility is also a limitation of soft law since there is no mechanism available to guarantee that States will abide by these instruments or that they will be fully implemented.

Wastes covered by the OECD Recommendation C(2004)100 are the same as those defined in the OECD Council Decision C(2001)107/FINAL, i.e., substances or objects, other than radioactive materials, subject to disposal or recovery operations whether hazardous or not.[46] The OECD Recommendation is, however, wider in scope since it is concerned with both disposal and recovery operations carried out in management facilities of OECD States whether public or privately owned. Additionally, no distinction is made in terms of the management of domestic or imported wastes. This is consistent with the principle of no discrimination, since the management of wastes depends on their physical and chemical characteristics rather than their place of origin.

The structure of the OECD Recommendation C(2004)100 can be divided into four parts: (a) objectives to be achieved by implementing standards related to the environmentally sound and economically efficient management of wastes; (b) recommendations that are general long-term aspirations regarding waste management; (c) six Core Performance Elements, which are suggestions covering the functioning, closure, and aftercare of waste management facilities; and (d) detailed technical guidelines for the management of certain types of wastes.

One objective of the OECD Recommendation C(2004)100 is to protect human health and the environment from the deleterious effects associated with

---

43 "This means that one must discard the assumption that nonbinding instruments are typically unspecific and vague. Nonbinding does not always mean soft and imprecise norms, but rather there is often a correlation between nonbinding norms and precise substance." Friedrich, *International Environmental "Soft Law": The Functions and Limits of Nonbinding Instruments in International Environmental Governance and Law*, 131.

44 Ibid., 140–41.

45 Grosz, *Sustainable Waste Trade under WTO Law*, 4, 179.

46 *See* footnote 2 of the OECD Recommendation C(2004)100. *See also* Organisation for Economic Co-Operation and Development (OECD), "Guidance Manual on Environmentally Sound Management of Waste," 12–13.

ESM and transboundary movement 159

wastes, while promoting the "sustainable use of natural resources and minimization of wastes".[47] Waste minimization could prove difficult to achieve considering that the OECD regime on transboundary movements of wastes provides incentives for trading wastes and protects well-established waste markets. Other objectives of the OECD Recommendation C(2004)100 are: (a) achieving fair competition between waste management facilities in the OECD area by the harmonization of environmental standards; and (b) minimizing the demand "for management facilities operating low-standards to facilities that manage waste in an environmentally sound and economically efficient manner".[48]

Member States have great latitude of discretion in going about accomplishing these objectives. For instance, they could enact regulations or establish subsidies on certain waste management technologies to make recovery more economically appealing than disposal alternatives. Some guidance can be found in the "recommendation" part of the instrument where the OECD Council suggests that Member States do not hinder transboundary movements of wastes destined for recovery operations, and that they consider the size of the waste management facility, type of waste, and required management operation. The recommendations include several mechanisms to achieve the objectives of the instrument that are not limited to enacting legislation, but also include economic incentives. Regulatory measures could consist of licensing schemes, monitoring coupled with noncompliance procedures, and the establishment of liability regimes for facilities carrying out risky activities.[49] Developing a liability regime is long overdue in respect of transboundary movement of wastes. It also marks a shift toward the internalization of environmental costs involved in waste management, as well as a manifestation of the polluter pays principle, but such internalization can also be achieved through economic measures, like taxation of landfill disposal. Member States should also provide incentives to "take part in environmentally sound recycling schemes",[50] including educational and communicational campaigns for waste separation and collection, subsidies, setting minimum recycling goals, among others. Waste recovery is seen as a device to minimize wastes by recovering and reusing materials. Nonetheless, further efforts are required to minimize the generation of wastes at source. In addition, the OECD Recommendation considers that waste management facilities should manage wastes according to the "best available techniques," i.e., BAT.[51] This includes *technology and methods of operation*, which not only seek to minimize the environmental and health risks associated with waste management, but also strive to be cost-efficient.[52]

---

47 *See* objective No. 1 of the OECD Recommendation C(2004)100.

48 Ibid., objective No. 3.

49 Ibid., Recommendations Nos. 1, 2 and 10.

50 Ibid., Recommendation 9.

51 Ibid., Recommendation 3.

52 *Note* that "best available techniques" could be understood as a constant process for "improving environmental performance" and should not be equated exclusively with a particular level of technology. Organisation for Economic Co-Operation and Development (OECD), "Guidance Manual on Environmentally Sound Management of Waste," 23–24. The Guidance Manual provides an overview of the understanding of the criterion "best available techniques" under EU law, and in the United States.

160   *The ESM of wastes*

The OECD Recommendation encourages States to implement six core performance elements provided in this instrument and to consider incentives for the facilities that fulfill those requirements.[53] The core performance elements are detailed guidelines covering the operation, closure, and aftercare of waste management facilities. Finally, Annexes II and III of the OECD Recommendation C(2004)100 include detailed technical guidelines and endorses several instruments adopted by the COP to the Basel Convention.

It is curious that neither the OECD Council Decision C(2001)107/FINAL nor the OECD Recommendation C(2004)100 defines the ESM of wastes. There is an OECD working definition, which reads as follows:

> scheme for ensuring that wastes and scrap materials are managed in a manner that will save natural resources, and protect human health and the environment against adverse effects that may result from such wastes and materials.[54]

Some of the elements of this definition have been phrased as objectives to be achieved in the implementation of waste management policies and regulations. The inclusion of scrap materials in the working definition is somewhat confusing, given that wastes are defined in relation to an operational approach. Consequently, all objects or substances subject to disposal or recovery operations are wastes for the purposes of the OECD Recommendation C(2004)100 independently of their designation. However, one should remember that the boundaries between waste and nonwaste are not evident, and many jurisdictions could try to disassociate certain materials or substances from the notion of wastes by labelling them "by products," "raw materials," "recyclable materials," "second hand products."

The OECD Council instructed the Environment Policy Committee to report on the implementation of Recommendation C(2004)100, after three years of its adoption, based on the information provided by Member States.[55] At present, there is no available data on this matter, so it is difficult to assess the impact of the Recommendation on waste management. The lack of submissions from Member States also reveals a limitation of soft law in the absence of enforcement mechanisms. However, even mandatory reporting obligations could prove difficult to enforce, especially when States do not have the appropriate resources to generate and transmit the required information. For instance, a report on the transboundary movement of wastes at an international level during the years 2004 to 2006 showed that only a third of the Parties to the Basel Convention provided data on the generation of hazardous wastes.[56]

---

53 *See* Recommendations 2, 5 and 6 of the OECD Recommendation C(2004)100.
54 Organisation for Economic Co-Operation and Development (OECD), "Guidance Manual on Environmentally Sound Management of Waste," 8.
55 *See* instruction No. 3 of the OECD Recommendation C(2004)100.
56 Wielenga, "Waste without Frontiers: Global Trends in Generation and Transboundary Movements of Hazardous Wastes and Other Wastes," 4. At the time the report was published, the

ESM at the EU level

The regulation of waste at the EU level is extensive. While the Waste Framework Directive provides for general obligations, other specific pieces of legislation deal with, for instance: shipments of wastes[57]; packaging of waste[58]; incineration of waste[59]; landfill of waste[60]; waste of electrical and electronic equipment.[61] The Waste Framework Directive is *lex generalis vis-à-vis* the legislation dealing with specific waste streams and disposal operations.[62] Article 2 of the Waste Framework Directive 2008/98/EC excludes from its scope several wastes, including radioactive waste and decommissioned explosives. It also provides for a *lex specialis* clause. Article 2(4) reads as follows:

> [s]pecific rules for particular instances, or supplementing those of this Directive, on the management of particular categories of waste, may be laid down by means of individual Directives.

From the wording of Article 2(4), it becomes apparent that legislation dealing comprehensively with wastes will take precedence over the Waste Framework Directive.[63] It does not mean, however, that the *lex generalis* ceases to have legal effects, or that it is set aside completely. On the contrary, everything that is not regulated by the *lex specialis* will be subject to the *lex generalis*, e.g., the concept of waste.

The Waste Framework Directive gives priority to a precautionary approach, since the minimization of waste ranks highly as a priority of the waste policy at the EU level. Article 13 imposes ESM as an underlying obligation in relation to wastes, i.e., management without endangering human health and the environment. In relation to Regulation 1013/2006/EC on Shipments of Wastes, every transboundary movement of waste must be assessed in accordance with the ESM obligation.[64]

Article 2(8) of Regulation 1013/2006/EC on Shipments of Wastes defines ESM. The definition closely follows that of the Basel Convention and the OECD working definition, i.e., "taking all practicable steps to ensure that waste is managed in a manner that will protect human health and the environment against adverse effects which may result from such waste." The protection of human health and the environment is not only fundamental in respect of ESM; it is also the main purpose of Regulation 1013/2006/EC on Shipments of Wastes as a whole.

Basel Convention had 175 parties and during the period 2004–2006 only 66 parties reported on the generation of hazardous wastes.

57 "Regulation (EC) 1013/2006 on Shipments of Waste," (OJ L 190, p. 1, 12.07.2006).

58 "Directive 94/62/EC on Packaging and Packaging Waste."

59 "Directive 2000/76/EC on the Incineration of Waste," (OJ L 332, p. 91, 28.12.2000).

60 "Directive 1999/31/EC on the Landfill of Waste," (OJ L 182, p. 1, 16.07.1999).

61 "Directive 2012/19/EU on Waste Electrical and Electronic Equipment (WEEE)" (OJ L 197/38, 24.07.2012.)

62 Van Calster, *EU Waste Law*, 1; Grosz, *Sustainable Waste Trade under WTO Law*, 4, 73.

63 This will be the case of wastes and management operations that are not excluded *ab initio* from the scope of application of the Waste Framework Directive 2008/98/EC.

64 *See* Articles 35, 41, 42, 44, and 49 of Regulation on Shipment of Wastes 1013/2006/EC.

162   *The ESM of wastes*

In the case *C-411/06*, the Commission of the European Communities challenged the choice made by the European Parliament and the Council of the European Union to exclusively base Regulation 1013/2006/EC on Shipments of Wastes on Article 175(1) of the EC Treaty,[65] i.e., environmental policy, instead of Article 133 of the EC treaty,[66] i.e., commercial policy, and Article 175(1). According to the Commission, Regulation 1013/2006/EC on Shipments of Wastes serves a dual purpose: the protection of the environment, and regulation of the "free movement of goods" within the EU.[67] The Commission also observed that the protection of the environment does not preclude the pursuing of other objectives, including trade. In fact, both the commercial and environmental policies are not just compatible but indissociable, "neither of which can be regarded as secondary".[68] The Court of Justice determined that Article 175(1) of the EC Treaty is the proper legal basis of Regulation 1013/2006/EC on Shipments of Wastes because it establishes procedures whereby transboundary movements of wastes could be restricted, and it is not concerned with enabling the free circulation of wastes "within the internal market or as part of commercial trade with third countries".[69]

Article 49 of Regulation 1013/2006/EC on Shipments of Wastes elaborates on the substantive content of the ESM of wastes. This is a general obligation applicable to all transboundary movements of wastes occurring within the EU and from or to third States. ESM applies to wastes subject to disposal and recovery operations including those subject to the PIC procedure or general information requirements. In fact, guaranteeing ESM is a fundamental prerequisite for any transboundary movement.[70]

An integral part of ESM includes the waste hierarchy established in Article 4 of the Waste Framework Directive. Thus, when assessing alternatives for waste management, the following priority order must be followed: prevention; preparing for reuse; recycling; other recovery; and disposal. Additionally, Article 49(2) of the Regulation 1013/2006/EC on Shipments of Wastes refers to several guidelines listed in Annex VIII that may serve as guidance to EU Member

---

65 The corresponding article is 192(1) of the "Treaty on the Functioning of the European Union."
66 The corresponding article is 207 of the Treaty on the Functioning of the European Union.
67 Paras 30 and 32. Case C-411/06. Commission of the European Communities v. European Parliament and Council of the European Union, ECR I-07585 (2009).
68 Ibid., paras 30–31.
69 Ibid., para 72. *See also Case C-187/93, ECR I-2874 (1994)*. In this case, the Court of Justice examined the legal basis of the Regulation on Shipment of Wastes (EEC) No. 259/93. Paragraph 26 indicates: "the aim of the Regulation is not to define those characteristics of waste which will enable it to circulate freely within the internal market, but to provide a harmonized set of procedures whereby movements of waste can be limited in order to secure protection of the environment." Regulation 1013/2006/EC on Shipment of Wastes repealed Regulation No. 259/93/EEC, but the legal basis and the analysis provided is applicable to the current Regulation.
70 *See*, for instance, Article 34(3)(b) where transboundary movements of wastes destined to disposal and to EFTA countries, must be prohibited if "the competent authority of dispatch has reason to believe that the waste will not be managed in an environmentally sound manner, as referred to in Article 49." *See also* Articles 35 (4)(d), 36(1)(g), and 42(4)(d). *See also* Grosz, *Sustainable Waste Trade under WTO Law*, 4, 189.

States in the implementation of ESM, including those adopted under the Basel Convention, by the OECD, the IMO and the ILO. This provides evidence of the emergence of international agreed standards in relation to ESM.

Article 49(2) of the Regulation 1013/2006/EC on Shipments of Wastes incorporates the principle of nondiscrimination in the following terms:

> [e]nvironmentally sound management may, *inter alia*, be assumed ... if the notifier or the competent authority in the country of destination can demonstrate that the facility which receives the waste will be operated in accordance with human health and environmental protection standards that are broadly equivalent to standards established in Community legislation.

The principle of nondiscrimination is also incorporated in Article 11(1)(b) related to transboundary movements of wastes destined for disposal operations, and Article 12(1)(b) and (c) concerning transboundary movements of wastes destined for recovery operations. According to the conditions established in these articles, the authorities of the State of export and import may object to a proposed shipment if it is not in accordance with "the national legislation relating to the environmental protection ... or health protection concerning actions taking place in the objecting country".[71] Subject to certain exceptions, Article 12(1)(c) also provides that an objection may be raised when wastes would be recovered in a facility "which has lower treatment standards for the particular waste than those of the country of dispatch."

Concluding remarks

The ESM of wastes comprises all the activities and measures that deal with wastes from a life-cycle approach. The activities included under ESM are regulatory, economic, and technological. In addition, ESM requires the participation and cooperation of governmental authorities, waste generators, carriers, brokers and dealers, management facilities, and civil society organizations.

The COP to the Basel Convention has played an important role in the development of a common framework of ESM that is not just applicable to wastes subject to transboundary movements. Overall, ESM should be understood as the development and implementation of waste management systems that take into account the waste management hierarchy. Such a hierarchy was originally developed at the EU level, and it is the point of departure for establishing agreed standards with regard to ESM.

---

71 Articles 11(1)(b) and 12(1)(b) of Regulation 1013/2006/EC on Shipment of Wastes.

8 The ESM of ship wastes: the sea/land interface

The ESM of ship wastes at the international level

Sea/land ship waste management and the duty not to transform pollution

The IMO manual on Port Reception Facilities provides guidelines for downstream treatment of wastes after their discharge at port reception facilities. Thus, the IMO is assisting States in complying with the obligation set in Article 195 of the LOSC, *i.e.*, to avoid the transformation of one type of pollution into another. This provision has an integrative function[1] that requires cooperation and coordination between stakeholders and legal regimes in order to prevent unintended consequences in one environmental media, *e.g.*, sea, while taking actions to prevent and control pollution in another environmental media, *e.g.*, land. The international regulation of the environment has a predominant sectoral approach, and Article 195 of the LOSC is an attempt to address fragmentation. The duty to not transfer or transform pollution has been incorporated in several treaties, including various regional sea conventions. The development of standards related to the ESM of wastes certainly operationalizes the duty to not transform pollution. Principle 6 of the Cairo Guidelines indicates that ESM cannot be achieved by the "mere transformation of one form of pollution into another."

Port reception facilities

According to Article 211(2) of the LOSC, the regulations adopted by States to prevent, control, and reduce ship-source pollution "shall at least have the same effect as that of generally accepted international rules and standards established through the competent international organization." These international

---

1 *See* the analysis of Article 195 in Kim Rakhyun and Harro van Asselt, "Global Governance: Problem Shifting in the Anthropocene and the Limits of International Law," in *Research Handbook on International Law and Natural Resources*, ed. Elisa Morgera and Kati Kulovesi (Cheltenham: Edward Elgar Publishing, 2016), 481–82.

ESM of ship wastes: the sea/land interface 165

rules –also known as GAIRS– refer, in this case, to MARPOL. State Parties to the LOSC and MARPOL have designed a regulatory system that aims to prevent marine pollution by reducing discharges of harmful substances into the marine environment. This regulatory system has two implications. On the one hand, since their holding capacity is limited, vessels using a port or terminal have not only the obligation *but also the right* to discharge residues at port reception facilities.[2] States, on the other hand, while exercising their sovereign right over the use of their territory and resources, have agreed to receive ship wastes and treat them on land without transforming one type of pollution into another. It is meaningless to require wastes to be kept on board unless they are eventually received on land.

Notwithstanding the crucial role of port reception facilities in the prevention of ship-source pollution, treaty obligations do not clearly identify whether the State or a private operator, *e.g.*, terminal operator, is responsible for the funding, construction, operation, maintenance, and decommissioning of a port reception facility. For instance, OILPOL 54, the predecessor of MARPOL, regulated exclusively oil pollution. Originally, Article VIII of the Convention established that States "shall ensure the provision ... of facilities." After the amendment of the Convention in 1962,[3] Article VIII prescribed that States shall take "appropriate steps to promote the provision of facilities." The article as amended is weaker than its original wording. Several State Parties, including the Commonwealth of the Bahamas, Chile, Fiji, and the United States, declared, in a similar way, that they "will urge port authorities, oil terminals or private contractors to provide adequate disposal facilities ... [but] shall not be obliged to construct, operate, or maintain shore facilities ... or to assume any financial obligation to assist in such activities".[4] Other States, such as Liberia, made a reservation in relation to Article VIII.[5] It is doubtful whether this reservation is valid because a State that does not accept the obligation related to the provision of port reception facilities is undermining the object and purpose of the Convention according to Article 19(c) of the Vienna Convention on the Law of the Treaties, 1969.

The obligation to "ensure" the provision of port reception facilities

The regulations in MARPOL requiring port reception facilities state in a similar fashion that each party "undertakes to ensure the provision of" *adequate*

---

2 de La Fayette, "The Sound Management of Wastes Generated at Sea: MARPOL, Not Basel," 211.

3 OIPOL 54 entered into force on 26 July 1958. Amendments to the Convention were adopted at the International Conference on Prevention of Pollution of the Sea by Oil, 1962, and at the Sixth Assembly of IMCO on 21 October 1969. Two further amendments were adopted in 1971 but did not enter into force.

4 "Declarations, Statements and Reservations of the Parties to the International Convention for the Prevention of Pollution of the Sea by Oil," (London: Informa UK Limited), available at: <www.i-law.com/ilaw/doc/view.htm?id=131464>, last accessed 23 March 2019.

5 Ibid.

166 *The ESM of wastes*

reception facilities to receive harmful substances of Annexes I, II, IV, V, and VI.[6] Unlike strict regulations prescribed in MARPOL and impinged directly on ship operators, *e.g.*, ships' construction standards, equipment, and discharge criteria, the obligation in relation to the funding and operation of port reception facilities remain vague. States explicitly avoided being bound by strict regulations under MARPOL, and "never meant to state clearly who – the states, the ports ... should pay for the facilities".[7] In fact, State Parties amend the Convention periodically and strongly support on-board treatment techniques,[8] but little has been done to establish binding obligations in relation to port reception facilities. According to the IMO, a State Party may provide reception facilities, but it is not an obligation imposed on a State *per se*; instead a Party could choose to require port authorities and terminal operators to provide the facilities.[9] However, the obligation "to ensure" the provision of port reception facilities goes beyond the adoption of regulations requiring operators to fund and operate such facilities.

The Arbitral Tribunal examined the obligation *"to ensure"* in *the South China Sea Arbitration* case. According to the Court, "ensure" is an obligation of conduct. It requires a State to be due diligent, *i.e.*, it must adopt "appropriate rules and measures, *but also a certain level of vigilance in their enforcement and the exercise of administrative control*"[10] (emphasis added). This case reproduces verbatim the concept of due diligence as analyzed by ITLOS in the *Request for an Advisory Opinion Submitted by the Sub-Regional Fisheries Commission*; and the Seabed Disputes Chamber in its advisory opinion concerning the *Responsibilities and Obligations of States Sponsoring Persons and Entities with Respect to Activities in the Area.*

The obligation to provide "adequate" port reception facilities

MARPOL does not define what constitute "adequate reception facilities," but the IMO considers that "adequacy"[11] serves to describe reception facilities with the following characteristics: satisfy the requirements of their users; prevent un-

---

6 *See* MARPOL, Annex I – Regulation 38; Annex II – Regulation 18; Annex IV – Regulations 12 and 13; Annex V – Regulation 8; and Annex VI – Regulation 17.

7 Tan, *Vessel-Source Marine Pollution: The Law and Politics of International Regulation*, 265. For Tan, the vague obligation under MARPOL in relation to port reception facilities "is a classic example of a serious and deliberate deficiency in the regime formation process which has inevitably affected compliance with the treaty."

8 For amendments and further regulation expected to enter into force before January 2024, *See* "Future IMO Legislation," (Southampton: Lloyd's Register, 2016).

9 International Maritime Organization (IMO), "MARPOL: How to Do It," (London: CPI Group, 2013), 97.

10 *Case No. 2013-19 the South China Sea Arbitration (the Republic of Philippines v. The People's Republic of China)*, para 944.

11 Marine Environment Protection Committee (MEPC), "Resolution MEPC.83(44): Guidelines for Ensuring the Adequacy of Port Waste Reception Facilities." MEPC.1/Circ.834 "Consolidated Guidance for Port Reception Facility Providers and Users." International Maritime Organization (IMO), "Port Reception Facilities – How to Do It."

ESM of ship wastes: the sea/land interface 167

due delays; avoid creating disincentives for using reception facilities; contribute to the improvement of the marine environment; and allow the "final disposal" of wastes generated on board ships on land in an environmentally appropriate way. These characteristics are explained below:

a *Satisfy the requirements of ships that usually use the port:* notwithstanding their size, all ports should be able to provide port reception facilities *for the types of ships using a particular port.* This does not mean, however, that a port should provide reception facilities for all types of ship wastes. It requires a previous study consistent with the waste management strategy to determine which type of vessels usually call to a port, and an assessment of the type and quantities of ship wastes.[12] Ports should carefully plan where to locate port reception facilities. If those facilities are inconveniently located, their use is subject to complex procedures or time-consuming, the facility cannot be considered adequate. The difficulties encountered by the users of port reception facilities include delays, the need to make use of a pilot, and "even the necessity of gas freeing before moving berth".[13]

b *Prevent undue delays of ships at ports:* vessels run on a tight schedule and if the use of reception facilities is time-consuming, incentives for illegal discharges at sea increase.[14] For this reason, "adequate" also means that the use of the facility must not go "beyond the normal turn-around time of the ship in that port".[15] The IMO recommends that the ship operator notify the "appropriate authority" in advance before the expected delivery of ship wastes at a port reception facility in order to plan the reception of ship wastes in a timely fashion. The IMO manual on Port Reception Facilities does not identify the authority that should be notified. If the notification system involves several authorities or individual terminals, this system could create practical problems in the assessment of quantities of wastes that are actually received at port reception facilities. It also creates difficulties in tracing the management of such wastes after they are discharged to a port reception facility.

c *Avoid creating disincentives for using reception facilities:* States are interested in developing cost recovery systems for the reception and further management on land of ship wastes. Based on the polluter pays principle, *i.e.,* "an economic policy for allocating the costs of pollution or environmental damage",[16] ship operators should pay, at least partially, for the costs involved in the operation of port reception facilities. In the case of port reception

---

12 *See* Chapter 5, "Planning port reception facilities," International Maritime Organization (IMO), "Port Reception Facilities – How to Do It."

13 Tom Westwood, "Poor Reception," *HS Safety at Sea* (2013): 32.

14 "failure to establish adequate facilities is a breach of international obligations and will increase the risk of illegal discharges from ships." International Maritime Organization (IMO), "Port Reception Facilities – How to Do It," 10.

15 Ibid., 20.

16 Birnie, Boyle, and Redgwell, *International Law and the Environment*, 322.

168 *The ESM of wastes*

facilities, many States have implemented the polluter pays principle by establishing diverse charge systems. If these charges become prohibitive, however, illegal discharges at sea increase.[17] Charges are useful to recover capital costs, personnel, maintenance, and other day-to-day operations of reception facilities. The IMO's manual on Port Reception Facilities includes several alternatives for allocating costs of port reception facilities, which are summarized in the following graphic (Figure 8.1).

Tax revenues or subsidies cover the operation of port reception facilities if State Parties have not implemented a recovery system.[18] In this case, incentives for illegal discharges are reduced, since ship operators must not pay anything for the discharge of wastes. However, if calling to a port causes delays, a ship may still choose to discharge ship waste into the marine environment. In addition, waste minimization on board is not encouraged in a free of charge system, and since the operation of facilities is covered by tax revenues or subsidies, ports will not have incentives to invest in best available technologies (BAT).[19]

In practice, States adopt several recovering mechanisms depending on, *e.g.*, type of ship, the frequency of calls of a particular kind of ship to a port, the type of wastes, the type of cargo handled in a port, and the length of voyage since the last port of call. For instance, in the Baltic Sea area, a direct fee is the most common recovery system in the case of cargo residues from MARPOL, Annexes I and II, *i.e.*, oil and hazardous chemicals, respectively.[20] As illustrated in the graphic above, direct fees may encourage illegal discharges. So, more resources need to be allocated for monitoring and enforcement mechanisms. Additionally, ships could hold wastes to discharge them at cheaper ports, which may affect ports' competitiveness.[21] In fact, direct fees could encourage "artificial price cutting" among ports, thereby triggering a race to the bottom. According to the IMO, States could impose "compulsory discharge for certain types of ship-generated wastes/residues"[22] to avoid ships to discharge their wastes elsewhere. Compulsory discharge criteria are unusual[23] because States face challenges not

---

17 Angela Carpenter and Sally Macgill, "Charging for Port Reception Facilities in North Sea Ports: Putting Theory into Practice," *Marine Pollution Bulletin* 42, no. 4 (2001): 258.

18 This is what the IMO calls "free-of-charge system." International Maritime Organization (IMO), "Port Reception Facilities – How to Do It," 160–61.

19 Dimitrios Georgakellos, "The Use of the Deposit-Refund Framework in Port Reception Facilities Charging Systems," *Marine Pollution Bulletin* 54, no. 5 (2007): 511.

20 Ramboll, "Final Report: EMSA Study on the Delivery of Ship-Generated Waste and Cargo Residues to Port Reception Facilities in EU Ports," 45.

21 Georgakellos, "The Use of the Deposit-Refund Framework in Port Reception Facilities Charging Systems," 511.

22 International Maritime Organization (IMO), "Port Reception Facilities – How to Do It," 156.

23 Regulation 8B of Annex IV of the Helsinki Convention: "[b]efore leaving port ships shall discharge all ship-generated wastes, which are not allowed to be discharged into the sea in the Baltic Sea Area ... to a port reception facility. Before leaving port all cargo residues shall be discharged to a port reception facility." Regarding this mandatory criteria, *See* Uwe Jenisch, "The Development of Environmental Standards for the Baltic Sea," in *Marine Issues: From a Scientific, Political*

ESM of ship wastes: the sea/land interface 169

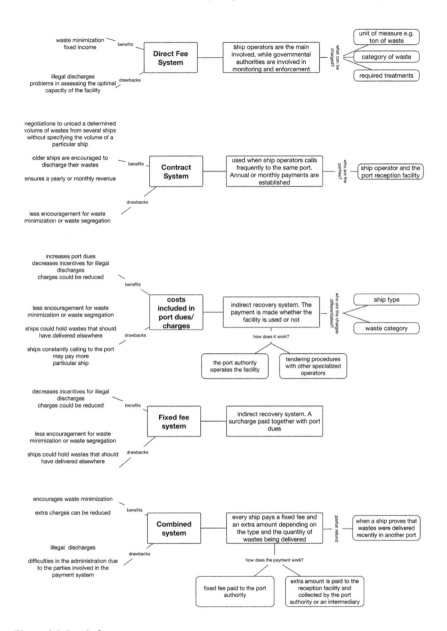

Figure 8.1 Port's fee system.

just in relation to the reception of ship wastes, but also in terms of their management on land.

For wastes generated in ships' machinery and living spaces, the recovery system is also varied. For instance, in the Baltic Sea area, several ports in Denmark,

170   *The ESM of wastes*

Estonia, Latvia, Lithuania, Poland, and Sweden have implemented an indirect fee system.[24] This could be the result of the implementation of HELCOM's recommendations on port reception facilities. HELCOM encourages State Parties to the Helsinki Convention to harmonize their fee systems based on "the no special fee" system, *i.e.*, "charging system where the cost of reception, handling and disposal of ship-generated wastes, originating from the normal operation of the ship … is included in the harbour fee or otherwise charged to the ship irrespective of whether wastes are delivered or not".[25] State Parties to the Helsinki Convention, except from Russia, are also Member States to the EU. Article 8 of Directive 2000/59/EC on Port Reception Facilities obliges State Parties to establish cost recovery systems for ship-generated wastes. The recovery system must include indirect fees, *i.e.*, included in port dues or as a surcharge paid together with port dues. In addition, costs that are not covered by indirect fees must be covered by direct fees.

d   *Contribute to the improvement of the marine environment*: the aim of establishing port reception facilities is to prevent and reduce marine pollution. This is closely connected with incentives to avoid illegal discharges at sea. At the same time, it relates to monitoring and enforcement mechanisms to punish illegal discharges.

e   *Allow the "final disposal" of wastes generated on board ships on land in an environmentally appropriate way*: a reception facility is adequate when it is integrated into national or regional waste management systems. Final disposal should not be understood only as operations without the possibility of recovery. According to the IMO's manual on Port Reception Facilities, "final disposal" includes operations of recycling, recovery.[26] The management of ship wastes on land shall follow the ESM principle. The IMO and the Secretariat of the Basel Convention have combined efforts to enhance the ESM of ship wastes on land.

At first glance, it is outside the IMO's competences to deal with the management of ship wastes after their discharge. According to Article 1(a) of the Convention on the International Maritime Organization, the purpose of the IMO is to provide the institutional machinery for cooperation among States and facilitate

---

and Legal Perspective, ed. Peters Ehlers, Elisabeth Mann-Borgese, and Rüdiger Wolfrum (The Hague: Kluwer Law International, 2002), 71.

24 Ramboll, "Final Report: EMSA Study on the Delivery of Ship-Generated Waste and Cargo Residues to Port Reception Facilities in EU Ports," 35.

25 Baltic Marine Environment Protection Commission (HELCOM), "Helcom Recomendation 28e/10: Application of the No-Special-Fee System to Ship-Generated Wastes and Marine Litter Caught in Fishing Nets in the Baltic Sea Area," (15 November 2007).

26 *See* Chapters 9 and 10 of "Port Reception Facilities – How to Do It."

the adoption of highest standards in relation to the prevention and control of ship-source pollution. In the Advisory Opinion regarding *Reparation of Injuries Suffered in the Service of the United Nations*, the ICJ discussed the powers vested in the United Nations and stated that:

> [u]nder international law, the Organization must be deemed to have those powers which, though not expressly provided in the Charter, are conferred upon it by necessary implication as being essential to the performance of its duties.[27]

The IMO's efforts to provide guidance regarding the discharge of ship wastes and the integration of port reception facilities into national waste management plans are justified because the legal regime adopted under the auspices of the IMO for the prevention, control, and reduction of ship-source pollution restricts discharges of harmful substances at sea and places a crucial role on the provision of "adequate reception facilities." Adequacy is closely linked with two major aspects: (a) prevention of illegal discharges at sea; and (b) the management of ship wastes on land to prevent the transformation of one type of marine pollution into another. The IMO cannot prescribe standards for waste streams and effluents, but it can guide States on how to integrate their port reception facilities into national waste management systems.

State Parties to MARPOL must provide reception facilities in every port according to the necessity of the users of such port. *Therefore, adequacy is assessed at port level.* However, under certain circumstances, States can join forces to provide at the regional level a system of reception facilities. This is currently the case of Small Island Developing States (SIDS), *i.e.*, a variety of States that share similar social, economic, and environmental vulnerabilities. Amendments to Annexes I, II, IV, V, and VI of MARPOL were adopted in 2012 to allow SIDS to establish regional arrangements for the provision of port reception facilities. The amendments entered into force in 2013.[28]

The provision of adequate port reception facilities is also fundamental in relation to Special Areas. These areas are usually closed or semi-enclosed seas and may encompass several maritime zones. In Special Areas, stricter discharge criteria apply due to their oceanographic, ecological conditions, and vessel

---

27 *Advisory Opinion: Reparation for Injuries Suffered in the Service of the United Nations*, 12.

28 Marine Environment Protection Committee (MEPC), "Resolution MEPC.216(63) – Amendments: Regional Arrangements for Port Reception Facilities under MARPOL Annexes I, II, IV and V," (2 March 2012). "Resolution MEPC.217(63) – Amendments: Regional Arrangements for Port Reception Facilities under MARPOL Annex VI and Certification of Marine Diesel Engines Fitted with Selective Catalytic Reduction Systems under the NOx Technical Code 2008," (2 March 2012).

172   *The ESM of wastes*

traffic characteristics[29] that make them particularly vulnerable. Through the amendment procedure established in Article 16 of MARPOL, Special Areas are designated under one or more of the following Annexes of MARPOL. The more stringent discharge criteria, however, will *only be applicable after States bordering the special area provide adequate port reception facilities.* In relation to Annex IV, air pollution, "Emission Control Areas" (ECAS) have been designated. In these areas, more stringent emission criteria apply for SO_x, NO_x, and particulate matter (PM). Currently, Special Areas, and Emission Control Areas under MARPOL are (Table 8.1).

Table 8.1 Special Areas MARPOL[a]

Annex I: Oil	*Annex II: Noxious substances carried in bulk*	*Annex IV: sewage*	*Annex V: Garbage*
More stringent discharge criteria apply in: the Baltic Sea, the Black Sea, the Mediterranean Sea, the "Gulfs" area, the Antarctic area, North West European waters	More stringent discharge criteria apply in: the Antarctic area[b]		More stringent discharge criteria apply in: the Baltic Sea, the Mediterranean Sea, "Gulfs" area, the North Sea, the Antarctic area; and the Wider Caribbean region including the Gulf of Mexico and the Caribbean Sea
More stringent criteria do not apply because adequate reception facilities are still lacking: the Red Sea, the Gulf of Aden, Oman area of the Arabian Sea		More stringent criteria do not apply because adequate reception facilities are still lacking: the Baltic Sea	More stringent criteria do not apply because adequate reception facilities are still lacking: the Black Sea and the Red Sea
MARPOL Annex VI: Air pollution (Emission Control Areas) For SO_x: the Baltic Sea and the North Sea For SO_x, NOx and PM: North American and United States Caribbean Sea			

a Marine Environment Protection Committee (MEPC), "MEPC.1/Circ.778/REV.1: List of Special Areas under MARPOL and Particularly Sensitive Sea Areas," (16 November 2012).

b In 2004, Annex II was extensively revised. Noxious liquid substances were recategorized and more strict discharge criteria were established. Since then, only the Antarctic Area is a Special Area under this Annex. "Resolution MEPC.118(52): Revised Annex II of MARPOL 73/78," (15 October 2004). The revised Annex entered into force on 1 January 2007. "Resolution MEPC.57(33) Designation of the Antarctic Area as a Special Area and Lists of Liquid Substances in Annex II," (30 October 1992).

29 International Maritime Organization (IMO), "Resolution A.1087(28): 2013 Guidelines for the Designation of Special Areas under MARPOL," in *Assembly, 28th session, Agenda Item 12* (4 December 2013), 3. *See also* MARPOL Annex I – Regulation 1(11). Annex V – Regulation 1(14).

Compliance challenges

Over the last four decades, inadequacy of port reception facilities has been on the agenda of the IMO's MEPC.[30] In developing States, technical capacities are still lacking[31] and environmental protection is not usually a priority within their agendas. For instance, the amendments establishing the Red Sea and the Gulf of Aden as Special Areas under MARPOL Annex I entered into force in 1983 and 1989, respectively.[32] However, after three decades, the strict discharge criteria are still not applicable because States surrounding these Special Areas have yet to provide adequate reception facilities. The World Bank in cooperation with the IMO commissioned a study into the provision of port reception facilities in Sub-Saharan African Ports. It revealed that States are reluctant to provide reception facilities not only because of investment and operational costs, but also due to the challenges related to the management on land of such wastes.[33] The World Bank noticed that, in many ports, ship wastes were poorly managed and were usually subject to scavenging operations. Furthermore, wastes usually end up in drainage systems and eventually end up back in the ocean.[34]

In 2006, the IMO approved the Action Plan to Tackle the Inadequacy of Port Reception Facilities. One of the activities of the Action Plan relates to the development of technical capabilities of developing States, including the downstream management of ship wastes.[35] Additionally, the IMO's Sub-Committee on Flag State Implementation identified six areas of concern:[36] (1) notification procedure between the ship operator and the facility concerning the intention to use a certain facility; (2) information on available port reception facilities; (3) technological challenges in relation to ship-to-shore operation and standardization of standards for garbage segregation; (4) revision of the type of wastes generated on board vessels, the capacity of available port reception facilities, and methodologies to establish the required capacity of port reception facilities; (5) revision

---

30 Björn Hassler, "Oil Spills from Shipping: A Case Study of the Governance of Accidental Hazards and Intentional Pollution in the Baltic Sea," in *Environmental Governance of the Baltic Sea*, ed. Michael Gilek et al. (Berlin: Springer, 2016), 140.

31 Saiful Karim, *Prevention of Pollution of the Marine Environment from Vessels: The Potential and Limits of the International Maritime Organizations* (Switzerland: Springer, 2015), 134–35. Tan, *Vessel-Source Marine Pollution: The Law and Politics of International Regulation*, 267.

32 Marine Environment Protection Committee (MEPC), "MEPC.1/Circ.778/REV.1: List of Special Areas under MARPOL and Particularly Sensitive Sea Areas."

33 John Lethbridge et al., "The MARPOL 73/78 Convention: The Economic Implications and Other Issues in Providing Reception Facilities for Ship Wastes in Sub-Saharan African Ports," (Washington: The World Bank, 1991), 2.

34 Ibid., 6. Sadler and King, "Study on Mechanisms for the Financing of Facilities in Ports for the Reception of Wastes from Ships," (MEPC Doc. 30/INF.32, 1990), 5.

35 Sub-Committee on Flag State Implementation (FSI), "Draft Action Plan to Tackle the Inadequacy of Port Reception Facilities (FSI 14/19)," (30 June 2006), 50.

36 These problem areas were highlighted by users and providers of port reception facilities. Sub-Committee on Flag State Implementation (FSI), "Report to the Maritime Safety Committee and the Marine Environment Protection Committee (FSI 14/19)," (30 June 2006), 46.

174 *The ESM of wastes*

of several IMO guidelines and other related regulations; and (6) technical assistance for developing countries.[37] The IMO's work on the Action Plan concluded with the adoption of several documents, including the Consolidated Guidance for Port Reception Facility Providers and Users and the revision of the Manual on Port Reception Facilities.

As part of the Action Plan to Tackle the Inadequacy of Port Reception Facilities, an updated version of the "advanced notification form" was adopted.[38] Ship operators are encouraged to give notification at least 24 hours in advance of their intention to use a reception facility. Such notification is useful in identifying the availability of a certain facility and avoiding possible delays. Furthermore, the provider of reception facilities is able to plan the discharge of wastes and, if necessary, arrange special handling requirements.[39] The notification intends to provide useful information to governmental authorities regarding the type of wastes received, the quantities that are discharged, and their hazardous characteristics. This information is also used to establish the required capacity and technical capabilities of port reception facilities, and to plan for further management operations on land. The use of a standard "advanced notification form" is intended to "provide uniformity of records throughout the world",[40] and potentially using this form will facilitate the submission of information to the IMO as required in Article 11(d) of MARPOL. Uniformity of records could also enable a comprehensive analysis of the availability and adequacy of port reception facilities.

In respect of funding mechanisms, States have devised recovery mechanisms to cover the day-to-day operations of port reception facilities and "investments pertaining to design and building of the facilities".[41] However, efforts to secure initial investment funds to build port reception facilities have been unsuccessful. In the early 1990s, an IMO proposal recommending cargo owners and charterers to secure funds for the provision port reception facilities did not find support.[42] Based on the polluter pays principle, this proposal suggested the establishment of a Fund for Port Reception Facilities whereby the "burden of financing [reception facilities would] fall on those who benefit from the economic activity which gives rise to the risk of pollution".[43] The financing mechanism of the Fund required charges to be fixed and included in charter-parties regardless

---

37 Sub-Committee on Flag State Implementation (FSI), "Draft Action Plan to Tackle the Inadequacy of Port Reception Facilities (FSI 14/19)."
38 *See* Annex II MEPC.1/Circ.834, "Consolidated Guidance for Port Reception Facility Providers and Users."
39 Ibid., 8.
40 Sub-Committee on Flag State Implementation (FSI), "Draft Action Plan to Tackle the Inadequacy of Port Reception Facilities (FSI 14/19)."
41 International Maritime Organization (IMO), "Port Reception Facilities – How to Do It," 153.
42 Sadler and King, "Study on Mechanisms for the Financing of Facilities in Ports for the Reception of Wastes from Ships."
43 Ibid., 2.

ESM of ship wastes: the sea/land interface 175

of whether or not port reception facilities were actually provided.[44] The Fund would be administered by an international entity with an institutional arrangement similar to the International Oil Pollution Compensation Fund.[45] Since no support was given to the establishment of an international Fund for Port Reception Facilities, the IMO no longer devotes its efforts to securing international financing mechanisms for port reception facilities. At present, there are several sources for financing the establishment of reception facilities, which include: "private sector investors/contractors; commercial banks; government; regional/ local authorities; multilateral donors (the World Bank, the United Nations, ...); and bilateral donors".[46]

In the decades following the entry-into-force of MARPOL, developed States have generally been able to provide port reception facilities for ships calling at their ports.[47] This has not been the case for many developing States. The unintended consequence of this development is the transfer of pollution from one place to another as exemplified in the *Probo Koala* affair. In the absence of compulsory standards that specify the location where ship wastes must be discharged, *e.g.*, the unloading port, ships with enough holding capacity can choose cheaper port reception facilities. In general, the poorest countries continue to be the most affected by pollution because illegal discharges also increase if reception facilities are not available. The lack of provision of port reception facilities is usually accompanied by weak monitoring and control of illegal discharges as well.

While States must regulate, monitor, and enforce laws in relation to port reception facilities, in practice port reception facilities are usually provided by private companies.[48] In Europe, waste reception and handling are generally undertaken by private operators. These operators are chosen through several mechanisms, *i.e.*, public tendering, framework contracts, contract with one operator, or the free market.[49] The IMO recommends that States establish a licensing system in cases where private operators provide reception facilities. A licensing system is helpful in establishing standards in relation to the type of waste that must be

---

44 "Balances would only be released when construction or upgrading of reception facilities are in progress, and agreement reached that appropriate receipts will be channeled into repayments." Ibid., 2 and 28.

45 Ibid., 24–28.

46 International Maritime Organization (IMO), "Port Reception Facilities – How to Do It," 170.

47 Angela Carpenter and Sally Macgill, "The EU Directive on Port Reception Facilities for Ship-Generated Waste and Cargo Residues: The Results of a Second Survey on the Provision and Uptake of Facilities in North Sea Ports," *Marine Pollution Bulletin* 50, no. 12 (2005): 1541–47. Ramboll, "Final Report: EMSA Study on the Delivery of Ship-Generated Waste and Cargo Residues to Port Reception Facilities in EU Ports."

48 *See* Section 6, "Waste Reception Facilities Available in the Port," Final Report: EMSA Study on the Delivery of Ship-Generated Waste and Cargo Residues to Port Reception Facilities in EU Ports, in Ramboll, "Final Report: EMSA Study on the Delivery of Ship-Generated Waste and Cargo Residues to Port Reception Facilities in EU Ports," 45–46. *See also* Chapter 3, Section 3.5. International Maritime Organization (IMO), "Port Reception Facilities – How to Do It."

49 Ramboll, "Final Report: EMSA Study on the Delivery of Ship-Generated Waste and Cargo Residues to Port Reception Facilities in EU Ports," 45.

176 *The ESM of wastes*

accepted.[50] Additionally, a licensing system provides the basis to "control and enforce the performance of treatment facilities, such as compliance with discharge standards, application of proper equipment".[51]

Judging the availability and adequacy of port reception facilities around the globe is a difficult task, since State Parties to MARPOL are reluctant to provide information. Article 11(d) of the MARPOL prescribes that the Parties must communicate to the IMO "a list of reception facilities including their location, capacity and available facilities and other characteristics." Reporting is a common feature in conventions adopted under the auspices of the IMO and in multilateral environmental agreements (MEAs) in general. The obligation to report serves as a monitoring compliance mechanism of MEAs.[52] In the case of MARPOL, *e.g.*, both the IMO and State Parties can collectively exercise supervisory functions and exert pressure on States that fail to implement, comply with, and enforce their international obligations. Extensive research has been undertaken regarding the relationship between reporting and transparency, as well as the influence of reporting on improving enforcement among State Parties.[53] Most noncompliance remedies under general public international law, including the possibility to terminate or suspend a treaty in cases of material breach, are essentially inadequate to deal with environmental problems because MEAs require the secure cooperation of States in addressing environmental concerns that are transboundary in nature. In other words, nonconfrontational procedures are preferred, since terminating or suspending MEAs would "primarily harm the international community, not the defaulting State".[54]

Overall, reporting enables one to access the necessary information and to assess how diverse treaty objectives are fulfilled. However, State Parties to MARPOL have constantly disregarded their reporting obligations.[55] The problem is further exacerbated by the limited powers vested in the supervisory body, *i.e.,* the IMO, to effectively deal with nonperforming State Parties. Where reports are actually provided, the accuracy, consistency, and quality of the information have

---

50 International Maritime Organization (IMO), "Port Reception Facilities – How to Do It," 37.
51 Ibid.
52 Günter Handl, "Compliance Control Mechanisms and International Environmental Obligations," *Tulane Journal of International and Comparative Law* 5 (1997): 32. *See also* Alan Boyle, "Saving the World? Implementation and Enforcement of International Environmental Law through International Institutions," *Journal of Environmental Law* 3 (1991): 229–45.
53 Jørgen Wettestad, "Monitoring and Verification," in *The Oxford Handbook of International Environmental Law*, ed. Daniel Bodansky, Jutta Brunnée, and Ellen Hey (Oxford: Oxford University Press, 2007). Abram Chayes and Antonia Handler Chayes, "Compliance without Enforcement: State Behavior under Regulatory Treaties," *Negotiation Journal* 7, no. 3 (July 1991): 311–30. Geir Ulfstein, "Dispute Resolution, Compliance Control Adn Enforcement in International Environmental Law," in *Making Treaties Work: Human Rights, Environment and Arms Control*, ed. Geir Ulfstein (Cambridge: Cambridge University Press, 2008), 129.
54 Boyle, "Saving the World? Implementation and Enforcement of International Environmental Law through International Institutions," 233.
55 Tan, *Vessel-Source Marine Pollution: The Law and Politics of International Regulation*, 271.

been brought into question.[56] The IMO has adopted several soft law instruments together with standard formats to facilitate the compliance of reporting obligations. In terms of port reception facilities, the "advanced notification form" and the form related to the "annual report on reception facilities"[57] seek to encourage reporting as well as the harmonization of information throughout the world.

In 2005, the Secretariat of the IMO launched the Global Integrated Shipping Information System (GISIS),[58] which includes the Port Reception Facilities Database[59] as one of its modules. GISIS aims at increasing the reporting rate among State Parties and enabling "coordination with relevant intergovernmental organizations ... research on trends [and] statistical analysis".[60] Additionally, GISIS provides information that is open to public scrutiny. Making this information available should persuade or pressure State Parties to provide the required information. Over time, GISIS should become the basis for monitoring and assessing the performance of MARPOL. In relation to the availability of port reception facilities, GISIS's success remains limited. For instance, as for wastes related to MARPOL, Annex II, only 27 percent of State Parties have included information on reception facilities.[61] Overall, reporting records continue to be poor. The compliance reporting rate for the year 2015 was 25 percent, *i.e.*, only 38 Parties have submitted reports.[62] In fact, according to the IMO, since 2010 around 60 percent of the Parties have not submitted any report.[63]

Information on available port reception facilities must be complemented with data concerning their adequacy. Based on a standard format prepared by the IMO, shipmasters are required to report inadequacies to their Flag State and, if possible, to the Port State.[64] Historical records show that IMCO and later on the

---

56 Mitchell, *Intentional Oil Pollution at Sea: Environmental Policy and Treaty Compliance*, 137.

57 *See* Part III of the Annex to "MEPC/Circ.318. Formats for a Mandatory Reporting System under MARPOL 73/78," (26 July 1996).

58 Secretariat of the International Maritime Organization (IMO), "Circular Letter No. 2639. Global Integrated Shipping Information System (GISIS) – Manual for Administration on the Use of Reporting Facilities," (8 July 2005).

59 MEPC incorporated this module in its 53rd Session. *See* para 9.6, Marine Environment Protection Committee (MEPC), "Report of the Marine Environment Protection Committee on Its Fifty-Third Session. (MEPC 53/24)," (25 July 2005).

60 Assembly of the International Maritime Organization (IMO), "Resolution A.1029(26) Global Integrated Shipping Information System (GISIS)," in *A 26/Res.1029* (18 January 2010).

61 According to the status of MARPOL, Annexes I and II have currently 157 parties. According to GISIS's database, 42 parties have provided information on reception facilities related to Annex II. A summary of the status of IMO conventions can be found at <www.imo.org/en/About/Conventions/StatusOfConventions/Documents/StatusOfTreaties.pdf>, last accessed 25 March 2019.

62 Marine Environment Protection Committee (MEPC), "Summary Reports and Analysis of Mandatory Reports under MARPOL for the Period 2010–2015 (MEPC.1/Circ.869)," (31 January 2017): 3.

63 Ibid.

64 The format of reporting is found in Appendix 1 of "MEPC.1/Circ.834 Consolidated Guidance for Port Reception Facility Providers and Users."

178 *The ESM of wastes*

IMO did not receive any reports during the 1960s, 1970s, and early 1980s.[65] Currently, reporting rates are low. In 2015, only seven Flag States reported on alleged inadequacies.[66] Several factors influence the low level of reporting rates regarding alleged inadequacies of port reception facilities. For instance, many State Parties do not distribute the formats provided by the IMO.[67] Shipmasters are not aware of the procedures for reporting inadequacies, and many have expressed a "fear of retaliation" from Port State authorities.[68] Port States receiving the highest number of reports on alleged inadequacies, during 2015, were the United States, Australia, Canada, Japan, Chile, and India.[69] This does not mean that inadequacies do not exist elsewhere; on the contrary, there is a lack of coordination and communication between private operators and public authorities, and several Port States have not implemented any system to receive and follow up reports regarding alleged inadequacies of port reception facilities.

In practice, several shipping organizations, including INTERTANKO and INTERCARGO, have provided information to the IMO regarding inadequate port reception facilities based on anonymous surveys submitted to their members.[70] In 2016, the bulk carriers informed that in relation to cargo residues and garbage, port reception facilities around the world remain inadequate.[71] Considering the tight schedules that ships are subject to, there is a common practice to wash and clean holds of MARPOL, Annex V, *i.e.*, garbage, in loading ports rather than unloading ports.[72] Thus, there is a growing need to provide reception facilities at loading ports.

In the absence of noncompliance mechanisms, State Parties to MARPOL usually fail to comply with their reporting obligations concerning the availability of port reception facilities and the adequacy of such facilities. Failing to report, however, does not *ipso facto* mean that States fail to provide adequate reception facilities, because there are cases in which State reports show noncompliance with substantive obligations. There is also evidence that developed States report in a higher proportion than developing States because the act of reporting

---

65 Mitchell, *Intentional Oil Pollution at Sea: Environmental Policy and Treaty Compliance*, 128–29.

66 These States were the Bahamas, Cyprus, Denmark, Liberia, Marshall Islands, the Netherlands, and Portugal. Sub-Committee on Implementation of IMO Instruments (IMO), "Annual Enforcement Reports on Port Reception Facilities for 2015 (III 3/3)," (16 May 2016), 2.

67 Sub-Committee on Flag State Implementation (FSI), "Study on the Low Level of Reporting on Alleged Inadequacy of Port Reception Facilities (FSI 13/19)," (International Maritime Organization (IMO), 3 December 2004), 5.

68 Ibid.

69 Annual Enforcement Reports on Port Reception Facilities for 2015 (III 3/3) Sub-Committee on Implementation of IMO Instruments (IMO), "Annual Enforcement Reports on Port Reception Facilities for 2015 (III 3/3)," 4.

70 *See*, for instance, International Maritime Organization (IMO), "Availability of Adequate Port Reception Facilities Submitted by Intercargo (III 3/3/1)," in *Sub-Committee on Implementation of IMO Instruments, Third Session, Agenda Item 3* (13 May 2016).

71 International Maritime Organization (IMO), "Availability of Adequate Port Reception Facilities Submitted by Intercargo (III 3/3/1)," 1.

72 Ibid., 2.

ESM of ship wastes: the sea/land interface 179

requires institutional capacity and entails costs that many States cannot afford.[73] There is also a lack of incentives to report. On the one hand, private operators want to maintain good relations with ports they use; as such, many do not report inadequacies due to fear of future retaliation. On the other hand, States may not have the necessary resources to report, or they may not want to provide evidence of noncompliance with other substantive norms.[74] However, reporting could also highlight the challenges faced by several State Parties in implementing and enforcing MARPOL.

Alternative incentives to improve compliance with MEAs need to be implemented. These incentives usually rely on supervisory mechanisms of international organizations, closer cooperation between several stakeholders, enhancement of transparency, *e.g.*, standardized forms, publicly available information, and shaming "lists". On a soft law basis, the IMO has indeed created a number of standard forms and utilized technological advances to enhance self-regulation. Nonetheless, the success of this soft approach has been modest. Much can be done to improve transparency and achieve the desired naming and shaming effect. Particularly, the IMO should provide a comprehensive and authoritative analysis of complying and noncomplying ports. At present, the information is scattered and provided by shipping organizations on an *ad-hoc* basis. In fact, there is a perception that reporting is irrelevant, since the IMO does not use the information received in any meaningful manner.[75] The analysis conducted by the IMO should also be complemented with recommendations to address challenges related to the provision of adequate port reception facilities. In general, the information received should be useful for both governments and the shipping industry. Otherwise, reporting becomes a burdensome and bureaucratic task.

Binding regulation could be a positive step forward in addressing some challenges in respect of port reception facilities, such as allowing developing States to provide regional reception facilities or establishing a fund for financing the design and construction of port reception facilities. This alternative seems, however, unrealistic given that States have consistently failed to establish regulations in relation to port reception facilities. Nonetheless, State Parties must consider strengthening the enforcement capabilities of the IMO, including providing the IMO Secretary with the power to begin rule-making processes and to conduct auditing schemes so as to improve supervision and scrutiny. Since 2003, a voluntary Member State Audit Scheme was developed to enhance the implementation and enforcement of several IMO treaties,[76] *e.g.*, MARPOL. Audit standards

---

73 Chayes and Handler Chayes, "Compliance without Enforcement: State Behavior under Regulatory Treaties," 325.

74 "In self-reporting systems, states or other actors will not report if they believe that revealing their own noncompliance will prove more costly that remaining silent." Mitchell, *Intentional Oil Pollution at Sea: Environmental Policy and Treaty Compliance*, 144.

75 Tan, *Vessel-Source Marine Pollution: The Law and Politics of International Regulation*, 373.

76 Assembly of the International Maritime Organization (IMO), "Resolution A. 946(23). Voluntary IMO Member State Audit Scheme Resolution A. 946(23)," (27 November 2003).

180 *The ESM of wastes*

are found in the IMO Instruments Implementation Code (III CODE). This code guides States in fulfilling their obligations as flag, port, or coastal States in relation to: safety of life at sea; prevention of pollution from ships; standards of training, certification, and watch keeping for seafarers; load lines; tonnage measurement of ships; and regulations for preventing collisions at sea.[77] III Code also aims at developing assessment and periodical review procedures to monitor the performance of MARPOL, and other treaties.[78] In January 2016, this voluntary audit scheme together with III Code became mandatory in several instruments, including MARPOL.[79] This initiative should be welcomed because it reflects a political commitment to strengthen the IMO and to increase its supervisory functions. If possible, the results of the audits should be publicly available for scrutiny.

For port reception facilities, other, stricter noncompliance mechanisms are necessary, including:

> conditioning a state's candidacy for Council membership upon satisfactory provision of port reception facilities. Financial incentives should also be used – for example, a member state's dues to IMO … may enjoy a discount if the State agrees to commit the corresponding sum toward the provision of reception facilities.[80]

Enhancing financial and technical assistance is also a priority. A positive step in this direction is the IMO's Integrated Technical Cooperation Programme, which included as a priority the provision of port reception facilities.[81] Finally, there is a need to establish channels of communication between public authorities and private operators, including shipmasters, port operators, and waste management providers. Knowing ship practices in relation to discharge practices at port reception facilities could affect the planning and provision of port reception facilities.

Strengthening the enforcement capacities of the IMO could also be seen as a countermeasure against threats of unilateral actions by single coastal States or the EU, for example. Unilateralism is often considered undesirable since shipping is a transboundary activity and ship operators strive for uniformity and certainty in the regulations applicable to them, no matter where they operate.[82]

---

77 "Resolution A.1070(28) IMO Instruments Implementation Code (III Code)," (December 2013).

78 Ibid.

79 "Resolution MEPC.247(66). Amendments to MARPOL Annex VI (to Make the Use of the III Code Mandatory)," (4 April 2014). "Resolution MEPC.246(66). Amendments to MARPOL Annexes I, II, III, IV and V to Make the Use of the III Code Mandatory," (4 April 2014).

80 Tan, *Vessel-Source Marine Pollution: The Law and Politics of International Regulation*, 379.

81 Marine Environment Protection Committee (MEPC), "Thematic Priorities for the Integrated Technical Co-Operation Programme (ITCP) for 2014–2015 (MEPC 65/15)," (8 February 2013).

82 There is an extensive literature on EU unilateralism. *See*, for example, Ringbom, *The EU Maritime Safety Policy and International Law*. Alan Boyle, "EU Unilateralism and the Law of the Sea," *The International Journal of Marine and Coastal Law* 21, no. 1 (2006): 31.

However, in the field of maritime regulation, EU law initiatives do not always compete with international regulation. On the contrary, EU law may enhance international obligations in two meaningful ways. First, EU law obligations include strong noncompliance mechanism procedures where Member States could be "brought before justice by the Commission and even being obliged to pay lump-sum penalties in case of continued non-compliance".[83] Second, the IMO's soft law instruments may become binding. This is the case, for instance, with Directive 2000/59/EC on Port Reception Facilities where detailed obligations regarding the provision of port reception facilities were drawn using IMO guidelines, *e.g.*, advanced notification and the establishment of a fee system to finance the operations of these facilities.

Concluding remarks: integration of port reception facilities with national waste management systems

The UN General Assembly in its annual review and evaluation regarding the implementation of the LOSC urged States to develop integrated waste management systems and infrastructure to deal with discharges from ships, among other things.[84] The UN General Assembly also encouraged cooperation between the COP to the Basel Convention and the IMO.[85] Such cooperation should lead to enhanced coordination and further development of cross-sectoral standards relating to the ESM of ship wastes drawing upon existing expertise and institutional capacity of both the IMO and the COP to the Basel Convention.

An integrated waste management strategy involves several private operators and public authorities, including port authorities, ship operators, cargo interests such as shippers and receivers of oil and chemicals, terminal operators, waste operators, civil society organizations, and society in general. The IMO calls for public participation[86] in order to involve different stakeholders in the decision-making processes regarding waste management, *e.g.*, the legislative process. Public participation gained significance in international environmental law

---

83 Ringbom, *The EU Maritime Safety Policy and International Law*, 7–8. Stronger non-compliance mechanisms, according to Ringbom, "explain the reluctance of Member States to adopt EU measures in a field traditionally regulated by means of international conventions, even where the EU measures only implement preexisting international obligations." *See also* Judith Van Leeuwen and Kristine Kern, "The External Dimension of European Union Marine Governance: Institutional Interplay between the EU and the International Maritime Organization," *Global Environmental Politics* 13, no. 1 (2013): 82–83.

84 *See* para 210 in which the General Assembly urged States to "integrate the issue of marine debris into national and, as appropriate, regional strategies dealing with waste management" "71/257. Oceans and the Law of the Sea," in *Resolution Adopted by the General Assembly on 23 December 2016* (A/RES/71/257, 20 February 2017), 38.

85 Ibid., para 234 on p. 42.

86 *See* Chapter 4 of International Maritime Organization (IMO), "Port Reception Facilities – How to Do It."

182 *The ESM of wastes*

after UNCED 1992.[87] It is not surprising that treaties predating UNCED made no reference to public participation, including the LOSC and MARPOL. Public participation is considered a procedural element of sustainable development, and in broad terms it includes mechanisms to access justice and information, as well as participation in decision-making processes.[88] At the international level, the most prominent "regional treaty" dealing with public participation is the Convention on Access to Information, Public Participation in Decision-Making and Access to Justice in Environmental Matters, 1998 (Aarhus Convention).[89] In general, the implementation of public participation procedures requires the development of legal, institutional, and educational frameworks. The incorporation of public participation procedures in relation to ship wastes could potentially have an impact on the legitimacy of waste regulation. Furthermore, if the expertise of several stakeholders is considered, positive effects on the environmental status can also be achieved.

The implementation of a waste management strategy requires the adoption of legal and administrative measures, the development of technological capabilities, and the establishment of adequate infrastructure. Among legal and administrative measures, States should establish legal standards for waste collection, storage, handling and management operations, alongside monitoring procedures, enforcement mechanisms to effectively address noncompliance, and liability and compensation schemes. A workable regulatory framework should link ship wastes to existing national legislation on waste, *e.g.*, pollution control, industrial and chemical control, land planning, sewage and drainage systems, pesticides, and occupational and public health. A good example of this approach can be found in Directive 2000/59/EC on Port Reception Facilities where "ship-generated waste" and "cargo residues" are considered wastes within the meaning of Article 3(1) of the Waste Framework Directive.[90] The relevance of this provision is in linking ship wastes to land management regulation. In fact,

---

87 *See* principle 10 of the Rio Declaration: United Nations General Assembly, "Rio Declaration on Environment and Development – a/CONF.151/26 (Vol. I)." After UNCED, several treaties provide for "public access to information and/or public participation, albeit with different degrees of ambition … [M]any of these treaties … support the notions of public awareness, public access to documents, and public participation in environmental matters at a rather abstract level." Jonas Ebbesson, "Principle 10: Public Participation," in *The Rio Declaration on Environment and Development: A Commentary,* ed. Jorge Viñuales (Oxford: Oxford University Press, 2015), 308.

88 *See* Chapter 2, "Sustainable Development," Birnie, Boyle, and Redgwell, *International Law and the Environment,* 116–23. *See also* Jonas Ebbesson, "The Notion of Public Participation in International Environmental Law," *Yearbook of International Environmental Law* 8, no. 1 (1998).

89 Convention on Access to Information, Public Participation in Decision-Making and Access to Justice in Environmental Matters, Aarhus, 25 June 1998, 2161 UNTS 447; 38 ILM 517. In force 30 October 2001. This Convention was concluded under the auspices of the United Nations Economic Commission for Europe (UNECE). In principle, this is a regional Convention for States Members of the Economic Commission for Europe (*See* Article 17). Nonetheless, Article 19(3) of the Convention allows other States to accede "to the Convention upon approval by the Meeting of the Parties."

90 *See* the final paragraph of Article 2 of Directive 2000/59/EC on Port Reception Facilities.

ESM of ship wastes: the sea/land interface   183

Article 12(1)(g) of Directive 2000/59/EC provides that management of ship wastes must be carried out in accordance with the relevant EU waste legislation.

The management of ship wastes requires a licensing system[91] for the providers of port reception facilities and waste operators. This system is essential to enable public authorities to trace the management of wastes once they are discharged from ships, and monitor whether the operators are complying with substantive standards. Licenses should be complemented with notification systems[92] covering the generation, storage, transport, and management of wastes. Procedures should also be in place to secure that notifications reach the designated public authority even when transactions take place exclusively between private operators.

The Manual on Port Reception Facilities provides assistance on the integration of port reception facilities within national waste management strategies, as well as the available alternatives to collect, store, and treat ship wastes, including recycling and final disposal operations. Downstream waste management has also been a concern for the Parties to the Basel Convention. Over the years, the COP to the Basel Convention has adopted numerous technical guidelines that have not only dealt with management alternatives, but also addressed particular types of wastes, particular hazardous characteristics or constituents, and waste streams. These guidelines could be relevant for managing ship wastes after they are discharged at port reception facilities. In fact, the COP to the Basel Convention required that any Party in close consultation with the IMO provides an assessment regarding how far the technical guidelines developed under the Basel Convention cover MARPOL wastes.[93] Such an assessment was conducted by the Public Waste Agency of Flanders, on behalf of Belgium.[94] This initiative is to be welcomed since it is a step toward developing cross-sectoral standards dealing with hazardous wastes from a life-cycle perspective. This assessment could potentially avoid the duplication of activities and address fragmentation in the international regulation of wastes.

In general, the Manual on Port Reception Facilities follows closely the common understanding of ESM developed through the Basel Convention. The foundation of an environmentally sound waste management system is to protect the

---

91 *See* Chapter 3 of International Maritime Organization (IMO), "Port Reception Facilities – How to Do It."

92 Ibid, Chapter 4.

93 *See* COP to the Basel Convention, "Decision BC-10/16: Cooperation between the Basel Convention and the International Maritime Organization." "Decision BC-11/17: Cooperation between the Basel Convention and the International Maritime Organization."

94 "Revised Assessment Prepared by the Public Waste Agency of Flanders, on Behalf of Belgium, on How Far the Current Basel Convention Technical Guidelines Cover Wastes Covered by the International Convention for the Prevention of Pollution from Ships, 1973, as Modified by the Protocol of 1978 Relating Thereto, and as Further Amended by the Protocol of 1997," in *Matters related to the implementation of the Convention: International cooperation, coordination and partnerships: cooperation with the International Maritime Organization (UNEP/CHW.12/INF/29/REV.1)* (2015).

184   *The ESM of wastes*

environment and human health. Waste management plans should consider the life-cycle of wastes and follow the waste management hierarchy. The ESM of wastes requires the participation of stakeholders and the development of regulatory schemes together with institutional and technical capabilities taking into account the social and economic conditions of a particular State. Responding to the revised Manual on Port Reception Facilities, the Secretariat of the Basel Convention developed a "guidance manual on how to improve the sea-land interface to ensure that wastes falling within the scope of MARPOL, once offloaded from a ship, are managed in an environmentally sound manner".[95] This instrument duplicates much of the work already undertaken by the IMO. It seems that the IMO and the COP to the Basel Convention are still developing parallel activities instead of enhancing cooperation and coordination in relation to the management of ship wastes. Any reluctance to engage in meaningful cooperation could undermine the effectiveness of both Conventions and prove to be a lost opportunity to develop international standards for the management of hazardous wastes.

The ESM of ship wastes at the EU level

The relationship between MARPOL and Directive 2000/59/EC

What triggered the adoption of Directive 2000/59/EC on Port Reception Facilities was a growing frustration at the lack of enforcement mechanisms of MARPOL's standards. The immediate catalyst, however, was the *Erika* affair.[96] As a result, the EU became more active in the regulation of maritime safety and marine environmental protection. Directive 2000/59/EC was welcomed as a way of implementing MARPOL because unlike international law, EU legislation is supported by noncompliance mechanisms against EU Member States. Furthermore, this Directive establishes additional binding obligations that have no parallel in MARPOL, with regard to: a) waste reception and handling plans; b) mandatory discharge criteria for ship-generated wastes; c) cost recovery systems, among others. These novel obligations follow, to some extent, soft law instruments adopted under the auspices of the IMO, and as such they could be seen as an effort to complement international obligations that do not *per se* compete with their international counterparts.

Since the objective of Directive 2000/59/EC is to strengthen MARPOL and be consistent with other regional treaties, including the Helsinki Convention,

---

95 "Revised Draft Guidance Manual on How to Improve the Sea-Land Interface (UNEP/CHW.13/INF/37)."

96 In 1999, the Maltese single-hull tanker, *Erika*, "broke in two and sank in the Bay of Biscay ... France. The tanker was carrying a cargo of 31,000 tonnes of heavy fuel oil, of which some 19,800 tonnes were spilt at the time of the incident ... Approximately 400 km of shoreline was affected by the oil, and the incident gave rise to nearly 7,000 claims for compensation for the cost of clean-up operations, other pollution preventive measures and economic losses sustained in the fishing and tourism industries." Rue and Anderson, *Shipping and the Environment: Law and Practice*, 74.

ESM of ship wastes: the sea/land interface   185

no serious doubts have been raised over the legitimacy and compatibility of the Directive *vis-à-vis* MARPOL.[97] The EU is not a Party to MARPOL, and in principle the Convention is not binding for the EU.[98] Nonetheless, MARPOL is not inconsequential within the EU legal order. The implementation of certain MARPOL obligations within Directive 2000/59/EC has a direct impact on how EU Member States comply with their international obligations, and it also has an effect on non-EU ships calling at EU ports. Furthermore, in the *Intertanko* case, the Court of Justice of the European Union recognized that in light of the customary international law principle of good faith, MARPOL is relevant for the interpretation of EU secondary legislation falling within the scope of MARPOL's application.[99] The following sections pursue the aforementioned logic with which Directive 2000/59/EC is interpreted taking MARPOL into account.

Regional regulatory framework of port reception facilities

Although the EU is not a Party to MARPOL, it is, however, a Party to several agreements[100] that deal with ship-source pollution and enhance the implementation and enforcement of MARPOL. These agreements consider the singular features of regional and closed and semi-enclosed seas in Europe. Regulation of port reception facilities has been particularly fruitful in the Baltic Sea area.

---

97 Frank, *The European Community and Marine Environmental Protection in the International Law of the Sea: Implementing Global Obligations at the Regional Level*, 248. Van Leeuwen and Kern, "The External Dimension of European Union Marine Governance: Institutional Interplay between the EU and the International Maritime Organization," 82–83. Ringbom, *The EU Maritime Safety Policy and International Law*, 258. Jörn-Ahrend Witt, *Obligations and Control of Flag States: Developments and Perspectives in International Law and EU Law* (Berlin: Lit Verlag, 2007), 151–59.

98 "It is true that all the Member States of the Community are parties to MARPOL 73/78. Nevertheless, in the absence of a full transfer of the powers previously exercised by the Member States to the Community, the latter cannot, simply because all those States are parties to MARPOL 73/78, be bound by the rules set out therein, which it has not itself approved." *C-308/06, Intertanko and Others* ECR I-4057; ECLI:EU:C:2008:312, para 49 (2008).

99 *C-308/06, Intertanko and Others*, para 52.

100 *Note* that Article 197 of the LOSC calls for global and regional cooperation, as appropriate, to develop rules, standards, practices, and procedures for the protection and preservation of the marine environment. These regional treaties (adopted under the auspices of the UNEP Regional Seas Programme) are: the Helsinki Convention that covers the Baltic area; the OSPAR Convention that covers the North-East Atlantic; and the Barcelona Convention that covers the Mediterranean marine and coastal environment. In relation to the Bucharest Convention that covers a part of the Black Sea, the EU has been granted an observer status. These conventions establish general obligations. They are also "umbrellas conventions." For this reason, the development of precise legal requirements is made through the adoption of protocols. *See* Convention for the Protection of the Marine Environment and the Coastal Region of the Mediterranean, Barcelona, 10 June 1995, 1102 UNTS 27. In force 9 July 2004. Convention on the Protection of the Black Sea against Pollution, Bucharest 21 April 1992, 32 ILM 1101; 1764 UNTS 3. In force 15 January 1994.

186   *The ESM of wastes*

Increasing regulation in this area is probably the result of the Baltic Sea's designation as a special area under Annexes I, IV and V of MARPOL. The stringent discharge criteria applicable in Special Areas include the correlated obligation of States to be able to receive ship wastes at port reception facilities and manage them on land. Article 2(8) of the Helsinki Convention provides for the application of harmonized standards in relation to port reception facilities. Such standards refer to those adopted by the IMO and those established in MARPOL.[101] Annex IV of the Convention also sets out specific obligations concerning the mandatory discharge of ship wastes.[102] Additionally, the Governing Body of the Helsinki Convention, *i.e.*, HELCOM, has adopted numerous soft law instruments covering various issues pertaining to the provision and functioning of port reception facilities, *e.g.*, the application of an indirect cost recovery system called "non-special fee system" for ship-generated waste, standards for the management of sewage,[103] and marine litter. A more in-depth analysis of the Helsinki Convention's obligations and soft law framework of port reception facilities is presented in subsequent sections of this chapter.

The OSPAR Convention covers the North-East Atlantic.[104] In principle, this instrument does not set out specific obligations regarding ship-source pollution. In fact, Article 7 does not impose regional cooperation requirements if there are "effective measures agreed by other international organizations or prescribed by other international conventions." In other words, the appropriate forum for the regulation of this source of marine pollution is the IMO and MARPOL. Article 7 implies that Parties to the OSPAR Convention may still cooperate and develop standards for ship-source pollution if the international standards "are not

---

101 *See* Regulations 1, 4, and 5 of Annex IV of the Helsinki Convention.
102 Ibid., Regulation 6.
103 Baltic Marine Environment Protection Commission (HELCOM), "Baltic Sea Sewage Port Reception Facilities: Helcom Overview 2014," (2015). Baltic Marine Environment Protection Commission (HELCOM), "Helcom Recommendation 10/6: Application by the Baltic Sea States of a Helsinki Convention Form for Reporting Alleged Inadequacy of Reception Facilities for Sewage," (1989). Other HELCOM recommendations on port reception facilities include: "HELCOM Recommendation 10/5: Guidelines for the Establishment of Adequate Reception Facilities in Ports," (1989). "HELCOM Recommendation 10/7: General Requirements for Reception of Wastes," (1989). "HELCOM Recommendation 19/12: Waste Management Plans for Ports," (1998). "HELCOM Recommendation 19/13: Basic Principles of Ashore Handling of Ship-Generated Wastes," in *HELCOM 19/98 15/1 (Annex 24)* (1998). "HELCOM Recommendation 22/3: Unified Interpretations to Ensure the Harmonized and Effective Implementation of the Strategy for Port Reception Facilities for Ship-Generated Wastes and Associated Issues," (2001). "HELCOM Recommendation 23/1: Notification of Ship's Wastes," in *HELCOM 23/2002 – Minutes of the Meeting (Annex 3)* (2002). "HELCOM Recommendation 28/2: Recording of Fuel Oil Bunkering Operations in the Oil Record Book and Documentation for the Use of Reception Facilities," (2007). These recommendations have a "valid" status since they have not been superseded. However, some of them need to be read considering current regulatory developments.
104 Convention for the Protection of the Marine Environment of the North-East Atlantic (OSPAR Convention), Paris, 22 September 1992, 2354 UNTS 67, 32 ILM 1072. In force 25 March 1998.

ESM of ship wastes: the sea/land interface 187

effective" and in the absence of criteria to assess this effectiveness, State Parties enjoy a wide latitude of discretion in this regard. The OSPAR Commission has adopted a plan for the reduction of marine litter, including the litter generated on board vessels.[105] The plan includes requirements for the reception of marine litter in port reception facilities.

The Barcelona Convention is an umbrella treaty concerned with the protection of the Mediterranean Sea's marine environment, including the prevention, abatement, and to the "fullest possible extent" the elimination of marine pollution.[106] Regarding ship-source pollution, Article 6 of the Convention provides for the implementation of measures "in conformity with international law," *i.e.*, MARPOL. The Convention is complemented by Protocols that set out detailed obligations.[107] In 2002, the State Parties adopted the Protocol Concerning Cooperation in Preventing Pollution from Ships and, in Cases of Emergency, Combating Pollution of the Mediterranean Sea.[108] Article 14 relates to port reception facilities. It includes only a general obligation regarding the provision of adequate reception facilities for all type of ships, but it does not elaborate on any specific standard regarding States' obligations in relation to the financing, provision, or operation of port reception facilities. Parties are also "invited to explore ways and means to charge reasonable costs for the use of these facilities".[109] This provision is weak in two respects. First, it is not a binding obligation of any sort. Second it includes a recommendation that is so wide in scope that in the absence of criteria to assess what constitutes reasonable charges, State Parties may decide to implement a cost recovery system based on, for instance, fixed fees, direct fees, or contract systems. Overall, Article 14 of this Protocol adds little to existing obligations on port reception facilities established in MARPOL.

The Bucharest Convention is also an umbrella treaty that aims to prevent, control, and reduce marine pollution in the Black Sea.[110] Although the EU is not a Party to the Convention, this organization has been granted an observer

---

105 OSPAR Commission, "Regional Action Plan for Prevention and Management of Marine Litter in the North-East Atlantic," (2014).

106 *See* Article 4(1) of the Barcelona Convention.

107 A comprehensive overview of the Barcelona Convention is found in Tullio Scovazzi, "Regional Cooperation in the Field of the Environment," in *Marine Specially Protected Areas: The General Aspects and the Mediterranean Regional System*, ed. Tullio Scovazzi (The Hague: Kluwer Law International, 1999).

108 Protocol Concerning Cooperation in Preventing Pollution from Ships and, in *Cases of Emergency, Combating Pollution of the Mediterranean Sea*, Valletta, 25 January 2002 OJ L 261, 6 August 2004, pp. 41–46. In force 27 March 2004.

109 Ibid., Article 14(1).

110 *See* Article V(2) of the Bucharest Convention. For a general overview of the Convention, *See* Gabino Gonzalez and Frédéric Hébert, "Conventions Relating to Pollution Incident Preparedness, Response, and Cooperation," in *The IMLI Manual on International Maritime Law: Volume III, Marine Environmental Law and Maritime Security Law*, ed. David Attard et al. (Oxford: Oxford University Press, 2016), 217–20.

188 *The ESM of wastes*

status since 2001.[111] This treaty, like the Barcelona Convention, requires that Parties take joint or individual measures regarding ship-source pollution in accordance with "generally accepted international rules and standards",[112] *i.e.*, MARPOL. Like other framework treaties, subsequent protocols impose more detailed obligations. In relation to port reception facilities, however, there are no specific obligations. In 2009, the IMO and the Commission on the Protection of the Black Sea against Pollution signed an agreement of cooperation[113] and in that same year, the Commission adopted the "Strategic Action Plan for the Environmental Protection and Rehabilitation of the Black Sea".[114] The Plan contains several targets including the provision of adequate reception facilities for wastes related to MARPOL – Annexes I, IV, and V. The overall objective is to reduce illegal discharges and increase the compliance with MARPOL.

The relation between ship wastes and wider EU waste legislation

Considering that ESM is a principle that deals with wastes from a life-cycle approach, there is a growing awareness that ship wastes cannot be handled in isolation from other "land wastes". According to Article 2 of Directive 2000/59/EC, ship-generated waste and cargo residues shall be considered wastes within the meaning of Article 3(1) of the Waste Framework Directive. This provision becomes relevant for the management of wastes once they are discharged to port reception facilities since while on board vessels, the management of these substances, including their accidental and operational discharges, are in principle governed by MARPOL.

In marine pollution incidents where compensation mechanisms are either unavailable or appraised as inadequate, reliance on EU waste legislation could be an alternative to bypass international regulation,[115] including international liabilities regimes, *i.e.*, CLC Conventions and the Fund Conventions. This was the case of the *Commune de Mesquer v. Total* where an accidental oil spillage from a ship was deemed as waste. The ship owner, for liability purposes, was considered as the holder of the waste within the meaning of Directive 75/442, which was in force when the incident occurred.[116] This case raised doubts regarding the relation between Directive 75/442 and international liability regimes. While the

---

111 This status was granted at the 7th Regular Black Sea Commission Meeting held in May 2001. *See* <www.blacksea-commission.org/_projects_observers_partners.asp>, last accessed 26 March 2019.
112 *See* Article VIII of the Bucharest Convention.
113 "Agreement of Cooperation between the International Maritime Organization (IMO) and the Commission on the Protection of the Black Sea against Pollution," (December 2009).
114 Permanent Secretariat of the Commission on the Protection of the Black Sea against Pollution, "Strategic Action Plan for the Environmental Protection and Rehabilitation of the Black Sea," (Bulgaria, April 2009).
115 Rosa Greaves, "The Impact of EU Secondary Legislation on Issues Concerning Ships: A Case Study of National Proceedings in Respect of Waste Liability and Insolvency," in *Jurisdiction over Ships: Post-UNCLOS Developments in the Law of the Sea*, ed. Henrik Ringbom, Publications on Ocean Development (Leiden: Brill Nijhoff, 2015).
116 This Directive was repealed by Directive 2008/98/EC.

ESM of ship wastes: the sea/land interface 189

CLC channels liability to the ship owner by imposing strict liability, the *Commune de Mesquer v. Total* case sought to impose liability on Parties other than those provided for in the CLC, *i.e.*, the producer of the oil and the charterer. This case potentially opens the door for further conflicts in compensation and liability matters and raises questions regarding the extent of the applicability of the Waste Framework Directive to ship wastes before being discharged at port reception facilities. After Directive 75/442 was repealed by Directive 2008/98/EC, Article 14(6) currently reads as follows:

1   In accordance with the polluter-pays principle, the costs of waste management shall be borne by the original waste producer or by the current or previous waste holders.
2   Member States may decide that the costs of waste management are to be borne partly or wholly by the producer of the product from which the waste came and that the distributors of such product may share these costs.

According to Langlet and Mahmoudi, "This can be seen as a step back from the Court's statement that the producer of the product from which the waste originated must be required to bear the costs if no other party later in the life-cycle of the product can be required to do so".[117] Additionally, the European Commission issued guidelines for the interpretation of the Waste Framework Directive. Regarding the management of oil spills, Member States can individually decide upon the measures to manage such spillages, including liability issues.[118]

Everything that is not governed by Directive 2000/59/EC will be subject to the Waste Framework Directive. Directive 2000/59/EC provides for the collection of wastes at port reception facilities, but management activities related to transport, recycling, reuse, recovery, and final disposal operations must follow the Waste Framework Directive and other relevant EU waste legislation. The management of wastes, including ship-generated waste and cargo residues, must be carried out in an environmentally sound manner, States are obliged to adopt measures so as to achieve such a general duty.[119] Directive 75/442 had a very similar obligation that was subject to judicial scrutiny in the *Comitato di Coordinamento per la Difesa della Cava and Others v. Regione Lombardia and others* case. The Court of Justice considered that this provision had no direct effect since it does not provide for "specific measures or a particular method of waste disposal. It is therefore neither unconditional nor sufficiently precise and thus is not capable of conferring rights on which individuals may rely as against the State".[120]

117 Langlet and Mahmoudi, *EU Environmental Law and Policy*, 57.
118 European Commission, "Guidance on the Interpretation of Key Provisions of Directive 2008/98/EC on Waste," 14.
119 Ibid., Article 13.
120 Michael Reddish, "ECJ Case Report: Case C-236," *European Environmental Law Review* 3, no. 10 (November 1994): 307–10.

190   *The ESM of wastes*

Waste hierarchy

Article 12(1)(g) of Directive 2000/59/EC provides that the recovery or disposal of ship-generated waste and cargo residues must be carried out in accordance with the waste hierarchy. For specific waste streams, Article 4(2) of the Waste Framework Directive 2008/98/EC gives Member States the capacity to depart from the priority order established in the waste management hierarchy if it is justified from a life-cycle approach. The strict application of the hierarchy may involve higher risks for the environment and human health. In this case, it is reasonable to depart from the priority order.[121] Several aspects should be considered when deciding if derogation from the waste management hierarchy is justified. These include: "precaution and sustainability, technical feasibility and economic viability, protection of resources ... and social impacts".[122] In practice, however, Member States choose – more or less freely – whether wastes are going to be composted, recycled, incinerated, or landfilled. For this reason, some scholars consider that the waste management hierarchy resembles more a recommendation than a binding obligation.[123] The European Commission deems such a hierarchy as binding, albeit subject to a certain degree of flexibility. From the wording of Article 4(1) of the Waste Framework Directive 2008/98/EC, it appears that following the waste management hierarchy is a legal obligation since States "shall apply" this priority order in their waste policy and legislation. Thus, Article 4(1) imposes a legal constraint,[124] but the exceptions to deviate from the hierarchy provided in Article 4(2) are so wide that in practice the enforcement of such an obligation is extremely difficult.

Waste minimization

The EU has taken certain subtle actions to prevent and minimize ship-generated waste, without establishing obligations related to on-board operations, equipment, or ship design. Article 8(2)(c) of Directive 2000/59/EC prescribes that fees for ship-generated wastes "may be reduced if the ship's environmental management, design, equipment and operation are such that the master of the ship can demonstrate that it produces reduced quantities of ship-generated waste." Although Member States have implemented such provision, few EU ports apply it[125] because in the absence of minimum criteria regarding actual on-board practices and potential waste handling mechanisms to reduce the generation of wastes, the provision remains of limited utility. In 2017, EMSA commissioned a study

---

121 European Commission, "Guidance on the Interpretation of Key Provisions of Directive 2008/98/EC on Waste," 49–50.

122 Ibid., 50.

123 Richard Moules, *Environmental Judicial Review* (Oxford: Hart Publishing, 2011), 300–3.

124 Elizabeth Fisher, Bettina Lange, and Eloise Scotford, *Environmental Law: Text, Cases, and Materials* (Oxford: Oxford University Press, 2013), 446, 703–4.

125 Panteia and PWC, "Ex-Post Evaluation of Directive 2000/59/EC on Port Reception Facilities for Ship-Generated Waste and Cargo Residues (Final Report)," 101.

ESM of ship wastes: the sea/land interface 191

regarding on-board waste management treatments, methods, and technologies used to reduce the quantities of ship-generated waste.[126] Given that Directive 2000/59/EC is being revised, the gathering of these data could inform the revision of this Directive in several ways. First, for every type of ship-generated waste, the Directive should include an Annex related to best available techniques that could serve as a basis on which to demonstrate waste minimization, and consequently ship operators may benefit from a reduced fee while using port reception facilities. Second, the EU can also introduce direct obligations relating to on-board practices to secure the prevention of ship-generated waste for vessels bound for EU ports. If these practices follow, *e.g.*, IMO recommendations in the field of waste prevention, binding obligations could become a welcome development.[127] Such a legislative approach could also exert pressure for the adoption of binding regulations at the international level. The history of MARPOL shows that States are more inclined to adopt strict regulations to improve on-board management practices and technological equipment of ships, rather than imposing obligations on the actual provision and functioning of port reception facilities.

Waste reception and handling plans

Ports either individually or in a regional setting must develop waste reception and handling plans.[128] The integration of port reception facilities within the broader context of waste management requires that port waste reception and handling plans are adopted and monitored considering national waste management plans set out in Article 28 of the Waste Framework Directive. Although each EU Member State has national waste management policies, the Waste Framework Directive includes several indications of the content of such plans. Public participation must be ensured in the development of such national plans. Ensuring public participation in decision-making activities regarding waste management is consistent with the Aarhus Convention and, at the EU level, the obligations of this Convention have been implemented in Directive 2003/35/EC.[129] National waste management plans should be instrumental in achieving a coherent EU waste policy. However, some commentators believe that EU waste policy is still inconsistent and subject to "political divergence within the European Union".[130]

---

126 CE Delft and CHEW, "The Management of Ship-Generated Waste On-Board Ships. EMSA/Op/02/2016."

127 Implementing soft law measures is "politically accepted given that the standards are international in origin and adopted by the maritime community as a whole; and their introduction is frequently even coupled with an exhortation encouraging State to apply them in a mandatory form at national level." Ringbom, *The EU Maritime Safety Policy and International Law*, 250.

128 *See* Article 5 of Directive 2000/59/EC.

129 *See* Article 2(2) and Annex I of the "Directive 2003/35/EC Providing for Public Participation in Respect of the Drawing up of Certain Plans and Programmes Relating to the Environment," (OJ L 156, p. 17, 25.06.2003).

130 Ludwig Krämer, *EU Environmental Law*, 8th edn (London: Sweet & Maxwell, 2015), 359–60.

192   *The ESM of wastes*

Waste separation

Separate collections of wastes may be necessary to ensure those wastes undergo recovery operations according to the Waste Framework Directive 2008/98/EC.[131] Port users and providers of port reception facilities encounter difficulties in waste separation and collection, since waste legislation among EU Member States varies considerably.[132] These differences are likely to persist for two reasons. First, standards for separate collection of waste differ between jurisdictions since the Waste Framework Directive 2008/98/EC leaves Member States with greater discretion for setting up such separate collections. Regarding recovery and recycling, Articles 10 and 11 provide, respectively, that wastes must be collected separately if *"technically, environmentally and economically practicable."* The Directive also includes specific obligations for the separation of waste oils[133] and paper, metal, plastic, and glass.[134] Second, the legal basis of the Waste Framework Directive 2008/98/EC is Article 192 TFEU. Consequently, and in accordance with Article 193 TFEU, there is no obligation of full harmonization, and States are entitled to enact more stringent measures. The limit, however, is that those "measures must be compatible with the Treaties".[135]

Port users and the providers of port reception facilities face further difficulties since waste classification, set out in MARPOL and Directive 2000/59/EC, is not always equivalent to the categories of waste legislation on land. The classification of wastes varies from one jurisdiction to another, and as such, it is necessary that port waste reception and handling plans include guidelines for providers of port reception facilities to identify the equivalent categories according to waste legislation on land. Currently, Annex I of Directive 2000/59/EC requires that waste reception and handling plans incorporate a "summary of relevant legislation." Such a summary is not entirely adequate without describing how the relevant legislation relates to ship-generated waste and cargo residues.

Waste oils, hazardous wastes, and recovery targets

Other obligations of the Waste Framework Directive 2008/98/EC that are particularly relevant for ship wastes pertain to: (a) waste oils, *e.g.*, ship-generated wastes from MARPOL Annex I – oil; (b) separate collection and recovery targets

---

131 *See* Articles 10, 11 and 21(1)(a) of the Waste Framework Directive 2008/98/EC.

132 Panteia and PWC, "Ex-Post Evaluation of Directive 2000/59/EC on Port Reception Facilities for Ship-Generated Waste and Cargo Residues (Final Report)," 104–5.

133 *See* Article 21(1)(a) of the Waste Framework Directive 2008/98/EC.

134 *See* the third paragraph of Article 11 of the Waste Framework Directive 2008/98/EC. Other EU legislation, include obligations on separate collection, including, for example, Article 5 of WEEE Directive 2012/19/EU and Article 6(3) of Directive 96/59/EC on PCB/PCT. "Directive 96/59/EC on the Disposal of Polychlorinated Biphenyls and Polychlorinated Terphenyls (PCB/PCT)," (OJ L 243, p. 31, 24.09.1996).

135 *See* Article 193 of TFEU. This article "only allows stricter measures to be taken. Consequently, the Member States may not adopt different measures from those adopted by the European Union." Krämer, *EU Environmental Law*, 123.

ESM of ship wastes: the sea/land interface   193

for paper, metal, plastic, and glass, *e.g.*, ship-generated waste from MARPOL Annex V – garbage; and (c) hazardous wastes, *e.g.*, cargo residues from MARPOL Annex II – harmful substances carried in bulk. Subject to certain exemptions, waste oils must be collected separately, and these wastes shall not be mixed with other wastes or with waste oils of different characteristics. Furthermore, Member States could enact laws regarding the regeneration of waste oils.[136] Member States are obliged to set up separate collections for paper, metal, plastic, and glass, and by 2020 the preparation for reuse or recycling of these waste materials must increase to at least 50 percent by weight.[137] These obligations are especially difficult to implement in respect of the management of ship-generated wastes from MARPOL Annex V, *i.e.*, garbage, because many port reception facilities are not usually "supportive of the on board separation efforts of solid waste".[138] The lack of waste segregation on board and at port reception facilities limits the possibility of waste recovery.

In terms of hazardous wastes, Member States are generally obliged, subject to some exceptions, to ensure that hazardous wastes are not mixed.[139] During their collection, transport, and temporary storage, hazardous wastes must be labelled and packaged according to international and EU law.[140] Member States are also obliged to ensure their traceability, *i.e.*, from production to final treatment.[141] To this end, producers and operators, including dealers and brokers, who collect and transport hazardous wastes must keep records detailing the quantity, nature, mode(s) of transport, destination, and treatment method of the waste.[142] In port reception facilities, the *traceability* of hazardous wastes, *e.g.*, cargo residues, is problematic since port authorities are generally not involved in any stage of hazardous waste management, *e.g.*, collection and transport. Even though Article 6 of Directive 2000/59/EC obliges shipmasters to provide information on ship wastes to the designated authority, EU ports generally lack adequate systems to collect, exchange, and monitor information regarding ship wastes in general and cargo residues in particular.

Overall, the inclusion of ship-generated waste and cargo residues as wastes within the meaning of wastes set out in the Waste Framework Directive 2008/98/EC should provide an adequate basis to achieve the ESM of ship wastes since the Directive embraces a life-cycle approach to wastes.[143] This approach is not just

---

136 *See* Article 21 of the Waste Framework Directive 2008/98/EC. Regeneration of waste oils means, according to Article 3(18) of this Directive, "any recycling operation whereby base oils can be produced by refining waste oils, in particular by removing the contaminants, the oxidation products and the additives contained in such oils."

137 Ibid., Articles 11(1) and (2)(a).

138 Panteia and PWC, "Ex-Post Evaluation of Directive 2000/59/EC on Port Reception Facilities for Ship-Generated Waste and Cargo Residues (Final Report)," 103.

139 *See* Article 18 of the Waste Framework Directive 2008/98/EC.

140 Ibid., Article 19(1).

141 Ibid., Article 17.

142 Ibid., Article 35.

143 "ESM has also been addressed by the European Union, although somewhat differently compared to the Basel Convention … The EU has not carried out, to date, specific work on ESM

194   *The ESM of wastes*

reflected in the inclusion of the waste management hierarchy; it is also evident in the requirement to develop waste management and waste prevention plans in which relevant stakeholders, including the public, must be able to participate. At the EU level, there are specific directives that deal with treatment operations, including landfilling and the incineration of waste.[144] These specific directives have an impact on the assessment of the waste treatment alternatives for ship wastes.

Port reception facilities: obligations and current challenges

This section provides an analysis of specific obligations related to the provision and operation of European port reception facilities. The discussion focuses mainly on Directive 2000/59/EC and the regulatory framework for port reception facilities developed under the auspices of HELCOM for the Baltic Sea area. In addition, this section examines the difficulties faced by States in the implementation of their obligations and the challenges associated with the ESM of wastes on land.

Waste reception and handling plans

According to Article 6 of Directive 2000/59/EC, Member States must develop – whether individually or in a regional context – waste reception and handling plans for ship-generated waste and cargo residues. The development of such plans on a regional basis does not imply, however, that States enjoy the right to provide port reception facilities on a regional basis as well. On the contrary, port reception facilities must be available at every single port.[145]

Annex I of Directive 2000/59/EC details the content of waste reception and handling plans. This Annex includes mandatory and optional requirements. It is obligatory to include: (a) an evaluation of the facilities required to satisfy the needs of ships usually calling at a particular port; (b) a description of the type and quantities of ship-generated wastes and cargo residues received on land; (c) a description of the technical capacity of facilities including the procedures for reception and collection of ship wastes; (d) a description of the cost recovery system; (e) mechanisms to report alleged inadequacies of port reception facilities, among others.

From a practical point of view, the assessment of the type of facilities needed should ideally be based on available data regarding the size and location of the port, volume of traffic, type of vessel calling at the port, and the amount of

---

but has indirectly addressed it through many EC Directives and Regulations related to waste and environmental protection, where managing waste in an environmentally sound manner is an underlying principle." Organisation for Economic Co-operation and Development (OECD), "Guidance Manual on Environmentally Sound Management of Waste," 18.

144 *See* "Directive 1999/31/EC on the Landfill of Waste," (OJ L 182, p. 1, 16.07.1999). "Directive 2000/76/EC on the Incineration of Waste."

145 *See* Article 5(2) of Directive 2000/59/EC.

wastes actually received. However, the vast majority of plans do not describe the type and quantities of ship-generated waste and cargo residues that are received at port reception facilities.[146] This is the result of poor collection data mechanisms at port level, and where this information is available, port authorities do not make use of it.[147]

Shipmasters, bound to an EU port, are obliged to notify the type and amount of ship-generated waste and cargo residues "to be delivered and/or remaining on board".[148] However, for many port authorities, collecting this information may be burdensome, especially where electronic means are not available.[149] To simplify data collection and to reduce administrative burdens for port authorities and shipmasters, from June 2015, EU Member States must "accept" that certain reporting obligations are transmitted electronically through a "single window"[150] in accordance with Article 5 of Directive 2010/65/EU on reporting formalities for ships arriving in and/or departing from ports of the Member States.

Directive 2010/65/EU is applicable to several reporting obligations applicable to ships that arrive at or depart from EU ports.[151] If these electronic means are indeed implemented, they could simplify the systematization and analysis of such data. It could also enhance the harmonization of data to assess, *e.g.*, the quantities and type of ship-generated waste not only at port level, but also at regional or EU level. The benefits of implementing the electronic means set forth in Directive 2010/65/EU are already noticeable in the Baltic Sea area. Currently, several ports have access to information on cargo residues because such information is notified through national single windows.[152] However, there are still problems with the management of the data collected. Many ports that collect the required information "act on the basis of their own data needs, using their own units of measurement".[153] Collecting and making use of the information on ship wastes that are actually received at port reception facilities is vital

---

146 "C/2016/1759 Commission Notice – Guidelines for the Interpretation of Directive 2000/59/EC on Port Reception Facilities for Ship-Generated Waste and Cargo Residues," 7.

147 *See Infra*, Appendix II.

148 *See* Article 6 and Annex II of Directive 2000/59/EC.

149 European Commission, "Roadmap. Inception Impact Assessment: REFIT Revision of EU Directive 2000/59/EC on Port Reception Facilities for Ship-Generated Waste and Cargo Residues," (2015), 5.

150 "Directive 2010/65/EU support the so-called 'ONCE paradigm', *i.e.,* the approach of implementing a single electronic transmission of data and a single control declaration formalities for ships arriving and for ship departing/arriving in/from ports of member states." Paolo Pagano et al., "Complex Infrastructures: The Benefit of Its Services in Seaports," in *Intelligent Transportation Systems: From Good Practices to Standards*, ed. Paolo Pagano (Boca Raton, FL: CRC Press, 2017), 174.

151 *See* Article 1(2) of Directive 2010/65/EU.

152 *See Infra*, Appendix II.

153 European Commission, "Roadmap. Inception Impact Assessment: REFIT Revision of EU Directive 2000/59/EC on Port Reception Facilities for Ship-Generated Waste and Cargo Residues," 5.

196 *The ESM of wastes*

not only in developing waste reception and handling plans, but also in monitoring and enforcing Directive 2000/59/EC in accordance with its Article 12(3).

The development of waste reception and handling plans requires the consultation of "relevant parties," *e.g.*, the shipping industry, terminal and waste management operators.[154] Nonetheless, many ports do not engage their users and service providers, or if they do so, such engagement occurs on a merely informal basis.[155] It is particularly challenging to evaluate whether waste reception and handling plans are integrated into national waste management systems. In principle, national waste management plans should be a good basis on which to evaluate the plans developed at port level. The information included in waste reception and handling plans, however, does not reflect whether the general duties set forth in the Waste Framework Directive 2008/98/EC inform their development and implementation, *e.g.*, the waste management hierarchy, separate collection of wastes, and obligations related to waste oils and hazardous wastes. Annex I of Directive 2000/59/EC includes optional requirements that should be included in waste reception and handling plans including, *e.g.*, "a description of how the ship-generated waste and cargo residues are disposed of." But such a general description fails to address how the disposal of ship wastes relates to other areas of EU waste law.

In the Baltic Sea area, HELCOM recommends that ports develop waste management plans that provide a "detailed description" of procedures related to the reception and collection of ship wastes.[156] The plans "must"[157] also include information regarding ship waste management on land, *i.e.*, storage, pretreatment and treatment operations. Waste management should be consistent with standards applicable to other wastes with the same characteristics. In other words, ship wastes must be treated as other similar wastes generated on land. HELCOM also endorses a life-cycle approach toward ship wastes. Every waste management plan must follow general principles for waste management, *e.g.*, application of the waste management hierarchy, requiring licenses to waste management operators, and application of BAT and BEP standards regarding treatment operations. These requirements are consistent with an ESM of wastes approach developed at both EU and international levels.

---

154 *See* Article 5 and Annex 1 of Directive 2000/59/EC.

155 "[I]n one-third of the Member States no documentary evidence could be provided of such stakeholder consultations. However, there is the possibility that such consultations have taken place informally, as part of normal daily contacts without a reporting routine." Panteia and PWC, "Ex-Post Evaluation of Directive 2000/59/EC on Port Reception Facilities for Ship-Generated Waste and Cargo Residues (Final Report)," 47.

156 Baltic Marine Environment Protection Commission (HELCOM), "HELCOM Recommendation 19/12: Waste Management Plans for Ports."

157 The recommendation of HELCOM regarding the elaboration of waste management plans uses binding language such as "shall." However, recommendations are not *per se* mandatory. The use of language that denotes a "law-like" provision should be understood as a normative commitment. The recommendation shows an intention to create legal relationships and if States decide to follow this recommendation, they are urged to implement it and to adopt it as a binding instrument.

ESM of ship wastes: the sea/land interface   197

Mandatory discharge criteria for ship-generated waste

Article 7 of Directive 2000/59/EC provides that ships calling at an EU port *must deliver all ship-generated waste* to port reception facilities before leaving said port. From the wording of this provision it is uncertain whether operational discharges at sea (which MARPOL allows) are still legal for ships calling at an EU port. According to the Commission, Directive 2000/59/EC aims at supporting the full implementation of MARPOL "instead of introducing new discharge rules for ships".[158] Thus, it is reasonable to conclude that this provision establishes a binding obligation for ships in ports, which does not affect the operational discharge standards established in MARPOL. Annex II of Directive 2000/59/EC removes any possible doubt as to whether or not the Directive restricts operational discharges at sea, at least as far as sewage is concerned. According to this Annex, sewage may be discharged according to the relevant regulation of MARPOL, and consequently shipmasters are not obliged to report on sewage "if it is the intention to make an authorized discharge at sea."

However, the position of the Commission seems to have changed. In the interpretative guidelines of Directive 2000/59/EC, the Commission takes a bold yet cautious step toward a zero-discharge standard, by stating:

> the overall delivery requirement should be interpreted in the light of the Directive's objectives of reducing ship-generated waste into the sea and enhancing the protection of the marine environment. Therefore, the Commission takes the view that what is allowed to be discharged under MARPOL cannot be automatically excluded from the delivery requirement in the Directive.[159]

If this policy is actually pursued, such action will disrupt the jurisdictional framework prescribed in the LOSC, since it would be an attempt to extend legislative jurisdiction beyond internal and territorial waters because many operational discharges allowed by MARPOL occur beyond 12 nm from the nearest land. Annex IV of the Helsinki Convention also incorporates a provision related to mandatory discharge criteria, which states: "[b]efore leaving port ships shall discharge all ship-generated wastes, which are not allowed to be discharged into the sea in the Baltic Sea Area in accordance with MARPOL 73/78." This provision unequivocally avoids imposing any discharge rule for ships while at sea.

If adequate port reception facilities are available and enforcement mechanisms are in place, then establishing compulsory discharge criteria is an effective

---

158 Commission of the European Communities, "Com(1998) 452 Final, Explanatory Memorandum: Proposal for a Council Directive on Port Reception Facilities for Ship-Generated Waste and Cargo Residues. 98/0249 (Syn)," (17.07.1998), 3, para 5. *See also* Ringbom, *The EU Maritime Safety Policy and International Law*, 330.

159 "C/2016/1759 Commission Notice – Guidelines for the Interpretation of Directive 2000/59/EC on Port Reception Facilities for Ship-Generated Waste and Cargo Residues," 10.

198 *The ESM of wastes*

mechanism through which to avoid illegal discharges at sea. There is, however, an exception regarding the general obligation to discharge ship-generated wastes at port reception facilities. According to Article 7(2) of Directive 2000/59/EC, if there is "sufficient dedicated storage capacity," the ship may keep on board the ship-generated waste and proceed to the next port of call regardless of whether this port is within the EU. Port authorities face many difficulties in assessing whether ships have sufficient dedicated storage capacity. Empirical evidence shows significant differences in the application of this provision between EU Member States, whereby interpretation is left to the discretion of port authorities.[160] Considering that the general provision demands that all ship-generated waste is delivered at port reception facilities, the exception cannot become the rule, and the application of such an exception must be strict. Nonetheless, port users fear that using port reception facilities in every port instead of keeping wastes on board could increase their operational costs.[161] The needs of port users must also be taken into account when applying the mandatory discharge criteria because it can translate into an incentive to discharge ship-wastes at sea, or to deliver them to a cheaper facility – whether "adequate" or otherwise.

The decision concerning this exception depends on the data provided by the ship-master in accordance with the information required by Directive 2000/59/EC. This poses a further challenge in terms of the mechanisms available to monitor the accuracy of such information. EMSA has adopted technical guidelines to assess, through different methods, the dedicated storage capacity of ships depending on the type of ship waste.[162] Dedicated storage capacity is not, however, the only relevant aspect when evaluating whether a ship is exempt from the application of the mandatory discharge criteria. Article 7(2) of Directive 2000/59/ EC prescribes:

> [i]f there are good reasons to believe that adequate facilities are not available at the intended port of delivery, or if this port is unknown, and that there is therefore a risk that the waste will be discharged at sea, the Member State shall take all necessary measures to prevent marine pollution, if necessary by requiring the ship to deliver its waste before departure from the port.

This article imposes a precondition to allow a vessel to proceed to its next port of call and that inevitably requires a case-by-case analysis based on general information available to port authorities. If the next port of call is outside the EU, this article raises some theoretical questions regarding extra-territorial jurisdiction since the provision calls for the assessment of the "adequacy" of port reception facilities located in another jurisdiction. However, the provision is of

---

160 Panteia and PWC, "Ex-Post Evaluation of Directive 2000/59/EC on Port Reception Facilities for Ship-Generated Waste and Cargo Residues (Final Report)," 90.
161 Ibid., 72.
162 European Maritime Safety Agency (EMSA), "Technical Recommendations on the Implementation of Directive 2000/59/EC on Port Reception Facilities," (2016), 14–18.

ESM of ship wastes: the sea/land interface   199

such a general nature that it can hardly be construed as an interference of the sovereignty or territorial integrity of other States. The situation will be different if Member States intend to monitor, supervise, or exercise control activities on port reception facilities outside their jurisdictions.

Article 9(1) of Directive 2000/59/EC contains another exemption from the application of the mandatory discharge criteria for ships "engaged in scheduled traffic with frequent and regular port calls and there is sufficient evidence of an arrangement to ensure the delivery of ship-generated waste … in a port along the ship's route." This exception could be granted in cases where the cost recovery system of port reception facilities is based on contracts and the payments for delivering wastes are made on a monthly or annual basis, for instance. However, several port authorities lack access to relevant information that could provide evidence of such arrangements.[163] Such relevant information includes, but is not limited to, contracts and receipts showing that such contractual arrangements are still valid.[164] This provision aims to prevent any undue burdens for port users and port authorities in cases where a vessel has recurring journeys between identified ports. The provision is silent on whether the exemption applies to a specific journey or is valid for a limited period of time while the vessel is engaged on the same scheduled traffic and while the arrangement for delivery of ship-generated wastes remains valid. Considering the rationale behind the establishment of such provision, it is reasonable to conclude that a port authority will provide an exemption for a determined period of time. That way, the ship-master is not obliged to require an exemption every time the vessel visits a determined port. The Commission recommends that such exception should last no longer than five years, and in any case should extend "beyond the duration of the waste management arrangement".[165] The exemption provided for in Article 9(1) of the Directive is also applicable to the obligations relating to the payment of fees for ship-generated waste and waste notification requirements.

In the Baltic Sea area, the Helsinki Convention also includes an exemption from the application of mandatory discharge of ship-generated waste. According to Regulation 6(B.3) of Annex IV of the Convention, a vessel can keep "on board minor amounts of wastes which are unreasonable to discharge to port reception facilities." The provision offers some latitude of discretion for its interpretation and application, but in principle it could be construed as a stricter exemption than that provided in Article 7(2) of Directive 2000/59/EC because a ship may have sufficient dedicated storage capacity, but could still be required to discharge ship-generated wastes if waste quantities are not considered "minor." HELCOM, however, relates minor amounts to storage capacity when assessing the delivery of oil and oily mixtures coming from the machinery spaces

163 Panteia and PWC, "Ex-Post Evaluation of Directive 2000/59/EC on Port Reception Facilities for Ship-Generated Waste and Cargo Residues (Final Report)," 68.
164 C/2016/1759 Commission Notice – Guidelines for the Interpretation of Directive 2000/59/EC on Port Reception Facilities for Ship-Generated Waste and Cargo Residues, 15.
165 Ibid., 16.

200   *The ESM of wastes*

of ships.[166] In relation to food wastes, all garbage, *i.e.*, MARPOL – Annex V, must be delivered according to HELCOM's interpretative guidelines.[167] Other exceptions regarding the application of mandatory discharge include the "need for special arrangements for, *e.g.*, passenger ferries engaged in short voyages",[168] and the absence of adequate port reception facilities.[169]

Discharge criteria for cargo residues

Article 10 of Directive 2000/59/EC does not impose mandatory discharge criteria for cargo residues, which must be discharged in accordance with MARPOL standards. MARPOL does not specify where or when "cargo residues" must be discharged. This means that ship operators can freely choose the port reception facility where they will discharge the residues. There are two exceptions to this general rule:

- Ships carrying substances, "which through their physical properties inhibit effective product/water separation, and monitoring, including asphalt and high-density oils," must discharge their residues at the unloading port.[170]
- Ships carrying MARPOL, Annex II, substances of category X need to prewash their tanks and discharge the residues at the unloading port.[171] If substances of categories Y or Z are not unloaded following the procedures established in Appendix IV of MARPOL, Annex II, tanks must also be prewashed.[172] However, if ships load the same substance, the relevant authority could make an exception for a prewash.

In general, dedicated terminals receive cargo and cargo residues with little or no involvement from port authorities.[173] Thus, the relevant authorities are not in charge of making exemptions from required prewashes, for instance, leaving this responsibility to the terminal. In the absence of information exchange between port authorities and terminals, it is difficult to assess how port authorities verify that ships are complying with the discharge criteria established in MARPOL, Annex II, and the procedures concerning the cleaning of cargo tanks, the discharge of residues, ballasting, and deballasting.

---

166 Baltic Marine Environment Protection Commission (HELCOM), "HELCOM Recommendation 22/3: Unified Interpretations to Ensure the Harmonized and Effective Implementation of the Strategy for Port Reception Facilities for Ship-Generated Wastes and Associated Issues," 30.
167 Ibid. *Note* that the guidelines are silent as to what constitutes "minor amounts" in relation to sewage.
168 Regulation 6(C.1) of Annex IV of the Helsinki Convention.
169 Ibid., Regulation 6(C.2).
170 *See* Regulation 2.4 of Annex I of MARPOL, and numerals 7 and 62 of the Unified Interpretations of Annex I of MARPOL.
171 *See* Regulation 13.6 of MARPOL, Annex II.
172 Ibid., Regulation 13.7.
173 *See Infra*, Appendix II.

The mandatory discharge criteria of the Helsinki Convention do not extend to cargo residues either.[174] Concerning harmful substances carried in bulk, *i.e.*, MARPOL, Annex II, unloading ports are encouraged to receive "tank washings resulting from the application of prewash procedures".[175] Furthermore, loading operations and tanker repairs should not take place if reception facilities are not equipped to receive "ballast water or ... tank washings containing cargo residues".[176]

Cost recovery system

Directive 2000/59/EC and the Helsinki Convention adopted the polluter pays principle that serves as the basis for establishing cost recovery systems. Day-to-day operations of port reception facilities generate environmental externalities derived from the reception and management of ship-generated wastes. These externalities must be internalized by port users rather than by other members of society. Concerning ship-generated wastes, Article 8(2) of Directive 2000/59/EC provides for the application of a combined cost recovery system, which incorporates both an indirect cost recovery mechanism in addition to an extra direct fee. In relation to cargo residues, Article 10 of Directive 2000/59/EC provides for a direct fee system.

Concerning the combined recovery system, Article 8(2)(a) of Directive 2000/59/EC provides that all ships[177] calling at an EU port must "contribute significantly to the costs" for the reception and treatment of ship-generated wastes. The costs can be included in port dues or as separate waste charges. The establishment of such a fee is based on several parameters, *e.g.*, ship type, size, on-board equipment, crew and/or passenger number, the type of ship-generated waste and the required treatment. According to the Commission, "significantly" means that the fee should cover at least 30 percent of the costs. Nonetheless, Member States have considerable discretion in deciding what should be deemed a significant contribution. The payments are made regardless of whether a ship uses a port reception facility. HELCOM encourages their Parties, including the EU, to implement a nonspecial-fee system for ship-generated waste. Such nonspecial-fee is a cost recovery system where *all the costs* must be included in port dues or "harbor fees".[178] It appears that article subparagraph (a) of Article 8(2) of Directive 2000/59/EC incorporates, to some extent, this recommendation

---

174 Regulation 6(B) of Annex IV of the Helsinki Convention provides that "[b]efore leaving port all cargo residues shall be discharged to a port reception facility in accordance with the requirements of MARPOL 73/78."

175 Baltic Marine Environment Protection Commission (HELCOM), "HELCOM Recommendation 10/5: Guidelines for the Establishment of Adequate Reception Facilities in Ports," letter (c).

176 Ibid., letters (d) and (e).

177 Article 8(2) of Directive 2000/59/EC includes all ships "other than fishing vessels and recreational craft authorised to carry no more than 12 passengers."

178 Baltic Marine Environment Protection Commission (HELCOM), "HELCOM Recomendation 28e/10: Application of the No-Special-Fee System to Ship-Generated Wastes and Marine Litter Caught in Fishing Nets in the Baltic Sea Area."

202 The ESM of wastes

by requiring a significant contribution to the costs of port reception facilities.[179] However, subparagraph (b) of this article also includes the possibility to charge an extra fee when the indirect fee does not cover the costs for the use and management of ship-generated wastes that are actually delivered at port reception facilities. Charging an extra direct fee does not discourage legal discharges at sea because the costs related to the use and management of ship-generated wastes will influence a ship operator's decision to discharge at sea or at a port reception facility. The implementation of this provision varies considerably among EU Member States and, in some cases, significant differences are also found at port level.[180] The following graphic summarizes general trends regarding cost recovery systems around Europe (Figure 8.2).

A direct fee system governs the reception and management of cargo residues. In relation to cargo residues subject to MARPOL, Annex II, the establishment of an indirect fee system may be difficult, given: (a) the variety of cargo residues and the specialization required for their management; and (b) the lack of knowledge by port authorities regarding the type and quantities of cargo residues that ships actually discharge at port reception facilities. In the Baltic Sea area, HELCOM has not actively pursued any policy regarding a cost recovery system for cargo residues. Parties to the Helsinki Convention are only encouraged to charge a reasonable cost[181] for the use of facilities related to cargo residues of noxious liquid substances. Ports in the Baltic Sea area generally apply a direct fee system for the collection of cargo residues subject to MARPOL, Annex II. In general, ship operators contact the terminal or waste operator in the "free market," or the operator is chosen through public tendering or framework contracts.[182]

Indirect or combined cost recovery systems should be preferred to avoid creating incentives for ships to discharge wastes at sea. The "administrative waste fee or contribution system" could be especially effective because ships are charged, either directly or indirectly, but the fee is at least partially refunded after ships discharge wastes at port reception facilities.[183] Thus, ships that deliver wastes are rewarded. In cases where direct recovery systems are in place, mandatory

---

179 According to Ringbom, "Article 8 represents a compromise between the (mainly northern) Member States who wished to introduce a 'no special fee' system whereby all ships pay the same irrespective of delivery and others who wished to maintain a link between the fee and types and quantities of waste which are actually delivered. The compromise is laid down in the form of 'principles,' through which all ships have to 'contribute significantly' to the costs of the reception facilities, while still leaving the possibility of a more direct fee system open." Ringbom, *The EU Maritime Safety Policy and International Law*, 259, footnote 30.

180 Ramboll, "Final Report: EMSA Study on the Delivery of Ship-Generated Waste and Cargo Residues to Port Reception Facilities in EU Ports."

181 Letter (f) of the Baltic Marine Environment Protection Commission (HELCOM), "HELCOM Recommendation 10/5: Guidelines for the Establishment of Adequate Reception Facilities in Ports."

182 *See Infra*, Appendix II.

183 Other factors that influence the quantities of wastes received at port reception facilities include: "traffic in the port, ship size calling in the ports, types of vessels calling at the port, price level, efficiency of waste operations, and the type of port operations." "Ex-Post Evaluation of

ESM of ship wastes: the sea/land interface 203

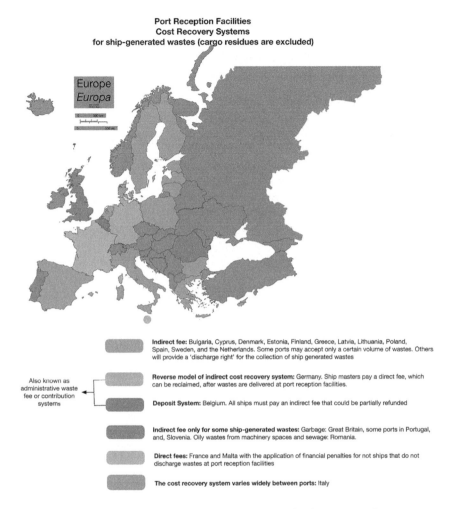

Figure 8.2 Port reception facilities: cost recovery systems for ship-generated wastes.

discharge criteria must also be implemented and coupled with effective monitoring and enforcement mechanisms not only to prevent illegal discharges, but also to avoid competitive distortions between ports.[184] In the case of cargo residues, where direct fee systems are implemented, establishing framework contracts with waste operators could enhance monitoring activities regarding this type of waste, as well as improving communication channels between port authorities

---

Directive 2000/59/EC on Port Reception Facilities for Ship-Generated Waste and Cargo Residues (Final Report)."
184 International Maritime Organization (IMO), "Port Reception Facilities – How to Do It," 156.

204 *The ESM of wastes*

and waste operators. Additionally, other incentives should be put in place, including the reduction of the fee whereby ships are engaged in waste minimization practices.[185]

Transparency in the provision of port reception facility services

According to Article 8(3) of Directive 2000/59/EC, the fees charged for the use of port reception facilities and for the subsequent management of ship wastes shall be "fair, transparent, and non-discriminatory." To assess such transparency, port users should have information concerning the fees and the mechanisms used to calculate them. The article, however, does not impose an obligation to provide such information. While many EU ports made information available regarding waste fees, the basis for their calculation is either not provided or unclear.[186] In ports where ship operators make contact with external operators to handle and manage wastes, the fees are not disclosed and ship operators must request a quote.[187]

In 1997, the Commission presented a Green Paper on Sea Ports and Maritime Infrastructure addressing port competitiveness in general and "port charges and market access" in particular.[188] This policy document attempted to develop a uniform framework for port dues, which drew strong criticisms. For instance, the Economic and Social Committee stated: "there is a great diversity among ports in terms of ownership, internal organization, and governmental involvement in the management of ports ... when it comes to financing and charging".[189] What was welcomed, however, was a policy on market access to port services.

---

185 *See* subparagraph (c) of Article 8.2 of Directive 2000/59/EC. *See* Panteia and PWC, "Ex-Post Evaluation of Directive 2000/59/EC on Port Reception Facilities for Ship-Generated Waste and Cargo Residues (Final Report)," 62–63, 101. CE Delft and CHEW, "The Management of Ship-Generated Waste On-Board Ships. EMSA/Op/02/2016." HPTI Hamburg Port Training Institute GmbH, "Study on Ships Producing Reduced Quantities of Ships Generated Waste – Present Situation and Future Opportunities to Encourage the Development of Cleaner Ships," (European Maritime Safety Agency (EMSA), 2007).

186 European Maritime Safety Agency (EMSA), "Horizontal Assessment Report – Port Reception Facilities (Directive 2000/59/EC)," 24–25. According to this report, the information is made available through a variety of methods, such as "leaflets, published legislative acts or notices, web/homepage."

187 *See Infra*, Appendix II. Only few ports in the Baltic provide information regarding the basis for calculating fees related to cargo residues subject to MARPOL, Annex II. *See also* European Maritime Safety Agency (EMSA), "Horizontal Assessment Report – Port Reception Facilities (Directive 2000/59/EC)," 25.

188 European Commission, "Green Paper on Sea Ports and Maritime Infrastructure," (Luxembourg: Office for Official Publications of the European Communities, 1997).

189 "Opinion of the Economic and Social Committee on the 'Green Paper from the Commission on Sea Ports and Maritime Infrastructure'," (OJ C 407, pp. 92–99, 28.12.1998), 98. *See also* Thomas Brinkmann, "Commentary on Directive 2000/59/EC of 27 November 2000 on Port Reception Facilities for Ship-Generated Waste and Cargo Residues," in *Brussels Commentary on EU Maritime Transport Law*, ed. Henning Jessen and Micheal Jürgen Werner (Münster: Nomos, 2016), 640.

In 2013, the Commission presented a Communication called "Ports: an engine for growth" that aims to improve the financial transparency of ports and to enhance efficiency in port infrastructure charges.[190] As a result of this policy, Regulation 2017/352/EU introduced a framework for the provision of port services and common rules on the financial transparency of ports.[191] However, given the diversity of ports, this Regulation does not impose a uniform regime. Overall, Regulation 2017/352/EU offers a procedure for the selection of port service providers including several reasons to justify limiting the number of such providers. Port authorities may impose minimum requirements as to the performance of a specific service, including the compliance of maritime safety and environmental obligations. Member States also have the capacity to impose public service obligations on port service providers.

The port services covered by this Regulation include the collection of ship-generated waste and cargo residues. Concerning port service charges, Article 12(1) prescribes:

> [t]he charges for the services provided by an internal operator under a public service obligation, the charges for pilotage services that are not exposed to effective competition and the charges levied by providers of port services, referred to in point (b) of Article 6(1), shall be set in a transparent, objective and non-discriminatory way, and shall be proportionate to the cost of the service provided.

The obligation applies to certain types of port service providers and may be of limited assistance in cases where such providers are chosen in the "free market." This provision could potentially have an impact on services related to cargo residues, since the obligation established in Article 8(3) of Directive 2000/59/EC to ensure transparency in the port charges is limited to ship-generated waste. Other than that, Article 12(1) of Regulation 2017/352/EU does not add much to the obligation established in Directive 2000/59/EC. In fact, the obligation contained in Directive 2000/59/EC is wider in two respects. First, Article 8(3) stipulates that fees must be "transparent, non-discriminatory and reflect the costs of the facilities." The article refers to fees in general without restricting its application to a certain type of port service provider. Second, port users "should" have access to the information related to the fees, *e.g.*, the amounts and the underlying basis for their calculation.[192]

---

190 European Commission, "Com(2013) 295 Final: Ports an Engine for Growth," (23.05.2013).
191 *See* "Regulation (EU) 2017/352 Establishing a Framework for the Provision of Port Services and Common Rules on the Financial Transparency of Ports," (OJ L 57, pp. 1–18, 03.03.2017).
192 Brinkmann, "Commentary on Directive 2000/59/EC of 27 November 2000 on Port Reception Facilities for Ship-Generated Waste and Cargo Residues," 642.

206 *The ESM of wastes*

Enforcement activities

According to Article 11 of Directive 2000/59/EC, port inspections must be in place to ensure that ships comply with their obligations. Considering that ships run on tight schedules, not all ships can be subject to port inspections without making the system extremely burdensome and ineffective. Additionally, authorities conducting such inspections face several constraints, *e.g.*, budget and time. Thus, port inspections should target vessels that pose a risk of noncompliance.

Article 11(2) contains two parameters to select ships for inspections. First, inspections will take place if shipmasters do not provide the information required in the waste notification form set out in Annex II of Directive 2000/59/EC. Second, inspections will also take place in cases where the information provided reveals "other grounds to believe"[193] that ships are not complying with their discharge obligations. Directive 2000/59/EC does not oblige Member States to conduct port inspections that are exclusively related to the compliance of discharge obligations. Therefore, inspections could be conducted, for instance, within the framework of Directive 2009/16/EC on Port State Control.[194] This Directive targets substandard vessels and aims at increasing the compliance of international[195] and EU legislation in the fields of maritime security and safety, marine environmental protection, and labor standards. Directive 2009/16/EC attributes a risk profile to all ships calling at an EU port which serves as the basis to choose which ships must be inspected. The risk profile is based on generic criteria, *e.g.*, type and age of ship, and historical criteria, *e.g.*, number of previous detentions. A factor that influences the decision as to whether a ship is subject to an inspection also relates to the noncompliance of the notification requirements established in Directive 2000/59/EC.

Regarding the compliance of discharge obligations at port reception facilities, the implementation of the provision related to port inspections has been diverse around ports in the EU. Some Member States conduct the inspections within the framework of Directive 2009/16/EC or within other specialized environmental inspections.[196] Some have also developed dedicated

---

193 *See* Article 11(2)(a) of Directive 2000/59/EC.

194 Ibid., Article 11(2)(b). The inspection system established in Directive 2009/16/EC follows closely the work of the Paris Memorandum of Understanding on Port State Control (Paris: MOU). The Directive and MOU Paris have developed a risk profile for ships and have abandoned the 25 percent fixed target.

195 *See* Articles 1 and 2 of the Directive 2009/16/EC on Port State Control, (OJ L 131, p. 57, 28.05.2009). Some of the international instruments covered by this instrument include MARPOL, SOLAS, and COLREGS. "[T]he conventions, through their 'no more favorable treatment' clauses, envisage the extension of such controls to ships flying the flag of non-Party States. These features ... should remove any doubts that may have existed as regard the legal legitimacy of a co-ordinated European regulatory approach to requiring compliance with the international conventions." Ringbom, *The EU Maritime Safety Policy and International Law*, 239–40.

196 Panteia and PWC, "Ex-Post Evaluation of Directive 2000/59/EC on Port Reception Facilities for Ship-Generated Waste and Cargo Residues (Final Report)," 79.

ESM of ship wastes: the sea/land interface   207

port inspections.[197] No matter the legal framework used to conduct port inspection, the application of the selection criteria, *i.e.*, "waste notification form," has proven to be challenging for several reasons. It is important to be aware that port authorities are not always in charge of conducting port inspections and that other specialized agencies could be responsible for conducting such inspections.[198] In general, the waste notification form does not serve as a basis on which to select ships for inspections because of the difficulties in collecting and actually monitoring such information; moreover, sometimes this information is not transmitted to the authorities in charge of the inspections.[199] When authorities conduct inspections within the framework of Directive 2009/16/EC, other generic or historical criteria are used to select the ships and in several cases the compliance of the discharge obligations set out in Directive 2000/59/EC are not included in the inspection.

To enable authorities to use the selection criteria established in Directive 2000/59/EC, EMSA is developing a module for inspections of port reception facilities within THETIS, *i.e.*, an information system for Port State Control, hosted by EMSA, which assists port authorities of the EU and the Paris Memorandum of Understanding on Port State Control (Paris MoU).[200] The module will include information provided by shipmasters on ship-generated wastes and cargo residues.[201] In accordance with Article 12(3) of Directive 2000/59/EC, this database should enable the identification of ships that are not delivering their wastes as provided in the Directive. As such, it is an important tool to facilitate port state control and monitoring activities. This database could also be useful in analyzing, for instance, the quantities and nature of cargo residues received at port reception facilities, and eventually this database could be a starting point to ensure the traceability of these hazardous wastes on land. THETIS must also be integrated into the SafeSeaNet (SSN),[202] *i.e.*, the traffic monitoring and information system that receives, stores, and exchanges data in relation to "maritime safety, port and maritime security, marine environment protection and the efficiency of maritime traffic and maritime transport".[203]

---

197 Ibid., 80.
198 European Maritime Safety Agency (EMSA), "Horizontal Assessment Report – Port Reception Facilities (Directive 2000/59/EC)," 28.
199 Ibid., 31–32.
200 *Note* that in relation to the Paris MoU, "[a] major change occurred in 2011 with the adoption of a New Inspection Regime which facilitates the selection of ships for a PSC [Port State Control] inspection with a central computer database, known as Thetis ... Each ship in the information system is attributed a ship risk profile. The ship risk profile determines the ship's priority for inspection, the interval between its inspections and the scope of the inspection." Philippe Boisson, "Law of Maritime Security," in *The IMLI Manual on International Maritime Law: Volume II, Shipping Law*, ed. David Attard et al. (Oxford: Oxford University Press, 2016), 203.
201 European Commission, "Com(2016) 168 Final REFIT Evaluation of Directive 2000/59/EC on Port Reception Facilities for Ship-Generated Waste and Cargo Residues," 14–15.
202 Ibid., 14.
203 *See* Annex III of "Directive 2002/59/EC Establishing a Community Vessel Traffic Monitoring and Information System," (OJ L 208, p. 10, 05.08.2002). *See also* Christodoulou-Varotsi,

208 *The ESM of wastes*

Difficulties in assessing the information contained in the waste notification form have a negative impact on the selection of ships for inspection. Concerning ship-generated wastes, ships may be exempted from their discharge obligations if they have "sufficient dedicated storage capacity".[204] The interpretation of this exemption varies around ports. For this reason, EMSA adopted guidelines on ship inspection that include several methods for the calculation of the dedicated storage capacity.[205] Regarding cargo residues, the selection of ships for inspection is also problematic because Directive 2000/59/EC does not impose any mandatory discharge criteria other than the standards set out in MARPOL.[206] Shipmasters, subject to some exceptions, are able to freely choose the reception facility for the discharge of these wastes. Authorities, even if they have access to the waste notification form, may not be able to assess the location of the reception facility where cargo residues must be discharged. They could also face difficulties in assessing whether a ship has enough storage capacity because the information provided in the waste notification form usually contains "estimations as the amounts will depend on the methods used to unload the cargo, which vary from port to port".[207] In cases of noncompliance, ships must be detained until they discharge wastes at port reception facilities.[208]

The Helsinki Convention does not provide for dedicated inspections to verify the compliance of the mandatory discharge criteria established in Regulation 6 of Annex IV of this instrument. The Convention calls instead for the application of the Paris MoU or Directive 2009/16/EC on Port State Control.[209] This latter instrument considers the inspection system developed by the Paris MoU.

Forthcoming regulation on port reception facilities

Directive 2000/59/EC is currently under revision and the Commission submitted a legislative proposal in January 2018 to repeal the current Directive.[210] Such revision is necessary to enhance the integration of ship-generated wastes and cargo residues into wider EU waste legislation. First, there is a need for terminology harmonization between MARPOL and EU legislation. The proposal takes a positive step in this direction by including a general definition

---

Maritime Safety Law and Policies of the European Union and the United States of America: Antagonism or Synergy?, 110–11.

204 *See* Article 7(2) of Directive 2000/59/EC.

205 European Maritime Safety Agency (EMSA), "Guidance for Ship Inspections under the Port Reception Facilities Directive (Directive 2000/59/EC)," (2016), 21–24.

206 *See* Article 10 of Directive 2000/59/EC.

207 European Maritime Safety Agency (EMSA), "Guidance for Ship Inspections under the Port Reception Facilities Directive (Directive 2000/59/EC)," 8, footnote 4.

208 *See* Article 11 (c) of Directive 2000/59/EC.

209 *See* Regulation 10 of Annex IV of the Helsinki Convention.

210 European Commission, "Com(2018) 33 Final: Proposal for a Directive of the European Parliament and of the Council on port reception facilities for the delivery of wastes from ships" (16.01.2018).

ESM of ship wastes: the sea/land interface 209

of 'waste from ships' that includes cargo residues as well as residues subject to MARPOL, Annex VI. This potential amendment is also the result of regulatory developments at the international level. Regulation 17 of MARPOL, Annex VI, requires that State Parties provide reception facilities for "exhaust gas cleaning residues and exhaust gas cleaning systems".[211]

Second, mandatory discharge criteria for all categories of ship wastes should be included. Compulsory discharge criteria include the correlated obligation of States to manage such waste on land in an environmentally sound manner without transforming one source of pollution into another. This could prove particularly challenging for cargo residues due to the diversity of these residues as well as for the practices around ports that leave the management of such residues to individual terminals. The discharge criteria set up in Article 7 of the legislative proposal is far from satisfactory. The general rule indicates that before leaving the port, the master of a ship delivers the wastes in accordance to MARPOL. As discussed in this Chapter, MARPOL does not impose compulsory standards that specify the location where ship wastes must be discharged, *e.g.*, the unloading port. Therefore, ships with enough holding capacity can freely choose, subject to some exceptions, the port reception facility for the discharge of wastes. However, the general rule set forth in the legislative proposal is subject to several caveats.[212] Article 7(5) prescribes that when the next port of call is unknown or it is not possible to determine whether adequate facilities are available in the next port of call, wastes must be delivered before departure. This seems to indicate that ship wastes must be deliver at least in an EU port where authorities should be able to verify in GISIS the availability of adequate port reception facilities.

The proposal in its Article 7(4) prescribes that ships may be exempted from their discharge obligations if they have "sufficient dedicated storage capacity." Currently, the challenges faced to implement such exception concerns the diverse interpretation around ports of the meaning and extent of 'sufficient storage capacity.' The legislative proposal confers implementation powers to the Commission to establish the methods to be used for the calculation of the storage capacity.[213]

Third, in order to improve the traceability of these wastes on land it is necessary to include obligations regarding cooperation and exchange of information between dedicated terminals, waste operators, and port authorities. It is positive that the legislative proposal includes reporting and exchange of information

---

211 In ports where ships undergo repairs or where ships are dismantled, facilities should be available for the reception of "ozone-depleting substances and equipment containing such substances when removing from the ship." Since repairs and ship breaking are not within the day-to-day operations of ships, this requirement will probably be left outside the scope of the Directive.

212 The comments of this section are based on the proposal as it stands after the first reading. Council of the European Union: "2018/0012(COD) Outcome of the European Parliament's first reading" (2019). The document can be found at <https://eur-lex.europa.eu/legal-content/EN/TXT/?uri=consil:ST_7175_2019_INIT>, last accessed 28 March 2019.

213 Ibid., 49th preambular paragraph.

210 *The ESM of wastes*

based on the Union Maritime Information and Exchange System (SafeSeaNet). This information will be transmitted to the IMO electronic database GISIS.[214]

Finally, transparency and waste management fees should also be addressed, especially in relation to cargo residues. Article 8 of the legislative proposal details that waste from ships other than cargo residues shall be covered by an indirect fee and if necessary, by a direct fee. The positive development of the proposal is the establishment of the basis for the calculation of waste fees. However, cargo residues continue to be excluded from the fee system. This implies that direct contractual arrangements between the ship operator and the terminal will continue to take place. Such scheme certainly hinders the monitoring of obligations, *e.g.*, discharge criteria.

The legislative proposal fails to reflect how the waste management hierarchy is going to be incorporated into waste reception and handling plans; (a) the support of waste-minimization practices on board ships; and (b) the provision of waste segregation and separate collection obligations. The inclusion of waste from ships within the meaning of the Waste Framework Directive 2008/98/EC has proven to be insufficient as previously discussed in this Chapter. In general, the integration of ship wastes with wider EU waste legislation will continue to be the major challenge. The revision of Directive 2000/59/EC on Port Reception Facilities must clarify how and to what extent the obligations of the Waste Framework Directive 2008/98/EC are applicable to these wastes in detail. The Current reference to general EU waste law is far from satisfactory since such measures are unrelated to daily shipping operations. The result is the inapplicability of such standards to ships.

---

214 Ibid., 42th and 43rd preambular paragraphs; Articles 2(14), and 7(5)(a).

Part IV
Conclusions

9 The management of ship wastes: the sea-land interface

Conflicts of law

Conflicting legal regimes are not uncommon in all fields of law. International environmental law, in particular, has experienced a rapid development, which has led to the adoption of a plethora of legal instruments.[1] This is the result of a regulatory growth in terms of both "expansion and differentiation".[2] Expansion relates to the regulation of areas previously unnoticed by the States, while differentiation refers to the continuous sophistication and enactment of detailed rules.[3] The expansion of areas of international law requires a high level of expertise, but usually this continuous sophistication of law comes at a price, *i.e.* (a) lack of coordination among different but related areas of law; (b) inconsistent and incompatible[4] obligations; (c) isolated and uncoordinated institutional practices; and (d) regulatory gaps, *e.g.*, sea-land waste management interface.

As Wolfrum and Matz-Lück explain, the phenomenon of regulatory growth is particularly challenging in international environmental law due to "ecological interdependencies".[5] The study of waste management, for instance, reveals that instruments dealing directly or indirectly with wastes could be concerned with: (1) a particular portion of the environment, *e.g.*, air, sea, and land; (2) a particular activity, *e.g.*, transboundary movements of wastes or dumping; or (3) a particular substance, *e.g.*, persistent organic pollutants. These instruments, although connected, may compete with one another, *e.g.*, the Basel Convention and MARPOL, either because they have different purposes or because the

---

1 Law is experiencing a growth in regulatory legal schemes, also known as juridification. *Note* that "juridification is described primarily as a growth phenomenon ... [or] rapid expansion of law." Gunther Teubner, "Juridification: Concepts, Aspects, Limits, Solutions," in *Juridification of Social Spheres: A Comparative Analysis in the Areas of Labor, Corporate, Antitrust and Social Welfare Law*, ed. Gunther Teubner (Berlin: Walter de Gruyter & Co., 1987), 6.

2 *See* Lars Blichner and Anders Molander, "Mapping Juridification," *European Law Journal* 14, no. 1 (2008).

3 Ibid., 42–43.

4 On incompatibility and inconsistency, *See also* Rüdiger Wolfrum and Nele Matz, *Conflicts in International Environmental Law* (Berlin: Springer, 2003), 6.

5 Ibid., 4–6.

214   *Conclusions*

underlying reasons behind their development differ.[6] These differences may translate into inconsistent and incompatible obligations. However, international law is not the aggregation of unrelated norms. There is a background of values[7] and principles against which international norms operate. These principles guide the interpretation in cases of conflicting regimes and ultimately lead to coherence and certainty of the legal system.

Alongside principles, treaties also have their own mechanisms to avoid conflicts of law, *i.e.*, conflict clauses. The Basel Convention contains such a clause, which excludes from their scope of application *wastes derived from the normal operations of ships that are covered by another convention*. A similar exclusion is found in Regulation 1013/2006/EC on Shipments of Wastes. The following subsections discuss the main reasons behind the conflict between transboundary movements of waste and ship-source pollution regimes, and the relationship between them.

The reason for the conflict between the transboundary movement of wastes and ship-source pollution regimes

The main cause of the conflict between the transboundary movement of wastes and ship-source pollution regimes stems from their different objectives. Such objectives are the result of historical and political considerations underlying the development of these regulatory regimes. On the one hand, at the international level, transboundary movements of wastes gained attention in the light of well-known incidents of transport and unsafe management of hazardous wastes from developed to developing countries. Consequently, transboundary movements of wastes were framed as a detrimental and negative activity, and therefore these transboundary movements were strictly regulated. On the other hand, ship-source pollution aims to protect the marine environment without hindering shipping activities, since shipping is considered a positive activity that is vital for international trade. Therefore, instruments governing ship-source pollution try to strike a balance between navigational freedoms and protection of the marine environment.

As a result of the underlying assumptions regarding the regulated activity, the legal obligations of these regimes are generally contradictory. One of the most striking differences between the regime dealing with transboundary movements of wastes and ships source pollution is that in the former, States have the right to prohibit the entrance of wastes into their jurisdiction, but in relation to ship wastes, States have an obligation to receive ship wastes and to ensure the provision of adequate reception facilities. In the case of transboundary movements of wastes, States invoke their sovereign right to decide whether or not they are

---

6 Ibid., 7–13.

7 For instance, in international environmental law, the sustainable development goals adopted in 2015 by the UN General Assembly could be generally considered as international values.

willing to accept a certain risk within their territorial boundaries. In relation to ship-source pollution, States in their efforts to protect the marine environment have agreed to receive ship wastes on land.

Another reason behind the incompatibility between these regimes comes from the very nature of these activities. A transboundary movement of wastes presupposes the existence of a land territory (State of export) where such wastes could, in principle, be managed. This is not the case of ship wastes. Ships operate in the marine environment and wastes coming from machinery, cargo, and living spaces are the result of such operation. There is also a limited capacity of ships to keep wastes on board before being discharged either at sea or into a port reception facility.

The relationship between the Basel Convention and MARPOL

Despite MARPOL's effectiveness in managing harmful substances at sea, including wastes, Parties to this Convention have given little attention to the extent and meaning of the obligation to ensure the provision of adequate port reception facilities. The *Probo Koala* and *Probo Emu* highlighted the deficiencies regarding waste management in the sea/land interface and ignited a conflict between MARPOL and the Basel Convention. However, after scrutinizing the evolution of the principles and substantive obligations of these treaties, it is submitted that these conventions are mutually exclusive.

Incompatible obligations

The relationship between MARPOL and the Basel Convention is an example of legal conflict resulting from incompatible obligations. According to Kelsen, incompatible obligations are those that generate a conflict *per se* between norms, since the "observance or application of one norm *necessarily* or *possibly* involves the violation of the other".[8] In international law there is no specific hierarchy among treaty norms that regulate closely related subject matter. However, the coherence of the legal system is preserved due to the application of principles such as *lex posterior, lex specialis* or through explicit conflict clauses.

Regarding MARPOL and the Basel Convention, Parties to the latter treaty attempted to avoid a possible conflict concerning the regulation of ship wastes with the incorporation of an exclusion clause found in Article 1(4) of the Basel Convention that excludes from the scope of this Convention wastes derived from the normal operation of ships whose discharge is governed by another instrument, *i.e.*, MARPOL. Shipping is in itself a transboundary activity. Thus, even in the absence of such an exclusion clause, or in cases where ship wastes could be characterized as abnormal or not covered by MARPOL, the Basel Convention

---

8 Hans Kelsen, *General Theory of Norms*, trans. Michael Hartney (Oxford: Oxford University Press, 1991), 123.

216   *Conclusions*

is still inapplicable to wastes generated during the operations of ships at sea. For instance, Article 4(2)(d) of the Basel Convention discourages transboundary movements of wastes. Movements are allowed only as an exception. Considering that ships operate at sea, wastes are continuously being generated during their operation within and outside national boundaries. Therefore, transboundary movements are the rule, not the exception. Furthermore, due to the proximity principle established in the Basel Convention, wastes must be disposed of as close as possible to their place of generation. Bearing in mind that the generation of wastes on board vessels is an ongoing activity, it is not feasible to precisely determine their place of generation to comply with the proximity principle. Additionally, rights and obligations related to transboundary movements of wastes are heavily reliant on the identification of exporting, transit, and importing States. In the case of ship wastes there is no State of export. Thus, it is not possible to establish where a transboundary movement of wastes begins and which State is ultimately responsible for the management of such wastes.

As examined in Chapter 6, the cornerstone control mechanism of the Basel Convention is the PIC procedure, which *is incompatible and contrary to the objectives of MARPOL* because ships operate at sea and have a limited capacity to maintain wastes on board vessels. If States do not consent to receiving wastes generated on board ships, discharging those wastes into the ocean is an unavoidable consequence. This is especially true in the absence of an "exporting State" to which wastes can be "returned" for their disposal. In addition, a complex and lengthy system, such as the PIC procedure, could hamper international trading by sea.

Overall, the Basel Convention appears inadequate to deal with ship wastes. These wastes were not within the concern of the States negotiating this instrument and, therefore, it is understandable why its obligations are not applicable to ships since they were not designed with daily ship operations in mind. This also explains why the exclusion contained in Article 1(4) of the Basel Convention was introduced to ensure legal certainty in relation to the applicable legal regime of ship wastes. It is also due to legal certainty that the applicability of the Basel Convention to ship wastes on board the vessel cannot be lightly assumed, especially in the absence of any evidence that supports that States envisaged the potential application of this Convention to ship-related wastes.

Inconsistent obligations

Despite the inapplicability of the Basel Convention to ship wastes while at sea, the Secretariat of the Basel Convention argues that ship wastes, independently of any characterization of normality, are subject to this treaty once they are discharged to port reception facilities. This basically relates to the ESM of wastes as established in the Basel Convention. This book argues that ESM has been transformed into a customary law principle, which is applicable to every category of waste, including ship wastes. However, it is a stretch to imply that obligations related to ESM under the Basel Convention are applicable to those wastes. ESM as a principle imposes an obligation to treat wastes from a life-cycle perspective by observing, for instance, the waste hierarchy. The application and enforcement of ESM could take various forms depending on the waste or activity regulated. Regarding transboundary movements of wastes, *the compliance of ESM obligations impinges directly on Parties involved in a transboundary movement, i.e.,* exporting, transit, and importing States. These Parties are nonexistent in relation to ship wastes. For instance, according to the Basel Convention, exporting States are the main party responsible for the ESM of wastes. Such an obligation cannot be transferred to any other State involved in the movements. In the case of ship wastes, States providing reception facilities are the main party responsible for the ESM of such wastes, regardless of whether these wastes were generated within or beyond their jurisdiction. ESM in the Basel Convention is interlinked with transboundary movements and cannot be applied independently. Furthermore, the scope of the Convention deals with hazardous and other wastes subject to a transboundary movement of wastes. Therefore, if no transboundary transfer takes place, no obligation remains applicable.

In relation to the management of ship wastes on land, the Basel Convention and MARPOL are inconsistent. According to Wolfrum and Matz-Lück, conflicts in a wider perspective "establish divergences or inconsistencies without establishing contradictory, absolute obligations".[9] The core obligation in relation to wastes relates to their ESM. This obligation is not contradictory. In fact, ESM is the connective thread of waste regulation from a holistic perspective. What is inconsistent is assuming that the Basel Convention as such is the applicable source to deal with ship wastes on land. In the transboundary movement of waste regime, ESM informs, for instance, which State is responsible for the management of such wastes and what actions could be taken (*e.g.,* reimportation of wastes) in cases where ESM cannot be guaranteed. Regarding ship wastes, ESM informs, *e.g.,* the meaning and extent of the obligation to ensure the provision of adequate port reception facilities. The solution to this conflict does not entail the derogation of the substantive norms of either of the regimes involved, since both have a common foundation, *i.e.,* the ESM of wastes. Detailed rules and standards to accomplish ESM must take into account the distinctive characteristic of a certain waste category.

The management of ship wastes at the EU level

Article 1(3) of Regulation 1013/2006/EC on Shipments of Wastes excludes from its scope of application "offloading to shore of waste … generated by the normal operation of ships … provided that such waste is subject to … MARPOL." The exclusion also extends to wastes generated in airplanes, trains, and vehicles "until such waste is offloaded in order to be recovered or disposed of." The text of the exclusion as well as the preparatory work of the Regulation indicate that the regime governing transboundary movements of wastes is not concerned with operational wastes generated in different transport modes. Such operations could involve a transboundary activity where waste disposal in several jurisdictions is

9 Wolfrum and Matz, *Conflicts in International Environmental Law,* 6.

218   *Conclusions*

incidental to transport operations. Transboundary movement of wastes is mainly focused on wastes that are deliberately transported, generally as cargo, to be disposed of in another jurisdiction.

Regulation 1013/2006/EC on Shipments of Wastes refers exclusively to wastes that are offloaded from a ship and is silent on the management of wastes while on board vessels. This is again an indication that waste generated on board vessels, while at sea, are to be regulated exclusively by MARPOL and Regulation 1013/2006/EC on Shipments of Wastes does not seek to impose any further obligation. The exclusion raises again the question as to whether MARPOL regulates wastes that are "offloaded to shore." As discussed in Chapter 8, MARPOL is also a relevant instrument in relation to wastes discharged on land. Although it is beyond the scope of the Convention to determine downstream management operations of ship wastes, MARPOL includes an obligation to ensure the provision of adequate port reception facilities. In light of the ESM of wastes, adequacy includes the integration of port reception facilities into regional or national waste management systems. Such integration must allow further management operations. At the EU level, there is also specific legislation on port reception facilities, *i.e.*, Directive 2000/59/EC. This piece of legislation does not compete with MARPOL, but rather complements it by establishing substantive content related to the provision of port reception facilities.

Directive 2000/59/EC attempts to take a step forward in respect of the integration of ship wastes into national waste management systems by including them within the scope of the Waste Framework Directive 2008/98/EC. The success of such inclusion, however, remains limited since it is not clear how the obligations of the latter Directive, *e.g.*, waste minimization or waste segregation, will be applied to ship wastes. This uncertainty is a common problem of what Ringbom calls "horizontal environmental requirements",[10] *i.e.*, "EU legislation of activities that could occur on board ships or that regulates substances that could be transported or generated by ships".[11] In the absence of an express provision regarding the relation of a piece of environmental legislation to ships, their applicability remains limited because the rationale behind the adoption of these "horizontal measures" may not always consider the particular features of maritime transport.[12] In relation to ship wastes, Directive 2000/59/EC on Port Reception Facilities is currently under revision and this is an opportunity to clarify how and to what extent the obligations of the Waste Framework Directive 2008/98/EC are applicable to these wastes.

Overall, the exclusion of ship wastes from Regulation 1013/2006/EC follows its international counterpart. Such exclusion gives priority to MARPOL. Nonetheless, even in the absence of such an exclusion clause, the transboundary movement of wastes regime remains inapplicable to ship wastes, since its regulatory approach does not take into account the particular operational activities of ships.

---

10 Ringbom, *The EU Maritime Safety Policy and International Law*, 189–93.
11 Ibid., 189.
12 Ibid., 189–91.

10 International law and waste management

The integrative function of ESM: possibilities and limitations

ESM has an integrative function since this principle provides legal coherence at both regulatory and sectoral levels. By regulatory level, the author refers to coherence within international law as well as between several regulatory levels, i.e., international and EU law. Sectoral integration refers to coordination between regulations governing different environmental media, e.g., land, sea, air. The study of ship wastes highlighted two legal issues that have had a negative effect on legal coherence. One related to a legal gap in the management of such wastes once discharged at port reception facilities, while the second relates to traceability challenges of ship wastes on land.

The quest for legal coherence

Concerning the legal gap, some could argue that ship wastes discharged to port reception facilities enter national jurisdiction, meaning that States are then free to decide how to manage such wastes. In other words, international law is not relevant in dealing with domestic matters. The life-cycle approach, which is at center of the ESM of wastes, highlights the relative nature of "domestic" environments and imposes an obligation on the management of wastes irrespective of their transboundary effects. In the case of ship wastes, the rise of ESM implies that port reception facilities must be, e.g., integrated into national waste management systems. Such waste management systems must follow the waste hierarchy. If port reception facilities are not integrated with national waste management systems, States are breaching their international obligations.

An initial effort to integrate ship wastes relates to the adoption of Directive 2000/59/EC on Port Reception Facilities, which imposes substantial obligations related to the functioning of such facilities. These obligations closely follow the soft law framework developed under the auspices of the IMO. Additionally, the substances regulated in Directive 2000/59/EC on Port Reception Facilities are defined as "wastes" for the purposes of the Waste Framework Directive 2008/98/EC. However, the reference at the EU level to horizontal measures is far from satisfactory since such measures are unrelated to daily shipping operations.

220 Conclusions

Environmental principles, including ESM, have a broad formulation. On the one hand, this makes these principles flexible and easy to adapt to novel legal scenarios and to prompt normative developments. On the other hand, such levels of abstraction are also a shortcoming, since the principle says nothing about the standards (e.g., liability schemes) necessary to accomplish ESM. Therefore, a principle cannot function in isolation and must be operationalized with the development of further soft and binding legal instruments.

Renewed impetus on regime interaction

The development of soft and binding legal instruments could have a potential drawback insofar as it might increase the risk of conflicts of law due to regulatory growth. Chapter 8 discussed the challenges faced in tracing the management of ship wastes after their discharge at port reception facilities. In facilities located in the Baltic Sea, traceability obstacles relate to the identification of quantities of cargo residues and their downstream management. This problem is not the result of a lack of regulations at the international or regional levels. Rather, it is the result of poor enforcement due to horizontal environmental measures that in practice are inapplicable to ships. It is also the result of the multiplicity of public authorities and private operators along horizontal and vertical levels dealing with different bodies of law, having separate spheres of competence with little or no communication and coordination. Finally, the problem of traceability stems from the diverse nature of residues arising from chemicals carried in bulk and from the actual practices of ports dealing with the discharge of these cargo residues. The challenges described, i.e., regulatory growth, multiplicity of actors involved in the implementation and enforcement of regulation, are increasingly common and are by no means unique to ship waste management. However, such legal challenges require a reexamination of the role of principles in the regime interaction. In respect of ESM, it is not just a legal source concerning waste management; it also provides the basis for moving from fragmented to comprehensive waste regulation. Legal principles are dynamic and provide renewed impetus to legal regimes. In the case of ship waste management, such impetus has implications for the interpretation of existing legal obligations, as well as for coordination between legal regimes as they deal with wastes.

The present: impact on existing obligations

Article 195 of the LOSC prohibits States from transforming one type of pollution into another. This obligation also has an integrative function since it intends to prevent unintended consequences in one environmental medium, e.g., sea, while preventing any environmental harm in another environmental medium, e.g., land. The ESM of wastes is an example of the operationalization of Article 195 in relation to ship waste management. States are not entirely free to dispose of ship wastes entering their national jurisdiction. On the one hand, such management shall not imply the transformation of ship-source pollution into land-based pollution. On the other hand, the management of ship wastes must take into account their life-cycle.

MARPOL imposes several obligations for the prevention of ship-source pollution concerning the construction, equipment, and manning of ships. In addition, operational discharges at sea are severely restricted or prohibited. Although MARPOL is not concerned with waste management on land, the accomplishment of its purpose will be defeated without the development of standards concerning port reception facilities given that such facilities are linked to both the prevention of illegal discharges at sea and the management of ship wastes on land to prevent the transformation of one type of marine pollution into another.

Taking into account that the marine environment is to ships as roads are to cars, operational wastes can be kept on board for a limited period of time before their discharge becomes unavoidable. Ship operators have not only the obligation, but also the right to discharge wastes to port reception facilities, since otherwise the inevitable consequence would be discharges at sea. In the light of both the prohibition prescribed in Article 195 of the LOSC and ESM, the "adequacy" of port reception facilities includes not only the reception of wastes, but also their downstream management. The interpretation of adequacy according to the ESM principle also implies that port reception facilities must be integrated into national waste management systems. Due to the conflict between MARPOL and the Basel Convention, the IMO revised the manual concerning port reception facilities. The regulatory history of MARPOL shows that State Parties amend the Convention periodically and strongly support on-board treatment techniques, but little has been done to establish binding obligations in relation to port reception facilities. Soft law has been exclusively used in relation to standards of port reception facilities. Soft law could, of course, be the precursor to adoption of binding obligations at an international level. It could also become binding if adopted as legislation at a national level.

At the EU level, the Commission adopted Guidelines for the Interpretation of Directive 2000/59/EC on Port Reception Facilities. Concerning the "adequacy" of port reception facilities, the Commission relies on the development of the concept at the international and regional level. In addition, the Commission clarified that the management of ship wastes on land must reflect the ESM principle enshrined in the Basel Convention. Recognizing ESM as a fundamental principle to deal with ship wastes is a positive step toward their management from a life-cycle perspective.

The future: coordination in the regulation of wastes management

The development of a common framework of ESM has been fundamental in addressing the management of wastes beyond the peculiarities surrounding the transboundary movement of wastes. An obvious advantage of building a legal framework from existing instruments is that one can draw upon their existing obligations, institutional structures, control mechanisms, and financing systems. It also contributes to the building of bridges between different regimes, enhancing cooperation among international institutions and other subjects of international law, and mitigating fragmentation in international law.

222 *Conclusions*

The broad formulation of ESM fostered cooperation between the IMO and the COP to the Basel Convention to improve the management of wastes in the sea/land interface. Such cooperation, however, remains limited. Although the IMO supports the collaboration with the COP to the Basel Convention, the Secretariat of the IMO has been emphatic in clarifying that the IMO is the adequate forum where State Parties to MARPOL should interpret to what extent MARPOL applies to ship wastes discharged to port reception facilities. This position could explain why the IMO and the COP to the Basel Convention have been issuing different sets of guidelines instead of promoting a joint forum where different actors could address common concerns and coordinate future activities.

The EU also has an important coordinating role by enhancing international regulation in two meaningful ways. First, EU law includes strong noncompliance mechanism procedures where the Commission can bring noncompliant States to Court. Second, soft law instruments may become binding if adopted by the EU.

In achieving coordination, the role of international institutions and treaty organs (i.e., COPS) should not be overlooked. At the center of contemporary international environmental law is the prevention of environmental harm. Cooperation is required to achieve such prevention. International organizations and treaty organs provide the administrative machinery to achieve such concerted actions. These institutions highlight and address potential legal conflicts and contribute to the normative development of legal regimes through the adoption of decisions, or soft law instruments, for example. Their role in implementation and enforcement depends on the powers vested in the organization. As discussed in Chapter 8, enforcement capabilities of the IMO should be strengthened; e.g., the IMO should be vested with powers to initiate rule-making processes and to conduct auditing schemes to improve supervision and scrutiny in cases of noncompliance.

Final reflection

This book challenges the role of international law concerning waste management. Current legal scholarship considers wastes to be relevant for international law only if they pose transboundary risks. However, the development of ESM exemplifies the relative nature of "pure domestic environments" and it contributes to the understanding of the evolving nature of sovereignty from independent to concerted actions in achieving environmental goals. ESM has transformed into an overarching principle to deal with the life-cycle of wastes. ESM is interpreted and applied on a case-by-case. The book also highlighted the integrative function of ESM. This function is common to all legal principles. In a decentralized legal system, such as international law, legal principles are the connective thread between specific rules and the foundation for achieving coherence. Additionally, due to their abstract formulation, principles provide the legal system with the dynamic approach required to adapt to novel situations. ESM provides the basis for establishing synergies among different regimes. Particularly, ESM triggered the cooperation between the IMO and the COP to the Basel Convention. However, such cooperation remains limited and too much work is being duplicated.

Appendix I

Management of cargo residues (MARPOL, Annex II) in the Baltic Sea area

Data required for questions 1 and 2: Available data for the years 2012–2014.

1 Volume of traffic of ships calling to the port carrying liquid bulk cargoes, especially noxious liquid substances?
2 Volume (m^3) of cargo residues "actually delivered" during the required year?

   a If data is not available, could you explain the reason why?

3 What is the applicable fee system for cargo residues?
4 In relation to the collection, handling, and management of cargo residues (MARPOL, Annex II):

   a What is the waste notification procedure in relation to cargo residues?
   b Who handles the collection of cargo residues? Please select the alternative(s) that apply.

     i   Port
     ii Individual terminal
     iii External waste management operator

        1 A ship agent is allowed to identify and contract a waste operator in the "free market"
        2 A ship agent contacts one or some waste operators, previously chosen by the port (*e.g.*, through public tendering or framework contracts)
        3 Other. Who?

     iv Other. Who?

   c If the collection of cargo residues is done through an external waste management operator or the individual terminal. What is the relationship or channels of communication, if any, between the port and the individual terminal/external waste management operator?

5 Which of the following statements would best describe port reception facilities for cargo residues?

   a The facilities are port owned and port operated.
   b The facilities are port owned, but privately operated.

224   *Appendix I*

    c   The facilities are port operated, but privately owned.

    d   The facilities are privately owned and operated.

    e   Other. How?

6   Is the port involved at any stage in the handling or management of cargo residues? *E.g.*, final disposal of residues, incineration, biological treatment, physico-chemically treatment.

Appendix II
Survey results concerning the collection of cargo residues (MARPOL, Annex II) in the Baltic Sea area

During this study, the author contacted 61 ports that receive noxious liquid cargoes in the Baltic Sea area:

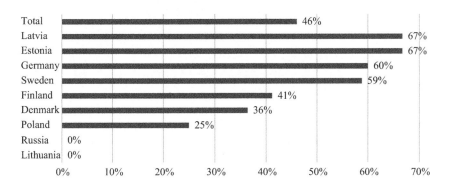

Figure a.1 Response rate (%). Ports that receive liquid bulk cargoes in the Baltic Sea area.

Contacted ports:

Denmark: Aalborg, Aabenraa, Aarhus, Copenhagen, Fredericia, Frederiks-havn, Grenaa, Horsens, Kalundborg, Randers, Vejle.
Estonia: Kunda, Sillamäe, and Tallin.
Finland: HaminaKotka, Hanko, Helsinki, Inkoo, Kantvik, Kaskinen, Kemi, Kokkola, Naantali, Oulu, Pietarsaari, Pori, Raahe, Rauma, Turku, Uusikaupunki, and Vaasa.
Germany: Lubmin, Lübeck, Rostock, Sassnitz, and Wismar.
Latvia: Liepaja, Riga, and Ventspils.
Lithuania: Klaipeda.
Poland: Gdansk, Gdynia, Kolobrzeg, and Szczecin.
Sweden: Gothenburg, Gävle, Halmstad, Kalmar, Karlshamn, Kristinehamn, Luleå, Malmö, Mälarhamnar, Norrköping, Oxelösund, Skellefteå, Stockholm, Södertälje, Sölvesborg, Uddevalla, and Varberg.
Russia: Vyborg and Kaliningrad.

226 Appendix II

The following graphs represent the data from the ports that responded to the survey either totally or partially:

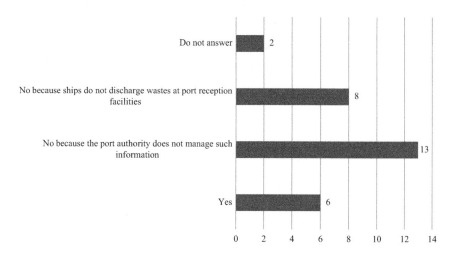

Figure a.2 Does the port authority have information regarding the volume (m^3) of cargo residues 'actually delivered'.

Yes: Kemi, Pietarsaari, Kolobrzeg, Halmstad, Södertälje, and Varberg: these ports have records of wastes that are delivered at port reception facilities.

No because the port authority does not manage such information: Copenhagen, Fredericia, Frederiks-havn, Randers, Kunda, Rauma, Lubmin, Riga, Ventspils, Gothenburg, Luleå, Malmö, and Norrköping: These ports explained that ship agents or terminals are responsible for the collection of cargo residues. Information is not available since the port authority is not engaged in the collection. One port declared that, on some occasions, vessels carrying noxious liquid substances in bulk call at the port, but port reception facilities are not available. Other ports explained that the authority does not file or handle these data.

No because ships do not discharge wastes at port reception facilities: Tallin, Hanko, Kokkola, Turku, Uusikaupunki, Gävle, Karlshamn, and Oxelösund: The ports know that ships have not made any discharge of cargo residues from MARPOL, Annex II, because: (a) vessels are loaded with the same cargo; (b) no tank washing is required; or (c) the vessels proceed to the next port of call and do not discharge any residue.

Do not answer: Lübeck and Rostock.

Direct fee paid to the operator: Copenhagen, Frederiks-havn, Kunda, Tallin, Kemi, Kokkola, Turku, Uusikaupunki, Lubmin, Riga, Gävle, Karlshamn, Luleå, Malmö, and Oxelösund.

Direct fee: Pietarsaari, Rostock, Halmstad, and Varberg.

Appendix II 227

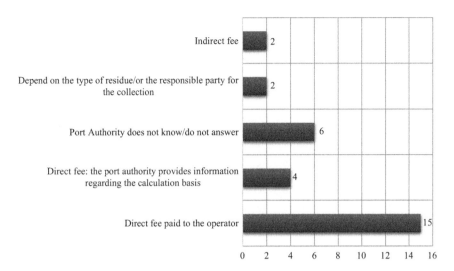

Figure a.3 Fee system: MARPOL – Annex II residues.

Port authority does not know/do not answer: Fredericia, Rauma, Lübeck, Ventspils, Norrköping, and Södertälje.
Depends on the type of residue/or the responsible party for the collection: Randers and Hanko.
Indirect fee: Kolobrzeg and Gothenburg.

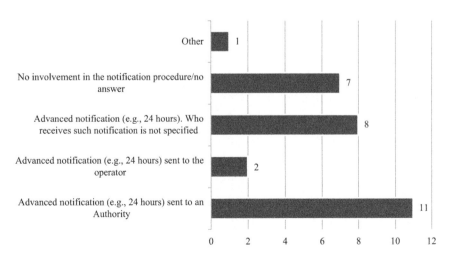

Figure a.4 Notification procedure regarding MARPOL Annex II residues.

228 Appendix II

Advanced notification sent to an authority: Copenhagen, Kunda, Tallin, Kokkola, Pietarsaari, Lubmin, Riga, Kolobrzeg, Halmstad, Malmö, and Varberg: In some ports, another authority receives the notification and then informs the port authority. For instance, the Swedish Maritime Administration sends the notification to the ports of Copenhaguen, Malmö, Halmstad and Varberg. In many ports the information can be accessed through national single windows.

Advanced notification sent to the operator: Kemi and Luleå.

Advanced notification – who receives such notification is not specified: Randers, Hanko, Turku, Lübeck, Gothenburg, and Karlshamn.

No involvement in the notification procedure: Fredericia, Frederiks-havn, Rauma, Uusikaupunki, Rostock, Norrköping, and Södertälje.

Other: Oxelösund: the port has not implemented any specific system. If required, the users send a notification via e-mail, for example.

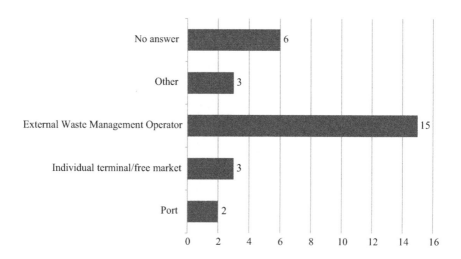

Figure a.5 Who handles the collection of MARPOL – Annex II residues?

Port: Halmstad and Varberg.

Individual terminal/free market: Copenhagen, Gothenburg, and Malmö.

External waste management operator: Frederiks-havn, Kunda, Tallin, Kemi, Kokkola, Pietarsaari, Turku, Uusikaupunki, Lubmin, Riga, Kolobrzeg, Gävle, Karlshamn, Luleå, and Södertälje.

Other: Randers, Hanko, and Oxelösund: either the port or a "free market" external operator could be in charge of the collection of MARPOL, Annex II, residues.

No answer: Fredericia, Rauma, Lübeck, Rostock, Ventspils, and Norrköping.

Appendix II 229

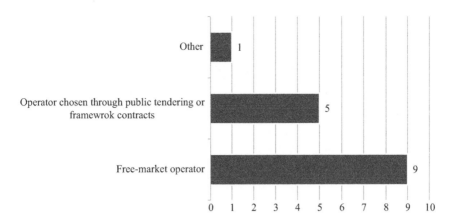

Figure a.6 Types of external waste management operators.

Free-market operator: Frederiks-havn, Kunda, Tallin, Kemi, Kokkola, Lubmin, Riga, Gävle, and Karlshamn.

Operator chosen through public tendering or framework contracts: Pietarsaari, Turku, Luleå, Kolobrzeg, and Södertälje.

Other: Uusikaupunki: The port contacts the operator.

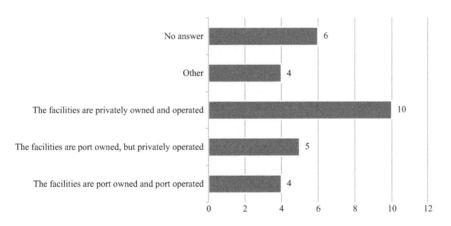

Figure a.7 Ownership and operation of port reception facilities.

The facilities are port owned and port operated: Randers, Gothenburg, Halmstad, and Varberg.

The facilities are port owned, but privately operated: Frederiks-havn, Kemi, Kokkola, Turku, and Kolobrzeg.

230 Appendix II

The facilities are privately owned and operated: Copenhagen, Tallin, Hanko, Pietarsaari, Uusikaupunki, Lubmin, Gävle, Luleå, Malmö, and Södertälje.

Other: Kunda, Karlshamn, Norrköping, and Oxelösund: The first three ports do not have these facilities. The port of Karlshamn, however, reported that trucks come to the port when needed to transport cargo residues subject to MARPOL, Annex II. In Oxelösund, the ownership and operation of port reception facilities depend on the cargo residues. Some facilities are owned and operated by the port, while others are privately owned and privately operated.

No answer: Fredericia, Rauma, Lübeck, Rostock, Riga, and Ventspils.

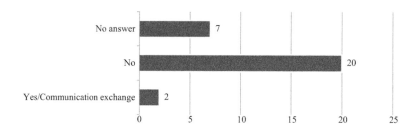

Figure a.8 Port involvement concerning handling or management of MARPOL – Annex II residues.

Yes/Communication exchange: Randers and Lubmin: The ports are informed regarding handling and management operations.

No: Copenhagen, Malmö, Frederiks-havn, Kunda, Tallin, Hanko, Kemi, Kokkola, Pietarsaari, Turku, Uusikaupunki, Kolobrzeg, Gävle, Halmstad, Varberg, Karlshamn, Luleå, Norrköping, Oxelösund, and Södertälje.

No answer: Fredericia, Rauma, Lübeck, Rostock, Riga, Ventspils, and Gothenburg.

References

International treaties

Statute of the International Court of Justice, San Francisco, 24 October 1945, 3 Bevans 1179; 59 Stat. 1031; T.S. 993; 39 AJIL Supp. 215.

Convention on the International Maritime Organization as amended, Geneva, 6 March 1948, 9 UST 621; 289 UNTS 48. In force 17 March 1958.

International Convention for the Prevention of Pollution of the Sea by Oil, London, 12 May 1954, 12 UST 2989; TIAS No. 4900; 327 UNTS 3. In force 26 July 1958.

Convention on Fishing and Conservation on the Living Resources of the High Seas, Geneva, 29 April 1958, 17 UST 138; 559 UNTS 285. In force 20 March 1966.

Convention on the Continental Shelf, Geneva, 29 April 1958, 15 UST 471; 499 UNTS 311. In force 10 June 1964.

Convention on the High Seas, Geneva, 29 April 1958, 13 UST 2312, 450 UNTS 82. In force 30 September 1962.

Convention on the Territorial Sea and Contiguous Zone, Geneva, 29 April 1958, 15 UST 1606; 516 UNTS 205. In force 10 September 1964.

International Convention on Civil Liability for Oil Pollution Damage, Brussels, 29 November 1969, 973 UNTS 3; 9 ILM 45. In force 19 June 1975.

Convention on the Law of Treaties, Vienna, 23 May 1969; 1155 UNTS 331; 8 ILM 689. In force 27 January 1980.

Convention on the Establishment of an International Fund for Compensation for Oil Pollution Damage, Brussels, 18 December 1971, 11 ILM 284; 1110 UNTS 57. In force 16 October 1978.

Convention on the Prevention of Marine Pollution by Dumping of Wastes and Other Matter, London, 29 December 1972, 26 UST 2403; 1046 UNTS 120; 11 ILM 1294. In force 30 August 1975.

International Convention for the Prevention of Pollution from Ships as amended by Protocol of 1978 (MARPOL 73/78), London, 17 February 1978, 1340 UNTS 184. In force 2 October 1983. Updated and consolidated text can be found in MARPOL Consolidated Edition 2017. 6th edn. London: International Maritime Organization (IMO), 2017.

International Convention for the Safety of Life at Sea, London, 1 November 1974, 32 UST 47; 1184 UNTS 278. In force 25 May 1980.

United Nations Convention on the Law of the Sea, Montego Bay, 10 December 1982, 1833 UNTS 396; 21 ILM 1261. In force 16 November 1994.

Convention on the Control of Transboundary Movements of Hazardous Wastes and their Disposal, Basel, 22 March 1989, 1673 UNTS 57; 28 ILM, 657. In force 24 May 1992.

232 *References*

International Convention on Oil Pollution Preparedness, Response and Co-Operation, London, 30 November 1990, 1891 UNTS 51; 30 ILM 733. In force 13 May 1995.

Convention on the Ban of the Import into Africa and the Control of Transboundary Movement and Management of Hazardous Wastes within Africa, Bamako, 29 January 1991, 30 ILM 775; 2101 UNTS 242. In force 22 April 1998.

Convention for the Protection of the Marine Environment of the North-East Atlantic (OSPAR Convention), Paris, 22 September 1992, 2354 UNTS 67, 32 ILM 1072. In force 25 March 1998.

Convention on Biological Diversity, Rio de Janeiro, 5 June 1992, 1760 UNTS 79; 31 ILM 818. In force 29 December 1993.

Convention on the Protection of the Black Sea against Pollution, Bucharest 21 April 1992, 32 ILM 1101; 1764 UNTS 3. In force 15 January 1994.

Convention on the Protection of the Marine Environment of the Baltic Sea Area, Helsinki, 9 April 1992, 2099 UNTS 195; 1994 OJ (L 73) 20; 13 ILM 546 (1974). In force 17 January 2000.

Protocol to amend the 1971 International Convention on the Establishment of an International Fund for Compensation for Oil Pollution Damage, London, 27 November 1992, 1953 UNTS 330. In force 30 May 1996.

Protocol to the International Convention on Civil Liability for Oil Pollution Damage, 1969, London, 27 November 1992, 1956 UNTS 255. In force 30 May 1996.

Convention for the Protection of the Marine Environment and the Coastal Region of the Mediterranean, Barcelona, 10 June 1995, 1102 UNTS 27. In force 9 July 2004.

Convention to Ban the Importation into Forum Island Countries of Hazardous and Radioactive Wastes and to Control the Transboundary Movement of Hazardous Wastes within the South Pacific Region, Waigani, 16 September 1995, 2161 UNTS 91. In force 21 October 2001.

Protocol on the Prevention of Pollution of the Mediterranean Sea by Transboundary Movements of Hazardous Wastes and their Disposal, Izmir, 1 October 1996, UNEP (OCA) ED/IG.4/4.11. In force 19 January 2008.

Protocol to the Convention on the Prevention of Marine Pollution by Dumping of Wastes and Other Matter, London, 7 November 1996, 36 ILM 7. In force 24 March 2006.

Convention on Access to Information, Public Participation in Decision-Making and Access to Justice in Environmental Matters, Aarhus, 25 June 1998, 2161 UNTS 447; 38 ILM 517. In force 30 October 2001.

Convention on the Prior Informed Consent Procedure for Certain Hazardous Chemicals and Pesticides in International Trade, Rotterdam, 10 September 1998, 38 ILM 1; 2244 UNTS 337. In force 24 February 2004.

Protocol on Liability and Compensation for Damage Resulting from Transboundary Movements of Hazardous Wastes and their Disposal, Basel, 10 December 1999, UNEP/CHW.5/29, Annex III. Not in force.

Convention on Persistent Organic Pollutants (POPs Convention), Stockholm, 22 May 2001, 40 ILM 532; 2256 UNTS 119. In force 17 May 2004.

International Convention on the Control of Harmful Anti-Fouling Systems of Ships, London, 5 October 2001, IMO Doc. AFS/CONF/26. In force 17 September 2008.

Protocol Concerning Cooperation in Preventing Pollution from Ships and, in Cases of Emergency, Combating Pollution of the Mediterranean Sea, Valletta, 25 January 2002, OJ L 261, 6 August 2004, pp. 41–46. In force 27 March 2004.

International Convention for the Control and Management of Ships' Ballast Water and Sediments, London, 13 February 2004, IMO Doc. BWM/CONF/36. In force 8 September 2017.

References 233

International Convention for the Safe and Environmentally Sound Recycling of Ships Hong Kong (Hong Kong Convention), 15 May 2009, 1672 UNTS 126. Not in force.

Minamata Convention on Mercury, Kumamoto, 10 October 2013. Available at: <http://www.mercuryconvention.org>. In force 16 August 2017.

European Union law

Primary sources

Consolidated versions of the Treaty on European Union and the Treaty on the Functioning of the European Union (2016/C 202/01), OJ C202/1, 07.6.2016.

Secondary sources

Directives

Council Directive 75/442/EEC of 15 July 1975 on Waste (Repealed), OJ L194/39, 25.07.1975.

Council Directive 91/156/EEC of 18 March 1991 amending Directive 75/442/EEC on Waste (Repealed), OJ L78/32, 26.03.1991.

Directive 94/62/EC of 20 December 1994 on Packaging and Packaging Waste, OJ L365/10, 31.12.1994.

Directive 96/59/EC of 16 September 1996 on the Disposal of Polychlorinated Biphenyls and Polychlorinated Terphenyls (PCB/PCT), OJ L243/31, 24.09.1996.

Directive 1999/31/EC of 26 April 1999 on the Landfill of Waste, OJ L182/1, 16.07.1999.

Directive 2000/59/EC of the European Parliament and of the Council of 27 November 2000 on Port Reception Facilities for Ship-Generated Waste and Cargo Residues, OJ L332/81, 28.12.2000.

Directive 2002/59/EC of the European Parliament and of the Council of 27 June 2002 Establishing a Community Vessel Traffic Monitoring and Information System and Repealing Council Directive 93/75/EEC, OJ L208/10, 05.08.2002.

Directive 2003/35/EC of the European Parliament and of the Council of 26 May 2003 Providing for Public Participation in Respect of the Drawing up of Certain Plans and Programmes Relating to the Environment and amending with regard to public participation and access to justice Council Directives 85/337/EEC and 96/61/EC – State ment by the Commission, OJ L 156/17. 25.06.2003.

Directive 2008/56/EC of the European Parliament and of the Council of 17 June 2008 Establishing a Framework for Community Action in the Field of Marine Environmental Policy (Marine Strategy Framework Directive), OJ L164/19, 25.06.2008.

Directive 2008/98/EC of the European Parliament and of the Council of 19 November 2008 on Waste and Repealing Certain Directives, OJ L312/3, 22.11.2008.

Directive 2009/16/EC of the European Parliament and of the Council of 23 April 2009 on Port State Control, OJ L131/57, 28.05.2009.

Directive 2010/65/EU of the European Parliament and of the Council of 20 October 2010 on Reporting Formalities for Ships Arriving in and/or Departing from Ports of the Member States and repealing Directive 2002/6/EC, OJ L283/1, 29.10.2010.

Directive 2010/75/EU of the European Parliament and of the Council of 24 November 2010 on Industrial Emissions (Integrated Pollution Prevention and Control), OJ L334/17, 17.12.2010.

234 *References*

Directive 2012/19/EU of the European Parliament and of the Council of 4 July 2012 on Waste Electrical and Electronic Equipment (WEEE), OJ L 197/38, 24.07.2012.

Commission Directive 2015/2087/EU of 18 Novemeber 2015 amending Annex II to Directive 2000/59/EC of the European Parliament and the Council on Port Reception Facilities for Ship-Generated Waste and Cargo Residues, OJ L302/99, 19.11.2015.

Regulations

Council Regulation (EEC) No. 259/93 of 1 February 1993 on the Supervision and Control of Shipments of Waste within, into and out of the European Community (Repealed), OJ L30/1, 06.02.1993.

Regulation (EC) No. 1406/2002 of the European Parliament and of the Council of 27 June 2002 Establishing a European Maritime Safety Agency, OJ L 208/1, 05.08.2002.

Regulation (EC) No. 1013/2006 of the European Parliament and of the Council of 14 June 2006 on Shipment of Waste, OJ L190/1, 12.07.2006.

Regulation (EU) No. 1257/2013 of the European Parliament and of the Council of 20 November 2013 on Ship Recycling and amending Regulation (EC) No. 1013/2006 and Directive 2009/16/EC, OJ L 330/1, 10.12.2013.

Regulation (EU) No. 2017/352 of the European Parliament and of the Council of 15 February 2017 Establishing a Framework for the Provision of Port Services and Common Rules on the Financial Transparency of Ports, OJ L57/1, 03.03.2017.

Table of cases

International arbitral awards

Trail Smelter arbitration *(United States v. Canada)*, 33 AJIL (16 April 1938), 182 & 35 AJIL (11 March 1941).

Lac Lanoux arbitration *(France v. Spain)*, 24 ILR 101 (16 November 1957).

Iron Rhine (Ijzeren Rijn) Railway arbitration *(Kingdom of Belgium v. Kingdom of the Netherlands)*, RIAA XXVII, pp. 35–125 (24 May 2005).

South China Sea arbitration *(The Republic of Philippines v. The People's Republic of China)*, PCA Case 2013-19, ICGJ 495 (12 July 2016).

Windstream Energy LLC v. Government of Canada, PCA Case 2013-22 (27 September 2016).

Permanent Court of International Justice

The Lotus case *(France v. Turkey)*, PCIJ, Series A No. 10 (7 September 1927).

International Court of Justice

Judgments

Corfu Channel case *(United Kingdom of Great Britain and Northern Ireland v. Albania)*, ICJ Reports 1949, p. 4 (9 April 1949).

Asylum case *(Colombia v. Peru)*, ICJ Reports 1950, p. 266 (20 November 1950).

Fisheries case *(United Kingdom v. Norway)*, (Dissenting Opinion of Judge J.E. Read), ICJ Reports 1951, p. 116 (18 December 1951).

Case Concerning Right of Passage over Indian Territory *(Portugal v. India)*, ICJ Reports 1960, p. 6 (12 April 1960).

References   235

South West Africa cases *(Ethiopia v. South Africa; Liberia v. South Africa)*, (Dissenting Opinion of Judge Tanaka), ICJ Reports 1966, p. 6 (8 July 1966).

North Sea Continental Shelf cases *(Federal Republic of Germany v. Denmark; Federal Republic of Germany v. Netherlands)*, ICJ Reports 1969, p. 3 (20 February 1969).

Fisheries Jurisdiction case *(Federal Republic of Germany v. Iceland)*, ICJ Reports 1974, p. 175 (25 July 1974).

Delimitation of the Maritime Boundary in the Gulf of Maine Area case *(Canada v. United States)*, ICJ Reports 1984, p. 246 (12 October 1984).

Case Concerning the Continental Shelf *(Libyan Arab Jamahiriya v. Malta)*, ICJ Reports 1985, p. 13 (3 June 1985).

Case Concerning Military and Paramilitary Activities in and against Nicaragua *(Nicaragua v. United States of America)*, ICJ Reports 1986, p. 14 (27 June 1986).

Gabčíkovo-Nagymaros Project case *(Hungary v. Slovakia)*, ICJ Rep, p. 7 (25 September 1997).

Gabčíkovo Nagymaros Project case *(Hungary v. Slovakia) (Separate Opinion of Vice-President Weeramantry)*, ICJ Rep, p. 7 (25 September 1997).

Maritime Delimitation and Territorial Questions between Qatar and Bahrain case *(Qatar v. Bahrain)*, ICJ Reports 2001, p. 40 (16 March 2001).

Armed Activities on the Territory of the Congo case *(Democratic Republic of the Congo v. Uganda)*, ICJ Reports, p. 168 (19 December 2005).

Pulp Mills on the River Uruguay case *(Argentina v. Uruguay)*, ICJ Reports 2010, p. 14 (20 April 2010).

Jurisdictional Immunities of the State case *(Germany v. Italy: Greece Intervening)*, ICJ Reports 2012, p. 99 (3 February 2012).

Questions Relating to the Obligation to Prosecute or Extradite case *(Belgium v. Senegal)*, ICJ Reports 2012, p. 422 (20 July 2012).

Territorial and Maritime Dispute case *(Nicaragua v. Colombia)*, ICJ Reports 2012, p. 624 (19 November 2012).

Advisory opinions

Reparation for Injuries Suffered in the Service of the United Nations, ICJ Reports 1949 p. 174; ICGJ 232 (11 April 1949).

Legal Consequences for States of the Continued Presence of South Africa in Namibia (South West Africa) notwithstanding Security Council Resolution 276 (1970), ICJ GL No. 53, [1971] ICJ Reports 1971, p. 16; ICGJ 220 (21 June 1971).

Legality of the Threat or Use of Nuclear Weapons, ICJ Reports 1996, p. 226 (8 July 1996).

Legality of the Threat or Use of Nuclear Weapons, *(Declaration of Judge Shi)*, ICJ Reports 1996, p. 226 (8 July 1996).

Legality of the Threat or Use of Nuclear Weapons, *(Dissenting Opinion of Judge Weeramantry)*, ICJ Reports 1996, p. 226 (8 July 1996).

International Tribunal for the Law of the Sea (ITLOS) and LOSC-Related arbitral tribunals

Advisory opinion

Request for an Advisory Opinion Submitted by the Sub-Regional Fisheries Commission, ITLOS Reports 2015, p. 4 (Advisory Opinion 2 April 2015).

Responsibilities and Obligations of States with Respect to Activities in the Area, ITLOS (Seabed Dispute Chamber), ITLOS Reports 2011, p. 10; ICGJ 449 (1 February 2011).

236 References

Provisional measures

MOX Plant case, *(Ireland v. United Kingdom)*, Order, (Request for Provisional Measures), ITLOS Case No. 10, ICGJ 343 (13 November 2001).

European Union cases

Joined Cases C-206/88 and C-207/88, *Vessoso and Zanetti* ECLI:EU:C:1990:145.
Case C-286/90, *Poulsen and Diva Navigation Corp* ECLI:EU:C:1992:453.
Case C-236/92, *Comitato di Coordinamento per la Difesa della Cava and Others v. Regione Lombardia and others* ECLI:EU:C:1994:60.
Case C-422/92, *Commision v. Germany* ECLI:EU:C:1995:125.
Case C-187/93, *European Parliament v. Council* ECLI:EU:C:1994:265.
Cases C-304/94, C-330/94, C-342/94, and C-224/95 *Criminal Proceedings against Euro Tombesi and others* ECLI:EU:C:1997:314.
Case C-129/96, *Inter-Environnement Wallonie ASBL v. Région Wallonne* ECLI:EU:C:1997:628.
Joined Cases C-418/97 and C-419/97 ARCO *Chemie Nederland Ltd. v. Minister van Volkshuisvesting, Ruimtelijke Ordening en Milieubeheer and Directeur van de dienst Milieu en Water van de Provincie Gelderland*, ECLI:EU:C:2000:318.
Case C-6/00, *Abfall Service AG (ASA) v. Federal Ministry of Economy, Family and Youth* ECLI:EU:C:2002:121.
Case C-9/00, *Palin Granit Oy and Vehmassalon Kansanterveystyön Kuntayhtymän Hallitus* ECLI:EU:C:2002:232.
Case C-1/03, *Criminal Proceedings v. Paul Van de Walle, Daniel Laurent, Thierry Mersch, and Texaco Belgium SA* ECLI:EU:C:2004:490.
Case C-252/05, *Thames Water Utilities Ltd. v. South East London Division, Bromley Magistrates' Court* ECLI:EU:C:2007:276.
Case C-308/06, *Intertanko and others* ECLI:EU:C:2008:312.
Case C-411/06, *Commission v. Parliament and Council* ECLI:EU:C:2009:518.
Case C-188/07, *Commune de Mesquer v. Total France SA and Total International Ltd.* ECLI:EU:C:2008:359.
Joined Cases C-241/12 and C-242/12, Shell Nederland Verkoopmaatschappij BV and Belgian Shell NV ECLI:EU:C:2013:821.

United Kingdom cases

Queen's Bench Division (Administrative Court) *on the Application of Friends of the Earth v. Environment Agency* [2003], Env. L.R. 31, EWHC 3193.

Bibliography

Books, book chapters, and monographs

Abecassis, David W. and Richard L. Jarashow. *Oil Pollution from Ships: International, United Kingdom and United States Law and Practice*. 2nd edn. London: Stevens & Sons Ltd., 1985.

Albers, Jan. *Responsibility and Liability in the Context of Transboundary Movements of Hazardous Wastes by Sea: Existing Rules and the 1999 Liability Protocol to the Basel Convention*. Hamburg Studies on Maritime Affairs, Vol. 29. Berlin: Springer, 2015.

Allot, Philip. "The Emerging Universal Legal System." In *New Perspectives on the Divide between National and International Law*, edited by Janne Nijman and André Nollkaemper, 63–83. Oxford: Oxford University Press, 2007.

Aust, Anthony. *Modern Treaty Law and Practice*. 3rd edn. Cambridge: Cambridge University Press, 2013.

Backes, Chris. *Law for a Circular Economy*. The Hague: Eleven International Publishing, 2017.

Barral, Virginie. "National Sovereignty over Natural Resources: Environmental Challenges and Sustainable Development." In *Research Handbook on International Law and Natural Resources*, edited by Elisa Morgera and Kati Kulovesi, 3–25. Cheltenham: Edward Elgar Publishing, 2016.

Baxter, Richard Reeve. *Treaties and Customs*. Vol. 129: Collected Courses of the Hague Academy of International Law. The Hague: The Hague Academy of International Law, 1970.

Berndsen, Stephan. "Between Error and Evil: The Dynamics of Deadly Governmental Accidents." PhD thesis, Vrije Universiteit Amsterdam, 2015.

Birnie, Patricia, Alan Boyle, and Catherine Redgwell. *International Law and the Environment*. 3rd edn. Oxford: Oxford University Press, 2009.

Bischoff, Jean-Marc. "The Territorial Limits of Public Law and their Implications in Regard to the Principles of Non-Discrimination and Equal Right of Access as Recognized in Connection with Transfrontier Pollution." In *Legal Aspects of Transfrontier Pollution*, edited by Organisation for Economic Co-Operation and Development (OECD), 128–45. Paris: OECD, 1977.

Boisson, Philippe. "Law of Maritime Security." In *The IMLI Manual on International Maritime Law: Volume Shipping Law*, edited by David Attard, Malgosia Fitzmaurice, Norman Martínez Gutiérrez, Ignacio Arroyo, and Elda Belja, 180–208. Oxford: Oxford University Press, 2016.

238   *Bibliography*

Boyle, Alan. "Further Development of the 1982 Convention on the Law of the Sea: Mechanisms for Change." In *The Law of the Sea: Progress and Prospects*, edited by David Freestone, Richard Barnes, and David Ong. Oxford: Oxford University Press, 2006.

Brinkmann, Thomas. "Commentary on Directive 2000/59/EC of 27 November 2000 on Port Reception Facilities for Ship-Generated Waste and Cargo Residues." In *Brussels Commentary on EU Maritime Transport Law*, edited by Henning Jessen and Micheal Jürgen Werner, 635–45. Baden-Baden: Nomos, 2016.

Byers, Michael. *Custom, Power and the Power of Rules: International Relations and Customary International Law*. Cambridge: Cambridge University Press, 1999.

Cheng, Bing. *Studies in International Space Law*. Oxford: Oxford University Press, 1997.

Christodoulou-Varotsi, Iliana. *Maritime Safety Law and Policies of the European Union and the United States of America: Antagonism or Synergy?* Berlin: Springer, 2009.

Churchill, Robin. "Coastal Waters." In *The IMLI Manual on International Maritime Law: Volume I: The Law of the Sea*, edited by David Attard, Malgosia Fitzmaurice, and Norman Martínez Gutiérrez. Oxford: Oxford University Press, 2014.

Churchill, Robin Rolf and Alan Vaughan Lowe. *The Law of the Sea*. 3rd edn. Manchester: Manchester University Press, 1999.Colombos, C. John. *The International Law of the Sea*. 6th edn. London: Longmans, 1967.

Crawford, James. *The Creation of States in International Law*. 2nd edn. Oxford: Oxford University Press, 2006.

Crawford, James. *Brownlie's Principles of Public International Law*. 8th edn. Oxford: Oxford University Press, 2012.

D'Amato, Anthony. *Concept of Custom in International Law*. Ithaca, NY: Cornell University Press, 1971.

De Sadeleer, Nicolas. *Environmental Principles: From Political Slogans to Legal Rules*. Oxford: Oxford University Press, 2002.

De Visscher, Charles. *Theory and Reality in Public International Law*. Princeton, NJ: Princeton University Press, 1957.

Dupuy, Pierre-Marie. "Formation of Customary International Law and General Principles." In *The Oxford Handbook of International Environmental Law*, edited by Daniel Bodansky, Jutta Brunnée, and Ellen Hey, 449–66. Oxford: Oxford University Press, 2008.

Dupuy, Pierre-Marie and Jorge Viñuales. *International Environmental Law*. Cambridge: Cambrigde University Press, 2015.

Dworkin, Ronald. *Law's Empire*. Cambridge, MA: Harvard University Press, 1986.

Ebbesson, Jonas. "Principle 10: Public Participation." In *The Rio Declaration on Environment and Development: A Commentary*, edited by Jorge Viñuales, 287–310. Oxford: Oxford University Press, 2015.

Fisher, Elizabeth, Bettina Lange, and Eloise Scotford. *Environmental Law: Text, Cases, and Materials*. Oxford: Oxford University Press, 2013.

Focarelli, Carlo. *International Law as a Social Construct: The Struggle for Global Justice*. Oxford: Oxford University Press, 2012.

Franckx, Erik, ed. *Vessel-Source Pollution and Coastal State Jurisdiction: The Work of the ILA Committee on Coastal State Jurisdiction Relating to Marine Pollution (1991–2001)*. The Hague: Kluwer Law International, 2001.

Frank, Veronica. *The European Community and Marine Environmental Protection in the International Law of the Sea: Implementing Global Obligations at the Regional Level*. Leiden: Martinus Nijhoff Publishers, 2007.

Friedrich, Jürgen. *International Environmental "Soft Law": The Functions and Limits of Nonbinding Instruments in International Environmental Governance and Law*. Berlin: Springer, 2013.

Bibliography 239

Gaskell, Nicholas, Charles Debattista, and Richard Swatton. *Chorley and Giles' Shipping Law*. 8th edn. London: Pitman Publishing, 1987.

Gillespie, Alexander. *Waste Policy: International Regulation, Comparative and Contextual Perspectives*. New Horizons in Environmental and Energy Law. Edited by Kurt Deketelaere and Zen Makuch. Cheltenham: Edward Elgar Publishing, 2015.

Gold, Edgar. *Gard Handbook on the Protection of the Marine Environment*. 3rd edn. Norway: Gard AS, 2006.

Goldsmith, Jack L. and Eric A. Posner. *The Limits of International Law*. New York: Oxford University Press, 2005.

Gonzalez, Gabino and Frédéric Hébert. "Conventions Relating to Pollution Incident Preparedness, Response, and Cooperation." In *The IMLI Manual on International Maritime Law: Volume III, Marine Environmental Law and Maritime Security Law*, edited by David Attard, Gerald Fitzmaurice, Norman Martinez, and Riyaz Hamza, 195–260. Oxford: Oxford University Press, 2016.

Greaves, Rosa. "The Impact of EU Secondary Legislation on Issues Concerning Ships: A Case Study of National Proceedings in Respect of Waste Liability and Insolvency." In *Jurisdiction over Ships: Post-UNCLOS Developments in the Law of the Sea*, edited by Henrik Ringbom. Publications on Ocean Development. Leiden: Brill Nijhoff, 2015.

Grosz, Mirina. *Sustainable Waste Trade under WTO Law: Chances and Risks of the Legal Framework's Regulation of Transboundary Movement of Wastes*. Nijhoff International Trade Law Series. Edited by Mads Andenas, Vol. 4. Leiden: Martinus Nijhoff Pulishers, 2011.

Handl, Günther. "Transboundary Impacts." In *The Oxford Handbook of International Environmental Law*, edited by Daniel Bodansky, Jutta Brunnée, and Ellen Hey, 532–48. Oxford: Oxford University Press, 2007.

Hardman Reis, Tarcísio. "Waste and International Law: Towards a Resource-Based Approach?" In *Waste Management and the Green Economy: Law and Policy*, edited by Katharina Kummer, Andreas R. Ziegler, and Jorun Baumgartner, 33–55. Cheltenham: Edward Elgar Publishing, 2016.

Hassler, Björn. "Oil Spills from Shipping: A Case Study of the Governance of Accidental Hazards and Intentional Pollution in the Baltic Sea." In *Environmental Governance of the Baltic Sea*, edited by Michael Gilek, Mikael Karlsson, Sebastian Linke, and Katarzyna Smolarz, 125–48. Berlin: Springer, 2016.

Henkin, Louis. *International Law: Politics and Values*. Developments in International Law, Vol. 18. Leiden: Martinus Nijhoff Publishers, 1995.

Hobe, Stephan. "Evolution of the Principle on Permanent Sovereignty over Natural Resources." In *Permanent Sovereignty over Natural Resources*, edited by Marc Bungenberg and Stephan Hobe, 1–14. Switzerland: Springer, 2015.

Jacobson, Timothy. *Waste Management: An American Corporate Success Story*. Washington, DC: Regnery Publishing, 1993.

Jenisch, Uwe. "The Development of Environmental Standards for the Baltic Sea." In *Marine Issues: From a Scientific, Political and Legal Perspective*, edited by Peters Ehlers, Elisabeth Mann-Borgese, and Rüdiger Wolfrum, 63–72. The Hague: Kluwer Law International, 2002.

Johnston, Douglas M. "The Environmental Law of the Sea: Historical Development." In *The Environmental Law of the Sea*, edited by Douglas M. Johnston. Gland: International Union for Conservation of Nature and Natural Resources (IUCN), 1981.

Kachel, Markus. *Particularly Sensitive Sea Areas: The IMO's Role in Protecting Vulnerable Marine Areas*. Berlin: Springer, 2008. doi:10.1007/978-3-540-78779-2.

240 *Bibliography*

Kaczorowska, Alina. *European Union Law*. 3rd edn. London: Routledge Taylor & Francis Group, 2013.

Karim, Saiful. *Prevention of Pollution of the Marine Environment from Vessels: The Potential and Limits of the International Maritime Organizations*. Switzerland: Springer, 2015.

Kelly, Patrick. "Customary International Law in Historical Context: The Exercise of Power without General Acceptance." In *Reexamining Customary International Law*, edited by D. Brian Lepard, 47–85. Cambridge: Cambridge University Press, 2017.

Kelsen, Hans. *General Theory of Norms*. Translated by Michael Hartney. Oxford: Oxford University Press, 1991.

Kiss, Alexander and Dinah Shelton. *Guide to International Environmental Law*. Leiden: Martinus Nijhoff Publishers, 2007.

Kohler, Juliette. "A Paradigm Shift under the Basel Convention on Hazardous Wastes." In *Waste Management and the Green Economy: Law and Policy*, edited by Katharina Kummer, Andreas R. Ziegler, and Jorun Baumgartner, 80–95. Cheltenham: Edward Elgar Publishing, 2016.

Kolb, Robert. *The Law of Treaties: An Introduction*. Cheltenham: Edward Elgar Publishing, 2016.

Koskenniemi, Martti. *From Apology to Utopia: The Structure of International Legal Argument*. Cambridge: Cambridge University Press, 2006.

Krämer, Ludwig. *EU Environmental Law*. 8th edn. London: Sweet & Maxwell, 2015.

Krueger, Jonathan. *International Trade and the Basel Convention*. London: Earthscan Publications Ltd., 1999.

Kummer, Katharina. *International Management of Hazardous Wastes: The Basel Convention and Related Legal Rules*. Oxford: Oxford University Press, 1995.

Kummer, Katharina, Andreas R. Ziegler, and Jorun Baumgartner, eds. *Waste Management and the Green Economy: Law and Policy*. Cheltenham: Edward Elgar Publishing, 2016.

Kuokkanen, Tuomas. *International Law and the Environment: Variations on a Theme*. Vol. 4. The Hague: Kluwer Law International, 2002.

Kwiatkowska, Barbara and Alfred Soons, eds. *Transboundary Movements and Disposal of Hazardous Wastes in International Law: Basic Documents*. Leiden: Martinus Nijhoff Publishers, 1993.

Langlet, David. *Prior Informed Consent and Hazardous Trade: Regulating Trade in Hazardous Goods at the Intersection of Sovereignty, Free Trade, and Environmental Protection*. Austin, TX: Wolters Kluwer Law & Business, 2009.

Langlet, David and Said Mahmoudi. *EU Environmental Law and Policy*. Oxford: Oxford University Press, 2016.

Lebefer, René. *Transboundary Environmental Interference and the Origin of State Liability*. The Hague: Kluwer Law International, 1996.

Lepard, D. Brian. *Customary International Law: A New Theory with Practical Implications*. Cambridge: Cambridge University Press, 2010.

Lesaffer, Randall. "Peace Treaties from Lodi to Westphalia." In *Peace Treaties and International Law in European History: From the Late Middle Ages to World War One*, edited by Randall Lesaffer, 9–44. Cambridge: Cambridge University Press, 2004.

Louka, Elli. *International Environmental Law: Fairness, Effectiveness, and World Order*. Cambridge: Cambridge University Press, 2006.

Magraw, Daniel and Lisa D. Hawke. "Sustainable Development." In *The Oxford Handbook of International Environmental Law*, edited by Daniel Bodansky, Jutta Brunnée, and Ellen Hey, 614–38. Oxford: Oxford University Press, 2007.

Bibliography 241

Maitre-Ekern, Eléonore. "The Choice of Regulatory Instruments for a Circular Economy." In *Environmental Law and Economics*, edited by Mathis Klaus and Bruce R. Huber, 305–34. Cham: Springer, 2017.

Marten, Bevan. *Port State Jurisdiction and the Regulation of International Merchant Shipping*. Hamburg Studies on Maritime Affairs. Hamburg: Springer, 2014. doi:10.1007/978-3-319-00351-1.

Matz-Lück, Nele. "Norm Interpretation across International Regimes: Competences and Legitimacy." In *Regime Interaction in International Law: Facing Fragmentation*, edited by Margaret Young, 201–34. Cambridge: Cambridge University Press, 2012.

Mish, Frederick C., ed. *Merriam-Webster's Collegiate Dictionary*. Springfield, MA: Merriam-Webster's Collegiate, 2011.

Mitchell, Ronald B. *Intentional Oil Pollution at Sea: Environmental Policy and Treaty Compliance*. Cambridge: MIT Press, 1994.

Moules, Richard. *Environmental Judicial Review*. Oxford: Hart Publishing Ltd., 2011.

Nordquist, Myron H., Shabtai Rosenne, Alexander Yankov, and Neal Grandy, eds. *United Nations Convention on the Law of the Sea 1982: A Commentary*. V vols. Vol. IV. Leiden: Martinus Nijhoff Publishers, 1991.

Nussbaum, Arthur. *A Concise History of the Law of Nations*. Revised edn. New York: The Macmillan Co., 1954.

Pagano, Paolo, Mariano Falcitelli, Silvia Ferrini, Francesco Papucci, Francescalberto De Bari, and Querci Antonella. "Complex Infrastructures: The Benefit of Its Services in Seaports." In *Intelligent Transportation Systems: From Good Practices to Standards*, edited by Paolo Pagano, 172–86. Boca Raton, FL: CRC Press, 2017.

Parrish, Austen L. "Sovereignty's Continuing Importance: Traces of *Trail Smelter* in the International Law Governing Hazardous Waste Transport." In *Transboundary Harm in International Law: Lessons from the Trail Smelter Arbitration*, edited by Rebecca M. Bratspies and Russell A. Miller, 181–94. Cambridge: Cambridge University Press, 2006.

Perrez, Franz Xaver. *Cooperative Sovereignty: From Independence to Interdependece in the Structure of International Environmental Law*. The Hague: Kluwer Law International, 2000.

Portas, Pierre. "The Basel Convention – A Promising Future." In *Chemicals, Environment, Health: A Global Management Perspective*, edited by Philip Wexler, Jan van der Kolk, Asish Mohapratra, and Ravi Agarwal, 121–34. Boca Raton, FL: CRC Press, 2012.

Proelss, Alexander. "The European Court of Justice and Its Role in (Re-)Defining EU Member States' Jurisdiction over Ships." In *Jurisdiction over Ships: Post-UNCLOS Developments in the Law of the Sea*, edited by Henrik Ringbom, 431–32. Publications on Ocean Development. Leiden: Brill Nijhoff, 2015.

Puthucherril, Tony. *From Ship Breaking to Sustainable Ship Recycling: Evolution of a Legal Regime*. Legal Aspects of Sustainable Development. Edited by David Freestone, Vol. 5. Leiden: Martinus Nijhoff Publishers, 2010.

Rakhyun, Kim and Harro van Asselt. "Global Governance: Problem Shifting in the Anthropocene and the Limits of International Law." In *Research Handbook on International Law and Natural Resources*, edited by Elisa Morgera and Kati Kulovesi, 473–95. Cheltenham: Edward Elgar Publishing, 2016.

Rayfuse, Rosemary. "Principles of International Environmental Law Applicable to Waste Management." In *Waste Management and the Green Economy: Law and Policy*, edited by Katharina Kummer, Andreas R. Ziegler, and Jorun Baumgartner, 18. Cheltenham: Edward Elgar Publishing, 2016.

242 *Bibliography*

Restatement of the Law, Third, of Foreign Relations Law of the United States. Vol. I. §§1 to 488, St. Paul, MN: The American Law Institute, 1987.

Ringbom, Henrik. *The EU Maritime Safety Policy and International Law.* Leiden: Martinus Nijhoff Publishers, 2008.

Rothwell, Donald and Tim Stephens. *The International Law of the Sea.* Oxford: Hart Publishing Ltd., 2010.

Rue, Colin De La and Charles B. Anderson. *Shipping and the Environment: Law and Practice.* 2nd edn. London: Informa Law, 2009.

Rummel-Bulska, Iwona. "The Basel Convention and the UN Convention on the Law of the Sea." In *Competing Norms in the Law of Marine Environmental Protection,* edited by Henrik Ringbom. International Environmental Law and Policy Series, 83–108. The Hague: Kluwer Law International, 1997.

Sachs, Wolfgang. "Environment." In *The Development Dictionary: A Guide to Knowledge as Power,* edited by Wolfgang Sachs, 26–37. London: Zed Books Ltd., 1992.

Sand, Peter. "The Evolution of International Environmental Law." In *The Oxford Handbook of International Environmental Law,* edited by Daniel Bodansky, Jutta Brunnée, and Ellen Hey, 31–43. Oxford: Oxford University Press, 2007.

Sands, Philippe, Jacqueline Peel, Adriana Fabra, and Ruth MacKenzie. *Principles of International Environmental Law.* 3rd edn. Cambridge: Cambridge University Press, 2012.

Schneider, Jan. "Pollution from Vessels." In *The Environmental Law of the Sea,* edited by Douglas Johnson, 203–17. Gland: International Union for Conservation of Nature and Natural Resources (IUCN), 1981.

Schrijver, Nico. *Sovereignty over Natural Resources: Balancing Rights and Duties.* Cambridge: Cambridge University Press, 1997.

Schrijver, Nico. "Fifty Years Permanent Sovereignty over Natural Resources: The 1962 UN Declaration as the Opinio Iuris Communis." In *Permanent Sovereignty over Natural Resources,* edited by Marc Bungenberg and Stephan Hobe, 15–60. Switzerland: Springer, 2015.Scotford, Eloise. *Environmental Principles and the Evolution of Environmental Law.* Oxford: Hart Publishing, 2017.

Scovazzi, Tullio. "Regional Cooperation in the Field of the Environment." In *Marine Specially Protected Areas: The General Aspects and the Mediterranean Regional System,* edited by Tullio Scovazzi, 82–100. The Hague: Kluwer Law International, 1999.

Shaw, Malcolm. "The International Court of Justice and the Law of Territory." In *The Development of International Law by the International Court of Justice,* edited by Christian Tams and James Sloan, 151–76. Oxford: Oxford University Press, 2013.

Shaw, Malcolm. *International Law.* 8rd edn. Cambridge: Cambridge University Press, 2017.

Södersten, Anna and Dennis Patterson. "The Nature of International Law." In *A Companion to European Union Law and International Law,* edited by Anna Södersten and Dennis Patterson, 16–25. Chichester: Wiley Blackwell, 2016.

Tan, Alan Khee-Jin. *Vessel-Source Marine Pollution: The Law and Politics of International Regulation.* Cambridge: Cambridge University Press, 2006.

Tesón, Fernando. "Fake Custom." In *Reexamining Customary International Law,* edited by D. Brian Lepard, 86–110. Cambridge: Cambridge University Press, 2017.

Teubner, Gunther. "Juridification: Concepts, Aspects, Limits, Solutions." In *Juridification of Social Spheres: A Comparative Analysis in the Areas of Labor, Corporate, Antitrust and Social Welfare Law,* edited by Gunther Teubner, 3–49. Berlin: Walter de Gruyter & Co., 1987.

Tolba, Mostafa K. and Iwona Rummel-Bulska. *Global Environmental Diplomacy: Negotiating Environmental Agreements for the World, 1973–1992*. Global Environmental Accords. Edited by Nazli Choucri. Cambridge: The MIT Press, 2008.

Tuori, Kaarlo. *Ratio and Voluntas: The Tension between Reason and Will in Law*. Applied Legal Philisophy. Farnham: Ashgate, 2011.

Ulfstein, Geir. "Dispute Resolution, Compliance Control and Enforcement in International Environmental Law." In *Making Treaties Work: Human Rights, Environment and Arms Control*, edited by Geir Ulfstein, 129. Cambridge: Cambridge University Press, 2008.

Van Calster, Geert. *EU Waste Law*. 2nd edn. Oxford: Oxford University Press, 2015.

Venkat, Aruna. *Environmental Law and Policy*. Delhi: PHI Learning Private Limited, 2011.

Verschuuren, Jonathan. "Overcoming the Limitations of Environmental Law in a Globalised World." In *Handbook of Globalisation and Environmental Policy: National Government Interventions in a Global Arena*, edited by Frank Wijen, Kees Zoeteman, Jan Pieters, and Paul van Seters, 616–40. Cheltenham: Edward Elgar Publishing, 2010.

Villiger, Mark E. *Customary International Law and Treaties*. Leiden: Martinus Nijhoff Publishers, 1985.

Wettestad, Jørgen. "Monitoring and Verification." In *The Oxford Handbook of International Environmental Law*, edited by Daniel Bodansky, Jutta Brunnée, and Ellen Hey, 975–93. Oxford: Oxford University Press, 2007.

Witt, Jörn-Ahrend. *Obligations and Control of Flag States: Developments and Perspectives in International Law and EU Law*. Berlin: Lit Verlag, 2007.

Wolfke, Karol. *Custom in Present International Law*. Wroclaw: Zaklad Narodowy im. Ossolinskich, 1964.

Wolfrum, Rüdiger and Nele Matz. *Conflicts in International Environmental Law*. Berlin: Springer, 2003.

Articles

Abrams, David. "Regulating the International Hazardous Waste Trade: A Proposed Global Solution." *Columbia Journal of Transnational Law* 28, no. 3 (1990): 801–45.

Akehurst, Michael. "Custom as a Source of International Law." *British Yearbook of International Law* 47, no. 1 (1976): 1–53.

Birnie, Patricia. "Environmental Protection and Development." *Melbourne University Law Review* 20 (1995): 66–100.

Blichner, Lars and Anders Molander. "Mapping Juridification." *European Law Journal* 14, no. 1 (2008): 36–54.

Bodansky, Daniel. "Customary (and Not So Customary) International Environmental Law." *Global Legal Studies Journal* 3 (1995): 105–19.

Boyle, Alan. "Marine Pollution under the Law of the Sea Convention." *The American Journal of International Law* 79, no. 2 (1985): 347–72.

Boyle, Alan. "Saving the World? Implementation and Enforcement of International Environmental Law through International Institutions." *Journal of Environmental Law* 3 (1991): 229–45.

Boyle, Alan. "Some Reflections on the Relationship of Treaties and Soft Law." *International and Comparative Law Quarterly* 48, no. 4 (1999): 901–13.

Boyle, Alan. "EU Unilateralism and the Law of the Sea." *The International Journal of Marine and Coastal Law* 21, no. 1 (2006): 15–31.

244   *Bibliography*

Brunnée, Jutta. "Coping with Consent: Law-Making under Multilateral Environmental Agreements." *Leiden Journal of International Law* 15 (2002): 1–52.

Carpenter, Angela and Sally Macgill. "Charging for Port Reception Facilities in North Sea Ports: Putting Theory into Practice." *Marine Pollution Bulletin* 42, no. 4 (2001): 257–66.

Carpenter, Angela and Sally Macgill. "The EU Directive on Port Reception Facilities for Ship-Generated Waste and Cargo Residues: The Results of a Second Survey on the Provision and Uptake of Facilities in North Sea Ports." *Marine Pollution Bulletin* 50 (2005): 1541–47.

Chayes, Abram and Antonia Handler Chayes. "Compliance without Enforcement: State Behavior under Regulatory Treaties." *Negotiation Journal* 7, no. 3 (1991): 311–30.

Cheyne, Ilona. "The Definition of Waste in EC Law." *Journal of Environmental Law* 14, no. 1 (2002): 61–73.

Choongh, Satnam and Martha Grekos. "Finding a Workable Definition of Waste: Is It a Waste of Time?" *Journal of Planning & Environmental Law* (2006): 463–79.

Cross, Frank B. and Brenda J. Winslett. "'Export Death': Ethical Issues and the International Trade in Hazardous Products." *American Business Law Journal* 25, no. 3 (1987): 487–521.

Curtis, Jeff B. "Vessel-Source Oil Pollution and MARPOL 73/78: An International Success Story?" *Environmental Law* 15 (1984): 679–710.

D'Amato, Anthony. "Is International Law Really 'Law'?" *Northwestern University Law Review* 79, nos. 5–6 (1984–85): 1293–314.

de La Fayette, Louise. "Access to Ports in International Law." *The International Journal of Marine and Coastal Law* 11, no. 1 (1996): 1–22.

de La Fayette, Louise Angélique. "The Sound Management of Wastes Generated at Sea: MARPOL, Not Basel." *Environmental Policy and Law* 39, nos. 4–5 (2009): 207–14.

Donald, J. Wylie. "The Bamako Convention as a Solution to the Problem of Hazardous Waste Exports to Less Developed Countries." *Columbia Journal of Environmental Law* 17 (1992): 419–58.

Dupuy, Pierre-Marie. "Soft Law and the International Law of the Environment." *Michigan Journal of International Law* 12 (1991): 8.

Dworkin, Ronald. "The Model of Rules." *The University Chicago Law Review* 35 (1967–68): 14–46.

Ebbesson, Jonas. "The Notion of Public Participation in International Environmental Law." *Yearbook of International Environmental Law* 8, no. 1 (1998): 51.

Fluck, Jürgen. "The Term 'Waste' in EU Law." *European Environmental Law Review* (1994): 79–84.

Georgakellos, Dimitrios. "The Use of the Deposit-Refund Framework in Port Reception Facilities Charging Systems." *Marine Pollution Bulletin* 54 (2007): 508–20.

Gipperth, Lena. "The Legal Design of the International and European Union Ban on Tributyltin Antifouling Paint: Direct and Indirect Effects." *Journal of Environmental Management* 90 (2009): 86–95.

Guruswamy, Lakshman. "The Promise of the United Nations Convention on the Law of the Sea (UNCLOS): Justice in Trade and Environment Disputes." *Ecology Law Quarterly* 25 (1998–99): 189–228.

Gwam, Cyril Uchenna. "*Travaux Preparatoires* of the Basel Convention on the Control of Transboundary Movements of Hazardous Wastes and their Disposal." *Journal of Natural Resources and Environmental Law* 18 (2003): 1–78.

Handl, Günter. "Compliance Control Mechanisms and International Environmental Obligations." *Tulane Journal of International and Comparative Law* 5 (1997): 29–49.

Bibliography 245

Handl, Günter and Robert Lutz. "An International Policy Perspective on the Trade of Hazardous Materials and Technologies." *Harvard International Law Journal* 30 (1989): 351–74.

Harjula, Henrik. "Hazardous Waste." *Annals of the New York Academy of Sciences* 1076 (2006): 462–77.

Henkin, Louis. "That 'S' Word: Sovereignty, and Globalization, and Human Rights, Et Cetera." *Fordham Law Review* 68, no. 1 (1999): 1–14.

Hilz, Christoph and Mark Radka. "Environmental Negotiation and Policy: The Basel Convention on Transboundary Movement of Hazardous Wastes and their Disposal." *International Journal of Environment and Pollution* 1, nos. 1–2 (1991): 55–72.

Kadens, Emily and Ernest A. Young. "How Customary Is Customary International Law?" *William and Mary Law Review* 54, no. 3 (2013): 885–920.

Kammerhofer, Jörg. "Uncertainty in the Formal Sources of International Law: Customary International Law and Some of Its Problems." *European Journal of International Law* 15, no. 3 (2004): 523–53.

Krueger, Jonathan. "Prior Informed Consent and the Basel Convention: The Hazards of What Isn't Known." *The Journal of Environment and Development* 7, no. 2 (1998): 115–37.

Kummer, Katharina. "Turning Wastes into Valuable Resources: Promoting Compliance with Obligations?" *Environmental Policy and Law* 41, nos. 4–5 (2011): 177–80.

Linné, Phillip. "Ships, Air Pollution, and Climate Change: Some Reflections on Recent Legal Developments in the Marine Environment Protection Committee." *SIMPLY: Scandinavian Institute of Maritime Law Yearbook*, no. 414 (2011): 13–32.

Liu, Nengye and Frank Maes. "Prevention of Vessel-Source Marine Pollution: A Note on the Challenges and Prospects for Chinese Practice under International Law." *Ocean Development and International Law* 42, no. 4 (2011): 356–67.

Long, Ronán. "The Marine Strategy Framework Directive: A New European Approach to the Regulation of the Marine Environment, Marine Natural Resources and Marine Ecological Services." *Journal of Energy and Natural Resources Law* 29, no. 1 (2011): 1–44.

Matsui, Yoshiro. "Some Aspects of the Principle of 'Common but Differentiated Responsibilities'." *International Environmental Agreements: Politics, Law and Economics* 2 (2002): 151–71.

McIntyre, Owen and Thomas Mosedale. "The Precautionary Principle as a Norm of Customary International Law." *Journal of Environmental Law* 9 (1997): 221–41.

Mehry, Cyrus. "Prior Informed Consent: An Emerging Compromise for Hazardous Export." *Cornell International Law Journal* 21 (1988): 365–89.

Mejía-Lemos, Diego. "Some Considerations Regarding '"Instant" International Customary Law', Fifty Years Later." *Indian Journal of International Law* 55, no. 1 (2015): 85–108.

Mendelson, Maurice. "The Subjective Element in Customary International Law." *The British Yearbook of International Law* 66, no. 1 (1996): 177–208.

Murray, Alan, Keith Skene, and Kathryn Haynes. "The Circular Economy: An Interdisciplinary Exploration of the Concept and Application in a Global Context." *Journal of Business Ethics* 140, no. 3 (2017): 369–80.

Nengye, Liu and Frank Maes. "The European Union and the International Maritime Organization: EU's External Influence on the Prevention of Vessel Source Pollution." *Journal of Maritime Law and Commerce* 41, no. 4 (2010): 581–94.

O'Brien, Martin. "Rubbish Values: Reflections on the Political Economy of Waste." *Science as Culture* 8, no. 3 (1999): 269–95.

246 *Bibliography*

Okowa, Phoebe N. "Procedural Obligations in International Environmental Agreements." *The British Yearbook of International Law* 67, no. 1 (1997): 275–336.

Park, Rozelia. "An Examination of International Environmental Racism through the Lens of Transboundary Movement of Hazardous Wastes." *Global Legal Studies Journal* 5 (1997–98): 659–710.

Peczenik, Aleksander. "A Theory of Legal Doctrine." *Ratio Juris* 14, no. 1 (2001): 75–105.

Perrez, Franz Xaver. "Efficiency of Cooperation: A Functional Analysis of Sovereignty." *Arizona Journal of International and Comparative Law* 15, no. 2 (1998): 515–82.

Pinzon, Lillian. "Criminalization of the Transboundary Movement of Hazardous Waste and the Effect on Corporations." *DePaul Business Law Journal* 7 (1994–95): 173–221.

Reddish, Michael. "ECJ Case Report: Case C-236." *European Environmental Law Review* 3, no. 10 (November 1994): 307–10.

Redgwell, Catherine. "Sustainable Development of National Energy Resources: What Has International Law Got to Do with It?" *AFE Babalola University: The Journal of Sustainable Development Law and Policy* 8, no. 1 (2017): 378–95.

Roberts, Anthea Elizabeth. "Traditional and Modern Approaches to Customary International Law: A Reconciliation." *The American Journal of International Law* 95 (2001): 757–91.

Rockström, Johan, Will Steffen, Kevin Noone, Åssa Persson, Stuart Chapin, Eric Lambin, Timothy Lenton, et al. "Planetary Boundaries: Exploring the Safe Operating Space for Humanity." *Ecology and Society* 14, no. 2 (2009): 32.

Rockström, Johan and Jeffrey D. Sachs. "Sustainable Development and Planetary Boundaries." *High Level Panel on the Post-2015 Development Agenda* (2013): 1–45.

Selin, Henrik. "Global Environmental Governance and Regional Centers." *Global Environmental Politics* 12, no. 3 (2012): 18–37.

Shearer, Russell. "Comparative Analysis of the Basel and Bamako Conventions on Hazardous Waste." *Environmental Law* 23 (1993): 45.

Simma, Bruno and Philip Alston. "The Sources of Human Rights Law: Custom, Jus Cogens, and General Principles." *Australian Yearbook of International Law* 12 (1988–89): 82–108.

Singh, Jang B. and V. Chris Lakhan. "Business Ethics and the International Trade in Hazardous Wastes." *Journal of Business Ethics* 8 (1989): 889–99.

Steffen, Will, Jacques Grinevald, Paul Crutzen, and John McNeill. "The Anthropocene: Conceptual and Historical Perspectives." *Philosophical Transactions of the Royal Society A* 368 (2011): 842–67.

Steffen, Will, Katherine Richardson, Johan Rockström, Sarah Cornell, Ingo Fetzer, Elena Bennett, R. Biggs, et al. "Planetary Boundaries: Guiding Human Development on a Changing Planet." *Science* 347, no. 6223 (2015): 1–15.

Teclaff, Ludwik A. and Eileen Teclaff. "Transfers of Pollution and the Marine Environment Conventions." *Natural Resources Journal* 31 (1991): 187–211.

Thakker, Nisha. "India's Toxic Landfills: A Dumping Ground for the World's Electronic Waste." *Sustainable Development Law and Policy* 58 (2006): 58–61.

Van Calster, Geert. "The EC Definition of Waste: The Euro Tombesi Bypass and the Basel Relief Routes." *European Business Law Review* 8, nos. 5–6 (May/June 1997): 137–43.

Van Leeuwen, Judith and Kristine Kern. "The External Dimension of European Union Marine Governance: Institutional Interplay between the EU and the International Maritime Organization." *Global Environmental Politics* 13, no. 1 (2013): 69–87.

Bibliography 247

Walden, Raphael. "Customary International Law: A Jurisprudential Analysis." *Israel Law Review* 13, no. 1 (1978): 86–192.

Westwood, Tom. "Poor Reception." *HS Safety at Sea* (2013): 32.

Wilkinson, David. "Time to Discard the Concept of Waste." *Environmental Law Review* 1 (1999): 172–95.

Worster, William Thomas. "The Transformation of Quantity into Quality: Critical Mass in the Formation of Customary International Law." *Boston University International Law Journal* 31 (2013): 1–78.

Worster, William Thomas. "The Inductive and Deductive Methods in Customary International Law Analysis: Traditional and Modern Approaches." *Georgetown Journal of International Law* 45 (2014): 445–521.

Conference proceedings

Mukherjee, Proshanto and Jingjing Xu. "The Legal Framework of Exhausts Emissions from Ships: A Selective Examination from a Law and Economics Perspective." In *Impacts of Climate Change on the Maritime Industry: The Proceedings of the Conference on Impacts of Climate Change on the Maritime Industry, 2–4 June 2008*, edited by Neil Bellefontaine and Olof Lindén. Malmö: WMU Publications, 2009.

International documentation

Baltic Marine Environment Protection Commission (HELCOM)

Helcom Recommendation 10/5: Guidelines for the Establishment of Adequate Reception Facilities in Ports. 1989.

Helcom Recommendation 10/6: Application by the Baltic Sea States of a Helsinki Convention Form for Reporting Alleged Inadequacy of Reception Facilities for Sewage. 1989.

Helcom Recommendation 10/7: General Requirements for Reception of Wastes. 1989.

Helcom Recommendation 19/12: Waste Management Plans for Ports. 1998.

Helcom Recommendation 19/13: Basic Principles of Ashore Handling of Ship-Generated Wastes. In *HELCOM 19/98 15/1 (Annex 24)*. 1998.

Helcom Recommendation 22/3: Unified Interpretations to Ensure the Harmonized and Effective Implementation of the Strategy for Port Reception Facilities for Ship-Generated Wastes and Associated Issues. 2001.

Helcom Recommendation 23/1: Notification of Ship's Wastes. In *HELCOM 23/2002 – Minutes of the Meeting (Annex 3)*. 2002.

Helcom Recomendation 28e/10: Application of the No-Special-Fee System to Ship-Generated Wastes and Marine Litter Caught in Fishing Nets in the Baltic Sea Area. 15 November 2007.

Helcom Recommendation 28/2: Recording of Fuel Oil Bunkering Operations in the Oil Record Book and Documentation for the Use of Reception Facilities. 2007.

Baltic Marine Environment Protection Commission, HELCOM. "Baltic Sea Sewage Port Reception Facilities: Helcom Overview 2014." 94, 2015.

Conference of the Parties (COP) to the Basel Convention

Decision I/13: Establishment of Regional Centres for Training and Technology Transfer. *First Meeting of the Conference of the Parties to the Basel Convention on the*

248   *Bibliography*

Control of Transboundary Movements of Hazardous Wastes and their Disposal (UNEP/CHW.1/24). Piriapolis, 1992.

Decision III/19: Establishment of Regional or Sub-Regional Centres for Training and Technology Transfer Regarding the Management of Hazardous Wastes and Other Wastes and the Minimization of their Generation. *Third Meeting of the Conference of the Parties to the Basel Convention on the Control of Transboundary Movements of Hazardous Wastes and their Disposal (UNEP/CHW.3/35).* Geneva, 28 November 1995.

Decision IV/9: Amendment and Adoption of Annexes to the Convention. *Fourth Meeting of the Conference of the Parties to the Basel Convention on the Control of Transboundary Movements of Hazardous Wastes and their Disposal* (UNEP/CHW.4/35). Kuching, 23–27 February 1998.

Decision V/1: Basel Declaration on Environmentally Sound Management. *Fifth Meeting of the Conference of the Parties to the Basel Convention on the Control of Transboundary Movements of Hazardous Wastes and their Disposal* (UNEP/CHW.5/29). Basel, 1999.

Decision V/32: Enlargement of the Scope of the Technical Cooperation Trust Fund. *Fifth Meeting of the Conference of the Parties to the Basel Convention on the Control of Transboundary Movements of Hazardous Wastes and their Disposal* (UNEP/CHW.5/29). Basel, 1999.

Decision VI/14: Interim Guidelines for the Implementation of Decision V/32 on Enlargement of the Scope of the Trust Fund to Assist Developing and Other Countries in Need of Technical Assistance in the Implementation of the Basel Convention. *Sixth Meeting of the Conference of the Parties to the Basel Convention on the Control of Transboundary Movements of Hazardous Wastes and their Disposal (UNEP/CHW.6/4)0.* Geneva, 2002.

Review or Adjustment of the Lists of Wastes Contained in Annexes VIII and IX to the Basel Convention, Note by the Secretariat. *Seventh Meeting of the Conference of the Parties to the Basel Convention on the Control of Transboundary Movements of Hazardous Wastes and their Disposal,* Item 6 of the Provisional Agenda (UNEP/CHW.7/15). Geneva, 2004.

Decision VIII/4: Basel Convention Regional and Coordinating Centres. *Report of the Conference of the Parties to the Basel Convention on the Control of Transboundary Movements of Hazardous Wastes and their Disposal on Its Eighth Meeting* (UNEP/CHW.8/16*). Nairobi, 2006.

Decision VIII/9: Cooperation between the Basel Convention and the International Maritime Organization (UNEP/CHW.8/16*). *Report of the Eighth Meeting of the Conference of the Parties to the Basel Convention on the Control of Transboundary Movements of Hazardous Wastes and their Disposal.* Nairobi, 2006.

Decision VIII/18: Harmonization of Forms for Notification and Movement Documents and Related Instructions. (UNEP/CHW.8/16*). *Eighth Meeting of the Conference of the Parties to the Basel Convention on the Control of Transboundary Movements of Hazardous Wastes and their Disposal.* Nairobi, 2006.

Decision IX/4: Review of the Operation of the Basel Convention Regional and Coordinating Centres. *Report of the Conference of the Parties to the Basel Convention on the Control of Transboundary Movements of Hazardous Wastes and their Disposal on Its Ninth Meeting* (UNEP/CHW.9/39). Bali, 2008.

Cartagena Declaration on the Prevention, Minimization and Recovery of Hazardous Wastes and Other Wastes. Annex IV: *Report of the Tenth Meeting of the Conference of* the Parties to the Basel Convention on the Control of Transboundary Movements of Hazardous Wastes and their Disposal (UNEP/CHW.10/28). Cartagena, 2011.

Decision BC-10/2: New Strategic Framework for the Implementation of the Basel Convention for 2012–2021 (UNEP/CHW.10/3). *Tenth Meeting of the Conference of the Parties to the Basel Convention on the Control of Transboundary Movements of Hazardous Wastes and their Disposal.* Cartagena, 2011.

Decision BC-10/16: Cooperation between the Basel Convention and the International Maritime Organization. *Report of the Tenth Meeting of the Conference of the Parties to the Basel Convention on the Control of Transboundary Movements of Hazardous Wastes and their Disposal* (UNEP/CHW.10/28). Cartagena, 2011.

Decision BC-10/17: Environmentally Sound Dismantling of Ships. *Report of the Tenth Meeting of the Conference of the Parties to the Basel Convention on the Control of Transboundary Movements of Hazardous Wastes and their Disposal* (UNEP/CHW.10/28). Cartagena, 2011.

Outcome Document of the Consultative Process on Financing Options for Chemicals and Wastes (UNEP/CHW.10/INF/54). *Tenth Meeting of the Conference of the Parties to the Basel Convention on the Control of Transboundary Movements of Hazardous Wastes and their Disposal.* Cartagena, 2011.

Revised Legal Analysis on the Application of the Basel Convention to Hazardous Wastes and Other Wastes Generated on Board a Ship (UNEP/CHW.10/INF/16). *Tenth Meeting of the Conference of the Parties to the Basel Convention on the Control of Transboundary Movements of Hazardous Wastes and their Disposal. Item 3 (C) (VI).* 23. Cartagena, 2011.

Framework for the Environmentally Sound Management of Hazardous Wastes and Other Wastes (UNEP/CHW.11/3/Add.1/REV.1). *Eleventh Meeting of the Conference of the Parties to the Basel Convention on the Control of Transboundary Movements of Hazardous Wastes and their Disposal.* Geneva, 2013.

Decision BC-11/17: Cooperation between the Basel Convention and the International Maritime Organization. *Report of the Eleventh Meeting of the Conference of the Parties to the Basel Convention on the Control of Transboundary Movements of Hazardous Wastes and their Disposal* (UNEP/CHW.11/24). Geneva, 2013.

Decision BC-12/11: Implementation of Decision V/32 on the Enlargement of the Scope of the Trust Fund to Assist Developing and Other Countries in Need of Technical Assistance in the Implementation of the Basel Convention. *Twelfth Meeting of the Conference of the Parties to the Basel Convention on the Control of Transboundary Movements of Hazardous Wastes and their Disposal (UNEP/CHW.12/27).* Geneva, 2015.

Decision BC-12/16: Cooperation between the Basel Convention and the International Maritime Organization. *Twelfth Meeting of the Conference of the Parties to the Basel Convention on the Control of Transboundary Movements of Hazardous Wastes and their Disposal* (UNEP/CHW.12/27). Geneva, 2015.

Updated Report on the Creation of a Baseline for the Mid-Term and Final Evaluations of the Strategic Framework (UNEP/CHW.12/INF/5). *Twelfth Meeting of the Conference of the Parties to the Basel Conventionon the Control of Transboundary Movements of Hazardous Wastes and their Disposal.* Geneva, 2015.

Cooperation between the Basel Convention and the International Maritime Organization (UNEP/CHW.13/18). *Thirteenth Meeting of the Conference of the Parties to the Basel Convention on the Control of Transboundary Movements of Hazardous Wastes and their Disposal. Item 4 (e) (ii) of the provisional agenda.* Geneva, 2016.

250 Bibliography

Public Waste Agency of Flanders, (OVAM). Revised Assessment Prepared by the Public Waste Agency of Flanders, on Behalf of Belgium, on How Far the Current Basel Convention Technical Guidelines Cover Wastes Covered by the International Convention for the Prevention of Pollution from Ships (UNEP/CHW.12/INF/29/REV.1). *Twelfth Meeting of the Conference of the Parties to the Basel Convention on the Control of Transboundary Movements of Hazardous Wastes and their Disposal. Agenda Item 4 (e) (iii)*, 13 July 2015.

Revised Draft Guidance Manual on How to Improve the Sea-Land Interface (UNEP/CHW.13/INF/37). *Thirteenth Meeting of the Conference of the Parties to the Basel Convention on the Control of the Transboundary Movements of Hazardous Wastes and their Disposal. Item 4 (e) (ii) of the Provisional Agenda*. 2017.

Strategic Framework: Note by the Secretariat (UNEP/CHW.13/3). *Thirteenth Meeting of the Conference of the Parties to the Basel Convention on the Control of Transboundary Movements of Hazardous Wastes and their Disposal*. 2017.

Reports

United Nations Environment Programme (UNEP), Secretariat of the Basel Convention, GRID-Arendal, and DEWA-Europe. *Vital Waste Graphics*. 2004.

United Nations Environment Programme (UNEP), Secretariat of the Basel Convention, Zoï Environment Network, and GRID-Arendal. *Vital Waste Graphics 2*. 2006.

Wielenga, Kees. "Waste without Frontiers: Global Trends in Generation and Transboundary Movements of Hazardous Wastes and Other Wastes." Commissioned by the Secretariat of the Basel Convention, 36. Geneva, 2010.

Secretariat of the Basel Convention, Zoï Environment Network, and GRID-Arendal. *Vital Waste Graphics 3*. France, 2012.

Other documents related to the Basel Convention

Guidance Document on the Preparation of Technical Guidelines for the Environmentally Sound Management of Wastes Subject to the Basel Convention. 1994. <www.basel.int/Implementation/TechnicalMatters/DevelopmentofTechnicalGuidelines/Adopted TechnicalGuidelines/tabid/2376/Default.aspx#>.

Revised Notification and Movement Documents for the Control of Transboundary Movement of Hazardous Wastes and Instructions for Completing These Documents. 2006. <archive.basel.int/techmatters/forms-notif-mov/vCOP8.pdf>.

Implementation of the Decision VIII/9 on Cooperation between the Basel Convention and the International Maritime Organization: Comments Received from the International Maritime Organization (UNEP/SBC/Bureau/8/1/INF/1). *First Meeting of the Expanded Bureau of the Eighth Meeting of the Conference: Report on the Hazardous Waste Incidents in Abidjan, Côte d'Ivoire: Of the Parties to the Basel Convention. Item 3 of the Provisional Agenda*. Geneva, 2007.

Cooperation between the Basel Convention and the International Maritime Organization (OEWG-VII/13). *Report of the Open-ended Working Group of the Basel Convention on the Control of Transboundary Movements of Hazardous Wastes and their Disposal. Seventh Session*. (UNEP/CHW/OEWG/7/21). Geneva, 2010.

Secretariat of the Basel Convention. The Application of the Basel Convention to Hazardous Wastes and Other Wastes Generated on Board Ships. 4 April 2011.

Bibliography 251

Controlling Transboundary Movements of Hazardous Wastes. Switzerland: United Nations,2011.<www.basel.int/Portals/4/Basel%20Convention/docs/pub/leaflets/leaflet-control-procedures-en.pdf>.

Secretariat of the Basel Convention. Third Legal Analysis of the Application of the Basel Convention to Hazardous Wastes and Other Wastes Generated on Board Ships. 30 April 2012.

Compilation of Environmentally Sound Management Criteria and Core Performance Elements under the Work of the Basel Convention and Other Relevant Organizations UNEP/CHW/CLI_TEG.1/INF/4. *Technical Expert Group to Develop a Framework for the Environmentally Sound Management of Wastes: Item 3 of the Provisional Agenda.* 2012.

Manual for Implementation of the Basel Convention. 2014. <http://www.basel.int/Default.aspx?tabid=4160>.

Guidance Manual on How to Improve the Sea-Land Interface to Ensure that Wastes Falling within the Scope of MARPOL, Once Offloaded from a Ship, are Managed in an Environmentally Sound Manner (UNEP/CHW/OEWG.10/INF/15). *Open-Ended Working Group of the Basel Convention on the Control of Transboundary Movements of Hazardous Wastes and their Disposal. Tenth Meeting, Item 3 (d) (ii) of the Provisional Agenda.* Draft of May 2016.

OEWG-10/11: Cooperation between the Basel Convention and the International Maritime Organization (UNEP/CHW/OEWG.10/13). *Open-Ended Working Group of the Basel Convention on the Control of Transboundary Movements of Hazardous Wastes and their Disposal. Tenth Meeting.* Nairobi, 24 June 2016.

International Law Association (ILA)

Committee on Formation of Customary (General) International Law, Statement of Principles to the Formation of General Customary International Law. London Conference, 2000.

New Delhi Declaration of Principles of International Law Relating to Sustainable Development. *70th Conference of the International Law Association (ILA).* India. International Environmental Agreements: Politics, Law and Economics 2. Kluwer Academic Publishers. 2002.

International Law on Sustainable Development, Final Report. Sofia Conference 2012. 75 Int'l L. Ass'n Rep. Conf. 821, 879 (2012).

International Law Commission (ILC)

Draft Articles on Prevention of Transboundary Harm from Hazardous Activities, with Commentaries (Fifty-Third Session A/56/10). 2001.

Fragmentation of International Law: Difficulties Arising from the Diversification and Expansion of International Law, Report of the Study Group of the International Law Commission (Fifty-Eighth Session A/CN.4/L.682). Geneva, 2006.

Conclusions of the Work of the Study Group on the Fragmentation of International Law: Difficulties Arising from the Diversification and Expansion of International Law (Fifty-Eighth Session). *Yearbook of the International Law Commission*, no II. Part 2. 2006.

Special Rapporteur, Michael Wood: *Second Report on the Identification of Customary International Law* (Sixty-Sixth Session a/Cn.4/672*). Geneva, 2014.

252   Bibliography

Identification of Customary International Law, Text of the Draft Conclusions Provisionally Adopted by the Drafting Committee (Sixty-Eighth Session a/Cn.4/L.872). Geneva, 2016.

International Maritime Organization (IMO)

Agreements

Agreement of Cooperation between the International Maritime Organization (IMO) and the Commission on the Protection of the Black Sea against Pollution. December 2009.

Assembly

Resolution A. 946(23), Voluntary IMO Member State Audit Scheme. 27 November 2003.
Resolution A.1029(26), Global Integrated Shipping Information System (GISIS). 2010.
Resolution A.1070(28), IMO Instruments Implementation Code (III Code). 2013.
Resolution A.1087(28), 2013 Guidelines for the Designation of Special Areas under MARPOL. 2013.

Marine Environment Protection Committee (MEPC)

MEPC Doc. 30/INF.32, Sadler, P., and J. King, Study on Mechanisms for the Financing of Facilities in Ports for the Reception of Wastes from Ships. 1990.
Resolution MEPC.57(33), Designation of the Antarctic Area as a Special Area and Lists of Liquid Substances in Annex II. 1992.
MEPC/Circ.318, Formats for a Mandatory Reporting System under MARPOL 73/78. 1996.
Resolution MEPC.83(44), Guidelines for Ensuring the Adequacy of Port Waste Reception Facilities. 2000.
Resolution MEPC.118(52), Revised Annex II of MARPOL 73/78.2004.
Report of the Marine Environment Protection Committee on Its Fifty-Third Session. (MEPC 53/24). 2005.
Resolution MEPC.153(55), Guidelines for Ballast Water Reception Facilities (G5). MEPC\55\23. Fifty-Fifth Session – Agenda Item 23. 2006.
MEPC.1/Circ.642, Revised Guidelines for Systems for Handling Oily Wastes in Machinery Spaces of Ships Incorporating Guidance Notes for an Integrated Bilge Water Treatment System (IBTS), as Amended. 2008.
MEPC.1/Circ.671, Guide to Good Practices for Port Reception Facility Providers and Users. 2009.
Resolution MEPC.184(59), Guidelines for Exhaust Gas Cleaning Systems. (MEPC 59/24/Add.1). 2009.
Resolution MEPC.201(62), Revised MARPOL Annex V. (MEPC 62/24, Annex 13). 2011
Resolution MEPC.216(63), Amendments: Regional Arrangements for Port Reception Facilities under MARPOL Annexes I, II, IV and V. 2012.
Resolution MEPC.217(63), Amendments: Regional Arrangements for Port Reception Facilities under MARPOL Annex VI and Certification of Marine Diesel Engines Fitted with Selective Catalytic Reduction Systems under the NOx Technical Code 2008. (MEPC 63/23/Add.1) (Annex 21). 2012.

MEPC.1/Circ.778/REV.1, List of Special Areas under MARPOL and Particularly Sensitive Sea Areas. 2012.

Thematic Priorities for the Integrated Technical Co-Operation Programme (ITCP) for 2014–2015 (MEPC 65/15). 2013.

Resolution MEPC.247(66), Amendments to MARPOL Annex VI (to Make the Use of the III Code Mandatory). 2014.

MEPC.1/Circ.834, Consolidated Guidance for Port Reception Facility Providers and Users. 2014.

Port Reception Facilities – How to Do It, Inadequacy of Reception Facilities Updated Version of the Draft Manual on Port Reception Facilities. MEPC 69/11. 2016.

MEPC.1/Circ.869, Summary Reports and Analysis of Mandatory Reports under MARPOL for the Period 2010–2015. 2017.

Maritime Safety Committee (MSC)

Prohibition of the Blending of Bulk Liquid Cargoes during the Sea Voyage (MSC 89/25). Report of the Maritime Safety Committee on Its Eighty-Ninth Session – Agenda Item 25. 2011.

Prohibition of Production Processes during the Sea Voyage – Exemption for Offshore Service Activities: Submitted by Liberia, the United States, Vanuatu, IADC, IMCA and OCIMF (MSC 90/14/2). Ninetieth Session – Agenda Item 14. 2012.

Regulation 5.2 – Prohibition of Blending of Bulk Liquid Cargoes during the Sea Voyage (MSC 90/28). Ninetieth Session – Agenda Item 28. 2012.

Sub-committee on bulk liquids and gases

Application of the Requirements for the Carriage of Bio-Fuels and Bio-Fuel Blends: Guidelines for Blending on Board Submitted by INTERTANKO (BLG 13/4/2). Thirteenth Session – Agenda Item 4. 2009.

Report to the Maritime Safety Committee and the Marine Environment Protection Committee (BLG 13/18). Thirteenth Session – Agenda Item 18. 2009.

Report to the Maritime Safety Committee and the Marine Environment Protection Committee: Outcomes of MSC 89 and MEPC 62 (BLG 16/16). Sixteenth Session – Agenda Item 16. 2012.

Sub-committee on Flag State Implementation (FSI)

Study on the Low Level of Reporting on Alleged Inadequacy of Port Reception Facilities (FSI13/19). 2004.

Draft Action Plan to Tackle the Inadequacy of Port Reception Facilities (FSI 14/19). 2006.

Report to the Maritime Safety Committee and the Marine Environment Protection Committee (FSI 14/19). 2006.

Sub-committee on implementation of IMO instruments

Availability of Adequate Port Reception Facilities Submitted by INTERCARGO (III 3/1). Third Session – Agenda Item 3. 2016.

Sub-Committee on Implementation of IMO Instruments. Annual Enforcement Reports on Port Reception Facilities for 2015 (III 3/3). 2016.

254 *Bibliography*

Others

Circular Letter No. 2639. Global Integrated Shipping Information System (GISIS) – Manual for Administration on the Use of Reporting Facilities. 8 July 2005.

International Maritime Organization (IMO). International Code for the Construction and Equipment of Ships Carrying Dangerous Chemicals in Bulk. (IBC Code). United Kingdom, 2007 Edition.

International Maritime Organization (IMO), MARPOL: How to Do It. London: CPI Group, 2013 Edition.

Answer to the Invitation to IMO to Comment on the Draft Assessment on How Far the Current Basel Convention Technical Guidelines Cover MARPOL Wastes. 2015.

Joint group of experts on the Scientific Aspects of Marine Environmental Protection (GESAMP)

Report of the First Session (GESAMP I/11). 1969.

The State of the Marine Environment: Report and Studies No. 39. 128, 1990.

Organisation for Economic Co-Operation and Development (OECD)

Decisions, resolutions, and recommendations

Recommendation of the Council on Principles Concerning Transfrontier Pollution C(74)224, 14 November 1974.

Recommendation of the Council on Equal Right of Access in Relation to Transfrontier Pollution C(76)55/Final, 1976.

Recommendation of the Council on a Comprehensive Waste Management Policy C(76)155/Final, 1976.

Recommendation of the Council for the Implementation of a Regime of Equal Right of Access and Non-Discrimination in Relation to Transfrontier Pollution C(77)28/Final, 1977.

Recommendation of the Council for Strengthening International Co-Operation on Environmental Protection in Frontier Regions C(78)77/Final, 21 September 1978.

Recommendation of the Council on the Assessment of Projects with Significant Impact on the Environment C(79)116, 8 May 1979.

Council Decision and Recommendation on Transfrontier Movements of Hazardous Wastes C(83)180/Final, 1 February 1984.

Resolution on the International Co-Operation Concerning Transfrontier Movements of Hazardous Wastes C(85)100, 20 June 1985.

Council Decision and Recommendation on Exports of Hazardous Wastes from the OECD Area, C(86)64/Final, 5 June 1986.

Council Decision on Transfrontier Movements of Hazardous Waste C(88)90/Final, 27 May 1988.

Resolution on the Control of Transfrontier Movements of Hazardous Wastes C(89)1/Final, 30 January 1989.

Resolution on the Control of Transfrontier Movements of Hazardous Wastes C(89)112/Final, 18–20 July 1989.

Council Decision-Recommendation on the Reduction of Transfrontier Movements of Wastes C(90)178/Final, 31 January 1991.

Council Decision Concerning the Control of Transfrontier Movements of Wastes Destined for Recovery Operations C(92)39/Final, 1992.

Bibliography 255

Decision of the Council Concerning the Control of Transboundary Movements of Wastes Destined for Recovery Operations C(2001)107/Final, 19 March 2001.

Council Recommendation on the Environmentally Sound Management of Wastes C(2004)100, 9 June 2004.

Reports and other publications

Survey Report prepared by the OECD Secratariat, Equal Right of Access in Matters of Transfrontier Pollution in OECD Member Countries. In *Legal Aspects of Transfrontier Pollution*. Organisation for Economic Co-Operation and Development (OECD), 54–127. Paris, 1977.

Monitoring and Control of Transfrontier Movements of Hazardous Wastes. Environment Monographs N.34, 1–112. Paris, 1993.

Trade Measures in the Basel Convention on the Control of Transboundary Movements of Hazardous Wastes and their Disposal. COM/ENV/TD(97)41/FINAL, Joint Session of Trade and Environment Experts, 1998.

Waste Management Policy Group. Final Guidance Document for Distinguishing Waste from Non-Waste. 18. Paris: Organisation for Economic Co-Operation and Development (OECD), 1998.

Guidance Manual on Environmentally Sound Management of Waste. 2007. <www.oecd-ilibrary.org/environment/guidance-manual-on-environmentally-sound-management-of-waste_9789264042049-en>.

Guidance Manual for the Control of Transboundary Movements of Recoverable Wastes. 2009. <www.oecd.org/env/waste/42262259.pdf>.

Resource Productivity in the G8 and the OECD. A Report in the Framework of the Kobe 3R Action Plan. 2011.

Material Resources, Productivity and the Environment. OECD Green Growth Studies. Paris, 2015.

Organization of African unity

Council of Ministers of the Organization of African Unity, Resolution on Dumping for Nuclear Wastes in Africa Cm/Res.1153 (XLVIII). Ethiopia, 1988.

OSPAR commission

Regional Action Plan for Prevention and Management of Marine Litter in the North-East Atlantic. 2014. <www.ospar.org/documents?v=34422>.

The commission on the protection of the Black Sea against pollution

Strategic Action Plan for the Environmental Protection and Rehabilitation of the Black Sea. Bulgaria, April 2009. <www.blacksea-commission.org/_bssap2009.asp>.

United Nations

Conference on the Human Environment, UN Doc. A/CONF.48/14/REV.1. Stockholm. 1972.

Rio Declaration on Environment and Development, UN Doc. A/CONF.151/26/REV.1. 1992

256 *Bibliography*

Agenda 21 – UN Doc. A/Conf.151/26 (Vol I). 1992.

Plan of Implementation of the World Summit on Sustainable Development, UN Doc. A/CONF.199/20*. 2002.

General Assembly resolutions

Resolution on Permanent Sovereignty over Natural Resources.A/Res/1803/XVII. 1962.

Institutional and Financial Arrangements for International Environmental Cooperation Resolution 2997 (XXVIII). 1972.

3201 (S-VI). Declaration on the Establishment of a New International Economic Order A/RES/S-6/3201. 1974.

3281 (XXIX). Charter of Economic Rights and Duties of States. A/Res/29/3281. 1974.

World Charter for Nature A/Res/37/7. 1982.

Law of the Sea. A/RES/49/28. 1994.

The Future We Want. A/Res/66/288. 2012.

Transforming Our World: The 2030 Agenda for Sustainable Development. A/Res/70/1. 2015.

Oceans and the Law of the Sea. A/RES/71/257. 2017.

Others

Brundtland Report of the World Commission on Environment and Development (Distr. General A/42/427). 1987.

Developments Relating to the United Nations Convention on the Law of the Sea. In *Report of the Secretary-General (A/49/631) Forty-Ninth Session, Agenda Item 35.* 1994.

Human Rights Council, Report of the Special Rapporteur on the Adverse Effects of the Movement and Dumping of Toxic and Dangerous Products and Wastes on the Enjoyment of Human Rights, Okechukwu Ibeanu, A/HRC/12/26/Add.2. *Twelfth Session, Agenda Item 3.* 2009.

UN Recommendations on the Transport of Dangerous Goods – Model Regulations. United Nations Publications, 17th rev. edition. 2011.

United Nations Conference on Trade and Development (UNCTAD)

Report by the UNCTAD Secretariat, *Review of Maritime Transport.* (UNCTAD/RMT/2011) United Nations Publications, 2011.

United Nations Environment Programme (UNEP)

Montevideo Programme for the Development and Periodic Review of Environmental Law. Ad Hoc Meeting of Senior Government Officials Expert in Environmental Law Montevideo Programme for the Development and Periodic Review of Environmental Law. United Nations Environment Programme (UNEP). 6 November 1981.

Governing Council. Decision 10/21: Adoption of the the Programme for the Development and Periodic Review of Environmental Law. 31 May 1982.

Cairo Guidelines and Principles for the Environmentally Sound Management of Hazardous Wastes. (UNEP/GC.14/17). 1987.

Towards a Green Economy: Pathways to Sustainable Development and Poverty Eradication, ISBN: 978-92-807-3143-9, layout by UNEP/GRID-Arendal. 2011.

Bibliography 257

Ad hoc working group of legal and technical experts with a
mandate to prepare a global convention on the control of transboundary
movements of hazardous wastes

Organizational Meeting – UNEP/WG.180/3. United Nations Environment Programme (UNEP), Budapest, 1987.

Report of the Working Group: First Session – UNEP/WG.182/L.1. United Nations Environment Programme (UNEP), 1988.

Second Session: Note from the Executive Director. UNEP/WG.186/2, United Nations Environment Programme (UNEP), Caracas, 1988.

Third Session: Fourth Revised Draft Convention on the Control of Transboundary Movements of Wastes. UNEP/WG.189/L.2/REV.1. 47. United Nations Environment Programme (UNEP), Geneva, 1988.

Fourth Session. Explanatory Notes with Recommendations for Amending Annexes I–IV of the Fifth Revised Draft Convention. UNEP/WG.190/3/Add.1. United Nations Environment Programme (UNEP), Luxembourg, 1989.

Fifth Session – Item 4 of the Provisional Agenda. Draft Convention on the Control of Transboundary Movements of Wastes. UNEP/WG.191/4. United Nations Environment Programme (UNEP), 1989.

Final Report of the Ad Hoc Working Group of Legal and Technical Experts with a Mandate to Prepare a Global Convention on the Control of Transboundary Movements of Hazardous Wastes, (UNEP/IG.80/4), 1989.

European Union documentation

Commission of the European Communities

Com(1998) 452 Final, Explanatory Memorandum: Proposal for a Council Directive on Port Reception Facilities for Ship-Generated Waste and Cargo Residues. 98/0249 (Syn), 1998.

European Commission

Green Paper on Sea Ports and Maritime Infraestructure, Luxembourg: Office for Official Publications of the European Communities, 1997.

Recommendation from the Commission to the Council in Order to Authorise the Commission to Open and Conduct Negotiations with the International Maritime Organization (IMO) on the Conditions and Arrangements for Accession by the European Community/* Sec/2002/0381 Final */.

Com(2003) 301 Final, Towards a Thematic Strategy on the Prevention and Recycling of Waste, Brussels, 2003.

Com(2005) 641 Final, Opinion of the Commission Regarding the Proposal for a Regulation of the European Parliament and of the Council on Shipments of Wast, Brussels, 2003/0139 (COD), 2005.

Directorate-General Environment, Guidance on the Interpretation of Key Provisions of Directive 2008/98/EC on Waste, 2012.

Com(2013) 295 Final, Ports an Engine for Growth, 2013.

Com(2015) 614 Final, Closing the Loop – An EU Action for the Circular Economy, Brussels 2015.

Roadmap. Inception Impact Assessment: REFIT Revision of EU Directive 2000/59/EC on Port Reception Facilities for Ship-Generated Waste and Cargo Residues. 2015.

258   *Bibliography*

<ec.europa.eu/smart-regulation/roadmaps/docs/2017_move_001_refit_directive 2000–59_port_reception_facilities_for_waste_en.pdf>.

C/2016/1759 Commission Notice – Guidelines for the Interpretation of Directive 2000/59/EC on Port Reception Facilities for Ship-Generated Waste and Cargo Residues. OJ C 115/5, 2016.

Com(2016) 168 Final REFIT Evaluation of Directive 2000/59/EC on Port Reception Facilities for Ship-Generated Waste and Cargo Residues, 2016.

Com(2017) 33 Final, on the Implementation of the Circular Economy Action Plan, 2017.

European Maritime Safety Agency (EMSA)

Guidance for Ship Inspections under the Port Reception Facilities Directive (Directive 2000/59/EC). 2016.

Technical Recommendations on the Implementation of Directive 2000/59/EC on Port Reception Facilities. 2016.

Reports

HPTI Hamburg Port Training Institute GmbH. Study on Ships Producing Reduced Quantities of Ships Generated Waste – Present Situation and Future Opportunities to Encourage the Development of Cleaner Ships. Prepared for the European Maritime Safety Agency, EMSA. 2007.

Ramboll, Final Report: EMSA Study on the Delivery of Ship-Generated Waste and Cargo Residues to Port Reception Facilities in EU Ports. EMSA/OP/06/2011. Prepared for European Maritime Safety Agency (EMSA). August 2012.

European Commission, Panteia and PWC. Ex-Post Evaluation of Directive 2000/59/EC on Port Reception Facilities for Ship-Generated Waste and Cargo Residues (Final Report). 2015.

CE Delft and CHEW. The Management of Ship-Generated Waste on Board Ships. EMSA/OP/02/2016. Prepared for the European Maritime Safety Agency (EMSA). 2017.

Others

European Commission, REFIT: Making EU Lighter, Simpler, and Less Costly, OIB, <ec.europa.eu/smart-regulation/docs/refit_brochure_en.pdf.>

European Union. Submission of the EU and Its Member States on the Legal Analysis of the Application of the Basel Convention to Hazardous Wastes and Other Wastes Generated on Board Ships (Document UNEP/CHW.10/INF/16). 5.

Opinion of the Economic and Social Committee on the Green Paper from the Commission on Sea Ports and Maritime Infrastructure, OJ C407/92 28.12.1998.

National documentation

Dutch Forensic Institute. *Expert Report: Odour Nuisance Incident Aps Amsterdam.* Ministry of Justice, 2007.

Ministerio de Relaciones Exteriores de la República de Colombia. Colombian Submission on the Third Analysis of the Basel Convention's Secretariat Regarding Hazardous and Other Wastes Generated on Board Ships.

Waste Reduction and Management Division Environment Canada. Comments to the Revised Legal Analysis on the Application of the Basel Convention to Hazardous Wastes and Other Wastes Generated on Board a Ship (K1A 0H3). 2012.

Miscellaneous

Basel Action Network (BAN). "Needless Risk: The Bush Administration's Scheme to Export Toxic Waste Ships to Europe." 63, 20 October 2003.

Batstone Roger, Smith James, and Wilson David, eds. *The Safe Disposal of Hazardous Wastes: The Special Needs and Problems of Developing Countries*, Vol. 1, World Bank Technical Paper No. 93. United States of America: The World Bank, WTO, and UNEP, 1989.

Declarations, Statements and Reservations of the Parties to the International Convention for the Prevention of Pollution of the Sea by Oil. i-law, Informa UK Limited.

Duffy, Noel, Dermot Cunningham, Jean Finn, and Eileen O'Leary. "Procedure for the Identification of the Hazardous Components of Waste." 57: Clean Technology Centre Cork Institute of Technology, 2001.

Friends of the Earth. "Ghost Fleet Ships, Toxicity and PCBS." December 2003.

Future IMO Legislation. Southampton: Lloyd's Register, 2016.

Greenpeace. "Toxic Death Ship Blocked." *Greenpeace International*, 2006.

Greenpeace and Amnesty International. "The Toxic Truth about a Company Called Trafigura, a Ship Called the Probo Koala and the Dumping of Toxic Waste in Côte D'ivoire." 2012.

Hughes, Richard. "The EU Circular Economy Package – Life Cycle Thinking to Life Cycle Law?" Paper presented at the 24th CIRP Conference on Life Cycle Engineering, 2017.

"Ivory Coast 'Toxic Ship' Inquiry." *BBC News*, September, 2006.

Koh, Tommy. "A Constitution for the Oceans." 1982.

Kummer, Katharina. "Basel Convention on the Control of Transboundary Movements of Hazardous Wastes and their Disposal." 10: United Nations Audiovisual Library of International Law, 2011.

Lethbridge, John, Jon Wonham, John Oestergaard, J.W. Klein, and M.J. Willekes. "The MARPOL 73/78 Convention: The Economic Implications and Other Issues in Providing Reception Facilities for Ship Wastes in Sub-Saharan African Ports." Policy, Planning, and Research Staff, The World Bank, 1991.

Minton, Treharne and Davies Ltd. "The Minton Report: Caustic Tank Washing, Abidjan, Ivory Coast." 2006.

Ofeibea, Quist-Arcton. "Ivory Coast Tragedy Exposes Toxic Flow to Poor." *NPR.org*, October, 2006.

Polgreen, Lydia and Marlise Simons. "Global Sludge Ends in Tragedy for Ivory Coast." *New York Times*, 2006.

Skjold, Trygve, Kees van Wingerden, Ronan Abiven, and Øystein Larsen. "Accident Investigation Following the Vest Tank Explosion at Sløvåg: Revision 03 – English Version." 67. Bergen: CMR Gexcon, 2008.

Spongeberg, Helena. "EU Prepares Environmental Crime Law after Africa Tragedy." *EUobserver*, October 2006.

The Center for International Environmental Law (CIEL). "CIEL Issue Brief: 'Normal Operations of a Ship' in MARPOL: A Review of MARPOL's *Travaux*." 4, 26 June 2012.

260 *Bibliography*

The Center for International Environmental Law (CIEL). "Comments on the Analysis of the Basel Convention's Secretariat Regarding Hazardous and Other Wastes Generated on Board Ships. The Presidential/Congressional Commission on Risk Assessment and Risk Management. 'Framework for Environmental-Health Risk Management.'" United States of America, 1997.

United Nations, Department of Public Information. "Historic New Sustainable Development Agenda Unanimously Adopted by 193 UN Members." News release, 2015.

Index

Note: **Bold** page numbers refer to tables; *italic* page numbers refer to figures and page numbers followed by "n" denote footnotes.

Aarhus Convention 182, 191
Abecassis, David W. 104
Action Plan to Tackle the Inadequacy of Port Reception Facilities 173, 174
AFS Convention 46–7
Agenda 21 14
Agenda 2030 8, 29, 37
Akehurst, Michael 19
Albers, Jan 93n101
amber control procedure 57, 92–7
amber list wastes 88–9
Amsterdam Port Services (APS) 122, 122n9, 123
Annex I of Directive 2000/59/EC 192, 194, 196
Annex I of MARPOL 111–12, 122, 123n13, 126
Annex I (IV) 2 of OECD Council Decision C(92)39/FINAL 88n82
Annex II of Directive 2000/59/EC 197
Annex II of MARPOL 110, 110n46, 112, 123, 200–1, 223–30
Annex III of MARPOL 112–13
Annex IV of the Helsinki Convention 197; Regulation 6(B.3) 199; Regulation 8B 168n23
Annex IV of MARPOL 113
Annex V of MARPOL 113, 193, 200
Annex VI of MARPOL 114, 209
APS *see* Amsterdam Port Services (APS)
ARCO Chemie-Nederland Ltd. and Epon case 59, 60
Article 1 of the Basel Convention 52–3
Article 1(1) of MARPOL 44
Article 1(1)(b) of the Basel Convention 53
Article 1(3) of the BWM Convention 47n24

Article 1(3) of Regulation 1013/2006/EC on Shipments of Wastes 143–5, 217–18
Article 1(4) of the Basel Convention 127, 128, 215, 216
Article 1(4)(2) of the London Dumping Convention (1972) 128
Article 2 of Directive 2000/59/EC 144, 188
Article 2 of the Waste Framework Directive 2008/98/EC 161
Article 2(1) of the Basel Convention 50
Article 2(2) of the Kyoto Protocol 114
Article 2(3) of the Basel Convention 134–5
Article 2(4) of the Basel Convention 51
Article 2(8) of the Basel Convention 32, 147, 153
Article 2(8) of the Helsinki Convention 186
Article 2(8) of Regulation 1013/2006/EC on Shipments of Wastes 161
Article 2(9) of the Basel Convention 135
Article 3(15) of the Waste Framework Directive 58
Article 4(1) of the Basel Convention 129
Article 4(1) of the Waste Framework Directive 2008/98/EC 190
Article 4(2)(a) of the Basel Convention 73
Article 4(2)(b) of the Basel Convention 75
Article 4(2)(d) of the Basel Convention 74, 216
Article 4(2)(e) of the Basel Convention 153–4
Article 4(2)(g) of the Basel Convention 154
Article 4(6) of the Basel Convention 75

262 *Index*

Article 4(10) of the Basel Convention 97, 135, 153
Article 4(12) of the Basel Convention 136, 136n64, 137
Article 6 of the Basel Convention 137
Article 6 of Directive 2000/59/EC 49, 193, 194
Article 6(2) of the Basel Convention 95
Article 6(3)(b) of the Basel Convention 79
Article 6(4) of the Basel Convention 95
Article 6(11) of the Basel Convention 93
Article 7 of Directive 2000/59/EC 197
Article 7(1) of Directive 2000/59/EC 48
Article 7(2) of Directive 2000/59/EC 198, 199
Article 8 of the Basel Convention 68, 135
Article 8(2) of Directive 2000/59/EC 201, 201n177
Article 8(2)(a) of Directive 2000/59/EC 201–2
Article 8(2)(c) of Directive 2000/59/EC 190
Article 8(3) of Directive 2000/59/EC 204, 205
Article 9(1) of Directive 2000/59/EC 199
Article 10 of the Basel Convention 155
Article 10 of Directive 2000/59/EC 123, 200
Article 10(2)(c) of the Basel Convention 73
Article 11 of the Basel Convention 86, 92, 100
Article 11 of Directive 2000/59/EC 206
Article 11(d) of MARPOL 115, 176
Article 12(1)(g) of Directive 2000/59/EC 183, 190
Article 12(3) of Directive 2000/59/EC 207
Article 13 of the Waste Framework Directive 20
Article 13(4) of the Basel Convention 78
Article 14 of the Basel Convention 155
Article 15 of the ILC Draft Articles 152
Article 16 of MARPOL 172
Article 16(2) of MARPOL 111n48
Article 19(2) of the LOSC 138
Article 23 of the LOSC 138
Article 24 of the High Seas Convention of 1958 105, 106
Article 38 of the Vienna Convention on the Law of Treaties 20
Article 49 of Regulation 1013/2006/EC on Shipments of Wastes 162–3

Article 175(1) of the EC Treaty 162
Article 191(2) of the TFEU 61
Article 192 of the LOSC 107
Article 193 of the TFEU 192
Article 194(1) of the LOSC 107, 108
Article 194(3)(b) of the LOSC 108
Article 194(5) 194, 195
Article 195 of the LOSC 62–3, 139, 164, 220, 221
Article 197 of the LOSC 108, 185n100
Article 202 of the LOSC 108
Article 203 of the LOSC 108
Article 211 of the LOSC 108–9
Article 211(2) of the LOSC 164
Article 212 of the LOSC 113
Article 216 of the TFEU 115–16
Article 300 of the LOSC 104
Article 351(1) of the TFEU 117n94
Asylum case 25

Baltic Sea area 220; cargo residues management 223–30; cost recovery system 168, 202; HELCOM recommendations in 186, 186n103, 196, 196n157, 202
Bamako Convention 70n10
Barcelona Convention 185n100, 187, 187n107, 188
Basel Action Network (BAN) 41
Basel Convention 6–7, 6n16, 6n17; Annex I 55; Annex II 57; Annex III 55; Annex VIII 52–3, 52n47, 55, 57; Annex IX 52n47, 53, 55, 56, 99; Article 1 52, 53; Article 1(3) 47n24; Article 1(4) 127, 128, 215, 216; Article 2(1) 50; Article 2(3) 134–5; Article 2(4) 51; Article 2(8) 32, 147, 153; Article 2(9) 135; Article 4(1) 129; Article 4(2)(a) 73; Article 4(2)(b) 75; Article 4(2)(d) 74, 216; Article 4(2)(e) 153–4; Article 4(2) (g) 154; Article 4(6) 75; Article 4(9)(a) and (b) 78; Article 4(9)(c) 78; Article 4(10) 97, 135, 153; Article 4(12) 136, 136n64, 137; Article 6 137; Article 6(2) 95; Article 6(3) (b) 79; Article 6(4) 95; Article 6(11) 93; Article 8 68, 135; Article 10 155; Article 10(2)(c) 73; Article 11 86, 92, 100; Article 13(4) 78; Article 14 155; Cairo guidelines in 14; compliance with ESM obligations 140–1, 151–3, 217; compromise approach 70; conflict clauses in 214; control procedure 78–81, *81*; "Cooperation

between the Basel Convention and the IMO" 142; criticism of 146; disposal operations 51; ESM within 30–2, 146–7, 217; hazardous wastes in 52–3, 57; negotiation of 75, 75n36, 80, 154; objectives of 69; OECD and 86–9, **87**, 97–8; Open-ended Working Group 129; perceived rigidity of 100; regional centers 155–6; regulatory tensions 70–2; sea/land interface waste management 215–17; second negotiation session of 135n62; transboundary movements 50–3, 69–81, *81*, 134–6; *travaux préparatoires* of 128; waste minimization 73; *see also* COP to the Basel Convention; MARPOL-Basel Convention legal conflict; Secretariat of the Basel Convention
Basel Protocol on Civil Liability (1999) 93
best available techniques (BAT) 156–7, 159, 159n52
best environmental practices (BEP) 156–7
Birnie, Patricia 109
blending operations on board ships 125–7
Bodansky, Daniel 18n28
Boyle, Alan 101, 105
Brian, Lepard, D. 28
Bucharest Convention 187–8
BWM Convention 47, 47n24

Cairo Guidelines 13–14, 14n10, 72; Principle 6 164
cargo residues 48–9, 123; in Baltic Sea area 223–30; discharge criteria for 200–1
Cartagena Declaration on the Prevention, Minimization and Recovery of Hazardous Wastes and Other Wastes 146
Case Concerning Military and Paramilitary Activities in and against Nicaragua 30, 34
Center for International Environmental Law (CIEL) 133
Churchill, Robin Rolf 104, 106n25, 109
circular economy 4, 4n9, 5, 5n13, 54n49
CLC Conventions 188, 189
Commune de Mesquer v. Total case 60, 188, 189
Comprehensive Waste Management Policy 12
compulsory discharge criteria 197–200, 209
"concerned countries" 85n72

Conference of the Parties (COP) *see* COP to the Basel Convention
conflict clauses 214
conflicts of law 213–18
contemporary environmental law 36, 36n106
control procedure(s): amber 57, 92–7; Basel Convention and 78–81, *81*; *ex ante* and *ex post facto* control 153–6; green 56, 91–2; OECD and 89–91, **90–1**
COP to the Basel Convention 61, 140n81; Eighth Meeting 80; Eleventh Meeting 148; and ESM 15, 19, 25, 31, 100, 141, 163; Fifth Meeting 140n81, 155; Fourth Meeting 52; framework documents 148, 148n8; IMO cooperation with 181, 184, 222; Sixth Meeting 155; technical guidelines 148, 183; Tenth Meeting 73, 132, 146, 147; Thirteenth Meeting 143, 147n6; Twelfth Meeting 142
Corfu Channel case 104
cost recovery system 167–8; EU law on 201–4, *203*
Council Decision C(88)90(Final) 85–6, 88
Council Decision C(92)39/FINAL 58n57, 86–9, **87**, 88n80, 88n82
Council Decision C(2001)107/FINAL 53–5, 74, 80, 86–97, 90, 99, 158, 160
Council Decision/Recommendation C(83)180(Final) 13, 83–4
Council Decision/Recommendation C(86)64(Final) 84–5
Council Decision/Recommendation C(90)178/FINAL 86
Council Recommendation C(74)224151n19, 152
Court of Justice 162, 162n69, 189; *ARCO Chemie-Nederland Ltd. and Epon* case 59, 60; *Commune de Mesquer v. Total* case 60; *Inter-environment Wallonie* case 59; *Intertanko* case 116, 117; *Thames Water* case 60, 60n75; *Van de Walle* case 60; *Vessoso and Zanetti* case 58
customary law 9, 16–17, 18n27; ESM as 30–1; "Identification of Customary International Law" 17; on marine pollution 104–5; "*opinio juris*" 17, 22, 27–30; "putative" 22; role of 33; State practice 17–27; of transboundary pollution 68

264 Index

D'Amato, Anthony 18, 21
Democratic Republic of the Congo v. Uganda 36
De Sadeleer, Nicolas 31, 32
De Visscher, Charles: Theory and Reality in Public International Law 23n55
direct fee system 168, 201–2
Directive 2000/59/EC on Port Reception Facilities 48–50, 48n29, 123, 144, 181, 182, 189, 206, 218, 219; Annex I 192, 194, 196; Annex II 197; Article 2 144, 188; Article 6 193, 194; Article 7 197; Article 7(2) 198, 199; Article 8(2) 201, 201n177; Article 8(2)(a) 201–2; Article 8(3) 204, 205; Article 9(1) 199; Article 10 123, 200; Article 11 206; Article 12(1)(g) 183, 190; Article 12(3) 207; MARPOL and 184–5; objective of 184; revision of 191, 210
Directive 2009/16/EC on Port State Control 206–7
Directive 2010/65/EU 195, 195n150
discarding concept 58–9, 58n63
discharge criteria: for cargo residues 200–1; for ship-generated waste 197–200
"domestic" environments 33, 37–9, 219
domestic wastes 8
due diligence concept 147n7, 157, 166
Dupuy, Pierre-Marie 9n26, 15

emission control system 114
Environmental and Construction Supervisory Agency 123
environmental legal principles 9–10, 9n26
environmentally sound management (ESM) 6, 7, 163; "adequacy" of port reception facilities 221; Agenda 21 14; Basel Convention compliance with 140–1, 151–3, 217; within Basel regime 30–2, 146–7, 217; Cairo Guidelines 13–14, 14n10; connecting thread of waste regulation 15–16; core meaning 25–7, 26, 31; as customary law 30–1; definition of 148; and "domestic" environments 33, 37–9, 219; at EU level 161–3; ex ante and ex post facto control 153–6; Framework Document 148–9; "The Future We Want" 14–15; hazardous wastes 12–15; integrative function of 219–22; in national legislation 20–1; as normative legal framework 31–2; obligations

147–8, 147n7; OECD and 12–13, 157–60; and "permanent sovereignty over natural resources" 35–7, 35n103, 39; and ship wastes 7–8, 139–43; soft law instruments 14, 14n10, 15, 148; sovereignty and 33–9; and sustainable development 8; technical guidelines for 141; as treaty obligation 15, 30–1; waste hierarchy 148, 150
European Commission 54, 145; "Green Paper on Sea Ports and Maritime Infrastructure" 204; "Ports: an engine for growth" 205
European Maritime Safety Agency (EMSA) 11, 190–1, 198, 207
Euro Tombesi case 58, 58n 63, 59
EU waste legislation 11, 148; cost recovery system 201–4, 203; Directive 75/442 188–9; Directive 2005/35 116–17; Directive 2009/16/EC 206–7; Directive 2010/65/EU 195, 195n150; discarding concept 58–9, 58n63; discharge criteria 197–201; ESM framework 161–3; on hazardous wastes 61–2; and international obligations 181; MARPOL within 115–17; and proximity principle 75; Regulation 1013/2006/EC 58, 61–2, 98–9, 99, 143–5, 217–18; Regulation 2017/352/EU 205; sea/land interface waste management 143–5; ship wastes and 47–50, 115–18, 188–94, 217–18; waste framework 58–61; waste hierarchy 190; waste minimization 190–1; waste reception and handling plans 191, 194–6; waste separation 192; see also Directive 2000/59/EC on Port Reception Facilities; Waste Framework Directive 2008/98/EC
exclusive economic zone (EEZ) 135–8

Fisheries case 18
Framework for the Environmentally Sound Management of Hazardous Wastes and Other Wastes 148–9, 156
Frank, Veronica 102n3
Friends of the Earth 41
Fund for Port Reception Facilities 174–5
"The Future We Want" 14–15

Gabčíkovo-Nagymaros Project 38
GAIRS 165

Garbage Management Plan 113
"general" State practice 21–7
Geneva Convention on the High Seas
    (1958) 105–6, 107n29
"ghost ships" 41
Gillespie, Alexander 149n12
Global Integrated Shipping Information
    System (GISIS) 177, 177n61
green control procedure 56, 91–2
green economy 4, 4n10, 5
green list wastes 57, 61, 88, 98
Greenpeace 124, 124n21
Grosz, Mirina 50, 51, 51n39, 56, 158
Group of Experts on the Scientific Aspects
    of Marine Environmental Protection
    (GESAMP) 101, 103n8
Guidance Manual for the Control
    of Transboundary Movements of
    Recoverable Wastes 91, 97

Handl, Günter 43n15
harmful substances 44
hazardous wastes 73n26; Basel
    Convention 6, 52–3, 57; categorisation
    of 40; environmentally sound
    management of 12–15; EU framework
    61–2; "highly hazardous wastes" 83;
    OECD framework 55–7; vs. "other
    wastes" 53; traceability of 193; unsafe
    disposal of 71; see also nonhazardous
    wastes; transboundary movements of
    wastes
HELCOM recommendations 170,
    170n25, 186, 186n103, 196, 196n157,
    200n166, 201, 202
Helsinki Convention 170, 184, 208;
    Annex IV 197; Article 2(8) 186;
    mandatory discharge criteria of 201;
    Regulation 6(B.3) of Annex IV 199;
    Regulation 8B of Annex IV 168n23
Henkin, Louis 34
Hong Kong Convention 43
"horizontal environmental
    requirements" 218
Hughes, Richard 5n12

ILA see International Law Association
    (ILA)
IMO Instruments Implementation Code
    (III CODE) 180
indirect fee system 170, 202
innocent passage of ships 138
inspection system 206–8

Integrated Technical Cooperation
    Programme 180
integrated waste management
    strategy 181–4
INTERCARGO 178
Inter-environment Wallonie case 59
Intergovernmental Oceanographic
    Commission (IOC) 101
Interim Guidelines for the implementation
    of Decision V/32 155, 155n31
International Conference on Tanker Safety
    and Pollution Prevention (1978) 110
International Convention for the Control
    and Management of Ships' Ballast Water
    and Sediments see BWM Convention
International Convention for the
    Prevention of Pollution from Ships see
    MARPOL
International Convention for the
    Prevention of Pollution of the Sea by
    Oil, 1954 see OILPOL 54
International Convention for the Safety of
    Life at Sea see SOLAS Convention
International Convention on the Control
    of Harmful Anti-Fouling Systems of
    Ships see AFS Convention
International Court of Justice (ICJ)
    33n92; and customary law 17, 20, 25;
    exercise of due diligence 157; Fisheries
    case 18; sustainable development 38
international environmental law 9, 16,
    31; due diligence in 157; ecological
    interdependencies 213; expansion and
    differentiation 213
international law 5, 22n47; customary
    law 9; decentralized character 16; ship
    wastes 43; waste management 219–22;
    waste regulation 6–7
International Law Association (ILA) 16,
    19, 109n37
International Law Commission
    (ILC) 10n31, 20, 24; draft articles
    67n3, 68; "general" State practice
    22; Identification of Customary
    International Law 17; opinio juris 28–9;
    Second Report on Identification of
    Customary International Law 29; State
    practice 19; sustainable development 38
International Maritime Organization
    (IMO) 50; Action Plan to Tackle the
    Inadequacy of Port Reception Facilities
    173, 174; "Cooperation between the
    Basel Convention and the IMO" 142;

266 *Index*

and COP to the Basel Convention 181, 184, 222; emission control system 114; free-of-charge system 168; Global Integrated Shipping Information System 177; Integrated Technical Cooperation Programme 180; licensing system 175–6; Manual on Port Reception Facilities 47, 139, 142, 164, 167, 170, 183–4; Maritime Safety Committee 126, 127; port reception facilities 170–1; restricted faculties of 115; rules and standards 108, 109, 109n43; soft law instruments 177, 181; Sub-Committee on Flag State Implementation 173–4; Sub-Committee on Liquids and Gases 126; World Bank cooperation with 173
International Oil Pollution Compensation Fund 175
International Tribunal for the Law of the Sea (ITLOS) 166; Seabed Dispute Chamber 157
International Waste Identification Code (IWIC) 85–6
INTERTANKO 178
Intertanko case 116, 185
Iron Rhine ("Ijzeren Rijn") Railway arbitration 38

Janus-like nature of wastes 41–3, 63
Jarashow, Richard L. 104
Johannesburg Plan of Implementation 14, 14n12
Judge Hercules 24
Judge Read 18
Judge Weeremantry 24, 38
juridification 213n1

Kelsen, Hans 215
Khian Sea waste disposal incident 71
Kohler, Juliette 6n17
Kummer, Katharina 4n8, 6n16, 53n48, 57, 71, 74, 91n94, 130, 136

Lac Lanoux arbitration 68–9
Langlet, David 189
Legality of the Threat or Use of Nuclear Weapons 24
Lesaffer, Randall 34n99
licensing system 175–6, 183
life-cycle approach 4–5, 219; and Basel Convention 6n17; legal challenges for 5–6
linear economy 4–5

Lomé Convention IV 98n114
LOSC *see* United Nations Convention on the Law of the Sea (LOSC)
Lotus case 18
Louka, Elli 78
Lowe, Alan Vaughan 104, 106n25, 109
Lutz, Robert 43n15

Mahmoudi, Said 189
mandatory discharge criteria 197–200, 209
Manual on Port Reception Facilities 47, 139, 142, 164, 167, 170, 183–4
Marine Environment Protection Committee (MEPC) 166n11, 171n28
marine pollution 101–2, 102n5; *see also* ship-source marine pollution
Maritime Safety Committee 126, 127
MARPOL 7, 103, 109, 132n56, 218, 221; Achilles heel 114–15; amendments 171, 173; Annex I 111–12, 122, 123n13, 126; Annex II 110, 110n46, 112, 123, 200–1, 223–30; Annex III 112–13; Annex IV 113; Annex V 113, 193, 200; Annex VI 114, 209; Article 11(d) 115, 176; Article 16 172; Article 16(2) 111n48; and Directive 2000/59/EC 184–5; history of 139; legal status in EU 115–17; prevention of ship-source pollution 111–14; regulations in 165–6; sea/land interface waste management 134, 139, 215–17; ship wastes **44–5**, 44–8; Special Areas 171–3, **172**; success of 115, 129; *travaux preparatoires* of 133
MARPOL 73 110
MARPOL-Basel Convention legal conflict 126; incompatible obligations 215–16; inconsistent obligations 216–17
Matsui, Yoshiro 73
Matz-Lück, Nele 10, 10n30, 213, 217
MEAs *see* multilateral environmental agreements (MEAs)
Ministry of Housing, Spatial Planning and the Environment 123
Montevideo Programme for the Development and Periodic Review of Environmental Law 13, 72
movement document 80, 94, 95
Mukherjee, Proshanto 108, 108n35, 114, 128
multilateral environmental agreements (MEAs) 155, 176, 179
municipal wastes 40, 53, 53n48

national waste management systems 142, 191, 196; port reception facilities within 181–4, 219, 221

navigational freedoms 136–8

New Strategic Framework for the Implementation of the Basel Convention for 2012–2021 147

no-harm rule 37, 37n109, 67–9

nondiscrimination principle 151–3, 151n18, 152n22, 163

nonhazardous wastes 56, 57, 88, 89; *see also* hazardous wastes

non-special fee system 186

normative chauvinism 23

norm-creation rules 21n45

North Sea Continental Shelf cases 23, 30–31, 33, 33n91

OECD *see* Organisation for Economic Co-Operation and Development (OECD)

OILPOL 54 165, 165n3

Open-ended Working Group (OEWG) 129

"*opinio juris*" 17, 22, 28n71; as a belief 27–8; International Law Commission and 28–9; UN General Assembly resolutions 29; voluntarist approach 27, 27n66

Organisation for Economic Co-Operation and Development (OECD) 3n6; amber control procedure 92–7; Appendix 1 55; Appendix 2 55; Appendix 3 56; Appendix 4 57; Appendix 6 56; and Basel Convention 86–9, **87**, 97–8; control procedures 89–91, **90–1**; Council Decision C(88)90(Final) 84–6, 88; Council Decision C(92)39/FINAL 58n57, 86–9, **87**, 88n80, 88n82; Council Decision C(2001)107/FINAL 53–5, 74, 80, 86–97, **90–1**, 99, 158, 160; Council Decision/Recommendation C(83)180(Final) 13, 83–4; Council Decision/Recommendation C(86)64(Final) 84–5; Council Decision/Recommendation C(90)178/FINAL 86; Council Recommendation C(74)224 151, 151n19; ESM framework 157–60; green control procedure 91–2; Guidance Manual for the Control of Transboundary Movements of Recoverable Wastes 56n56,

91, 97; hazardous wastes 55–7; nondiscrimination principle 151, 153; Recommendation C(76)155 FINAL 12; Recommendation C(2004)100 on the Environmentally Sound Management of Wastes 156, 158–60; recovery operations 54; Regulation 1013/2006/EC on Shipments of Wastes 157; soft law instruments 157–8; transboundary movements 53–7, 81–98; waste classification system 86–8; waste framework 53–5; waste generation 4, 4n7

Organization of African Unity (OAU) 71, 154

OSPAR Convention 186–7

"other wastes" category 53

"Our Common Future" 37–8

Paris Memorandum of Understanding on Port State Control (Paris MoU) 207, 207n200

Parrish, Austen L. 69

Part XII of the LOSC 101, 108

"The Penal Law of Ship-Source Marine Pollution: Selected Issues in Perspective" 108n35

Permanent Court of International Justice (PCIJ) 18

"permanent sovereignty over natural resources" 35–7, 35n103, 39

PIC procedure *see* prior informed consent (PIC) procedure

planetary boundaries 3

polluter pays principle 167–8, 174, 189, 201

port reception facilities 219; Action Plan to Tackle the Inadequacy of Port Reception Facilities 173, 174; "adequacy" of 166–7, 171, 197–8, 221; advanced notification form 174, 177; Article 8 of Directive 2000/59/EC 170; auditing schemes 179–80; binding regulation 179; characteristics 166–7; cost recovery system 167–8, 201–4, *203*; discharge criteria for cargo residues 200–1; enforcement activities 206–8; fee systems 168, *169*, 170; forthcoming regulation on 208–11; Fund for Port Reception Facilities 174–5; Global Integrated Shipping Information System 177, 177n61; HELCOM's recommendations 170,

170n25, 186, 186n103; IMO's guidance 170–1; inadequacies of 177–8; inspection system 206–8; Integrated Technical Cooperation Programme 180; licensing system 175–6, 183; mandatory discharge criteria 197–200, 209; Manual on Port Reception Facilities 47, 139, 142, 164, 167, 170, 183–4; within national waste management strategies 181–4; noncompliance mechanism 178, 180, 181; obligations and current challenges 194–208; polluter pays principle 167–8, 174; private operators 175, 179; provision of 165–6; public participation procedures 181–2; regional regulatory framework 185–8; reporting system 176–9, 179n74; ship wastes and EU framework 188–94; Special Areas 171–3, **172**; Sub-Committee on Flag State Implementation (FSI) 173–4; THETIS 207; transparency in 204–5; waste hierarchy 190; waste minimization 190–1; waste notification form 207; waste reception and handling plans 191, 194–6; waste separation 192; *see also* Directive 2000/59/EC on Port Reception Facilities

port State jurisdiction 117–18

Principle 2 of the Rio Declaration 37

Principle 4 of the Rio Declaration 38

Principle 6 of the Cairo Guidelines 164

Principle 6 of the Stockholm Declaration 12, 12n1

Principle 19 of the Rio Declaration 77

Principle 21 of the Stockholm Declaration 36

prior informed consent (PIC) procedure 75–7, 137, 138, 216; criticisms of 78; legal nature of 77–8; for transboundary movements of wastes 69, 94–6

prior informed consultation 77–8

Probo Emu incident 125, 215

Probo Koala incident 121–5, 215

proximity principle 75

Public Waste Agency of Flanders 142, 142n94, 183

Pulp Mills case 38, 157

"purely domestic affairs" 34–5

"putative" customary law 22

Rayfuse, Rosemary 5n14

Recommendation C(2004)100 on the Environmentally Sound Management

of Wastes 156; Annexes II and III 160; objective of 158–9; structure of 158

red list wastes 88

regime interaction 10–11; coherence 10, 10n32

regional centers 155–6

Regulation 8B of Annex IV of the Helsinki Convention 168n23

Regulation 1013/2006/EC on Shipments of Wastes 58, 61–2, 98–9, *99*, 143–5, 157, 218; Article 1(3) 217; Article 2(8) 161; Article 4 162; Article 49 162–3; purpose of 162

Regulation 2017/352/EU 205

regulation of waste 4–6

Reparation of Injuries Suffered in the Service of the United Nations 171

Resolution 1803 (XVII), UNGA 36

Ringbom, Henrik 181n83, 202n179, 218

Rio Declaration 14; Principle 2 37; Principle 4 38; Principle 19 77

Rio+20 14n13

Rothwell, Donald 109

Schrijver, Nico 37

sea/land interface waste management: blending operations on board ships 125–7; conflicting legal regimes 213–18; environmentally sound management 139–43; EU law 143–5; IMO assistance 164; innocent passage of ships 138; Manual on Port Reception Facilities 47, 139, 142; navigational freedoms 136–8; normal *vs.* abnormal operations 128–31; *Probo Emu* incident 125; *Probo Koala* incident 121–5; Secretariat of the Basel Convention's legal analysis 129–34; ship operations 134–6; transit States' rights 136–8, 136n64; *see also* MARPOL-Basel Convention legal conflict

"secondary raw materials" 54

Secretariat of the Basel Convention 71, 73, 78, 126, 141, 184; cycle of wastes 130; first legal analysis 129–30; Guidance Manual 142; second legal analysis 131–2; third legal analysis 132–4

self-contained regimes 10

self-sufficiency principle 75, 78

Seveso accident (1976) 82

Shaw, Malcolm 28, 33n94

ship-source marine pollution: customary law rules 104–5; EU law 115–18;

Geneva Convention on the High Seas (1958) 105–6; LOSC 107–10; MARPOL 110–15; OILPOL 54 106; oil spills 103; operational discharges 103; regulatory scheme 103; transboundary movement and 214–15

ship wastes 7–8; AFS Convention 46–7; BWM Convention 47, 47n24; cargo residues 48; environmentally sound management 139–43; EU waste legislation 47–50, 188–94, 217–18; IMO's manual on port reception facilities 47; international law 43; management of 11; MARPOL **44–5**, 44–8; transboundary movements of wastes 62–3; tributyltin discharge 46, 46n21

single notification document 94, 95

Small Island Developing States (SIDS) 171

SOLAS Convention 126, 131

South China Sea Arbitration case 102, 107, 166

sovereignty 33–4, 33n93; internal 34n99; "permanent sovereignty over natural resources" 35–7, 35n103, 39

Special Areas under MARPOL 171–3, **172**

State of export 78–80, 91, 95, 135, 151–5

State of import 76, 79, 80, 96, 151–5

State of transit 80, 91

State practice 19n33; Akehurst's account of 19; "general" 21–7; general considerations 17–18; meaning and evidence of 18–21

Stephens, Tim 109

Stockholm Declaration 36n107; Principle 6 12, 12n1; Principle 21 36

"Strategic Action Plan for the Environmental Protection and Rehabilitation of the Black Sea" 188

Strategic Framework for the Implementation of the Basel Convention (2012–21) 155

sustainable development 9n26; Agenda 2030 8, 29, 37; "domestic" environments and 37–9; ESM and 8

Thames Water case 60, 60n75

Theory and Reality in Public International Law (De Visscher) 23n55

THETIS 207

Tolba, Mostafa K. 52n44

Trail Smelter Arbitration 68, 104

transboundary movements of wastes 6–7, 13, 146n1; and Basel Convention 50–3, 69–81, 134–6; contracts 92–3, 97; EU law 58–62; minimization of 74–5; movement document 80, 94, 95; nondiscrimination principle 151–3; notice system 96, 96n106; OECD framework 53–7, 81–98; PIC procedure 69, 75–8, 94–6; pre-notification system 84; proximity principle 75; self-sufficiency principle 75, 78; and ship-source pollution regimes 214–15; and ship wastes 62–3; single notification document 94, 95; stages in 79; waste minimization 73–4; *see also* control procedure(s)

transboundary pollution 67–9

transfrontier pollution 152

transit States' rights 136–8, 136n64

Treaty on the Functioning of the European Union (TFEU): Article 191(2) 61; Article 193 192; Article 216 115–16; Article 351(1) 117n94

tributyltin (TBT) discharge 46, 46n21

United Nations Conference on Environment and Development (UNCED) 182, 182n87

United Nations Convention on the Law of the Sea (LOSC) 115n84; Article 19(2) 138; Article 23 138; Article 192 107; Article 194(1) 107, 108; Article 194(3)(b) 108; Article 195 139, 164, 220, 221; Article 197 108, 185n100; Article 202 108; Article 203 108; Article 211 108–9; Article 211(2) 164; Article 212 113; Article 300 104; "constitution of the oceans" 107–10; and marine pollution 102; Part XII 101, 108

United Nations Environment Programme (UNEP) 4n10, 36, 76, 155; Cairo Guidelines 13–14, 14n10, 72

United Nations General Assembly (UNGA) 29, 181; Resolution 1803 (XVII) 36; Transforming our World 37

Van Calster, Geert 59, 59n65

Van de Walle case 60

Vessoso and Zanetti case 58

Vienna Convention on the Law of Treaties 20

Viñuales, Jorge 15

270 *Index*

Waigani Convention 70n10

waste(s): conception of 40–1; EU framework 58–61; Janus-like nature of 41–3, 63; OECD framework 53–5; value of 41–3, 42n9; *see also* ship wastes; transboundary movements of wastes

waste classification system 86–9, **87**

Waste Framework Directive: Article 3(1) 182, 188; Article 3(15) 58; Article 4 162; Article 13 20; Article 16 156; Article 28 191; and hazardous wastes 61; inclusion of ship wastes 144; and waste hierarchy 148

Waste Framework Directive 2008/98/ EC 98, 144, 193, 196, 210, 218, 219; Article 2 161; Article 4(1) 190; Article 4(2) 190; legal basis of 192

waste generation 3; OECD framework 4, 4n7

waste hierarchy 148, *150*, 162, 190, 210

waste minimization 73–4, 159, 190–1

waste notification form 207

waste oils 192–3

waste reception and handling plans 191, 194–6

waste recovery 159

waste separation 192

waste trade 72, 140

Wilkinson, David 42

Wolfrum, Rüdiger 213, 217

World Bank-IMO cooperation 173

World Commission on Environment and Development 37

Xu, Jingjing 114